Visual Basic and COM+ Programming

BY EXAMPLE

que®

201 West 103rd Street
Indianapolis, Indiana 46290

Peishu Li

Visual Basic and COM+ Programming

International Standard Book Number: 0-7897-2458-8

Library of Congress Catalog Card Number: 00-107936

Printed in the United States of America

First Printing: November, 2000

01 00 99   4   3   2   1

Trademarks

Warning and Disclaimer

Acquisitions Editor
Gretchen Ganser

Development Editor
Sean Dixon

Managing Editor
Tom Hayes

Project Editor
Heather McNeill

Copy Editor
Chuck Hutchinson

Indexer
Chris Barrick

Proofreader
Harvey Stanbrough

Technical Editors
Vince Mayfield
Steve White

Team Coordinator
Cindy Teeters

Interior Designer
Karen Ruggles

Cover Designer
Rader Design

Copywriter
Eric Borgert

Editorial Assistant
Angela Boley

Contents at a Glance

Table of Contents

About the Author

Peishu Li is a Microsoft Certified Solution Developer who has more than 10 years' experience in developing enterprise and Internet solutions using Microsoft tools and technologies. Peishu's areas of expertise include COM, DCOM, MTS, COM+, MSMQ, IBM MQSeries, SQL Server, Visual Studio tools, ASP, EAI, XML, and UML.

Peishu is currently working at edeagroup.com as a technical development manager. A Dallas-based e-business solution leader, edeagroup.com assists its clients in building e-business relationships by providing innovative consulting solutions for e-business strategies, creative services, and Internet-enabled information technology.

Dedication

To my Dad and Mom, who gave me life, wisdom, and love.

To my wonderful wife, Xiaofang, and my lovely son, Jeff.

Acknowledgments

This book is a product of teamwork. I would like to thank the entire editorial team at Que for their help and efforts on this project. Special thanks to Acquisitions Editor Gretchen Ganser, Technical Editors Steve White and Vincent MayField, Development Editor Sean Dixon, Project Editor Heather McNeill, Copy Editor Chuck Hutchinson, and Proofreader Harvey Stanbrough for their patience and guidance.

Special thanks to Holly Allender, the original acquisitions editor of this book, who hired me for this exciting and challenging project.

Tell Us What You Think!

As the reader of this book, *you* are our most important critic and commentator. We value your opinion and want to know what we're doing right, what we could do better, what areas you'd like to see us publish in, and any other words of wisdom you're willing to pass our way.

As an Associate Publisher for Que, I welcome your comments. You can fax, email, or write me directly to let me know what you did or didn't like about this book—as well as what we can do to make our books stronger.

Please note that I cannot help you with technical problems related to the topic of this book, and that due to the high volume of mail I receive, I might not be able to reply to every message.

When you write, please be sure to include this book's title and author as well as your name and phone or fax number. I will carefully review your comments and share them with the author and editors who worked on the book.

Fax: 317-581-4666

Email: dean.miller@macmillanusa.com

Mail: Dean Miller
            Que
            201 West 103rd Street
            Indianapolis, IN 46290 USA

Introduction

The Component Object Model, or COM, dramatically changed the programming paradigm and made the life of developers who use Microsoft programming tools, such as Visual Basic and Visual C++, much easier. Microsoft Transaction Server, or MTS, further simplified the programming model by sheltering developers from the complex programming tasks, such as system level services and transaction management, letting them focus on solving business problems rather than struggling with writing plumbing code.

COM+ combines the power of both COM and MTS and adds a whole set of new services, which makes programming using Microsoft Visual Studio tools more configuration or attributes based. COM+ adds more infrastructure services at the operating system level and becomes an integral part of Windows 2000. Understanding COM+ services and mastering its programming paradigm is imperative since COM+ is the essential enabling technology for building Windows Distributed interNet Applications, or Windows DNA 2000.

About This Book

To build Windows DNA 2000 applications using COM+ services, you can choose any programming language that is COM compatible, such as Microsoft Visual Studio tools. This book teaches on building COM+ applications using Microsoft Visual Basic 6.0, Enterprise Edition. There are dozens of COM+ related books on the market now. Most of them are targeted for Visual C++ developers. Very few are for Visual Basic developers. Most books that do use Visual Basic as the programming language either do not really focus on COM+ itself or do not cover every aspect of COM+ from a Visual Basic developers' perspective like this book does.

Throughout the book, other tools and technologies are introduced wherever appropriate. These technologies include Unified Modeling Language (UML), Active Server Pages (ASP), eXtensible Markup Language (XML), and so on. The code examples for this book are available for download from Que's Web site at http://www.mcp.com/sourcecode.cfm?item=0789724588.

Who Should Use This Book

The intended audience for this book is Visual Basic programmers. Previous knowledge of COM or MTS is not required in order to follow the examples in this book. This book teaches beginning and intermediate programmers techniques for writing efficient COM+ components so that they can enjoy the benefits of the COM+ services provided by the Windows 2000 platform. It uses easy-to-follow, real-world, field-tested code samples to walk readers through the entire journey of building COM+ applications. It presents many useful tips and warns of possible pitfalls using the author's extensive real-world experiences in the COM developing arena. This book will also teach readers how to put to use the skills they learned to develop a complete Windows DNA application using COM+ services.

This Book's Organization

This book is divided into three parts.

Part I, "Welcome to COM+," introduces the reader to the world of COM+ services. It covers the basic COM+ and related technologies that readers need to understand to be able to work with the examples presented in this book.

Part I starts with Chapter 1, "What COM+ Is All About," which describes how COM+ evolved from COM/DCOM and MTS. It then introduces the core COM+ services that this book will cover.

Chapter 2, "Windows DNA 2000 and COM+," introduces Windows DNA and tells the reader how COM+ is related to Window DNA as an enabling technology. It also covers ActiveX Data Access Objects (ADO) with several code examples and introduces Active Server Pages (ASP).

Chapter 3, "Introduction to Microsoft Message Queuing Services (MSMQ)," compares and contrasts synchronous and asynchronous programming models and explains how message queuing can add robustness to distributed computing systems. It introduces Microsoft Message Queuing Server (MSMQ), which is a key component in several COM+ services, such as Queued Components (QC). It covers basic MSMQ programming with plenty of code examples.

Chapter 4, "Introduction to Visual Basic COM Programming," teaches Visual Basic programmers who have no previous COM programming experience how to write COM components. It will also help Visual Basic programmers who have some past COM exposure by demonstrating good COM programming practices and some pitfalls to watch out for. This chapter establishes a baseline for readers for working with code examples covered in the following chapters.

Part I ends with Chapter 5, "Using the Component Services MMC Snap-In," which teaches readers to use the Component Services administration tool to manage and configure COM+ applications and components.

Part II, "Developing COM+ Application Components," provides the meat and potatoes of this book. A fictitious ordering application, Northwind, adapted from the Northwind sample database that ships with Microsoft SQL Server 7.0, is used in several chapters of Part II to demonstrate how to use Visual Basic to build solutions using key COM+ features.

Chapter 6, "Writing Transactional Components," describes Atomicity, Consistency, Isolation, and Durability (ACID) transaction properties, Microsoft

Distributed Transaction Coordinator (DTC), and COM+ automatic transaction services.

Chapter 7, "Compensating Resource Manager (CRM)," describes how to leverage the power of COM+ to extend MTS transaction to nontransactional resources.

Chapter 8, "COM+ Securities," discusses how COM+ handles securities for components. This chapter also introduces administratively configured, or declarative, role-based security.

Chapter 9, "Queued Components," teaches readers how to take advantage of the Queued Components services of COM+ to asynchronously interact with the remote components. This chapter extends the knowledge readers learned in previous chapters, especially Chapter 3.

Chapter 10, "COM+ Events," introduces the Loosely Coupled Events (LCE) service of COM+. LCE allows a publisher to send event notifications to subscribers without knowing anything about the subscribers beforehand.

Chapter 11, "Administering COM+ Applications Programmatically," introduces the COM+ Admin object model and teaches readers how to use this COM interface to perform COM+ administration automatically. It also introduces the use of the Windows Scripting Host (WSH).

Chapter 12, "More on COM+ Programming," ends Part II. This chapter introduces COM+ enhancement in Visual Basic IDE debugging. It also describes some other COM+ services that were originally available in the Beta 3 of Windows 2000 but removed from the final Windows 2000 release, such as In Memory Database (IMB) and Component Load Balance (CLB). It also introduces the component pooling service, which is not supported by current versions of Visual Basic.

Part III, "Building Real-World COM+ Services Applications," presents two complete real-world COM+ sample applications.

Chapter 13, "Northwind Traders Online: A COM+ Enabled Windows DNA 2000 Application," pushes the Northwind application built in several chapters of Part II to the Internet. Here, readers build a complete Windows DNA 2000 application with all the COM+ services enabled. This chapter also discusses several important design considerations of Windows DNA applications.

Chapter 14, "A Case Study: COM+ and Enterprise Application Integration (EAI)," introduces EAI and how to use COM+ to resolve the issues involved in a real-world EAI case study. This chapter also introduces the eXtensible Markup Language (XML) and uses it as the standard data exchange format.

Part I

Welcome to COM+

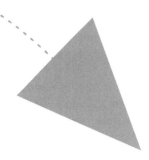

What COM+ Is All About

COM+ is not a radical departure from Microsoft's existing component-based technologies, such as COM, DCOM, and MTS. Rather, COM+ builds on the success of its predecessors by improving, extending, and unifying them, and providing several significant new services. In addition, COM+ services are deeply integrated into the Windows 2000 operating system and have become part of system services. To unleash the power of COM+ services, you need a solid understanding of COM, DCOM, and MTS.

This chapter teaches you the following:

- The fundamentals of the Component Object Model (COM), Distributed COM (DCOM), and Microsoft Transaction Server (MTS)

- The evolution of COM+ from its predecessors

- The core COM+ services

- The COM+ programming model

COM: The Component Object Model

In this section, you learn the basics of Microsoft's component software architecture, COM, which stands for *Component Object Model*. COM is designed to help resolve problems related to software reuse and component interoperability, allowing developers to build component-based applications. You learn about interfaces and COM threading models.

What Is COM?

Before you delve deeper into COM internals, you'll look at the problems of software reuse and the issues involved in component (or application) inter-operability. Then you'll see how COM addresses these problems and issues.

So, what is software reuse? As a software developer, you might find yourself repeatedly writing some common routines in project after project. For example, most enterprise applications require some mechanism to check users' security credentials, such as identification, permissions, and so on. It would be most efficient if you could simply reuse the routines you wrote earlier to save yourself the time and effort of developing and testing new code. You could probably use the Windows Clipboard to copy and paste the code you wrote. Some object-oriented programming languages, such as C++, allow you to reuse the source code in several ways, including *inheritance*, or *sub-classing*. But having copied and pasted multiple copies of the same code, what are you going to do when you want to enhance the security-checking functionality? Unfortunately, you will have to modify the same routines everywhere you use them.

Also, code reuse works only when two projects are written in the same pro-gramming language. Unfortunately, this is often not the case and that pre-sents a second problem. For instance, if your original security-checking routine was written in Visual Basic and the next project uses Java, you have to rewrite the same routines in Java, meaning you have to "translate" the code from one programming language to another. What a pain!

As you can see, code reuse is not an elegant solution in software reuse. It would be nice if there were some mechanism that would allow you to write the security routines just once and wrap them into some form of software. Later, you could simply plug this software into other applications and use it regardless of the programming languages' differences. The mechanism I am talking about here is called *software reuse*. The difference between code reuse and software reuse is that the former is language specific and the lat-ter is language independent—reuse happens at the binary level.

Fortunately, such a mechanism does exist. That mechanism is the COM architecture. COM provides a binary standard for software reuse in a language-independent manner. What does this mean? COM allows you to write security-checking logic just once, in any language you prefer, as long as the language meets the minimum requirements of COM.

NOTE

Any programming languages that support pointers (or pointers to functions) can be used to write COM components. You can write COM components in C++, Java, Visual Basic, PowerBuilder, Delphi, or even Microfocus COBOL. *Pointer* is an unfamiliar term to most Visual Basic programmers. A pointer is a variable that stores a memory address of another variable. In Visual Basic, you don't need to explicitly use pointers; this job is handled by the Visual Basic runtime behind the scene.

After you finish writing your security-checking routine, you just need to compile (wrap) the code into a binary file. This binary file is called a COM *component* (a piece of software). Later, you can simply register (plug) this COM component into the System Registry and start using this functionality without worrying about which language was used to build the COM component or which language is reusing it.

Put in COM terminology, the security-checking functionalities are the *services* exposed by a COM component, called a COM *server*. The application that uses the service of a COM server is called a COM *client*.

NOTE

Some COM literature uses the terms *COM component* and *COM object* interchangeably. This use is confusing and, strictly speaking, incorrect. In this book, I use either *COM components* or *COM servers* to refer to the physical binary file, whereas I use the term *COM objects* to refer to instances of activated COM classes. COM objects and COM classes will be covered in Chapter 4, "Introduction to Visual Basic COM Programming."

Another benefit of using a COM component is that when you need to enhance its functionality, you can simply modify the component itself, without recompiling existing client applications, as long as the contract between the COM component and the client remains the same. This contract between a COM component and the outside world is called an *interface*. Client applications access the services of COM components through their interfaces. Figure 1.1 shows a client application interacting with a COM object through a COM interface.

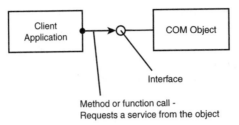

Figure 1.1: *A client application interacts with a COM object through an interface.*

COM Interfaces

A COM interface is a group of functions that define a set of behaviors of a COM component. The functions defined by an interface are called *methods*. The attributes of an interface are called *properties*. A COM component can have more than one interface. By convention, interface names start with an *I*. For example, the interface that defines the security COM component can be named ISecurity. This interface defines two methods. One method is called CheckIdentity(), and the other method is called CheckPermission(). Figure 1.2 is a Unified Modeling Language (UML) diagram of the ISecurity interface.

EXAMPLE

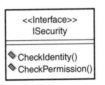

Figure 1.2: *The ISecurity interface has two methods: CheckIdentity() and CheckPermission().*

NOTE

Microsoft uses the "I" naming convention in most of their published COM interfaces (not all of them, though). The advantage of using a consistent naming convention for the interfaces is that you can differentiate them (abstract classes) from concrete implementations.

NOTE

UML, which stands for Unified Modeling Language, is a standard object-modeling language that is supported by various visual modeling tools such as Microsoft Visual Modeler and Rational Rose. In UML, an interface diagram is similar to a class diagram. It contains three sections. From the top to the bottom, the first section is the interface name (or the class name in case of a class diagram), the second section contains properties (the ISecurity interface doesn't have any properties, so in Figure 1.2 this section is empty), and the third section contains methods.

The COM specification requires that all COM components must support a special interface: IUnknown. COM further specifies that all other interfaces must be derived from this IUnknown interface. Therefore, IUnknown is the root interface of all other COM interfaces. It has three methods: QueryInterface(), AddRef(), and Release(). Figure 1.3 is a UML diagram of the IUnknown interface.

EXAMPLE

Figure 1.3: The IUnknown interface.

The QueryInterface() method of the IUnknown interface is used by the client application at runtime to figure out whether a specific interface is supported by the COM object. If the COM component supports the interface being queried, it will return a pointer to the requested interface back to the client application. Otherwise, it returns an error. AddRef() and Release() are used for tracking the reference count of running instances of the COM interface.

Each time a client creates a new instance of a COM object, the AddRef() method is called (often behind the scenes); it increments the reference count of the object's default interface by one. Similarly, whenever the client releases its reference to an instance of the COM object, the Release() method is called; it decrements the count by one. When the internal reference count reaches zero, the COM object destroys itself. When a COM server's objects have all destroyed themselves, the server (typically a DLL) will unload itself from memory to free up resources.

COM relies on this reference counting mechanism to track the running instances of objects and determine when is appropriate to release resources that are not used any more to avoid possible memory leaks.

The IUnknown interface is an entry point for a client to discover additional interfaces supported by a COM component.

EXAMPLE

All interfaces must be uniquely identified to avoid possible collision from any human-readable names. COM uses a special algorithm that generates a 128-bit integer. The numbers generated by this algorithm are guaranteed to be unique in the world across space and time. They are called *Globally Unique Identifiers* (GUIDs, also called *Universally Unique Identifiers* or

UUIDs). You can manually generate a GUID with a utility called GUID-GEN. To use the GUIDGEN utility, click Start, Run and type **GUIDGEN** to open the screen shown in Figure 1.4.

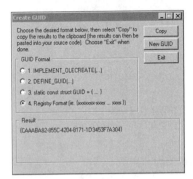

Figure 1.4: *Use the GUIDGEN utility to create a GUID.*

TIP

The GUIDGEN.EXE utility comes with Windows 2000 installation. It is not available, however, in the default installation of Windows NT or 9.x platforms. To get GUIDGEN.EXE for these platforms, you can run a custom setup of Visual Studio 6.0, Enterprise Edition.

For purposes of this book, the most useful GUID format is the Registry format, which looks something like this:

{CAAABA82-855C-4204-8171-1D3453F7A304}

This is the format used in the IDL (Interface Identification Language) files, and internally by Visual Basic, when you compile your COM components.

When you click the New GUID button, the GUID changes in the Result frame. You can copy the GUID being generated by GUIDGEN to the Clipboard by clicking the Copy button and pasting it in your code.

In Visual Basic, you usually don't have to generate GUIDs manually by yourself. When you compile your COM components, Visual Basic automatically generates these GUIDs for your class (called a *Class ID* or CLSID) and interfaces (called an *Interface ID* or IID). Chapter 4, "Introduction to Visual Basic COM Programming," discusses Class IDs and the Registry in greater detail.

Figure 1.5 shows how the CLSID for the Microsoft Word application (a COM object) looks in the Registry.

EXAMPLE

Figure 1.5: *The CLSID for the Microsoft Word application component in the Registry.*

An interface defines what methods (functions) and properties (attributes) it supports, the parameters and their data types in the methods, and the return types of the methods. These details are collectively known as the *method signatures* of an interface. COM requires that interfaces are immutable. When an interface is defined (or *published* in COM parlance), this interface (and its signatures) should never be changed because interfaces are the contract between a COM component and the client. Changing an interface after it has been published will cause the client to break.

A COM interface only defines its method signatures but never carries concrete implementation. This is a very important point to keep in mind. This forced separation of implementation from the interface itself differentiates COM from object-oriented languages where such separation is possible but often neglected. This separation offers several benefits.

For example, to improve the security-checking functionality of the COM security component shown earlier, you can simply change the code inside the CheckIdentity() and CheckPermission() methods. All changes you make are invisible to the clients that actually use the component. Of course, you do need to keep the interface itself, the contract, unchanged. That is, make sure that the Security component still supports the CheckIdentity() and CheckPermission() methods, and that the parameters and their data types and the return types of these two methods all stay the same.

Another benefit of this separation is that you can implement the same interface in different COM components in different ways. This is called *polymorphism*. Chapter 4 shows some examples of how interfaces are implemented.

The Virtual Function Table (vtable)

EXAMPLE

COM provides a binary standard using a double indirection mechanism through a *virtual function table* (*vtable*). All COM objects contain a vtable for each of their interfaces. The object also has a pointer to the vtable—a vtable pointer—for each interface. When an interface pointer is returned to the client, it is in fact a pointer to a pointer. It points to the object's vtable pointer for the interface. This is called *double indirection*. Figure 1.6 demonstrates how this type of indirection works. By convention, pointer variables are declared as pVariableName or m_pVariableName, depending on their scope.

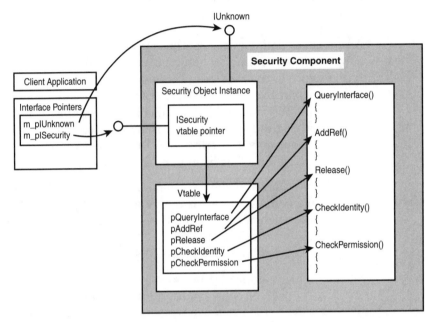

Figure 1.6: A client accesses the actual methods in an interface through the virtual function table (vtable).

TIP

In Figure 1.6, the prefix p in a variable's name indicates that the variable is a pointer; the prefix m_ indicates that the variable is a member of a class. Class member variables are said to be at *class scope*. Variables at global scope should be prefixed with g_, and variables inside methods, at local scope, should be of the form pVariableName. This is a convention known as Hungarian notation, developed at Microsoft by Charles Simonyi.

You'll learn more about vtables in Chapter 4, which discusses bindings.

COM Threading Models

Before starting our discussion on COM threading models, let's take a moment to introduce the *process* concept. A process is a running instance of an executable. A process is also a collection of memory space, code, data, and system resources along with one or more threads of execution. In this section, you'll look at a few more terms, *threads* and *apartments*, and examine the threading models that COM supports.

A *thread* is a scheduled, time-sliced context of execution within a process that is executed serially.

Processors execute code at thread level, not at process level. All processes must have at least one thread. You can view a thread as an execution unit inside a process. Threads actually interact with objects to perform a job in response to requests from clients. A process has one or more threads. In DOS or earlier Windows operating systems, all applications ran on a single thread of execution. Windows 9.x and NT rely on multiple threads of execution to support multitasking. The system kernel provides a thread scheduler to dynamically schedule and execute threads according to certain priority settings at both the process and thread levels.

Threads and objects reside in logical containers called *apartments*. An apartment is a conceptual association that describes the relationship between objects and threads, defines the rules that govern the concurrency pattern among objects, and provides a means by which the access to objects is handled.

EXAMPLE

COM supports two apartment models: the *Single-Threaded Apartment* model, or STA, and *Multi-Threaded Apartment* model, or MTA. An STA can have only a single thread. All objects inside the STA are associated with this particular thread, as shown in Figure 1.7.

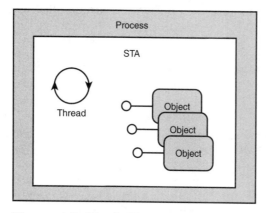

Figure 1.7: *Single-Threaded Apartment (STA) model.*

All calls to the objects inside an STA must be made through the thread in that STA. This applies to any call from any thread outside the STA, including calls from clients or other COM objects. Direct calls to objects in an STA are not allowed from threads outside the STA. Calls from one apartment to another are marshaled. The process of packaging calls is referred to as *marshaling*. This is illustrated in Figure 1.8.

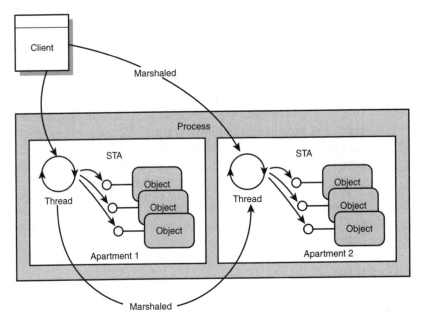

Figure 1.8: *Calls from a client are made through the thread. Calls from one apartment to another need to be marshaled.*

Synchronization and concurrency in STAs are handled by the COM system through a hidden Windows messaging mechanism. STA is therefore a thread-safe model.

The first STA created in a process is called the *main STA*. The STA model is sometimes called the *Apartment model*. A special kind of STA model is the *Single-Threading* model, in which only one thread exists in a process. An MTA can have one or more threads. In an MTA model, any threads in the apartment can call all the objects within the apartment, even objects on another thread. Calls that are made inside the apartment need not be marshaled. Figure 1.9 illustrates an MTA model.

Although a process can have any number of STAs, it can have only one MTA. MTA models are sometimes called *Free-threaded models*. With these models, unlike STA models, however, simultaneous calls are allowed and the synchronization is not handled by the COM system. Rather, the developer is responsible for handling the synchronization and concurrency issues that may arise.

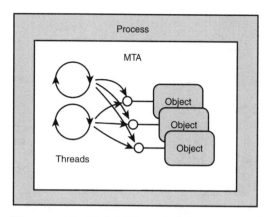

Figure 1.9: *Multi-Threaded Apartment (MTA) model.*

Although STA provides an easy, thread-safe mechanism for dealing with synchronization and concurrency issues, MTA offers better responsiveness to clients because it allows objects to be called from multiple threads at the same time.

A process can choose to support either STA, MTA, or both. This is called the *both-threaded* or *mixed-threaded model.*

The both-threaded model is illustrated in Figure 1.10.

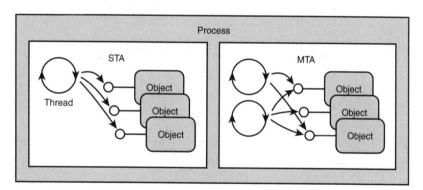

Figure 1.10: *Both-threaded model.*

An out-of-process COM component can store threading-model information inside the executable, whereas in-process COM components use the System Registry to provide threading-model information to their clients. Threading-model information in the Registry is stored under the HKEY_CLASSES_ROOT\CLSID\InprocServer32 subkey inside the ThreadingModel named value, as shown in Figure 1.11.

Figure 1.11: *The* ThreadingModel *value in the Registry.*

Table 1.1 lists possible values that can be stored in ThreadingModel and the corresponding threading models they support.

Table 1.1   **ThreadingModel** *Values and Their Meanings*

Value of ThreadingModel	Supported Threading Models
No value	Single-threading Model
Apartment	STA
Both	STA and MTA
Free	MTA

Distributed COM (DCOM)

The Distributed COM (DCOM) protocol extends COM to support communication between client applications and COM components across machine boundaries, and makes the distributed application development and deployment easier. As explained earlier in this chapter, a *process* is a running instance of an application that is loaded into the memory.

In-Process Servers Versus Out-of-Process Servers

There are two types of COM servers, depending on the memory address space where they are running. COM servers running at the address space of a client process are called *in-process* servers, whereas COM servers running at their own process address are called *out-of-process* servers. Physically, in-process servers are compiled as dynamic linking libraries (DLL files, sometimes called ActiveX DLLs), whereas out-of-process servers are compiled as executables (EXE files, sometimes called ActiveX EXEs).

NOTE

In-process servers (ActiveX DLLs) offer better performance over out-of-process servers (ActiveX EXEs) because they don't have the overhead of crossing the process boundaries and data marshaling.

DCOM Architecture

DCOM achieves this interprocess or intermachine communication through a proxy-stub mechanism with the help of a COM library. Figure 1.12 depicts the DCOM architecture.

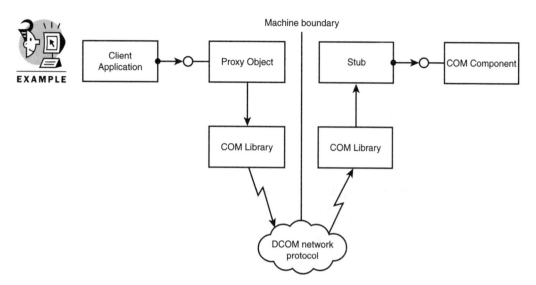

Figure 1.12: DCOM architecture.

When a client application (the client) makes a call to a COM component (the server) that resides either in a different process on the same machine or on a different machine, the COM library (OLE32.dll) reads the configuration information from the System Registry and creates a proxy object in the address space of the client application. It also creates a stub object in the address space of the server. The COM library communicates between these different processes (or machines) using either LPC (local procedure call) protocols or RPC (remote procedure call) protocols, depending on whether the client and the server reside on the same machine. The proxy object takes the call from the client, marshals (packs) the data, and sends it across the process or machine boundary to the stub. The stub object unmarshals (unpacks) the data, initializes the server on the behavior of the client, and makes the actual call for the server to process. The COM library handles all these tasks transparently from the client and the server. This location independency (or location transparency) offers several significant benefits for distributed applications, such as easier deployment and improved scalability. The COM component developer, on the other hand, does not need to do anything special to the component to take advantage of these benefits.

TIP

The proxy and stub objects are in fact identical to one another, but they behave differently in their different roles. The proxy is designed to imitate the server, so the client believes it is communicating directly with the server. The point of proxies is that all COM calls must be made to an object in the client's process. In-process COM servers (DLLs) are already in the client's process, but out-of-process and remote servers must have a "representative" in their client's process, which looks exactly like them—the stub. This stub then uses interprocess communication (of which cross-machine calls are a special case) to communicate with the server's process.

Microsoft Transaction Server (MTS)

Although COM and DCOM provide a binary standard and location independency for building component-based, distributed applications, developers still have to face numerous challenges, such as thread management, transaction support, database connection pooling, and security. To shield developers from these complicated programming tasks so that they can be more productive in building applications to solve the business problems of their organization, Microsoft introduced Microsoft Transaction Server (MTS). MTS was originally shipped as a standalone product, but it soon became a family member of NT 4.0 Option Pack along with other servers, including Internet Information Server (IIS) and Microsoft Message Queuing Server (MSMQ). IIS will be introduced in Chapter 2, "Windows DNA 2000 and COM+," and MSMQ will be covered in Chapter 3, "Introduction to Microsoft Message Queuing Services (MSMQ)."

MTS is a component-based, transaction-process system. It provides an infrastructure for building and deploying robust, distributed, enterprise applications, including Internet and intranet applications. In addition to transaction, MTS also offers other services, such as thread pooling, database connection pooling, declarative security, and just-in-time (JIT) object activation.

MTS provides a GUI tool for its administration tasks: the Microsoft Transaction Server Explorer, as shown in Figure 1.13.

MTS Architecture

MTS provides its services through a runtime environment. It also provides a server process for hosting COM components. For example, Figure 1.14 illustrates how a client application interacts with a series of COM components and a back-end database to perform user security credential checking.

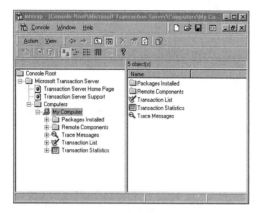

Figure 1.13: *The Microsoft Transaction Server Explorer.*

In this example, a client application makes a request to the COM security component to check a user's security credentials by creating an object (an instance) of the security component. The security object, in turn, creates a data-access object and makes a request. Finally, the COM data access object makes a query through the ADO/OLE DB interface to the User table on a SQL server database. Both the security component and the data-access component are hosted in the MTS process; they participate in the same transaction.

As shown in Figure 1.14, a typical MTS application consists of several components. The MTS server process (mtx.exe) hosts the execution of the COM components and manages object initiation and deactivation. The MTS executive (mtxex.dll) provides runtime services. The Resource Dispenser Manager manages the interaction between COM components and the resource dispenser. (The resource dispenser in this case is the OLE DB provider.) The resource manager manages the durable data store (the SQL Server database in this example). The Microsoft Distributed Transaction Coordinator (MS DTC) is responsible for coordinating the transactions.

MS DTC will be covered in Chapter 6, "Writing Transactional Components." Resource managers and resource dispensers will be discussed in Chapter 7, "Compensating Resource Manager (CRM)."

MTS Programming Model

In MTS, components are hosted (installed) in *packages*. An MTS package is a collection of components that run in the same process. A package also defines security boundaries. Figure 1.15 shows some installed packages in the MTS Explorer.

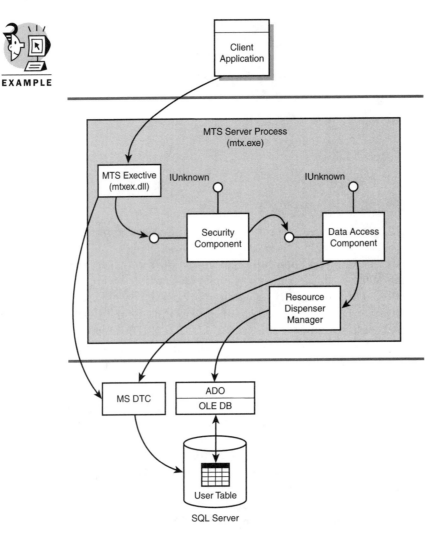

Figure 1.14: *A client accesses a database back end through MTS components.*

The two types of MTS packages are the *library package* and the *server package*. A library package runs in the process address of the client that creates it. A server package runs in its own process address on the local computer where the package resides.

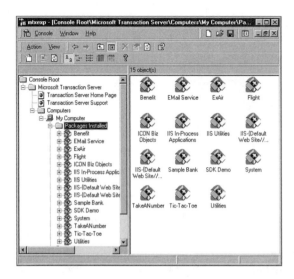

Figure 1.15: Installed packages shown in the MTS Explorer.

EXAMPLE

When an object (an instance of an MTS component) is created, MTS creates an associated wrapper object, called a *context object* (see Figure 1.16), through the IObjectContext interface. This context object allows the object to check the identity of the client. It also lets the object vote for the possible transaction output—either to commit the transaction by calling the SetComplete() method or roll back the transaction by calling the SetAbort() method.

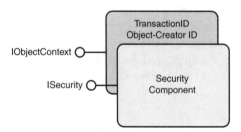

Figure 1.16: MTS creates an associated context object for each COM object it hosts.

An MTS component can have transactional attributes that can be set at design time and reconfigured during deployment. At runtime, MTS executive reads the transactional attributes of a component and decides whether the component should participate in a transaction, create a new transaction, or no transaction at all. Figure 1.17 shows how the transactional attributes look in the MTS Explorer. You'll learn how to set transactional attributes of COM components at design time in Visual Basic in Chapter 6.

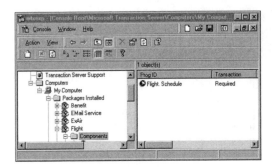

Figure 1.17: *Transactional attributes of an MTS COM object.*

MTS provides a just-in-time (JIT) object activation mechanism, which reduces the lifetime of an object and thus improves scalability. However, this also implies that the client should initiate the object as late as possible, preferably right before calling its methods. Similarly the client should also destroy the object as soon as possible, preferably right after the completion of the last method call.

To take advantage of the scalability provided by MTS, you should design the interface of MTS components as *stateless* instead of *stateful*. Stateless objects do not retain any state information, in contrast to stateful objects. You'll see some examples of stateful and stateless objects when you look at the interface design in Chapter 4, "Introduction to Visual Basic COM Programming."

MTS Security Model

MTS introduces a role-based security model. A *role* in MTS is a collection of NT users and groups. Each role defines which users are allowed to invoke which interfaces of a component. MTS also allows the security to be managed both declaratively and programmatically.

MTS Limitations

Although MTS provides numerous services to developers so that they can focus on resolving business problems; it does have several limitations, however.

MTS is not part of COM. Rather, it is built on top of COM, which places some restrictions on the way the client can create an instance of COM components hosted in MTS. For example, if you use the Visual Basic keyword New or the CreateObject() method to create an instance of COM components, you do not get the reference of the context object. Therefore, the object cannot participate in the existing transaction, even if its transactional attributes say it should do so. For the COM object to be enlisted in

an existing transaction, you have to create it by calling the
CreateInstance() method instead.

Another limitation of MTS is that it requires that the components inside
MTS must be a specific threading model—the Single-Threaded Apartment
(STA) model. This means that the object is tied to its creating thread
throughout its entire lifetime, thus preventing the object from being used
by other threads. This decreases performance and scalability. As you saw
earlier in this chapter, STA allows only one method call at a time because
calls are executed serially.

In addition, the role-based security model of MTS works only for server
packages. You cannot set roles for library packages.

What Is COM+?

Now that you have read through the preceding discussion on COM, DCOM,
MTS, and their limitations, you probably want to know exactly what COM+
is. COM+ is a set of component services that ship with Microsoft Windows
2000. COM+ combines and enhances all the services available in COM,
DCOM, and MTS and unifies them into a new integrated entity with many
great new services. The following sections introduce some core COM+ services and the new COM+ programming model.

Core COM+ Services

In addition to the enhancement of existing MTS services, such as automatic
thread pooling, database connection pooling, transaction management,
declarative security, and state management, COM+ also provides several
significant new services, including Queued Components (QCs), Loosely
Coupled Events (LCEs), object pooling, object construction, and
Compensation Resource Managers (CRMs).

The following sections briefly review both enhanced features and new services offered by COM+.

SECURITY MODEL

COM+ extended role-based security to library applications in addition to
server applications.

TIP

Former MTS packages are now called *applications* in COM+. COM+ applications will be
discussed in Chapter 5, "Using the Component Services MMC Snap-In."

COM+ also supports process access permissions security through authentication and impersonation. COM+ security will be covered in Chapter 8, "COM+ Securities."

THREADING MODEL

As you learned earlier, MTS restricts the threading model of its components to the Single-Threaded Apartment (STA) model. COM+ now supports a new threading model called Neutral-threading Apartment (NTA), which allows execution of objects on any thread types.

TRANSACTION MANAGEMENT

In addition to the MTS transaction semantics, COM+ now introduces an "auto-done" transaction management mechanism that allows the system to automatically call SetComplete() or SetAbort() if the developer didn't code these calls explicitly. Transaction will be covered in Chapter 6, "Writing Transactional Components."

SIMPLIFIED ADMINISTRATION

Whereas MTS uses the System Registry for storing the metadata that describes components, COM+ now provides a new registration database called RegDB for this purpose. RegDB offers better management capability than the System Registry. Information in RegDB can be accessed programmatically through a transactional, scriptable COM interface called the *COM+ catalog*. Additionally, the Component Services MMC snap-in provides a better centralized administrative tool than the MTS Explorer for administering and deploying components.

RegDB and the COM+ catalog will be discussed in Chapter 11, "Administering COM+ Applications Programmatically". The Component Services MMC snap-in will be covered in Chapter 5, "Using the Component Services MMC Snap-in."

New COM+ Services

In addition to enhancing and improving existing COM and MTS services, COM+ also provides a lot of powerful new services, such as Queued Components (QC), Loosely Coupled Events (LCE), Object Pooling, and Compensating Resource Manager (CRM).

QUEUED COMPONENTS (QC)

The COM+ Queued Components (QC) service extends the asynchronous programming model of MSMQ to the component level. QC is one of the most important COM+ component services. By using QC, a client is no longer blocked by the server process after making a call because the call is now processed asynchronously. As a result, scalability is improved. Moreover, QC allows clients to make the call even when the server components are not available. This capability makes enterprise applications more robust. Queued components will be discussed in Chapter 9, "Queued Components."

LOOSELY COUPLED EVENTS (LCE)

COM+ provides a Loosely Coupled Event model, using a publisher-subscriber metaphor. In contrast to traditional Tightly Coupled Events (TCE), the COM+ event model offers several advantages. Event publishers and subscribers don't need to know about each other (or they don't care). In COM+ events, publishers and subscribers can be developed, deployed, and executed independently. They do not need to be running at the same time either. You'll learn about LCE in Chapter 10, "COM+ Events."

OBJECT POOLING

COM+ provides the object pooling service to reduce the overhead incurred in object creation by maintaining a pool of objects instead of destroying and re-creating objects each time after using them. For the object to be pooled, it must meet several requirements. For example, the object must have no thread affinity. As you learned earlier in this chapter, the object must support the MTA or Free-threading model. Visual Basic 6.0 supports only single apartment threading (STA), so you can't use VB6 to create pooled objects yet. Microsoft promised that the next version of Visual Basic will support free threading. Until then, to create pooled objects, you have to use a tool that meets the requirements, such as Visual C++. Object pooling will be discussed in Chapter 12, "More on COM+ Programming."

COMPENSATING RESOURCE MANAGER (CRM)

Although MTS allows components to participate in database transactions through MTC, COM+ now extends the transactional support to nontransactional resources, such as some legacy systems. This result is achieved through the Compensation Resource Manager (CRM) architecture. You'll learn about CRM in Chapter 7, "Compensating Resource Manager (CRM)."

COM+ Programming Model

COM+ provides a significantly simplified programming paradigm over MTS. MTS introduced the attribute-based programming model. COM+ greatly enhances this model by supporting many more configurable attributes. Configuration is now becoming an essential part when you develop your COM+ applications.

For example, the *Synchronization* attribute allows you to specify what type of synchronization you want when your components are activated. The *Object pooling* attribute lets you decide whether the component should be pooled. For pooled objects, you can further specify the pool sizes and time-out value. You can control whether the JIT should be enabled. The Queuing and Events attributes allow you to control the behavior of Queued Components and Loosely Coupled Events, respectively.

One of the most noticeable new COM+ attributes is *Object construction*. This feature enables parameterized object construction with an administratively specified construction string. When this feature is enabled, constructor strings are passed in during object creation. Components can access these strings during runtime through the `IobjectConstruct` interface. In Chapter 5, you will see more detailed discussion and examples about object construction.

What's Next

By now, you should have a firm understanding of what COM+ and its services are, as well as the importance of COM+ services in building scalable, distributed enterprise applications. The next chapter describes Microsoft's framework for building three-tier applications: the Windows Distributed interNet Application (DNA) architecture. You'll also see how COM+ plays a significant role in the DNA architecture as an enabling technology and a glue for sticking all the different pieces together.

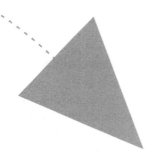

Windows DNA 2000 and COM+

Microsoft Windows Distributed interNet Application (DNA) is a framework and blueprint for developers to quickly and easily build scalable, high-performance, distributed, and robust enterprise and Internet applications. Windows 2000 is the next generation of Windows DNA. For purposes of this discussion, I'll simply use the term *Windows DNA* or just *DNA* although I am implying *Windows DNA 2000*.

This chapter teaches you the following:

- The basics of Windows DNA 2000

- How COM+ is related to Windows DNA

- Microsoft data-access strategies and how to use Microsoft ActiveX Data Objects (ADO) in Windows DNA applications

- The basics of Internet Information Services (IIS 5.0) and Active Server Pages (ASP)

Windows DNA 2000 Architecture

At the core of Windows DNA 2000 is a three-tiered application architecture, surrounded by a rich set of development tools and abundant infrastructure services that are integrated into the Windows 2000 operating system. Here, you'll first look at what challenges today's enterprise and Internet applications have to face. Then you'll see how Windows DNA addresses and resolves these challenges through its application architecture and infrastructure services.

Internet Applications and Their Challenges

The explosion of the Internet, especially the World Wide Web, has brought about tremendous business opportunities. To stay competitive, companies and organizations are urged to get their businesses on the Web to extend their reach to more customers who are simply impossible to reach by traditional means and to conduct business with partners more efficiently. All these aspects pose many unique challenges to today's application development. These challenges include scalability, availability, reliability, security, maintainability, and ease of development and deployment.

SCALABILITY

The more successful an Internet application becomes, the more potential users it will reach. The potential number of users can grow dramatically overnight in orders of magnitude. The application must be able to handle the increases in number of users without significantly degrading its performance.

AVAILABILITY

Today's Internet applications must be kept up and running all the time, 24 hours a day, 7 days a week. A possible system shutdown in an Internet environment could cause a significant financial loss. No business can afford such a loss.

RELIABILITY

Internet applications must be rock-solid. Data processed or generated by an application must be reliable and consistent. Inconsistent data in a system could cause disastrous consequences to the business.

SECURITY

Internet applications have a much higher security requirement than traditional applications. An Internet application must be able to protect its sensitive data against unauthorized access. An Internet application also must be able to determine what group of users are allowed to perform what operations or to access what part of data based on their given privileges to the application.

MAINTAINABILITY

Applications must be easy to support and maintain. They also must be easy to modify and enhance to accommodate business evolution and keep an organization competitive.

FAST AND EASY DEVELOPMENT AND DEPLOYMENT

Time is money. "Yesterday" is almost the standard answer to the question "When do you need this application?" In today's fast-paced business environment, an Internet application must be developed and deployed very quickly. Delivering an application late may mean lost business in most cases.

Now that you've reviewed some of the unique challenges today's Internet applications present, you'll next see how Windows DNA 2000 addresses these challenges through its three-tiered application architecture and its core infrastructure services provided by the underlying Window 2000 operating system. Let's start by looking at the three-tiered application architecture.

Three-Tiered Application Architecture

At a high level, all applications share some basic characteristics. They all contain three common components. First, an application must interact with its users, so it must provide a user interface or a presentation component. Second, an application needs to store its data somewhere in some form, such as a database, a file, or the Windows Registry. So, an application also needs a data-store component. Finally, an application must have some logic or rules upon which data can be retrieved from the data store, manipulated, and presented to the users or saved back to the data store. As a result, an application requires a business-logic component.

Depending on where these components reside, you can categorize an application as either a two-tiered application or a three-tiered application.

TWO-TIERED APPLICATIONS

EXAMPLE

Traditional client/server applications are typically two-tiered applications. In a two-tiered application, all clients directly access the data store on the server through a network such as a local area network (LAN), as illustrated in Figure 2.1.

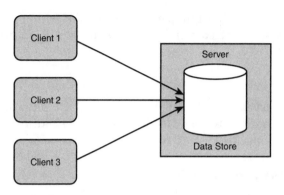

Figure 2.1: *A two-tiered application architecture.*

EXAMPLE

You'll find two variations to the two-tiered architecture, depending on where the application logic resides. The application logic can include both business logic and data-access logic. If the application logic resides in the presentation tier, the architecture is called a *fat client* architecture. As you can see in Figure 2.2, a Visual Basic client application contains both presentation logic (as VB forms) and application logic code (such as embedded SQL statements in the routines). When a user clicks the Log On button (Step 1), the click event of the button fires. This event calls the ValidateUser() function (Step 2; this function may be declared in the Generation Declaration section of the form), which directly accesses the database through embedded SQL statements (Step 3).

Another variation to the two-tiered application architecture is called a *fat server* architecture. As opposed to the fat client architecture, in a fat server two-tiered application, the application logic resides on the server side, usually in the form of stored procedures. Figure 2.3 illustrates a fat client two-tiered application model. As in the fat client example, when a user clicks the Log On button (Step 1), the events behind the button fire and call the ValidateUser() function (Step 2). This time, however, instead of accessing the database on the server using embedded SQL statements, the ValidateUser() function accesses the database table (Step 4) indirectly through a stored procedure, proc_ValidateUser (Step 3) on the server.

In the previous two examples, the user validation is the business logic, which implements both *business rules* and data access mechanisms. A business rule could be a specific business requirement, an organizational policy, a business specific computation algorithm, and so on. For example, a user validation business rule can be expressed as "A valid user is one who has an entry in the login table of the user's database."

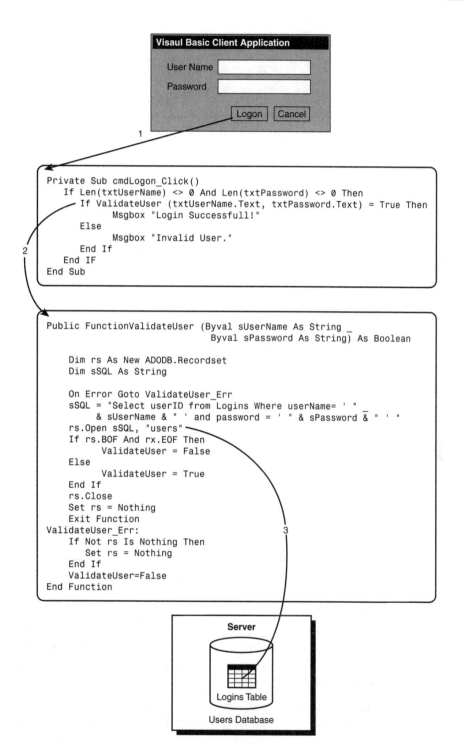

Figure 2.2: *A fat client two-tiered application.*

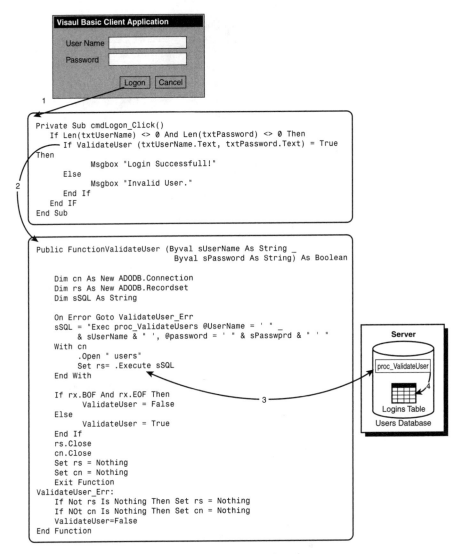

Figure 2.3: A fat server two-tiered application.

Two-tiered applications usually work fine in departmental scale applications in which only limited numbers of users (usually below 100) use the application. Clients usually access a single database on the server with fast, reliable networks such as a LAN. Most applications in use today are two-tiered client/server applications.

The two-tiered client/server architecture does present a number of limitations, however, especially when an application is developed for the Internet or Web.

First, a two-tiered application scales poorly when the number of users exceeds a certain limit. Some of the server resources, such as database connections, are very limited and expensive. In a two-tiered application, each user consumes some dedicated server resource, such as a database connection. As the number of users increases, the server resources are stolen away and the performance degrades dramatically. When the server resources are completely exhausted, the system crashes.

Second, two-tiered applications are not reliable in an Internet environment. Two-tiered applications rely on direct, fast, reliable local networks (such as a LAN). In Internet applications, most users use inexpensive, slow connections, such as dial-up connections through a telephone modem. These slow connections are not always reliable and sometimes even unavailable. Because the connections in two-tiered applications are usually direct, there is no guarantee of their availability. If the server shuts down for some reason, such as scheduled periodical maintenance, it is not available to the clients during that period of time.

Finally, two-tiered applications are hard to maintain. Because business logic is embedded in the client applications as in the fat client model, it is very difficult to modify the business logic and redeploy applications. Say you have thousands of users using your application. If you make some changes to the application, you have to reinstall the new version of the application to thousands of desktops or workstations. Besides, it is extremely difficult, if not impossible, to reuse the business logic in other applications.

The stored procedure mechanism in the fat server model somehow relieves the redistribution pain and also improves the performance and scalability a little bit. This configuration also has its own limitations. First, because stored procedures are written in some database-specific SQL languages that are not as powerful as full programming languages such as Visual Basic, its functionality is limited. Second, stored procedure languages are vendor-dependent, so they are not portable. For example, if you migrate your database from SQL Server to Oracle, you have to rewrite all these Transact-SQL stored procedures in PL/SQL, the SQL dialect used in Oracle databases.

THREE-TIERED APPLICATIONS

Due to the limitations with the two-tiered application model, Microsoft DNA presents a three-tiered application architecture. In a three-tiered model, the business logic is separated from both the client and the database as a separate tier, called the *business tier* or sometimes the *middle tier*.

TIP

In some Microsoft documentation, the three different tiers are called *services*. For example, the presentation tier is called *User Services*, the middle tier (or business tier) is called *Business Services*, and the data tier is called *Data Services*.

EXAMPLE

Figure 2.4 illustrates a three-tiered application architecture.

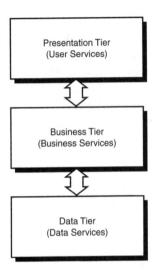

Figure 2.4: *The three-tiered application architecture.*

As shown in Figure 2.4, in a three-tired architecture, the business logic tier is separated from both the presentation tier and the data tier. The business tier sits between the presentation tier and the data tier. The business tier is responsible for implementing business rules, accessing data stored in the data tier on behalf of the presentation tier. The business tier also retrieves data from the data store and passes the data to the presentation tier, which in turn displays the data to the end user in a meaningful format.

In the Windows DNA three-tiered configuration, the business tier, or Business Services, contains COM components that implement business logic and data access mechanisms. The presentation layer, or User Services, can be either a traditional Windows application (sometimes called a Win32 application, such as a Visual Basic application) or a browser-based Web application. The data tier, or Data Services, can be a data store in a variety of forms, including a relational database system such as a SQL Server or Oracle database, a mainframe system such as an IBM DB2 system, a file system, or even an email system.

The presentation tier accesses the business components in the business tier directly through either the DCOM protocol, as in the case of a Win32 application, or indirectly through the Active Server Pages (ASP) on a Web server, such as the Internet Information Services (IIS) using the HTTP protocol, as in the case of a Web browser application. ASP and IIS will be discussed later in the section "Internet Information Services (IIS) and Active Server Pages (ASP)."

The business tier can further be partitioned as a *Business Logic Layer (BLL)* and *Data Access Layer (DAL)*. The DAL components access data stored in the data tier typically through Microsoft ActiveX Data Objects (ADO). ADO is an important component in Microsoft Data Access Components (MDAC). You'll see many ADO examples later, in the section "Microsoft Data Access Components (MDAC)."

CAUTION

Don't confuse the Data Access Layer (or DAL) with the data tier. The Data Access Layer is a subtier within the business tier; it is part of the Business Services. Because the data tier is the place where data stores (such as databases) reside, it is the data service.

EXAMPLE

Figure 2.5 illustrates the Windows DNA architecture.

Let's look at the example used earlier in the discussion of two-tiered architectures. As shown in Figure 2.6, the business logic (validate a user account) is separated from the presentation tier (refer to Figure 2.2) or the data tier (refer to Figure 2.3) and put in the business tier. This business tier is implemented as a BLL component (bus_User.Validation) and a DAL component (db_User.Validation).

As you can see in Figure 2.6, in a three-tired DNA architecture,

- The code in the Presentation Layer (the click event procedure of the command button, Step 1) no longer directly interacts with the database.

- Rather, it creates a BLL object and calls the ValidateUser() method of the BLL object (Step 2).

- The BLL object, in turn, creates a DAL object and calls the ValidateUser() of the DAL object (Step 3).

- The DAL object encapsulates all the database access details from the BLL and the client. It calls the stored procedure proc_ValidateUser (Step 4) and

- Retrieves a result set from the database table (Step 5).

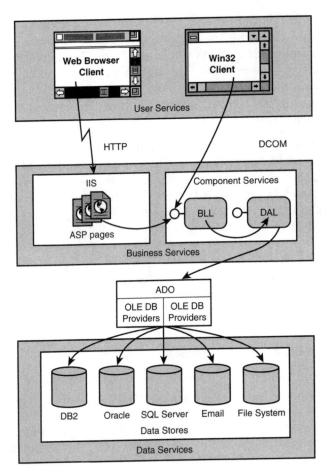

Figure 2.5: *Windows DNA architecture.*

You don't have to worry about the detail design of the COM objects and the implementation of code. You'll learn about them in depth in Chapter 4, "Introduction to Visual Basic COM Programming." The purpose here is simply to demonstrate the concept of Windows DNA three-tiered application architecture.

In the Windows DNA three-tiered architecture, the business tier is separated from the presentation and data tiers. It can be used by any number of clients. Because business components (BLL and DAL) are centralized in the business tier, they are more easily deployed and maintained. The clients now can't directly access the database, so you can enhance the security by setting appropriate security configurations at the component level, at the interface level, or even at the methods level. So, the security of the application is improved. The scalability of the three-tiered application is also improved because the component can serve a lot more clients and the server resources (such as database connections) can now be pooled and reused.

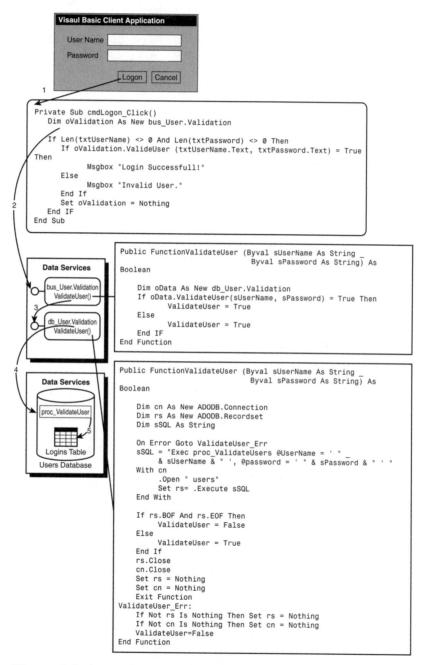

Figure 2.6: A sample three-tiered DNA application.

Infrastructure Services

The preceding section discussed the benefits of the three-tiered application architecture of Windows DNA. This section briefly introduces you to the rich set of infrastructure services provided by the Windows 2000 operating system and shows how these services enhance the three-tiered architecture, addresses the issues of enterprise and Internet applications, and helps developers focus on providing business solutions rather than developing "plumbing" code.

COMPONENT SERVICES

The heart of Windows DNA is the *component services*, or COM+, which is what this book is all about. The component services of Windows DNA provide the following:

- Distributed transactions
- Extended transaction support for nontransactional systems (the Compensation Resource Manager, or CRM)
- Security
- Queued Components (QC)
- Loosely Coupled Events (LCE)
- Object pooling
- Object construction
- Transient state management
- Shared Property Manager (SPM)

Part II of this book will teach you all the component services through plenty of Visual Basic code examples.

DATA SERVICES

Microsoft Data Access Components (MDAC) provides a universal strategy for accessing all kinds of data across the enterprise. MDAC consists of a set of programming interfaces, including OLE DB, ActiveX Data Objects (ADO), and Open Database Connectivity (ODBC). OLE DB and ADO are COM-based interfaces that offer easier programming models and better performance over ODBC. Microsoft integrates OLE DB and ADO support into all the programming languages in Visual Studio. OLE DB and ADO are described later, in the section "Microsoft Data Access Components (MDAC)."

Message Services

Message queuing is an industry standard that allows different applications or their components to interact in a loosely coupled, asynchronous manner. The Microsoft Message Queue (MSMQ) 1.0 was originally introduced as a component in the Windows NT 4.0 Option Pack. In Windows 2000, MSMQ 2.0 is integrated as part of system services. MSMQ will be discussed in Chapter 3, "Introduction to Microsoft Message Queuing Services (MSMQ)."

Web Services

Microsoft also integrated its powerful Web server, Internet Information Service (IIS 5.0), and the Active Server Pages (ASP) technology into the Windows 2000 operating system. IIS and ASP allow developers to build powerful script applications that run on the server side to produce dynamic, interactive Web pages. IIS and ASP will be discussed in the section "Internet Information Services (IIS) and Active Server Pages (ASP)."

Security Services

Windows DNA provides integrated security services, including authentication, authorization, data integrity, and data privacy services. Security will be discussed in Chapter 8, "COM+ Securities."

Where COM+ Fits In

By now, you should have a clear idea of where COM+, or the component services, fits in the big picture of Windows DNA architecture. It's the core service among all other services in Windows DNA. It's also a glue that enables different services and components of Windows DNA to work together to form an integrated enterprise or Internet application.

The Heart of Windows DNA Services

COM+ is the heart of Windows DNA. All Windows DNA Services expose their interfaces through the COM binary standard. COM+ services, such as Queued Components (QC), transaction services, events services (such as LCE), and so on, are the building blocks of every Windows DNA application.

A Glue That Enables Different Tiers to Work Together

COM+ also acts as the "glue" between all tiers of a Windows DNA application (refer to Figure 2.5). COM+ enables different parts of a Windows DNA application to communicate with each other to build robust, efficient, and integrated enterprise and Internet applications.

Microsoft Data Access Components (MDAC)

Microsoft Data Access Components (MDAC) is an important part of Microsoft's Universal Data Access (UDA) strategy that is used to interact with any kind of data stores, including relational database management systems, flat files, and emails. In this section, we will introduce MDAC and discuss the important component of MDAC, the ActiveX Data Objects (ADO), in great details by examples.

MDAC and Universal Data Access (UDA)

EXAMPLE

Microsoft Data Access Components (MDAC) is the heart of Microsoft's Universal Data Access (UDA) strategy, which is part of Windows DNA. UDA is the Microsoft strategy for providing access to information data throughout the enterprise, regardless of where it is stored and in what format. Figure 2.7 describes the UDA architecture.

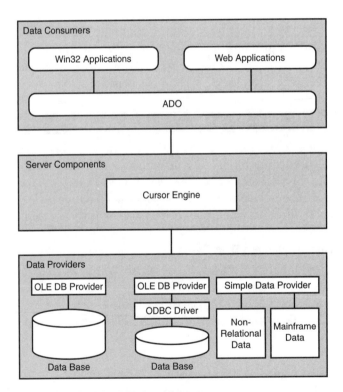

Figure 2.7: *The UDA architecture.*

As shown in Figure 2.7, UDA consists of three components: data providers, service components, and data consumers. Data providers represent data stores, such as databases, file systems, email systems, or mainframe systems. Service components consume and produce OLE DB data. Cursor engines and query processors are examples of these components. Data consumers consume OLE DB data provided by the service components. ADO itself is an OLE DB data consumer. Other data consumer examples include Win32 applications (for example, Visual Basic applications) and ASP applications.

MDAC provides a set of technologies that provide the basic framework for general-purpose data access on Microsoft platforms. MDAC was designed to provide high performance, better reliability, and the broadest-access range of data stores.

MDAC supports three major technologies. The first technology is OLE DB, which is a low-level, high-performance interface to a variety of data stores. The second technology in MDAC is the Microsoft ActiveX Data Objects (ADO), which is a high-level, easy-to-use interface to OLE DB. ADO and OLE DB can both work with relational as well as nonrelational data stores. The third technology MDAC supports is Open Database Connectivity (ODBC), which is another low-level, high-performance interface that is designed specifically for relational data stores. MDAC 2.5 ships with Windows 2000 and is available in default Windows 2000 installations.

ACTIVEX DATA OBJECTS (ADO)

EXAMPLE

As you have already seen from this discussion, ActiveX Data Objects is an OLE DB consumer. It's a set of COM-based interfaces that provide a simple programming model for developers to meet their data access needs. Figure 2.8 illustrates the object model of ADO 2.5.

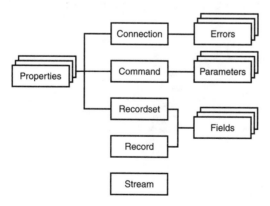

Figure 2.8: *ADO 2.5 object model.*

As shown in Figure 2.8, ADO 2.5 introduces a couple of new objects: the `Record` and `Stream` objects. The `Record` object represents and manages directories and files in a file system, for example, or folders and messages in an email system. It can also represent a row in a recordset. The `Stream` object is used to read, write, and manage the binary stream of bytes or text that comprise a file or message stream.

Compared to previous Microsoft data access object models, such as DAO and RDO, ADO has a relatively "flat" object model, as shown in Figure 2.8. That is, no restrictive hierarchical relationships exist between the top-level objects. Among the three objects—`Connection`, `Command`, or `Recordset`—you can create any one of them without explicitly creating the other two.

A thorough coverage of ADO 2.5 is beyond the scope of this book. This discussion focuses on the practical aspects of ADO that are most important in programming the Data Access Layer of business components. This chapter describes the `Connection`, `Command`, and `Recordset` objects, which are the most important and most used ADO objects. I will teach you how and when to use them. I will also show you some advanced ADO techniques. To follow the examples here, you need to use the pubs SQL Server sample database.

TIP

The pubs database should be installed by default when you install the SQL Server. If it is not installed for some reason, you can run the SQL script file, instpubs.sql, using the Query Analyzer of SQL Server 7.0. The `instpubs.sql` script file is located under the install subdirectory of your SQL Server installation, such as C:\MSSQL7\Install\.

EXAMPLE

To work with ADO in Visual Basic, you need to set a reference to the ADO Object Library, as shown in Figure 2.9. This process is called *early binding*. You can also use *late binding* to create and use ADO objects, without referencing the ADO Object Library in your Visual Basic project. You'll learn about object binding in Chapter 4, "Introduction to Visual Basic COM Programming."

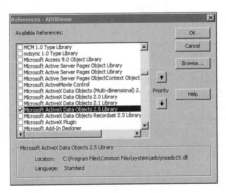

Figure 2.9: *Setting a reference to the ADO Object Library in Visual Basic.*

OPENING A DATABASE CONNECTION

The ADO Connection object enables you to establish a connection to the database by using the Open method. Data retrieved from the database is stored in a Recordset object. Use the Close method to close an open connection. You can use either a native OLE DB provider for a specific data store or OLE DB provider for ODBC to connect to the database. For SQL Server, you can use both.

Listing 2.1 shows how to open a database connection using OLE DB provider for ODBC.

EXAMPLE

Listing 2.1   Opening a Database Connection Using the OLE DB Provider for ODBC

```
Private Sub cmdConnection1_Click()
    'Enable the error handler
    On Error GoTo Connection1_Err
    'Declare and create an instance of
    'a Connection object.
    Dim oConnection As ADODB.Connection
    Set oConnection = New ADODB.Connection

    With oConnection
        'Specify the Provider property,
        'MSDASQL is the default provider.
        .Provider = "MSDASQL"
        'Set the ConnectionString property
        .ConnectionString = "Driver={SQL Server};" & _
                            "Server=(local);" & _
                            "Database=pubs;" & _
                            "UID=sa;" & _
                            "PWD=;"
        'Open the connection.
        .Open
    End With

    MsgBox "Connection Opened!"

    'Now close the connection and release the resource.
    oConnection.Close
    Set oConnection = Nothing

    'If everything is fine, get out the sub.
    Exit Sub
Connection1_Err:
    'Something is wrong, release the resource if not yet.
    If Not oConnection Is Nothing Then
```

Listing 2.1   continued

```
        Set oConnection = Nothing
    End If
    MsgBox Err.Description
End Sub
```

Listing 2.1 specifies the `Provider` property of the connection object as
`"MSDASQL"`. This is optional if you open the connection using OLE DB
provider for ODBC data sources. If this property is not specified, `"MSDASQL"`
is the default value. Notice that the `Server` attributes of the
`ConnectionString` property are set to `"(local)"`, assuming that the database is on the local machine. If the database is located on a remote server,
use the machine name of the server instead.

The syntax used in the `ConnectionString` property

```
.ConnectionString = "Driver={SQL Server};" & _
                    "Server=(local);" & _
                    "Database=pubs;" & _
                    "UID=sa;" & _
                    "PWD=;"
```

is called "DSN-less" syntax, because here we provided all the connection
information (dirver, server, database, user id and password) to the
ConnectionString property without explicitly creating or using a DSN.
Alternatively, if a DSN (Data Source Name) has been set up, you can use
the following syntax instead:

```
.ConnectionString = "DSN=pubs;" & _
                    "UID=sa;" & _
                    "PWD=;"
```

DSN is the Data Source Name. To run some of the sample code in this section, you need to set up a System DSN on your machine, name it *pubs*, and
point to the pubs database on the SQL Server. Toss set up a DSN in
Windows 2000, open the Control Panel and click the Administrative Tools
applet to open the Administrative Tools window. There, you can access the
Data Sources (ODBC) utility to set up the DSN (see Figure 2.10).

Figure 2.10: *Accessing the Data Sources (ODBC) utility in Windows 2000.*

Listing 2.2 uses the OLE DB provider for SQL Server, the native SQL Server provider.

Listing 2.2   Opening a Database Connection Using the OLE DB Provider for SQL Server

```
Private Sub cmdConnection2_Click()
    'Enable the error handler
    On Error GoTo Connection2_Err
    'Declare and create an instance of
    'a Connection object.
    Dim oConnection As ADODB.Connection
    Set oConnection = New ADODB.Connection

    With oConnection
        'Specify the Provider property.
        .Provider = "SQLOLEDB"
        'Set the ConnectionString property
        .ConnectionString = "Data Source=(local);" & _
                            "Initial Catalog=pubs;" & _
                            "User ID=sa;" & _
                            "Password=;"
        'Open the connection.
        .Open
    End With

    MsgBox "Connection Opened!"

    'Now close the connection and release the resource.
    oConnection.Close
    Set oConnection = Nothing

    'If everything is fine, get out the sub.
    Exit Sub
Connection2_Err:
    'Something is wrong, release the resource if not yet.
    If Not oConnection Is Nothing Then
        Set oConnection = Nothing
    End If
    MsgBox Err.Description
End Sub
```

In this case, the Provider property is set to "SQLOLEDB". Also, notice that the syntax for ConnectionString is different from Listing 2.1:

```
.ConnectionString = "Data Source=(local);" & _
                    "Initial Catalog=pubs;" & _
                    "User ID=sa;" & _
                    "Password=;"
```

In this syntax, the Data Source is the server, and Initial Catalog is the database. SQL Server has another important optional parameter, Trusted_Connection, which indicates the User Authentication mode. The default value of Trusted_Connection is No. In this case, the OLEDBSQL provider uses the Mixed mode to authorize user access to the SQL Server database. The SQL Server login and password are specified in the User Id and Password properties. If you set this property to Yes, SQLOLEDB uses the NT Authentication mode to authorize user access to the SQL Server database.

TIP

These examples are for demonstration purposes. When possible, always use the native OLE DB providers because they are optimized for the target data stores. Use the OLE DB provider for ODBC only when no native OLE DB provider for a specific data store is available.

EXECUTING A SQL COMMAND

The ADO Command object defines a command that you can execute against a data source. The command can be a SQL statement or a SQL stored procedure.

EXAMPLE

Listing 2.3 demonstrates how to execute a SQL statement to insert a row in the authors table in the pubs database.

Listing 2.3   Executing a SQL Statement Through the ADO Command Object

```
Private Sub cmdCommand_Click()
    'Enable the error handler
    On Error GoTo Command_Err
    'Declare variables.
    Dim oConnection As ADODB.Connection 'the Connection object
    Dim oCommand    As ADODB.Command    'the Command object
    Dim sSQL        As String           'the SQL statement
    'Initialize the Connection and Command objects.
    Set oConnection = New ADODB.Connection
    Set oCommand = New ADODB.Command

    'Construct the SQL statement
    sSQL = "Insert authors (au_id, au_lname, au_fname, contract)" & _
           "values ('123-45-6789','Li','Peishu',1)"
    'Open the connection.
    oConnection.Open "pubs"
    'Set up the properties of the Command object
    'and execute the SQL statement
    With oCommand
        .CommandType = adCmdText
```

Listing 2.3   continued

```
        .CommandText = sSQL
        .ActiveConnection = oConnection
        .Execute
    End With

    MsgBox "A row is inserted to the authors table!"

    'If everything is fine, release the resources
    'and get out the sub.
    Set oCommand = Nothing
    Set oConnection = Nothing
    Exit Sub
Command_Err:
    'Something is wrong, release the resource if not yet.
    If Not oCommand Is Nothing Then
        Set oCommand = Nothing
    End If
    If Not oConnection Is Nothing Then
        Set oConnection = Nothing
    End If
    MsgBox Err.Description
End Sub
```

In Figure 2.11, a SQL Server Query Analyzer window shows that the new row is inserted into the authors table in the pubs database.

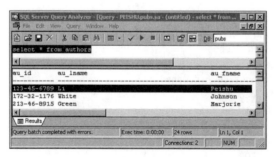

Figure 2.11: *A new row is inserted into the authors table.*

Notice that Listing 2.3 explicitly uses an ADO connection object and sets it as the ActiveConnection property. ADO allows you to use the Command object without explicitly creating a Connection object, by setting the ActiveConnection property to a connection string. There are a couple of downsides to using this approach. First, ADO automatically creates a new Connection object for you instead of using an existing connection, thus consuming additional server resources. Second, the Connection object has an associated `Errors` collection, which stores any OLE DB provider errors during the session. The `Errors` collection is very valuable for debugging and troubleshooting. However, this `Errors` collection is available to you only through the explicitly created `Connection` object.

The ADO `Command` object has a `Parameters` collection, which allows you to execute parameterized queries or stored procedures. You'll see how to use the `Parameters` collection later in this chapter when you examine how to execute stored procedures using ADO.

WORKING WITH RECORDSETS

An ADO `Recordset` object represents a set of records returned from a SQL query or a stored procedure. You can create an ADO `Recordset` in three ways.

The first way to create an ADO `Recordset` is to call the `Open` method of the `Recordset` object (see Listing 2.4.)

Listing 2.4   Creating an ADO `Recordset` Using the `Open` Method

EXAMPLE

```
Private Sub cmdRecordset1_Click()
    'Enable the error handler.
    On Error GoTo Recordset1_Err
    'Declare and inilialize an ADO objects
    Dim oConnection  As ADODB.Connection
    Dim oRecordset   As ADODB.Recordset
    Set oRecordset = New ADODB.Recordset

    'Initialize the connection object and open the connection
    Set oConnection = New ADODB.Connection
    oConnection.Open "pubs"
    With oRecordset
        .ActiveConnection = oConnection
        'Open the recordset.
        .Open "Select au_fname, au_lname from authors"

        'Loop through the recordset and display the results.
        Do Until .EOF
            Debug.Print !au_lname & ", " & !au_fname
            oRecordset.MoveNext
        Loop
        'Close the recordset
        .Close
    End With
```

Listing 2.4 continued

```
    'Close the connection
    oConnection.Close

    'If everything is fine, release the resources
    'and get out the sub.
    Set oRecordset = Nothing
    Set oConnection = Nothing
    Exit Sub
Recordset1_Err:
    'Something is wrong, release the resources if not yet.
    If Not oRecordset Is Nothing Then
        Set oRecordset = Nothing
    End If
    If Not oConnection Is Nothing Then
        Set oConnection = Nothing
    End If

    MsgBox Err.Description
End Sub
```

Figure 2.12 shows the results of Listing 2.4 in Visual Basic's debug window.

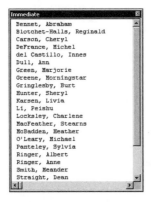

Figure 2.12: *The results of Listing 2.4 in Visual Basic's debug window.*

The other two methods of creating ADO Recordsets include calling the Execute method against either the Connection or Command object.

Listing 2.5 demonstrates how to create an ADO Recordset by calling the Execute method of the Connection object.

EXAMPLE

Listing 2.5 Creating an ADO Recordset Using the Execute Method of the Connection Object

```
Private Sub cmdRecordset2_Click()
    'Enable the error handler.
    On Error GoTo Recordset2_Err
    'Declare and initialize ADO object variables.
    Dim oRecordset  As ADODB.Recordset
    Dim oConnection As ADODB.Connection
    Set oConnection = New ADODB.Connection

    'Open the connection.
    oConnection.Open "pubs"

    'Create the recordset object
    Set oRecordset = oConnection.Execute _
                    ("Select au_fname, au_lname from authors")
    'Loop through the recordset and display the results.
    With oRecordset
        Do Until .EOF
            Debug.Print !au_lname & ", " & !au_fname
            oRecordset.MoveNext
        Loop
        'Close the recordset
        .Close
    End With

    'If everything is fine, release the resources
    'and get out the sub.
    Set oRecordset = Nothing
    Set oConnection = Nothing
    Exit Sub
Recordset2_Err:
    'Something is wrong, release the resources if not yet.
    If Not oConnection Is Nothing Then
        Set oConnection = Nothing
    End If
    If Not oRecordset Is Nothing Then
        Set oRecordset = Nothing
    End If
    MsgBox Err.Description
End Sub
```

EXAMPLE

The way the Execute method works against the ADO Command object is similar to the way it works with the ADO Connection object. Listing 2.6 shows how to do this.

Listing 2.6   Creating an ADO Recordset Using the Execute Method of the Command Object

```
Private Sub cmdRecordset3_Click()
    'Enable the error handler.
    On Error GoTo Recordset3_Err
    'Declare and initialize ADO object variables.
    Dim oRecordset   As ADODB.Recordset
    Dim oConnection As ADODB.Connection
    Dim oCommand     As ADODB.Command
    Set oConnection = New ADODB.Connection
    Set oCommand = New ADODB.Command

    'Open the connection.
    oConnection.Open "pubs"

    With oCommand
        'Set command properties.
        .ActiveConnection = oConnection
        .CommandType = adCmdText
        .CommandText = "Select au_fname, au_lname from authors"
        'Create the recordset object
        Set oRecordset = .Execute
    End With

    'Loop through the recordset and display the results.
    With oRecordset
        Do Until .EOF
            Debug.Print !au_lname & ", " & !au_fname
            oRecordset.MoveNext
        Loop
        'Close the recordset
        .Close
    End With

    'If everything is fine, release the resources
    'and get out the sub.
    Set oRecordset = Nothing
    Set oCommand = Nothing
    Set oConnection = Nothing
    Exit Sub
Recordset3_Err:
    'Something is wrong, release the resources if not yet.
    If Not oConnection Is Nothing Then
        Set oConnection = Nothing
    End If
    If Not oCommand Is Nothing Then
        Set oCommand = Nothing
    End If
    If Not oRecordset Is Nothing Then
```

Listing 2.6   continued

```
        Set oRecordset = Nothing
    End If
    MsgBox Err.Description
End Sub
```

The output of Listings 2.5 and 2.6 is the same as that of Listing 2.4, as shown in Figure 2.12.

Given these three different methods for creating an ADO recordset, which one should you choose? If the recordset is the result of a SQL Select statement, as shown in the examples, use the first method (see Listing 2.4). If the recordset is the result returned by a stored procedure without output parameters or a return value, use the second method (see Listing 2.5). If the recordset is the result of executing a stored procedure that takes output parameters or a return value, or if the SQL statement is a parameterized query, use the third method (see Listing 2.6). Calling stored procedures using ADO will be discussed next.

ADVANCED ADO TECHNIQUES

In previous sections, I briefly introduced some basic ADO operations. In this section, I will teach you some advanced ADO techniques, such as calling a SQL stored procedure, using a disconnected recordset, and creating a shorthand recordset. I will also discuss ADO error handling.

EXAMPLE

Let's first look at how to call stored procedures. A *stored procedure* is a piece of code that resides on the database server. Stored procedures are compiled so they can improve performance. You are going to create a simple stored procedure on the pubs database of SQL Server. This stored procedure inserts a title record to the titles table of the pubs database. It returns a message to the caller as an output parameter and a counter as a return value to indicate how many computer titles are in the titles table after the insertion. The purpose here is to demonstrate an ADO technique rather than try to teach you how to write stored procedures.

Listing 2.7 shows the stored procedure.

Listing 2.7   The NewTitle Stored Procedure

```
use pubs
go

If exists(select * from sysobjects where id=object_id("NewTitle"))
  Drop Procedure NewTitle
go

Create Procedure NewTitle
 @title_id varchar(6),
```

Listing 2.7   continued

```
@title varchar(80),
@message varchar (255) out
As

/* This stored procedure tries to insert a new   *
 * row in the titles table. It sends a messagae  *
 * back to the caller and then returns the       *
 * number of total computer books in the table.  */

/* Declare an integer variable to store the      *
 * maxium computer titles after the adding the   *
 * new title.                                    */
Declare @count int

/* Insert the new title. */
Insert titles (title_id, title)
Values (@title_id, @title)

Select @message = 'New title ' + @title + ' has been added!'
Select @count=count(title_id) from titles where title_id like 'BU%'

Return @count
Go
```

EXAMPLE

To create a stored procedure, open SQL Server Query Analyzer, type the script code as shown in Listing 2.7, and then press Ctrl+E.

Listing 2.8 contains sample Visual Basic code that shows how to process the stored procedure you just created.

Listing 2.8   Visual Basic Code for Processing the Stored Procedure

```
Private Sub cmdStoredProc_Click()
    'Enable the error handler
    On Error GoTo StoredProc_Err
    'Declare variables.
    Dim oConnection As ADODB.Connection 'the Connection object
    Dim oCommand    As ADODB.Command    'the Command object
    Dim oParameter  As ADODB.Parameter  'the Parameter object
    Dim sSQL        As String           'the stored procedure
    Dim sMessage    As String           'string variable for holing the output
parameter.
    'Initialize the Connection and Command objects.
    Set oConnection = New ADODB.Connection
    Set oCommand = New ADODB.Command

    'Prepare the stored procedure.
    sSQL = "NewTitle"
```

Listing 2.8   continued

```
    'Open the connection.
    oConnection.Open "pubs"

    'Process the stored procedure.
    With oCommand
        .CommandType = adCmdStoredProc
        .CommandText = sSQL
        .ActiveConnection = oConnection
        'Prepare the return value and parameters
        'and append them to the Command object.
        Set oParameter = .CreateParameter("Return", adInteger, _
                            adParamReturnValue)
        .Parameters.Append oParameter
        Set oParameter = .CreateParameter("@title_id", adVarChar, _
                            adParamInput, 6,"BU8000")
        .Parameters.Append oParameter
        Set oParameter = .CreateParameter("@title", adVarChar, _
                            adParamInput, 80, _
                            "All you need to know about COM+")
        .Parameters.Append oParameter
        Set oParameter = .CreateParameter("@message", adVarChar, adParamOutput,
255)
        .Parameters.Append oParameter
        'Execute the stored procedure.
        .Execute
        MsgBox .Parameters("@message") & vbNewLine & vbNewLine & _
                "We've got " & .Parameters("Return") & _
                " computer titles so far."

    End With

    'If everything is fine, release the resources
    'and get out the sub.
    Set oCommand = Nothing
    Set oConnection = Nothing
    Exit Sub
StoredProc_Err:
    'Something is wrong, release the resource if not yet.
    If Not oCommand Is Nothing Then
        Set oCommand = Nothing
    End If
    If Not oConnection Is Nothing Then
        Set oConnection = Nothing
    End If
    MsgBox Err.Description
End Sub
```

As you may notice, in Listing 2.8, input parameters, output parameters, and the return value are all treated in the same way: They are assigned to the Parameter object by the CreateParameter method of the Command object and then added to the Parameters option by the Append method. The syntax of the CreateParameter method is as follows:

```
Set parameter = command.CreateParameter (Name, Type, Direction, Size, Value)
```

For the Name argument, you use the actual parameter names of the stored procedure, such as @title_id and @title for both input and output parameters, but you use Return for the return values. You specify the Direction argument as adParamInput, adParamOutput, and adParamReturnValue for input parameters, output parameters, and return values, respectively. The return value has to be the *first* parameter object to be appended to the Parameters collection. When you run the code in Listing 2.8, you see a message box like the one shown in Figure 2.13.

Figure 2.13: *The results of executing the code in listing 2.8.*

If the stored procedure takes neither output parameters nor return values, you can use the execute methods of either the Connection or Command object, followed by the stored procedure statement, as shown in the following code segments:

```
OConnection.Execute "Exec AddTitle @title_id = 'BU8000', " & _
                  " @title = 'All You Need to Know About COM+'"
```

or:

```
OCommand.Execute "Exec AddTitle @title_id = 'BU8000', " & _
               " @title = 'All You Need to Know About COM+'"
```

In the "Working with Recordsets" section, you saw some basic VB code examples for dealing with ADO recordsets. Now see what else you can do about ADO recordsets.

The *disconnected recordset* feature of ADO allows you to work with a recordset offline and later synchronize the changes to database in a Batch Update mode. To create a disconnected recordset, you need to specify three properties of the ADO Recordset object. First, you set the CursorLocation property to adUserClient. Then you set the CursorType property to adOpenStatic. Finally, you set the LockType property to adLockBatchOptimistic. Listing 2.9 creates a disconnected recordset, manipulates data, reconnects to the database, and submits the changes. This offline modification and batch updating capability greatly improves scalability.

Listing 2.9 Using a Disconnected ADO Recordset

```
Private Sub cmdDisconnectRS_Click()
    'Enable the error handler.
    On Error GoTo DisconnectedRS_Err
    'Declare and inilialize an ADO Recordset object
    Dim oRecordset As ADODB.Recordset
    Set oRecordset = New ADODB.Recordset

    'Set recordset properties, open the recordset
    'and close the database connection.
    With oRecordset
        .CursorLocation = adUseClient
        .CursorType = adOpenStatic
        .LockType = adLockBatchOptimistic
        'Open the recordset.
        .Open "Select * From Authors", "Pubs"
        'Close the database connection.
        Set .ActiveConnection = Nothing
    End With

    'Loop through the recordset and change the phone number
    'to 800-123-4567 for those unknown phone numbers. This is
    'completely done offline.
    With oRecordset
        Do Until .EOF
            If Trim(!phone) = "UNKNOWN" Then
                !phone = "800-123-4567"
            End If
            oRecordset.MoveNext
        Loop
        'Now we are ready for submit our changes to the database.
        'Re-open the connection.
        .ActiveConnection = "Pubs"
        'Submit changes in batch mode.
```

Listing 2.9   continued

```
            .UpdateBatch
        End With

        'If everything is fine, release the resources
        'and get out the sub.
        MsgBox "Batch update succeed!"
        Set oRecordset = Nothing
        Exit Sub
DisconnectedRS_Err:
        'Something is wrong, release the resources if not yet.
        If Not oRecordset Is Nothing Then
            Set oRecordset = Nothing
        End If
        MsgBox Err.Description
End Sub
```

In addition to the disconnected recordset, ADO also allows you to create a recordset from scratch (called a *shorthand* recordset). To create a shorthand recordset, you declare and initialize an ADO Recordset object, define all the field objects, and append them to the Fields collection. Then you open the recordset and populate it with data. Shorthand ADO recordsets can be used in several scenarios. For example, you can create a shorthand recordset that maps to a database table structure for temporarily storing data without actually interacting with the database at all. Later, when the recordset is fully populated, you can save this recordset to a persistent file or open a database connection and transfer the data to a database. You can even send the recordset as an MSMQ message to a queue and let another application pick it up and process it later, and transfer the data to the database asynchronously. You will see MSMQ examples in Chapter 3, "Introduction to Microsoft Message Queuing Services (MSMQ)."

EXAMPLE

Listing 2.10 demonstrates the technique for creating a shorthand recordset. This example creates a Publishers recordset and populates it with three Macmillan publishing houses: Que, Sams, and BradyGames. It then loops through the recordset and displays its content in the debug window. Finally, the recordset is saved to a file.

Listing 2.10   Creating a Shorthand ADO Recordset

```
Private Sub cmdFirstHandRS_Click()
    'Enable the error handler.
    On Error GoTo FirstHand_Err
    'Declare and inilialize an ADO Recordset object
```

Listing 2.10   continued

```
Dim rsPublishers As ADODB.Recordset
Set rsPublishers = New ADODB.Recordset

With rsPublishers
    'Define fields and append them to the recordset.
    .Fields.Append "pub_id", adChar, 4
    .Fields.Append "pub_name", adChar, 10
    .Fields.Append "city", adVarChar, 20
    .Fields.Append "state", adChar, 2
    .Fields.Append "country", adVarChar, 30
    'Open the recordset
    .Open
    'populate the recordset with AddNew and Update methods.
    'Add Que to the publisher recordset.
    .AddNew
    !pub_id = "1111"
    !pub_name = "Que"
    !city = "Indianapolis"
    !State = "IN"
    !country = "USA"
    .Update
    'Add Sams to the publisher recordset.
    .AddNew
    !pub_id = "2222"
    !pub_name = "Sams"
    !city = "Indianapolis"
    !State = "IN"
    !country = "USA"
    .Update
    'Add BradyGames to the publisher recordset.
    .AddNew
    !pub_id = "3333"
    !pub_name = "BradyGames"
    !city = "Indianapolis"
    !State = "IN"
    !country = "USA"
    .Update

    'Loop through the recordset file and display its content
    'in the debug window.
    rsPublishers.MoveFirst
    Do Until .EOF
        Debug.Print !pub_id & _
                vbTab & !pub_name & _
                vbTab & !city & _
                vbTab & !State & _
```

Listing 2.10   continued

```
                 vbTab & !country
           .MoveNext
       Loop


       'Save the recordset to a file
       .Save App.Path & "\rsPublishers.rs"


       'Close the recordset.
       .Close
     End With


     'If everything is fine, release the resources
     'and get out the sub.
     Set rsPublishers = Nothing
     Exit Sub
FirstHand_Err:
     'If file already exists, delete it and move on.
     If Err.Number = 58 Then
         Kill App.Path & "\rsPublishers.rs"
         Resume
     End If
     'Something is wrong, release the resources if not yet.
     If Not rsPublishers Is Nothing Then
         Set rsPublishers = Nothing
     End If
     MsgBox Err.Description
End Sub
```

After the execution of code in Listing 2.10, the Visual Basic debug window looks like the one in Figure 2.14.

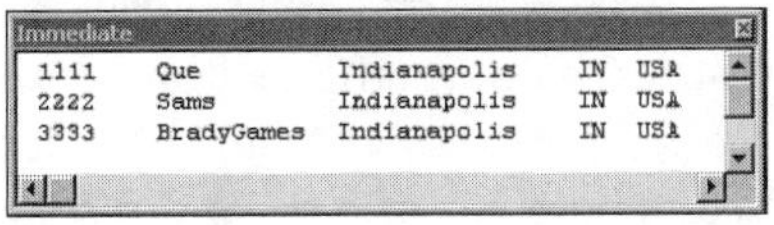

Figure 2.14: *Three publishers have been added to the shorthand recordset.*

Before finishing this journey through ADO, let's spend a little time on ADO error handling. Whereas Chapter 12, "More on COM+ Programming," will discuss COM+ error handling techniques in general, this section focuses on ADO- and OLE DB-specific error handling issues.

As you saw earlier, the ADO Connection object has an associated Errors collection. Errors generated by the OLE DB provider are added to this Errors collection. If ADO itself encounters an error, however, it stores the error information in the Visual Basic Err object, so the error handling code has to take care of both errors. Now you can expand the error handling section of Listing 2.8 to see how to appropriately handle ADO errors, as shown in the following code segment:

```
Private Sub cmdStoredProc_Click()
'See code in Listing 2.8
'for details
'. . . . . .
StoredProc_Err:
Dim sErrorInfo As String
Dim oErr        As Error
    If Not oConnection Is Nothing Then 'Make sure the Coonection object
                                        'is not destroyed yet.
        For Each oErr In oConnection.Errors
            sErrorInfo = sErrorInfo & oErr.Description vbCrLf
        Next
        'Now we are ready to destroy the Connection object.
        Set oConnection = Nothing
    End If
    'Destroy the Command Object
    If Not oCommand Is Nothing Then
        Set oCommand = Nothing
    End If
    If len(sErrorInfo) <> 0 Then
        MsgBox sErrorInfo 'Report OLE DB provider error.
    Else
        MsgBox Err.Description 'Report regular error.
    End IF
End Sub
```

Internet Information Services (IIS) and Active Server Pages (ASP)

Windows 2000 is a fully Web-aware operating system. Internet Information Services (IIS 5.0), formerly called Internet Information Server, is now a built-in Web server. IIS 5.0 runs as a set of enterprise services within Windows 2000.

In this section, I will introduce you to IIS and its server-side scripting technology, Active Server Pages (ASP).

INTERNET INFORMATION SERVICES (IIS 5.0)

In addition to those Web services available in IIS 4.0, such as security, administration, programmability, and support for Internet standards, IIS 5.0 provides improvements in reliability, performance, application protection, and support for clustering.

You can access Internet Information Services through the Computer Management Console or Internet Services Manager. You can access both by choosing Start, Programs, Administrative Tools. Figure 2.15 illustrates the Internet Information Services under Internet Information Manager.

Figure 2.15: *Managing Internet Information Services using the Internet Information Manager.*

ACTIVE SERVER PAGES (ASP)

Active Server Pages is a server-side scripting technology that allows you to generate dynamic, interactive Web pages. With ASP, you can read information from an HTTP request, send an HTTP response back to a Web client, store user information, and detect browser capabilities of the Web client.

An ASP page is an ASCII file with an .asp extension. When IIS detects a request on an .asp file, it executes the scripts inside the file on the server, generates a pure HTML page, and displays it in the browser. ASP supports both Visual Basic Script (or VBScript) and JavaScript scripting languages.

ASP has the following five built-in objects:

- The `Server` object allows you to manage the server resources. It supports the `CreateObject()` method, which lets you create an instance of a COM object.

- The `Application` object stores and manages information at the application level.

- The `Session` object stores and manages information specific to a user session.

- The `Request` object allows you to collect information that is sent through an HTTP request.

- The `Response` object allows you to send information back to the client through HTTP.

Inside an ASP page, you use <SCRIPT> tags or the inline equivalent <%> to indicate the scripts so that the Web server knows which part of the code should be executed on the server.

EXAMPLE

Let's look at an ASP example to see how it works. Listing 2.11 is an ASP page that retrieves the author names from the authors table of the pubs database on the SQL Server using ADO and displays the results in an HTML table.

Listing 2.11 Retrieving Author Names and Displaying Them in an HTML Table

```
<%@ Language=VBScript %>
<html>
<head>
<title>ASP ADO Demo</title>
<h3>Authors</h3>
<% dim rsAuthors 'ADO recordset for holding authors.%>
<% set rsAuthors = server.CreateObject("ADODB.Recordset")%>
<table width =300 border=2>
<tr><td><b>First Name</b></td><td><b>Last Name</b></td></tr>
<%
    'Set the ActiveConnection property
    rsAuthors.ActiveConnection  = "Provider=SQLOLEDB;" & _
                                  "Data Source=(local);" & _
                                  "Initial Catalog=pubs;" & _
                                  "User ID=sa;" & _
                                  "Password=;"

    'Open the recordset.
    rsAuthors.Open "Select au_fname, au_lname from authors"

    'Loop through the recordset and display the results in a table.
    do until rsAuthors.EOF
        Response.Write "<tr><td>" & rsAuthors("au_fname") & _
                       "</td><td>" & rsAuthors("au_lname") & "</td></tr>"
        rsAuthors.MoveNext
    loop

    'Close the recordset and release resources.
    rsAuthors.Close
    set rsAuthors = nothing
%>
</table>
</body>
</html>
```

The first line specifies that you are going to use VBScript as your scripting language. VBScript is the default language used in ASP. You create an ADO Recordset object by calling the CreateObject() method of the Server object.

Then you call the Open method of the ADO recordset, just as you do in the Visual Basic examples. Now you loop through the ADO recordset using the MoveNext() method and write the results as an HTML table through the Response object.

To see this ASP page in action, open a text editor such as Windows Notepad, type the code in Listing 2.11, and save the file as ADODemo.asp. In the Web server's root directory (C:\Inetpub\wwwroot\), create a subdirectory called ASPDemo, and copy ADODemo.asp to it. Now launch a Web browser such as Internet Explorer 5.0. In the Address line, type **http://<YourMachineName>/ASPDemo/ADODemo.asp**. You should see something like the result shown in Figure 2.16. Here, *<YourMachineName>* is the name of the IIS Server; in my case, the server name is Peishu.

Figure 2.16: *The result of an ASP page.*

TIP

You can also use Microsoft Visual InterDev 6.0 to create ASP pages. Visual InterDev is part of the Visual Studio family. It supports a rich set of IDE functionalities that make creating a Web page a lot easier.

In Windows DNA architecture, ASP pages are considered part of the User Services, or the presentation tier. In Chapter 13, "Northwind Traders Online: A COM+ Enabled Windows DNA 2000 Application," you will use ASP pages as the client application.

What's Next

In this chapter, you explored Windows DNA 2000 architecture. You also spent a great deal of time on Active Data Objects (ADO) because this topic is fundamental to the Data Access Layer of the entire business logic middle tier. In the next chapter, "Introduction to Microsoft Message Queuing Services (MSMQ)," you will shift gears a little bit and look at the asynchronous processing world of Windows 2000 message queuing services. Knowledge of how MSMQ works is essential for understanding some advanced COM+ services—for example, Queued Components (QC).

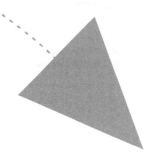

Introduction to Microsoft Message Queuing Services (MSMQ)

Distributed applications run on two or more computers. They communicate with one another by passing data over machine boundaries through appropriate network protocols. Most of these protocols use synchronous technologies, such as *Remote Procedure Calls* (RPC) and DCOM. The synchronous process model has a number of limitations, however. Message queuing provides an asynchronous programming model and a loosely coupled environment for different components of distributed applications.

This chapter teaches you the following:

- The limitations of synchronous processing
- Message queuing technology and Microsoft Message Queuing Services (MSMQ)
- MSMQ architecture
- How to write MSMQ applications in Visual Basic

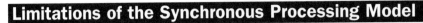

Limitations of the Synchronous Processing Model

EXAMPLE

In a synchronous processing model, components interact with one another in a tightly coupled manner. DCOM applications are examples of synchronous processing, as shown in Figure 3.1.

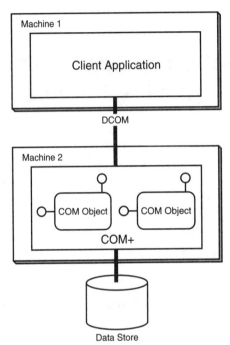

Figure 3.1: DCOM applications use the synchronous processing model.

In Figure 3.1, the client application in machine 1 interacts with the COM objects that are running on machine 2 using DCOM. This synchronous processing model has several limitations:

- A synchronous processing system requires a reliable network connection. As in Figure 3.1, the client has no way to communicate with the server when the network is disconnected.

- In a synchronous processing system, both communicating parties must be available at the same time. In Figure 3.1, if the COM objects on machine 2 are not up and running, calls from the client application fail.

- In Figure 3.1, when the client application makes a call to the COM object on the server, it must wait for the server to finish its processing. If the server takes a long time to process a client call, the client application is blocked (or frozen) until the server finishes processing.

- If machine 2 in Figure 3.1 is shut down for some reason, the calls from the client to the server fail. Therefore, the synchronous processing model is not fault tolerant and thus is not a robust architecture.

Message Queuing and MSMQ

This section introduces message queuing and MSMQ and explains why message queuing technology and products can overcome the shortcomings of the synchronous processing model.

Asynchronous Processing and Message Queuing

As you can see from the previous discussion, a tightly coupled architecture is not suitable for today's distributed applications, such as Windows DNA applications. In a typical DNA application, having a reliable network connection, available servers, and so on is not always feasible. Message queuing, on the other hand, provides an *asynchronous* processing model that addresses the limitations of the synchronous processing model.

EXAMPLE

Message queuing products use a *store-and-forward* mechanism to handle the interaction between different applications. In a typical message queuing system, like the one in Figure 3.2, instead of calling the server directly as in DCOM applications, the client sends data in the form of a message to a temporary data store, which is called a *queue*. The underlying message queuing service internally forwards the message to another queue on the server. A receiver application on the server then picks up the message from the queue and invokes the server to process.

As shown in Figure 3.2, the request of the client is processed in a loosely coupled, asynchronous manner. An asynchronous system such as message queuing can be configured in such a way that if the network is down, the message stays in the queue on the client machine and the data is not lost. The message queuing service forwards the message to the server queue if the network connection becomes available again. The receiver application on the server machine can pick up and process the message at another time. Finally, as long as the client application sends the message to the queue, it is ready to do whatever else it needs to do because it's not blocked by the server process any more.

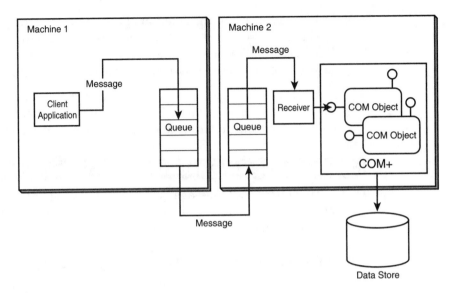

Figure 3.2: *A message queuing system.*

NOTE

The terms *client* and *client application* here simply mean the message *sender*. They are relative terms. The roles of the sender and the receiver can be reversed.

TIP

The configuration described here is called an *independent client* in MSMQ. In the IBM MQSeries system, you can use clustering queue managers to achieve the same results. IBM MQSeries, which is IBM's message queuing product, offers capabilities comparable to MSMQ. I will discuss only MSMQ in this book, because this chapter is intended to give you all the background information for Chapter 9, "Queued Components." Queued Components is an important COM+ services that uses MSMQ to achieve messaging queuing functionality.

MSMQ

Message queuing products are sometimes referred to as *Message-Oriented Middleware* (MOM). Microsoft Message Queue Services 2.0 is now an integrated part of Windows 2000 component services; it is the Microsoft implementation of MOM technology.

Applications developed for MSMQ can communicate across heterogeneous networks and with computers that may be offline. MSMQ provides guaranteed message delivery, efficient routing, security, transactional support, and priority-based messaging.

TIP

In Microsoft Windows 2000 documentation, MSMQ 2.0 is referred to as *message queuing*. In Microsoft Platform SDK documentation, both terms (MSMQ, and message queuing) are used.

MSMQ Architecture

Depending on your Windows 2000 configuration, MSMQ can be used in a domain environment or a workgroup environment. The difference is that for MSMQ, a domain environment includes domain controllers that provide a directory service, such as Active Directory, whereas a workgroup environment does not provide such a directory service.

Domain Environment

In a domain environment, an MSMQ network is a group of Windows 2000 *sites*, connected by *routing links*. Sites map the physical structure of a network, whereas domains map the logical structure of an organization. Sites and domain structures are independent of each other. A single site can have multiple domains, whereas a single domain can also have multiple sites. In Windows 2000, a site is defined as a set of computers in one or more IP subnets. Routing links are logic communication links created by MSMQ to route messages between different sites. In MSMQ, a computer that can provide message queuing, routing, and directory services to client computers is called an *MSMQ server*. A routing link is made up of MSMQ servers, one on each site.

CAUTION

Don't confuse routing links with *site links*. Routing links are used by MSMQ to route messages between sites, whereas site links are used by domain controllers to replicate Active Directory between sites.

Workgroup Environment

An MSMQ computer can also run in a workgroup environment that is not part of a domain. There are several restrictions, however. All the benefits provided by Active Directory Services are not available.

First, messages cannot be routed by an MSMQ server; a direct connection with the destination server is required.

Second, you can create and manage only *private queues* on a local computer. You cannot view or manage *public queues*. You can, however, send messages to or read messages from private queues, provided that a direct connection to the destination MSMQ server is specified.

Finally, you cannot use internal certificates to send authenticated messages. Instead, you must use an external certificate.

Queues

In MSMQ, queues are temporary storage locations for different types of messages. Queues can be logically divided into two groups: *application queues* and *system queues*. Application queues are created by applications. System queues are created by MSMQ.

TIP

Application queues can also be created using the Computer Management MMC snap-in.

EXAMPLE

Figure 3.3 shows the different types of queues in the Message Queuing services in the Computer Management snap-in.

Figure 3.3: *Message Queuing services in the Computer Management snap-in.*

TIP

If the Message Queuing service is not started yet for some reason, you cannot see it under the Services and Applications node in the Computer Management snap-in. You can manually start the Message Queuing service by using the Component Services snap-in. From Services, locate and right-click the Message Queuing service; then select Start (as shown in Figure 3.4).

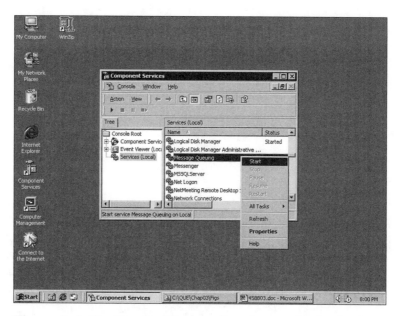

Figure 3.4: *Starting the Message Queuing service in the Component Services snap-in.*

In Figure 3.3, you may have noticed another type of queue: the *outgoing queue*. Those queues are used for offline operations in which directory service is not available. When MSMQ on a client machine is configured for offline use, it is called an *independent client*. When MSMQ on a client machine is configured for real-time access support, it is called a *dependent client*.

APPLICATION QUEUES

Application queues include *message queues*, *administration queues*, *response queues*, and *report queues*. These queues are created by applications.

EXAMPLE

Message queues allow applications to exchange data through messages. Applications can send messages to and receive them from message queues. Message queues can be either public or private. Figure 3.5 shows an example of a message queue called TestQueue that is created as a private queue.

CAUTION

When you create a queue from an application, it is always displayed in lowercase under Message Queuing in the Computer Management snap-in. However, the names in MSMQ are case sensitive, so be extremely careful in your code when you refer to a queue. For example, if you create a queue called MyQueue, it shows up in MSMQ as myqueue. In your code, however, you still need to access this queue by using MyQueue. You get an error if you refer it as myqueue.

Figure 3.5: A message queue.

EXAMPLE

Administration queues, which are specified by the sending application, store system-generated acknowledgment messages sent by MSMQ. If you specify the administration queue when you send a message, MSMQ generates an acknowledgment message and sends it to the administration queue specified, indicating whether the original message was successfully sent (see Figure 3.6).

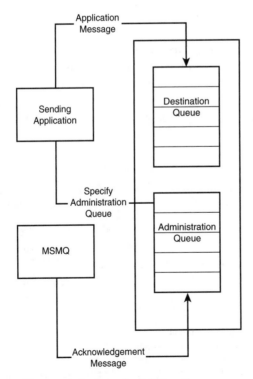

Figure 3.6: An administration queue.

Response queues are specified by the sending application and used by the receiving application to send response messages back to the sending application (see Figure 3.7).

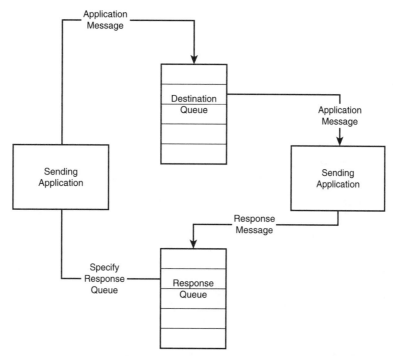

Figure 3.7: A response queue.

Report queues track the progress of messages as they move through the enterprise. When the sending application enables tracking and specifies a report queue, MSMQ sends *report messages* to the report queue. A report message is a system message that is generated each time an application message passes through an MSMQ routing server.

System Queues

System queues are created either by MSMQ or the MSMQ administrator. System queues contain *journal queues* and *dead-letter queues*. Whenever an application queue is created, MSMQ automatically create a journal to track the messages that are removed from the queue. Dead-letter queues store messages that could not be delivered. MSMQ provides two dead-letter queues for each computer: one for nontransactional messages and the other for transactional messages. Figure 3.8 shows system queues.

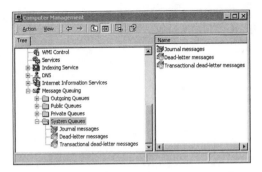

Figure 3.8: System queues.

Messages

MSMQ messages are data exchanged between applications. Messages can be generated by MSMQ applications or by MSMQ itself. This chapter addresses only application-generated messages and some of their important properties.

EXAMPLE

For each message, MSMQ generates and assigns a *message identifier*. The identifier, or ID, of a message is unique on the computer where the message resides and can be used along with other message properties to identify a message. Figure 3.9 shows the property page of a message with its message identifier highlighted.

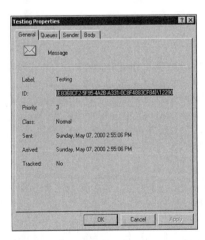

Figure 3.9: A message identifier (ID).

A message identifier is composed of the machine GUID of the computer that sent the message and an identifier that is unique to the computer. For example, in Figure 3.9, the message identifier is

{E8368CF2-5F95-4A2B-A331-0C8F4883CF84}\12290

The Label property of a message is used to describe the message, much like the subject of an email. The Label of the message in Figure 3.9 is Testing.

Unlike an email message, however, the Body property of a message is not limited to string data types. The body of a message is a variant data type. It can be literally any data type, including string, date, numeric, currency, or array of bytes. The body of a message can be a persistent object such as an Excel spreadsheet or even an ADO recordset.

Journaling

MSMQ journaling allows you to keep track of messages. The two types of MSMQ journaling are *source journaling* and *target journaling*. Source journaling tracks messages sent by a computer, whereas target journaling tracks messages removed from a queue.

Programming MSMQ in Visual Basic

MSMQ provides both API functions and a COM interface for developers to interact with it programmatically. This book focuses on the COM interface. I'll first introduce MSMQ COM objects. Then I'll show you some basic MSMQ examples followed by a couple of advanced MSMQ programming examples. Finally, I'll give you an asynchronous ordering example to demonstrate how to use MSMQ in real-world scenarios.

MSMQ COM Object Model

EXAMPLE

MSMQ provides a set of COM objects that allow applications to access and manage message queuing. The three most important MSMQ COM objects are MSMQQueueInfo, MSMQQueue, and MSMQMessage. Their relationship is illustrated in Figure 3.10.

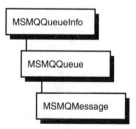

Figure 3.10: Important MSMQ COM objects.

MSMQQueueInfo, which provides queue management, allows you to create or delete a queue, open an existing queue, or manipulate the properties of a queue.

MSMQQueue represents an open instance of an MSMQ queue. It provides a cursor-like mechanism for traversing the messages in an open queue. Like a database cursor, at any give moment, it points to a particular message in the queue.

MSMQMessage provides properties to define the behavior of a message and the methods for sending the message to the queue.

Other MSMQ COM objects support additional functionalities:

- The MSMQApplication object provides methods or properties to retrieve information from the MSMQ machine. For example, the IsDSEnabled property tells you whether MSMQ is using the directory service on the computer.

- The MSMQQueueInfos and MSMQQuery objects allow you to get information on public queues. The MSMQQueueInfos object represents a set of MSMQ public queues and allows you to select a specific public queue from a collection of queues. The MSMQQuery object allows you to query the directory service for existing public queues.

- The MSMQEvent object provides an interface for you to implement a single event handler that supports multiple queues.

- The MSMQTransaction, MSMQTransactionDispenser, and MSMQCoordinatedTransactionDispenser objects allow you to manage internal and external MSMQ transactions.

Basic MSMQ Examples

EXAMPLE

To work with MSMQ, you need to set a reference to the Microsoft Message Queue Object Library in a Visual Basic project, as shown in Figure 3.11. Later, in the code samples, you will notice the syntactical difference between creating public and private queues.

The first example, Listing 3.1, creates a queue, opens the queue for send access, and puts a testing message in the queue.

> **CAUTION**
>
> Depending in which directory you put the sample code of this chapter, when you load the source code you may experience an error, "Could Not Create Reference...." If this error occurs, you should reset the references to "Microsoft Message Queue 2.0 Object Library" by select Project, References menu option. This object library is usually located in "\WINNT\system32\MQOA.dll".

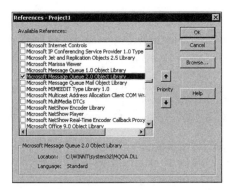

Figure 3.11: *Setting a reference to the Microsoft Message Queue Object Library.*

Listing 3.1   Creating and Opening a Queue and Sending a Message

```
Public Sub SendQueueMessage()
    '=================================================
    'In this sub routine, we will create a queue, open
    'the queue and send a testing message to the queue.
    '=================================================
    'Enable the error handler
    On Error GoTo SendQueueMessage_Err
    'Declare variables for MSMQ objects.
    Dim oQInfo       As MSMQ.MSMQQueueInfo
    Dim oQueue       As MSMQ.MSMQQueue
    Dim oMessage     As MSMQ.MSMQMessage

    'Initialize the MSMQQueueInfo object.
    Set oQInfo = New MSMQQueueInfo
    'we use a conditional compilation constant
    'to take care of both public and private queues.
    #If bUseDS Then
        'If directory service is used, we can create
        'a public queue.
        oQInfo.PathName = ".\TestingQueue"
    #Else
        'Else we can only create a private queue.
        oQInfo.PathName = ".\PRIVATE$\TestQueue"
    #End If
    'Now we are ready to create the queue.
    oQInfo.Label = "Testing Queue"
    oQInfo.Create
    'Open the queue for send access.
    Set oQueue = oQInfo.Open(MQ_SEND_ACCESS, MQ_DENY_NONE)
```

Listing 3.1 continued

```
    'If the queue is opened sccessfully, we send a
    'testing messge to it.
    If oQueue.IsOpen Then
        'Initialize the MSMQMessage object.
        Set oMessage = New MSMQMessage
        'Prepare the message and send to the queue.
        With oMessage
            .Label = "Testing Message"
            .Priority = 5 'Default priority is 3.
            .Body = "Testing Message"
            .Send oQueue
        End With
    Else
        'Queue is not open, report the error and get out.
        MsgBox "The queue is not open!"
        Exit Sub
    End If
    'If everything is ok, close the queue and get out.
    oQueue.Close
    MsgBox "The message is sent!"
    Exit Sub
SendQueueMessage_Err:
    'If the queue already exist when we try to create it, '
    'ignore the error and move on.
    If Err.Number = MQ_ERROR_QUEUE_EXISTS Then
        Resume Next
    End If
    'Handling other errors.
    MsgBox Err.Description
End Sub
```

In Listing 3.1, you use a Visual Basic *conditional compilation constant* that you set on the Make tab of the project's property page (see Figure 2.12). This way, you can have a single code base to handle creating both public and private queues.

The Open method of the MSMQQueueInfo object takes two parameters: Access Mode and Shared Mode. Access Mode can be MQ_SEND_ACCESS, MQ_RECEIVE_ACCESS, or MQ_PEEK_ACCESS. Shared Mode can be MQ_DENY_NOEN (the default) or MQ_DENY_RECEIVE_SHARE. Note that you set the priority to 5 to overwrite the default priority (3). MSMQ puts a message with higher priority in front of a message with lower priority. MSMQ message priorities range from 0 to 7. Also note that in the error handler, you test whether the error was caused by trying to create an already existing queue; then you ignore the error and continue execution of the next line of code. Figure 3.13

shows that the queue is created, and a testing message with a priority of 5 appears in the queue.

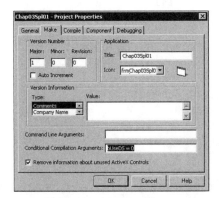

Figure 3.12: *Setting the conditional compilation constant.*

Figure 3.13: *A message is sent to the queue.*

EXAMPLE

The next example, Listing 3.2), opens an existing queue, retrieves a message from the queue, and prints the contents of the message (label and body) in the debug window.

Listing 3.2   Opening an Existing Queue and Receiving a Message

```
Public Sub ReceiveQueueMessage()
    '================================================
    'In this sub routine, we open an existing queue
    'retrieve the message and print to debug window.
    '================================================
    'Enable the error handler
    On Error GoTo ReceiveQueueMessage_Err
    'Declare variables for MSMQ objects.
    Dim oQInfo      As MSMQ.MSMQQueueInfo
    Dim oQueue      As MSMQ.MSMQQueue
    Dim oMessage    As MSMQ.MSMQMessage

    'Initialize the MSMQQueueInfo object.
    Set oQInfo = New MSMQQueueInfo
```

Listing 3.2   continued

```
'we use a conditional compilation constant
'to take care of both public and private queues.
#If bUseDS Then
    oQInfo.PathName = ".\TestingQueue"
#Else
    oQInfo.PathName = ".\PRIVATE$\TestQueue"
#End If
'Open the queue for receive access.
Set oQueue = oQInfo.Open(MQ_RECEIVE_ACCESS, MQ_DENY_NONE)
'If the queue is opened sccessfully,
'we retrieve the messge.
If oQueue.IsOpen Then
    'Retrieve the message and print it.
    Set oMessage = oQueue.ReceiveCurrent(ReceiveTimeout:=1000)

    Debug.Print "Message Label: " & oMessage.Label & vbCrLf
    Debug.Print "Message Body:  " & oMessage.Body
Else
    'Queue is not open, report the error and get out.
    MsgBox "The queue is not open!"
    Exit Sub
End If
'If everything is ok, we are out of here.
Exit Sub
ReceiveQueueMessage_Err:
    MsgBox Err.Description
End Sub
```

CAUTION

The code in Listing 3.2 will only work if there is a message in the queue. Otherwise you will get an "Object variable or With block variable not set" error message. This is because if there is no message in the queue, the `ReceiveCurrent()` will time out and the next line tries to access the `oMessage` object which is set to `Nothing`.

In Listing 3.2, you use the `Receive` method of the `MSMQQueue` object. Messages are removed from the queue after the `Receive` method is called. This procedure is called *dequeuing*. Note that you use a Visual Basic named argument syntax to specify the timeout value to one minute. Figure 3.14 shows the result.

Figure 3.14: *A message is received from the queue.*

The following example, Listing 3.3, shows you how to locate a public queue that is registered in Active Directory and delete it if you find one.

Listing 3.3   Locating a Public Queue and Deleting It

```
Public Sub DeleteTestQueue()
    '==================================================
    'In this sub routine, we locate an pubic queue
    'in the Active Directory and delete it.
    '==================================================
    'Enable the error handler
    On Error GoTo DeleteTestQueue_Err
    'Declare variables for MSMQ objects.
    Dim oQuery      As MSMQ.MSMQQuery
    Dim oQInfos     As MSMQ.MSMQQueueInfos
    Dim oQInfo      As MSMQ.MSMQQueueInfo
    Dim oQueue      As MSMQ.MSMQQueue

    'Get MSMQQueueInfo objects and search for
    'the TestingQueue.
    Set oQuery = New MSMQ.MSMQQuery.
    Set oqinfor = oQuery.LookupQueue(Label:="TestingQueue")
    'Get the first MSMQQueueInfo object.
    Set oQInfo = oQInfos.Next

    'If the queue is not found, report it and get out.
    If oQInfo Is Nothing Then
        MsgBox "TestingQueue is not found!"
        Exit Sub
    End If

    'Delete the TestingQueue queue.
    oQInfo.Delete

    'If everything is ok, we are out of here.
    MsgBox "The queue is deleted!"
    Exit Sub
DeleteTestQueue_Err:
    MsgBox Err.Description
End Sub
```

In Listing 3.2, you used the Receive method to read the message and remove it from the queue. In Listing 3.4, you will use another technique to read the message selectively and remove only certain messages that meet certain criteria. Before you test the code in Listing 3.3, though, send two messages to the queue. Send the first message by running the code in Listing 3.1 without any modification. Then add .AppSpecific = 25 to Listing 3.1 between the line .Priority = 5 'Default priority is 3 and the line .Body = "Testing Message". The code should now read as shown in the following segment:

```
Public Sub SendQueueMessage()
    '=================================================
    'In this sub routine, we will create a queue, open
    'the queue and send a testing message to the queue.
    '=================================================
        'Code is omitted here, see listing 3.1 for details.
        '. . . . . .
        'Prepare the message and send to the queue.
        With oMessage
            .Label = "Testing Message"
            .Priority = 5 'Default priority is 3.
            .AppSpecific = 25
            .Body = "Testing Message"
            .Send oQueue
        End With
        'The rest of the code is omitted, see Figure 3.1.
End Sub
```

Then run the modified code, and a message with the AppSpecific property set to 25 is sent to the queue. Figure 3.15 shows the two messages sent to the queue.

Figure 3.15: *Two messages in the queue.*

EXAMPLE

Listing 3.4 uses *Peek* methods (PeekCurrent and PeekNext) to search the queue for specific messages that meek certain criteria without removing them. If a specific message is found, the code will remove the message from the queue using the ReceiveCurrent method and also print the label and body of the message in the Debug window.

Listing 3.4   Searching for Specific Messages to Remove from the Queue

```
Public Sub FilterMessages()
    '=================================================
    'In this sub routine, we open an existing queue
    'and selectively retrieve a message.
    '=================================================
    'Enable the error handler
```

Listing 3.4   continued

```
On Error GoTo FilterMessages_Err
'Declare variables for MSMQ objects.
Dim oQInfo        As MSMQ.MSMQQueueInfo
Dim oQueue        As MSMQ.MSMQQueue
Dim oMessage      As MSMQ.MSMQMessage

'Initialize the MSMQQueueInfo object.
Set oQInfo = New MSMQQueueInfo
'we use a conditional compilation constant
'to take care of both public and private queues.
#If bUseDS Then
    oQInfo.PathName = ".\TestingQueue"
#Else
    oQInfo.PathName = ".\PRIVATE$\TestQueue"
#End If
'Open the queue for receive access while deny shared receive.
Set oQueue = oQInfo.Open(MQ_RECEIVE_ACCESS, MQ_DENY_RECEIVE_SHARE)
'If the queue is opened sccessfully,
'we process the messges.
If oQueue.IsOpen Then
    'Peek at the first message in the queue.
    Set oMessage = oQueue.PeekCurrent(ReceiveTimeout:=1000)
    'Search for specific messages with AppSpecific set to 25.
    'If found, Retrieve the message and print it.
    Do Until oMessage Is Nothing
        If oMessage.AppSpecific = 25 Then
            Set oMessage =
oQueue.ReceiveCurrent(ReceiveTimeout:=1000)
            Debug.Print "Message Label: " & oMessage.Label & vbCrLf
            Debug.Print "Message Body:  " & oMessage.Body
            'Keep searching.
            Set oMessage = oQueue.PeekCurrent(ReceiveTimeout:=1000)
        Else
            Set oMessage = oQueue.PeekNext
        End If
    Loop
Else
    'Queue is not open, report the error and get out.
    MsgBox "The queue is not open!"
    Exit Sub
End If
'If everything is ok, we are out of here.
Exit Sub
FilterMessages_Err:
    MsgBox Err.Description
End Sub
```

After executing the code in Listing 3.4, you get results similar to those shown in Figure 3.14. If you open the Computer Management snap-in, you will notice that the second message you saw in Figure 3.15 is gone, as you can see in Figure 3.16.

Figure 3.16: *The message with* `AppSpecific = 25` *is removed from the queue.*

Listing 3.4 filters messages based on the `AppSpecific` property. You can also use other message properties to look for specific messages. For example, you can use the `MsgClass` property to filter out report messages. To do so, simply change the line `.AppSpecific = 25` in Listing 3.4 to

`.MsgClass = MQMSG_CLASS_REPORT`

Advanced MSMQ Techniques

In this section, you will look at some more advanced MSMQ techniques. The first example demonstrates how to use the `MSMQEvent` object to retrieve messages asynchronously. In this example, you will create two Visual Basic applications: one to act as a message sender and another to act as a message receiver, as illustrated in Figure 3.17.

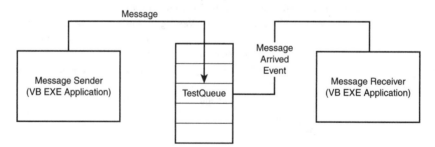

Figure 3.17: *An MSMQ event example.*

The Message Sender application in Figure 3.17 is a standard Visual Basic EXE project that contains a single form with a text box and a command button (see Figure 3.18).

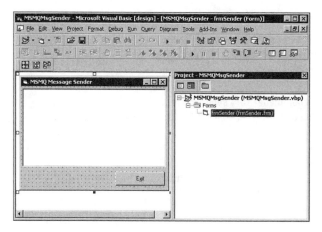

Figure 3.18: *The* MSMQMsgSender *Visual Basic project.*

The MultiLine property of the text box is better set to True so that it will function more like a text editor.

Listing 3.5 contains the code for the Message Sender application.

EXAMPLE

Listing 3.5   The MSMQMsgSender Project

```
'===================================================
'This is a sample MSMQ message sender application.
'It is paired with another MSMQ Receiver
'application to demonstrate how MSMQ event works.
'===================================================
Option Explicit


'===================================================
'The Change event of the text box tracks your key
'stroke and sends a message to the TestQueue every
'time when you press a key on the keyboard
'===================================================
Private Sub txtMessage_Change()
    'Enable the error handler
    On Error GoTo MessageSend_Error
    'Declare variables for MSMQ objects.
    Dim oQInfo As New MSMQ.MSMQQueueInfo
    Dim oQMsg  As New MSMQ.MSMQMessage
    Dim oQueue As MSMQ.MSMQQueue

    'Set the path name to the TestQueue.
    #If bUseDS Then
        oQInfo.PathName = ".\TestQueue"
```

Listing 3.5 continued

```
#Else
    oQInfo.PathName = ".\PRIVATE$\TestQueue"
#End If

'Open the queue for send access.
Set oQueue = oQInfo.Open(MQ_SEND_ACCESS, MQ_DENY_NONE)

'Prepare the message and send the queue.
With oQMsg
    .Label = "MSMQ Event Testing"
    .Body = txtMessage.Text
    .Send oQueue
End With
'If everything is ok, close the queue and get out.
oQueue.Close
Exit Sub
MessageSend_Error:
    MsgBox Err.Description
End Sub


'===================================
'The Click event of the Exit button.
'===================================
Private Sub cmdExit_Click()
    'Exit the program.
    Unload Me
End Sub
```

The code in Listing 3.5 is very straightforward. In the txtMessage_Change()
event of the text box, you put some code to send the content of the text box
as a message to the TestQueue created in previous sections.

The Message Receiver application in Figure 3.17 is another Standard
Visual Basic EXE project that has a single form with a text box and command button on it. It looks similar to the Message Sender application with
the text box grayed out and locked to prevent editing (see Figure 3.19).

The size of each MSMQ message is limited to 4MB. As you learned earlier,
however, the data type of the message can be almost anything. In the next
example, you will create a disconnected ADO recordset from the database
and send the recordset as a message to the queue. Later, you'll retrieve the
message (ADO recordset) from the queue and display its content in the
Visual Basic debug window. For details about ADO programming, see
Chapter 2, "Windows DNA 2000 and COM+."

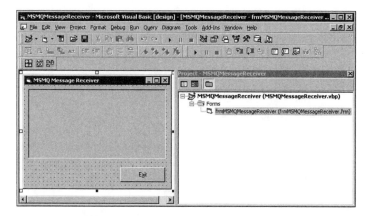

Figure 3.19: *The MSMQMessageReceiver Visual Basic project.*

Listing 3.6 shows the code for the Message Receiver application.

Listing 3.6   The MSMQMessageReceiver Project

```
'========================================================
'This is a sample MSMQ message receiver application.
'It is paired with the MSMQ Sender
'application to demonstrate how MSMQ event works.
'========================================================
Option Explicit
'Declare some model level variables for MSMQ objects.
Dim oQInfo As New MSMQ.MSMQQueueInfo
Dim oQReceive As MSMQ.MSMQQueue
Dim WithEvents oQEvent As MSMQ.MSMQEvent


'=========================================
'The form load event then opens the
'TestQueue and enables event notification.
'=========================================
Private Sub Form_Load()
    'Enable error handler.
    On Error GoTo Load_Err
    'Set the PathName of the queue.
    #If bUseDS Then
        oQInfo.PathName = ".\TestQueue"
    #Else
        oQInfo.PathName = ".\PRIVATE$\TestQueue"
    #End If
    'Open the queue for receive access.
    Set oQReceive = oQInfo.Open(MQ_RECEIVE_ACCESS, MQ_DENY_NONE)
    'Set the MSMQEvent object.
```

Listing 3.6   continued

```
    Set oQEvent = New MSMQ.MSMQEvent
    'Enable MSMQ event notification.
    oQReceive.EnableNotification oQEvent
    Exit Sub
Load_Err:
    MsgBox Err.Description
End Sub


'===================================
'The Click event of the Exit button.
'===================================
Private Sub cmdExit_Click()
    'Exit the program.
    Unload Me
End Sub


'=================================================
'The Arrived event of the MSMQEvent object.
'Whenever this event fires, we update the content
'of the text box. Remember to enable the event
'notification for ensuring the firing of the
'subsequent events.
'=================================================
Private Sub oQEvent_Arrived(ByVal Queue As Object, _
                            ByVal Cursor As Long)
    'Enable error handler.
    On Error GoTo Event_Arrived_Err
    'Declare the MSMQMessage object.
    Dim oQMsg As MSMQ.MSMQMessage
    'Retrieve the message and display its contents in the text box.
    Set oQMsg = oQReceive.ReceiveCurrent(ReceiveTimeout:=1000)
    txtMessage = oQMsg.Body
    'Important!!!---Enable event notification before exiting the event.
    oQReceive.EnableNotification Event:=oQEvent, Cursor:=MQMSG_FIRST
    Exit Sub
Event_Arrived_Err:
    MsgBox Err.Description
End Sub


'=======================================================
'The ArrivedError event of MSMQEvent object.
'This event will be fired when the EnableNotification
'of the message object is called and an error has
'been generated. The ErrorCode is the return code
'of the ReceiveCurrent call of the MSMQQueue object.
'=======================================================
```

Listing 3.6 continued

```
Private Sub oQEvent_ArrivedError(ByVal Queue As Object, _
                                ByVal ErrorCode As Long, _
                                ByVal Cursor As Long)
    MsgBox "Error event fired!" & vbCrLf & _
           "Error: " & Hex(ErrorCode)
End Sub
```

In Listing 3.6, the Load event of the form opens the queue, initializes the
event object, and enables event notification. The Arrived event receives the
message, updates the content of the text box with the message, and enables
event notification before you exit the event procedure. To see how this listing works, run two separate instances of the Message Sender and the
Message Receiver applications. Arrange the screens so that you can see
both of them at the same time. Notice that whenever you type something in
the text box of the Send application, its content also appears in the text box
of the Receiver application, as shown in Figure 3.20.

Figure 3.20: *An MSMQ event in action.*

The event notification capability of MSMQ enables you to develop some
very powerful applications that are event-driven rather than message
pulling (such as frequently checking the message according to a predefined
time interval).

The next example demonstrates another powerful feature of MSMQ: sending an ADO recordset as a message. In this example, you will use a simple
Visual Basic form with two command buttons: cmdSendRecordset and
cmdReadRecordset (see Figure 3.21).

EXAMPLE

In the click event of cmdSendRecordset, you will create a disconnected
recordset with six programming titles from the pubs database of SQL
Server and send the recordset as a message to the TestQueue created earlier. In the click event of the cmdReadRecordset, you will receive the message of the recordset and display its contents in the debug window. Listing
3.7 illustrates the code for this example.

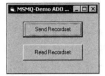

Figure 3.21: *An MSMQ ADO recordset example.*

Listing 3.7   ADO Recordset as the MSMQ Message

```
'================================================
'In this example, we demonstrate how to send
'a disconnected recordset as a MSMQ message.
'================================================
Option Explicit

Private Sub cmdSendRecordset_Click()
    'Enable the error handler.
    On Error GoTo SendRecordset_Err

    'Declare variables.
    Dim rsTitles    As New ADODB.Recordset
    Dim oQinfo      As New MSMQ.MSMQQueueInfo
    Dim oQueue      As MSMQ.MSMQQueue
    Dim oMessage    As New MSMQ.MSMQMessage
    Dim sConnection As String
    Dim sSQL        As String

    'Set connection string and SQL statement.
    sConnection = "pubs"
    sSQL = "select title from titles where title_id like 'BU%'"

    'Create a disconnected recordset.
    With rsTitles
        .CursorLocation = adUseClient
        .CursorType = adOpenStatic
        .LockType = adLockBatchOptimistic
        .Open sSQL, sConnection
    End With

    'Set the PathName of the MSMQQueueInfo object.
    #If bUseDS Then
        oQinfo.PathName = ".\TestQueue"
    #Else
```

Listing 3.7   continued

```
        oQinfo.PathName = ".\PRIVATE$\TestQueue"
    #End If

    'Open the queue for send access.
    Set oQueue = oQinfo.Open(MQ_SEND_ACCESS, MQ_DENY_NONE)

    'Send the ADO recordset to the queue.
    With oMessage
        .Label = "ADO recordset"
        .Body = rsTitles
        .Send oQueue
    End With

    'If everything is okay, clean up and get out of here.
    oQueue.Close
    rsTitles.Close

    MsgBox "Recordset sent!"
    Exit Sub
SendRecordset_Err:
    MsgBox Err.Description
End Sub

Private Sub cmdReadRecordset_Click()
    'Enable the error handler.
    On Error GoTo ReadRecordset_Err

    'Declare object variables.
    Dim rsTitles    As ADODB.Recordset
    Dim oQinfo      As New MSMQ.MSMQQueueInfo
    Dim oQueue      As MSMQ.MSMQQueue
    Dim oMessage    As MSMQ.MSMQMessage

    'Set the PathName of the MSMQQueueInfo object.
    #If bUseDS Then
        oQinfo.PathName = ".\TestQueue"
    #Else
        oQinfo.PathName = ".\PRIVATE$\TestQueue"
    #End If

    'Open the queue for read access.
    Set oQueue = oQinfo.Open(MQ_RECEIVE_ACCESS, MQ_DENY_NONE)

    'Read the message.
    Set oMessage = oQueue.Receive(ReceiveTimeout:=1000)
```

Listing 3.7   continued

```
    If Not oMessage Is Nothing Then
        'Assign the message body to an ADO recordset.
        Set rsTitles = oMessage.Body
        'Loop through the recordset and display its contents.
        Do Until rsTitles.EOF
            Debug.Print rsTitles("title")
            rsTitles.MoveNext
        Loop
        rsTitles.Close
    End If
    oQueue.Close
    'If everything is okay, we are out of there.
    Exit Sub
ReadRecordset_Err:
    MsgBox Err.Description
End Sub
```

Run this example, and click the Send Recordset button. A disconnected ADO recordset is then placed on the TestQueue (see Figure 3.22).

Figure 3.22: *The ADO recordset is put in the queue.*

NOTE

The size of the message on your machine may be a little different from the size you saw in Figure 3.22.

If you then click the Read Recordset button, the recordset is dequeued, and its contents are listed in the debug window (see Figure 3.23).

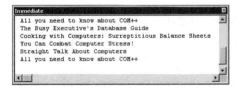

Figure 3.23: *The content of the recordset in the debug window.*

Creating a disconnected ADO recordset is a very efficient means by which you can pass data between different tiers in DNA applications. With this technique, combined with the asynchronous processing power of MSMQ, you can build more scalable and robust enterprise and Internet applications.

An Asynchronous Ordering Application

So far, I have introduced all MSMQ programming techniques in Visual Basic. In this section, you will use a more complicated example, an asynchronous ordering system, to learn how to use MSMQ in the real world.

Figure 3.24 illustrates the workflow of this ordering system. An ordering application sends the order data to OrderQueue as a message (step 1), which specifies OrderResponseQueue as the response queue (step 2). When the order message arrives in the OrderQueue, an event fires in the order processing application (step 3), which in turn inserts the order into the Orders table in the database by calling a stored procedure (step 4). When the order processing application finishes processing, it sends a confirmation message back to the OrderResponseQueue (step 5). When the confirmation message arrives in the OrderResponseQueue, an event fires and the results are displayed (step 6).

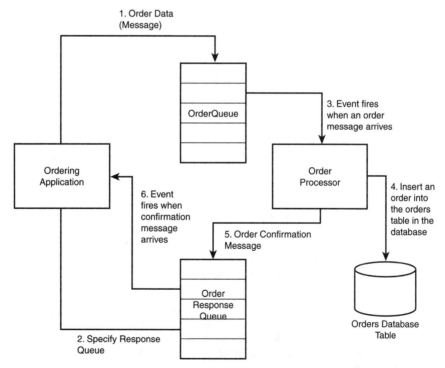

Figure 3.24: *The workflow of the asynchronous ordering system.*

EXAMPLE

The purpose of this example is to demonstrate how to leverage the asynchronous processing power of MSMQ to build highly scalable and robust applications. You will use the Orders table in the Northwind database that comes with SQL Server 7.0 in this example. For the sake of simplicity, you can ignore the Order Details table. To follow this example in Listing 3.8 and Listing 3.9, you need to create a system DSN named Northwind, which points to the Northwind database. You also need to create a stored procedure that inserts a row in the Orders table and returns the current `OrderID` as an output parameter.

Listing 3.8   Stored Procedure `PlaceOrder`

```
Use Northwind
go

if exists (select * from sysobjects where id = object_id('PlaceOrder'))
  drop proc PlaceOrder
go

create proc PlaceOrder
 @Order varchar(300),
 @OrderID int out
as
declare @sql varchar(600)

select @sql= 'insert Orders ('
          + 'CustomerID, '
        + 'EmployeeID, '
        + 'OrderDate,'
        + 'RequiredDate,'
        + 'ShippedDate,'
        + 'ShipVia,'
        + 'Freight,'
        + 'ShipName,'
        + 'ShipAddress,'
        + 'ShipCity,'
        + 'ShipPostalCode,'
        + 'ShipCountry'
        + ') values (' + @Order + ')'

--Insert the order to the Orders table.
exec(@sql)
--Return the OrderID for the newly inserted order.
select @OrderID = max(OrderID) from Orders
go
```

You can use the Computer Management snap-in to create the two queues for this example: the OrderQueue and the OrderResponseQueue (see Figure 3.25).

Figure 3.25: *The OrderQueue and the OrderResponseQueue.*

Figure 3.26 shows the asynchronous ordering system with the ordering application on the left and the order processing application on the right.

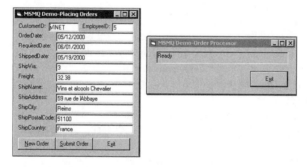

Figure 3.26: *The asynchronous ordering system.*

When you fill up the order information on the form and click the Submit Order button, the status of the ordering processing application briefly changes to Processing order and then back to Ready. Depending on the CPU speed and how much RAM you have on your machine, you may hardly notice the status change. Soon a message box pops up and confirms that your order (with an OrderID) is processed (see Figure 3.27).

Figure 3.27: *The confirmation message of the asynchronous ordering system.*

EXAMPLE

Listings 3.9 and 3.10 provide the complete code for this application and reveal what's happening behind the scenes.

Listing 3.9   The Ordering Application

```
'==================================
'The ordering application of the
'asynchronous ordering system
'==================================


'==============================
'General Declarations section
'==============================
Option Explicit
'Declare module level variables.
Dim oQinfoOrder          As New MSMQ.MSMQQueueInfo
Dim oQInfoOrderResponse As New MSMQ.MSMQQueueInfo
Dim oQueueResponse       As MSMQ.MSMQQueue
Dim WithEvents oQEvent   As MSMQ.MSMQEvent


'===========================
'The Load event of the form
'===========================
Private Sub Form_Load()
    'In the load event of the form, specify PathNames for
    'both OrderQueue and OrderResponseQueue.
    On Error GoTo Load_Err
    #If bUseDS Then
        oQinfoOrder.PathName = ".\OrderQueue"
        oQInfoOrderResponse.PathName = ".\OrderResponseQueue"
    #Else
        oQinfoOrder.PathName = ".\PRIVATE$\OrderQueue"
        oQInfoOrderResponse.PathName = ".\PRIVATE$\OrderResponseQueue"
    #End If

    'Open the OrderResponseQueue and prepare to receive events.
    Set oQueueResponse = oQInfoOrderResponse.Open(MQ_RECEIVE_ACCESS, _
                                                  MQ_DENY_NONE)

    Set oQEvent = New MSMQ.MSMQEvent

    'Enable message notification.
    oQueueResponse.EnableNotification oQEvent
    Exit Sub
Load_Err:
    MsgBox Err.Description
End Sub


'======================================
'The Click event of the New Order button
'======================================
```

Listing 3.9 continued

```vb
Private Sub cmdNewOrder_Click()
    'Clear all input boxes.
    Dim oControl As Control
    For Each oControl In Me.Controls
        If TypeOf oControl Is TextBox Then
            oControl.Text = ""
        End If
    Next oControl
End Sub


'============================================
'The Click event of the Submit Order button
'============================================
Private Sub cmdSubmit_Click()
    On Error GoTo SubmitOrder_Err
    Dim oQueue              As MSMQ.MSMQQueue
    Dim oMessage            As New MSMQ.MSMQMessage
    Dim sMessage            As String

    'Simple client side data validation.
    If Len(txtCustomerID) + _
       Len(txtEmployeeID) + _
       Len(txtOrderDate) + _
       Len(txtRequiredDate) + _
       Len(txtShipDate) + _
       Len(txtShipVia) + _
       Len(txtFreight) + _
       Len(txtShipName) + _
       Len(txtShipAddress) + _
       Len(txtShipCity) + _
       Len(txtShipPostalCode) + _
       Len(txtShipCountry) = 0 Then

        MsgBox "Incomplete order!", vbCritical
        Exit Sub
    End If

    'Gather information from the order form
    'and pad them into a message.
    sMessage = "'" & txtCustomerID & "'," _
            & txtEmployeeID & "," _
            & "'" & txtOrderDate & "'," _
            & "'" & txtRequiredDate & "'," _
            & "'" & txtShipDate & "'," _
            & txtShipVia & "," _
            & txtFreight & "," _
```

Listing 3.9 continued

```
                        & "'" & txtShipName & "'," _
                        & "'" & txtShipAddress & "'," _
                        & "'" & txtShipCity & "'," _
                        & "'" & txtShipPostalCode & "'," _
                        & "'" & txtShipCountry & "'"

        Screen.MousePointer = vbHourglass

        'Open the OrderQueue for send access and send the order
        'message to the queue.
        Set oQueue = oQinfoOrder.Open(MQ_SEND_ACCESS, MQ_DENY_NONE)
        sMessage = sMessage
        With oMessage
            .Label = "Order"
            .Body = sMessage
            'Specify the response queue.
            Set .ResponseQueueInfo = oQInfoOrderResponse
            .Send oQueue
        End With
        oQueue.Close
        Screen.MousePointer = vbDefault

        Exit Sub


SubmitOrder_Err:
        Screen.MousePointer = vbDefault
        MsgBox Err.Description
End Sub


'===========================================
'The Arrived event of the OrderResponseQueue
'===========================================
Private Sub oQEvent_Arrived(ByVal Queue As Object, ByVal Cursor As Long)
        'Display the response message when it arrives.
        On Error GoTo Event_Arrived_Err

        Dim oMessage As New MSMQ.MSMQMessage
        Set oMessage = oQueueResponse.ReceiveCurrent(ReceiveTimeout:=1000)
        MsgBox oMessage.Body

        'Enable message notification before exiting the event.
        oQueueResponse.EnableNotification oQEvent

        Exit Sub
Event_Arrived_Err:
```

Listing 3.9   continued

```
    MsgBox Err.Description
End Sub


'===================================================
'The ArrivedError event of the OrderResponseQueue
'===================================================
Private Sub oQEvent_ArrivedError(ByVal Queue As Object, _
                                 ByVal ErrorCode As Long, _
                                 ByVal Cursor As Long)
    MsgBox "Error event fired!" & vbCrLf & _
           "Error: " & Hex(ErrorCode)
End Sub


'===================================
'The Click event of the Exit button
'===================================
Private Sub cmdExit_Click()
    Unload Me
End Sub
```

Listing 3.10   The Order Processing Application

```
'===================================
'The order processing application of
'the asynchronous ordering system
'===================================


'============================
'General Declarations section
'============================
Option Explicit
'Declare module level variables.
Dim oQinfoOrder       As New MSMQ.MSMQQueueInfo
Dim oQueue            As MSMQ.MSMQQueue
Dim WithEvents oQEvent As MSMQ.MSMQEvent


'===========================
'The Load event of the form
'===========================
Private Sub Form_Load()
    'Listen to the event of the OrderQueue.
    #If bUseDS Then
        oQinfoOrder.PathName = ".\OrderQueue"
    #Else
```

Listing 3.10   continued

```
            oQinfoOrder.PathName = ".\PRIVATE$\OrderQueue"
    #End If

    Set oQueue = oQinfoOrder.Open(MQ_RECEIVE_ACCESS, MQ_DENY_NONE)
    Set oQEvent = New MSMQ.MSMQEvent

    lblStatus = "Ready"

    'Enable message notification.
    oQueue.EnableNotification oQEvent

End Sub

'=====================================
'The Arrived event of the OrderQueue
'=====================================
Private Sub oQEvent_Arrived(ByVal Queue As Object, ByVal Cursor As Long)
    'Process the order message when it arrives and
    'send a response message when the process is finished.
    On Error GoTo Event_Arrived_Err

    Dim oMessage        As New MSMQ.MSMQMessage
    Dim oQueueResponse  As MSMQ.MSMQQueue
    Dim oResponseMessage As New MSMQ.MSMQMessage
    Dim oConnection     As New ADODB.Connection
    Dim oCommand        As New ADODB.Command
    Dim iOrderID        As Integer
    Dim sMessage        As String

    'Update the status.
    Screen.MousePointer = vbHourglass
    lblStatus = "Processing order..."
    DoEvents
    'Read the message.
    Set oMessage = oQueue.ReceiveCurrent(ReceiveTimeout:=1000)
    sMessage = oMessage.Body

    'Connect to the Northwind database.
    oConnection.Open "Northwind"

    'Call the stored procedure "PlaceOrder".
    With oCommand
        .ActiveConnection = oConnection
```

Listing 3.10 continued

```
            .CommandType = adCmdStoredProc
            .CommandText = "PlaceOrder"
            .Parameters.Append .CreateParameter("@Order", _
                                                adVarChar, _
                                                adParamInput, _
                                                300)
            .Parameters.Append .CreateParameter("@OrderID", _
                                                adInteger, _
                                                adParamOutput)
            .Parameters("@Order") = sMessage
            .Execute
            iOrderID = .Parameters("@OrderID")
        End With


        'If the response queue is specified then send a confirmation mes-
sage.
        If Not oMessage.ResponseQueueInfo Is Nothing Then
            Set oQueueResponse = _
                oMessage.ResponseQueueInfo.Open(MQ_SEND_ACCESS, _
MQ_DENY_NONE)
            With oResponseMessage
                .Label = "Order Confirmation Message"
                .Body = "Order " & CStr(iOrderID) & " has been processed!"
                .Send oQueueResponse
            End With
        End If
        lblStatus = "Ready"


        'Enable message notification.
        oQueue.EnableNotification oQEvent
        Screen.MousePointer = vbDefault


    Exit Sub
Event_Arrived_Err:
    Screen.MousePointer = vbDefault
    lblStatus = "Ready"
    MsgBox Err.Description
End Sub


'=========================================
'The ArrivedError event of the OrderQueue
'=========================================
Private Sub oQEvent_ArrivedError(ByVal Queue As Object, _
```

Listing 3.10   continued

```
                                     ByVal ErrorCode As Long, _
                                     ByVal Cursor As Long)

    MsgBox "Error event fired!" & vbCrLf & _
           "Error: " & Hex(ErrorCode)

End Sub


'====================================
'The Click event of the Exit button
'====================================
Private Sub cmdExit_Click()
    Unload Me
End Sub
```

When the form of the ordering application is loaded, it establishes the pathnames for both OrderQueue and OrderResponseQueue, opens OrderResponseQueue, and enables the event for receiving order confirmation messages (refer to Listing 3.9). After you fill in the order form and click the Submit Order button, the click event packs the order into a string message and sends the message to the OrderQueue, specifying OrderResponseQueue as the response queue (refer to Listing 3.9). When the order processing application starts, the Load event of the form establishes a pathname for the OrderQueue and enables the event to receive ordering messages (refer to Listing 3.10). When an ordering message arrives, it triggers the Arrived event. The code in the event calls a stored procedure that inserts the order to the Orders table in the Northwind database and returns an order ID. Then a confirmation message is sent to OrderResponseQueue (refer to Listing 3.10), which in turn triggers the event of the ordering application to display the confirmation message (refer to Listing 3.9).

To better understand how the system works, run the applications in a slow motion mode. Stop the order process application if it is running. Then start the ordering application, fill in the form, and click the Submit Order button. If you look at both OrderQueue and OrderResponseQueue at this point, you will find that the order message you just sent stays in OrderQueue, whereas no messages appear in OrderResponseQueue (see Figure 3.28).

Now stop the ordering application and start the order processing application. If you check the queues, you will notice that the order message on OrderQueue is gone and a confirmation message appears in OrderResponseQueue (see Figure 3.29).

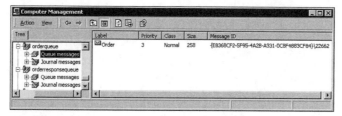

Figure 3.28: An order message in OrderQueue.

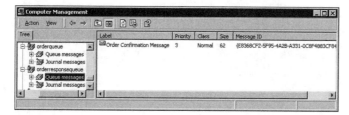

Figure 3.29: A confirmation message in OrderResponseQueue.

Now start the ordering application again. This time, you will see a confirmation message box. If you check the queues again, you will notice that no messages appear in OrderQueue or OrderResponseQueue.

What's Next

This chapter introduced MSMQ and showed you how to program MSMQ in Visual Basic. The knowledge you learned will be essential for you to understand important COM+ services, such as Queued Components (QC). In Chapter 4, "Introduction to Visual Basic COM Programming," you will learn how to develop COM components in Visual Basic.

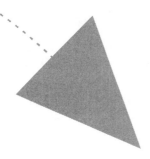

Introduction to Visual Basic COM Programming

In previous chapters, you learned how to work with ADO and MSMQ through their COM interfaces. In this chapter, you'll learn how to build your own COM components in Visual Basic to provide services to other applications.

This chapter teaches you the following:

- Basic COM programming techniques
- How to create in-process servers
- How to design COM components
- Important COM design decisions

Visual Basic COM Programming Primer

Chapter 1, "What COM+ Is All About," covered all the COM fundamentals. In Chapters 2 and 3, you learned how to access ADO and MSMQ functionalities using their COM object models. In this chapter, you'll learn how to create COM components in Visual Basic.

Types of COM Components

As you learned in Chapter 1, COM components are binary files that provide functionalities through COM interfaces. COM components can be either in-process components or out-of-process components.

As I discussed earlier in this book, in-process components usually provide better performance because they run in the process address space of the client application, and there is no process boundary overhead when making calls. On the other hand, out-of-process components offer fault isolation because they run as separate processes from the client. If the out-of-process components experience an abnormal shutdown, the client application can handle the situation gracefully without being fatally affected.

In Visual Basic, in-process components are compiled as ActiveX DLLs (or COM DLLs), whereas out-of-process components are compiled as ActiveX EXEs (or COM EXEs). Yet another variation of in-process COM components supported by Visual Basic are the ActiveX controls that usually have a user interface and are primarily used for building rich graphical user interfaces (GUI) with extended functionalities. When you start a new Visual Basic project, you see all three types, as shown in Figure 4.1.

Figure 4.1: *Types of COM components supported in Visual Basic.*

In COM+ applications, components have to be compiled as ActiveX DLLs. Therefore, here the discussion focuses on ActiveX DLLs. Let's look at a Visual Basic ActiveX DLL project.

A Visual Basic COM DLL Project

When you choose the ActiveX DLL project type as you start a new Visual Basic project, a new class module is inserted into your Visual Basic project and named Class1 (see Figure 4.2).

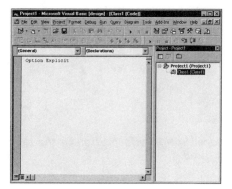

Figure 4.2: *A new ActiveX DLL project in Visual Basic.*

Now you are ready to set properties for the project and the classes.

PROJECT PROPERTIES

You can access the Project Properties sheet by choosing Project, Project1 Properties. Alternatively, you can just right-click Project1 in the Project Browser and choose Project1 Properties. Either way, you go to the General tab of the Project Properties sheet. I'll describe only those project properties that are important for ActiveX DLL components here.

Figure 4.3 shows the General tab with the project name COMDLLDemo. The project name becomes the DLL filename after you compile your project. In this case, you end up with a DLL file called COMDLLDemo.dll.

Figure 4.3: *The General tab of the Project Properties sheet.*

The information you put in the Project Description field will be displayed in the References property sheet as one of the Available References (see Figure 4.4). It will also appear in the Object Browser (see Figure 4.5).

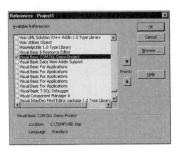

Figure 4.4: *The project description information in the References property sheet.*

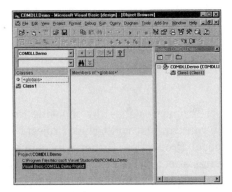

Figure 4.5: *The project description information in the Object Browser.*

The Unattended Execution option of the Project Properties sheet suppresses all message boxes raised by your components and writes their contents to the Windows Event Log. This option is preferable because the COM components you are going to develop for COM+ applications do not have any user interfaces and need not interact with users directly.

With the Upgrade ActiveX Controls option checked, Visual Basic automatically loads the most recent version of the ActiveX controls used in your project. This option is not, however, especially useful for your purposes because you are not likely to use any ActiveX controls in COM DLLs.

The Retained in Memory option prevents the object from being physically destroyed after the client releases all the references to it (for example, sets the reference to the object to Nothing). This can reduce the overhead accrued by object creation.

For the Threading Model option, you have only two choices: Single Threaded and Apartment Threaded. As you learned in Chapter 1, Single Threaded is the single-threaded model, whereas Apartment Threaded means the STA model. For COM+ applications built in Visual Basic, Apartment Threaded is the default threading model for ActiveX DLL projects.

CAUTION

Visual Basic ActiveX DLL project uses a slightly different terminology than COM specifications to describe the threading models. The Single-Threaded threading option in a Visual Basic ActiveX project corresponds to the COM single-threaded model. Apartment Threading, however, corresponds to the COM STA model, not the MTA model, which can be confusing.

Now look at the Component tab of the Project Properties sheet (see Figure 4.6). The Remote Server Files option in the Remote Server group generates two extra files when you compile your ActiveX DLL: VBR and TLB files with the same filenames as the DLL file. The VBR file contains information for the Windows Registry to run the component on a remote machine, and the TLB file is a separate type library file. If you don't select this option, the type library is embedded in the DLL file.

Figure 4.6: The Component tab.

NOTE

A type library provides information about the interfaces, methods, properties, and events of a component. Type library information is stored in the Windows Registry in HKEY_CLASSES_ROOT under the TypeLib folder.

The Version Compatibility options are sometimes quite confusing to Visual Basic developers. When you compile a component, Visual Basic generates all the GUIDs for the component, including CLSIDs, IIDs, and type library IDs. These GUIDs are stored in the Windows Registry and are used by the COM library at runtime to identify and use the functionality of your component. CLSIDs and IIDs are used to uniquely identify the classes and interfaces of COM components. Type library IDs are also used by Visual Basic to populate the Available References list of the References window (refer to Figure 2.9 of Chapter 2, "Windows DNA 2000 and COM+"). Each option in the Version Compatibility group has a different level of preservation of these GUIDs for each time you compile your components, as outlined in Table 4.1.

Table 4.1   Version Compatibility Options

Option	Description
No Compatibility	CLSIDs, IIDs, and type library IDs are re-created.
Project Compatibility	CLSIDs and IIDs are re-created, but type library IDs remain constant.
Binary Compatibility	CLSIDs, IIDs, and type library IDs remain constant.

As you can see from Table 4.1, setting the option to No Compatibility breaks all the compatibilities of any existing client applications of your component. Project Compatibility (the default option) preserves the type library ID for your components when you are testing and debugging your components, so you don't have to refresh the reference to your component in the client application each time you make minor changes to your component and recompile it. However, because the CLSIDs and IIDs are re-created each time you recompile the component, practically speaking, Project Compatibility is no different from No Compatibility. The last option, Binary Compatibility, preserves all the GUIDs for you (this feature is new in Visual Basic 6.0). Therefore, you should make sure not to change the interfaces of your component (that is, classes, properties, methods, and all the signatures) when you choose Binary Compatibility.

I recommend that, after you compile your component for the first time, you set the option to Binary Compatibility (see Figure 4.6). Remember from Chapter 1 that interfaces are immutable as soon as they are published. Therefore, if you have to change the interfaces to meet some specific needs, you should create new interfaces rather than change existing interfaces.

TIP

Figure 4.6 shows the physical pathname for the component file, which is the default when you set the path through the Browse button. Change it to a relative path; that is, use only the filename without the path. For example, use COMDLLDemo.dll instead of D:\QUE\Chap04\Src\COMDLLDemo.dll. Using the relative path helps Visual Basic to automatically locate the DLL file if you move the project source code to a different location, as long as you put the DLL file in the same folder as the project file (the VBP file).

CLASS PROPERTIES

Chapter 1 introduced interfaces as the contracts between COM components and the outside world. Classes are a concrete implementation of specific interfaces. Objects are individual instances of classes. The relationship between classes and objects is similar to the relationship between blueprints and houses. A blueprint defines the shape, dimensions, and different elements of houses, whereas each individual house can have a specific implementation of elements. For example, each house from the same blueprint can have different colored walls and use different materials for the windows. Similarly, each Employee object can have different attributes, such as names, ages, hiring dates, and so on, that are defined by the Employee class.

Some programming languages, such as C++ and Java, separate the interface definition from the classes. They define the interface through the Interface Definition Language (IDL), save it as a separate file, and then compile the IDL file to generate source files. In Visual Basic, however, this procedure is all handled behind the scenes.

Visual Basic uses class modules to define and implement classes. You can define your classes in two ways. One way is to define *abstract classes* without any implementations. Another way is to directly implement the interfaces using class modules. You'll learn different ways of implementing classes later in this chapter. For now, let's focus on some important properties of class modules.

The Name property defines the identification of the class in a human-readable manner. For this example, change the Name property of your class in the COMDLLDemo project from Class1 to SayHi. Another important class property is Instancing. The sample project is an ActiveX DLL, so you can choose from four possible options for the Instancing property, as shown in Figure 4.7.

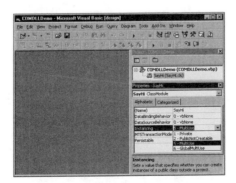

Figure 4.7: *The Instancing property of a class module.*

Table 4.2 summarizes these Instancing properties.

*Table 4.2 The **Instancing** Properties*

Option	Description
Private	Other applications cannot access the class, nor can they create objects from a class that are marked as Private.
PublicNotCreatable	Other applications cannot directly create an object from a class that is marked PublicNotCreatable. They can, however, access this class through other classes whose Instancing properties are set to either MultiUse or GlobalMultiUse. This option is useful for creating hierarchical object models.
MultiUse	Classes marked as MultiUse can be created and accessed by other applications. One instance of the component can be used by any number of client applications.
GlobalMultiUse	This property is similar to MultiUse; plus, you can access methods and properties of the component without explicitly creating an instance of the component. Setting the Instancing property to GlobalMultiUse is *not* a good practice. When possible, always explicitly create instances of components so that your code is consistent and more readable.

In this case, the Instancing property is set to MultiUse.

Writing a Simple COM Component

EXAMPLE

Now you can create a simple ActiveX DLL component using the ActiveX DLL project you started in the preceding section. Open the code window of the SayHi class module and create a public function called Hello(), as shown in Listing 4.1.

Listing 4.1   The Hello Function of the SayHi Class

```
Public Function Hello(ByVal sName As String) As String
    On Error GoTo Hello_Err
    If Len(sName) <> 0 Then
        Hello = "Hello, " & sName & "!"
    Else
        Hello = "Hello, there!"
    End If
    Exit Function
Hello_Err:
    MsgBox Err.Description
End Function
```

The `Hello()` function takes one string input parameter, which is the name of the person you want to greet. If you use an empty string, the function returns the generic greeting message `"Hello, there!"`. Otherwise, it returns a customized greeting message for a given name.

Save the project and compile the ActiveX DLL by choosing the File, Make COMDLLDemo.dll menu option. Then set the Version Compatibility to Binary Compatibility for the created DLL. Now you have a fully functional COM component ready for use. Start a new Visual Basic Standard EXE project and set a reference to the COM component you just created (see Figure 4.8).

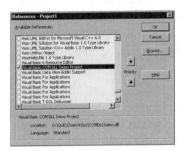

Figure 4.8: *Set a reference to the* `SayHi` *type library.*

Put a command button on the form and double-click it to open the code window. Now type the code in Listing 4.2.

Listing 4.2   Sample Client Code for Using the `SayHi` COM Component

```
Private Sub Command1_Click()
    On Error GoTo SayHi_Err
    Dim oSayHi As New COMDLLDemo.SayHi
    MsgBox oSayHi.Hello("Peishu")
    Set oSayHi = Nothing
    Exit Sub
SayHi_Err:
    MsgBox Err.Description
End Sub
```

Now press F5 to run the project. Click the command button to see a message box with a greeting message returned from the `Hello()` function of the `SayHi` component (see Figure 4.9).

Figure 4.9: *Using the* SayHi *COM component in a Visual Basic client application.*

Building Visual Basic ActiveX DLLs

In the preceding section, you created a simple ActiveX DLL component to get a general idea how it works. This section discusses the semantics involved in building an ActiveX DLL in Visual Basic.

Interfaces Revisited

Chapter 1 introduced COM interfaces and discussed several important interfaces, such as IUnknown. Earlier in this chapter, you learned that, in Visual Basic, you can define and implement interfaces in two ways. This section introduces more COM interfaces and shows you how to implement interfaces in Visual Basic.

THE DEFAULT INTERFACE

The simple ActiveX DLL named COMDLLDemo.dll uses a class module to define and implement the interface. When you compile the DLL, Visual Basic automatically creates an interface for you behind the scenes. Figure 4.10 shows the SayHi interface from the OLE/COM Object Viewer, which can be installed from the Visual Studio CD. You can access it by choosing Start, Programs, Microsoft Visual Studio 6.0, Microsoft Visual Studio 6.0 Tools, OLE View.

This tool is very handy for working with COM components. If you double-click the SayHi node on the left pane, a small dialog box appears with the name and IIDs of the _SayHi interface. When you click the View TypeInfo button, you go to the ITypeInfo Viewer window (see Figure 4.11). The right pane displays the Interface Definition Language (IDL) of this interface. Interfaces created in this way are called *default interfaces*.

CUSTOM INTERFACE AND MULTIPLE INTERFACES

Another way to define an interface is to create an abstract class and define its methods without any specific implementation.

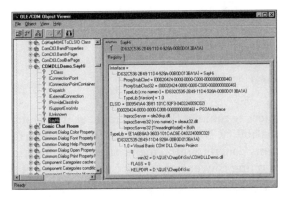

Figure 4.10: *The OLE/COM Object Viewer.*

Figure 4.11: *The ITypeInfo Viewer window.*

For this section, extend the SayHi example and create an abstract class that defines an interface. To do so, start a new ActiveX DLL project. Set the project properties as in Figure 4.12.

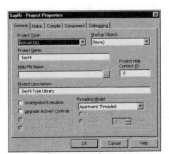

Figure 4.12: *Project property of* SayHi.

Change the name of Class1 to **ISayHi** and add a public function definition for Hello(), as in Listing 4.3. Notice that no code appears inside the Hello() function.

Listing 4.3 Defining the Hello() Function for the ISayHi Interface

```
Option Explicit

Public Function Hello(ByVal sName As String) As String
    'Abstract Class, no implementation here.
End Function
```

Compile the project to make a SayHi.dll and set its Version Compatibility as Binary Compatibility. Now you have an abstract interface definition for ISayHi without any concrete implementation of the function Hello(). Here, you follow the naming convention using *I* as the prefix of the interface name. Figure 4.13 shows the ISayHi interface in the OLE/COM Object Viewer.

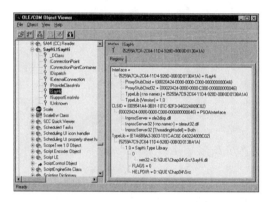

Figure 4.13: The ISayHi interface.

Now create two ActiveX DLL components that implement the ISayHi interface. To do so, start a new ActiveX DLL project and name the project **SayHi1**, set the project description to **SayHi Type Library Implementation 1**, and change Class1 to Hello1. Then set a reference to the ISayHi interface (see Figure 4.14).

Open a code window; then, in the General Declarations section, type **Implements ISayHi**. The Visual Basic Implements keyword makes the ISayHi interface available in the Object drop-down list so that you can implement specific functionalities. Click the Object drop-down list and select ISayHi. Visual Basic then generates the skeleton code for the ISayHi_Hello() function. Type the code as highlighted in Figure 4.15.

Compile the project to create the SayHi1.dll. Similarly, create a SayHi2.dll project as described in Table 4.3.

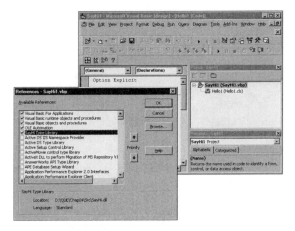

Figure 4.14: *A class that implements the ISayHi interface.*

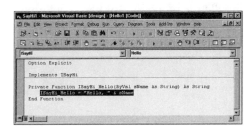

Figure 4.15: *Implement the ISayHi_Hello() function.*

Table 4.3 **SayHi2** Project Settings

Property/Function	Description
Project Name	SayHi2
Project Description	SayHi Type Library Implementation 2
Class Name	Hello2

Set a reference to the ISayHi interface as in the previous example and implement the Hello() function as in Listing 4.4.

Listing 4.4 Implementing the Hello() Function of the ISayHi Interface

```
Option Explicit

Implements ISayHi

Private Function ISayHi_Hello(ByVal sName As String) As String
    ISayHi_Hello = "Hello, " & sName & ". How are you?"
End Function
```

Compile the project to create the SayHi2.dll.

Now you can start testing your interface and its implementations. Start a new Standard EXE project and set references to the ISayHi interface and the two COM DLLs you just created (see Figure 4.16).

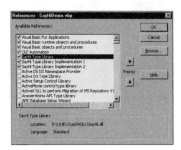

Figure 4.16: *Setting references in the client application.*

Add two command buttons to the form and name them **cmdSayHi1** and **cmdSayHi2**, respectively.

Next, write the code as in Listing 4.5.

Listing 4.5   Client Application Code That Uses Components to Implement the ISayHi Interface

```
Option Explicit

Private Sub cmdSayHi1_Click()
    Dim oHello As SayHi.ISayHi
    Set oHello = New SayHi1.Hello1
    MsgBox oHello.Hello("Peishu")
End Sub

Private Sub cmdSayHi2_Click()
    Dim oHello As SayHi.ISayHi
    Set oHello = New SayHi2.Hello2
    MsgBox oHello.Hello("Peishu")
End Function
```

Press F5 to run the application; then click the SayHi 1 button. The greeting shown in Figure 4.17 then appears. Clicking the SayHi 2 button generates the greeting shown in Figure 4.18. These messages match the different implementations of the ISayHi interface in SayHi1.dll and SayHi2.dll. The capability of implementing different behavior from the same interface is called *polymorphism,* as introduced in Chapter 1.

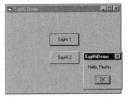

Figure 4.17: Greeting received by clicking the SayHi 1 button.

Figure 4.18: Greeting received by clicking the SayHi 2 button.

If you carefully look at the code in Listing 4.5, you'll notice that the syntax for declaring and creating objects is a little different from what you used before. You used the following syntax:

```
Dim oHello As SayHi.ISayHi
Set oHello = New SayHi2.Hello1
```

Alternatively, you can also use the following syntax:

```
Dim oHello As SayHi.ISayHi
Dim oHello1 As SayHi1.Hello1
Set oHello = oHello1
```

In either case, you create an object from the class that implements the interface, not from the interface itself.

Another benefit of using abstract classes is that you can implement multiple interfaces in your components so that they can evolve to meet new business requirements over time.

THE IDispatch INTERFACE

You may have noticed that among the many interfaces on the left pane of the OLE/COM Object Viewer in Figures 4.10 and 4.13 is an IDispatch interface. This interface is designed specifically for exposing object information to a client. Among the IDispatch interface's functions are GetTypeInfoCount, GetTypeInfo, GetIDsOfNames, and Invoke (see Figure 4.19).

Figure 4.19: The IDispatch *interface.*

The GetTypeInfoCount function returns either 1 or 0, indicating whether or not the object provides type information. The GetTypeInfo function returns the type information of an object, and this type information in turn can be used to get the type information of an interface. The GetIDsOfNames function takes one or more properties and/or methods and returns the dispatch IDs (or *dispIDs*) that are defined in the type library. A dispID is a unique number assigned to every property or method in an interface. The Invoke function takes a dispID and a variant array of parameters and invokes the corresponding property or method.

The rest of the functions in the IDispatch interface are inherited from the IUnknown interface. See Chapter 1 for more information about the IUnknown interface.

DUAL INTERFACE

The IDispatch interface provides a way for client applications to access the functionality of a COM component. This interface is slow, however, because it involves two functions, GetIDsOfNames and Invoke, to execute an actual call. A dual interface provides a more efficient way of communicating between a client application and the component. Figure 4.20 illustrates a typical dual interface.

A dual interface is actually a custom interface that implements all the functions of the IDispatch and IUnknown interfaces, as well as any functions that are specific to the object you are building (see Figure 4.20). An object that supports a dual interface allows different types of client applications to access its functionalities by the most efficient means possible. When you're writing your objects in Visual Basic, you don't explicitly implement the IDispatch interface nor dual interfaces. When you compile your component that contain the objects you built, Visual Basic automatically implements the dual interfaces for you.

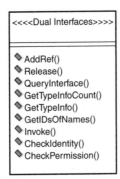

Figure 4.20: *A dual interface.*

Properties, Methods, and Events

COM+ has both properties and methods. You can also raise events from your components. The following sections describe how properties, methods, and events work.

PROPERTIES

Properties define the attributes of a class. In Visual Basic, properties are implemented either as module-level public variables or as public property procedures. As a COM developer, you should always implement properties using property procedures instead of public variables so that a client application can never directly access the data. In this way, you can have complete control over how your data is accessed and manipulated.

To continue with the example, add a `Name` property and a new `Greeting()` function to the COMDLLDemo component you started earlier in this chapter. Add some code in the `SayHi.cls` class module, as shown in Listing 4.6.

EXAMPLE

Listing 4.6   Adding a `Name` Property and a New `Greeting()` Function to the `SayHi.cls` of the COMDLLDemo Project

```
Option Explicit

Private m_sName As String

Public Property Let Name(ByVal sName As String)
    m_sName = sName
End Property

Public Function Greeting() As String
    On Error GoTo Greeting_Err
    If Len(m_sName) <> 0 Then
        Greeting = "Hello, " & m_sName & "!"
```

Listing 4.6 continued

```
    Else
        Greeting = "Hello, there!"
    End If
    Exit Function
Greeting_Err:
    MsgBox Err.Description
End Function
```

Listing 4.6 declares a module-level private string variable, m_sName, and provides a Let property procedure for manipulating the value of m_sName. Notice the naming convention used here: m_ indicates that you're using a module-level variable. Using a Let property procedure without a corresponding Get property procedure implements a write-only property for the component. Similarly, you can implement a read-only property for your component by using a Get property procedure without a corresponding Let property procedure. The Greeting() function takes no parameters.

Now recompile COMDLLDemo.dll. Start a new Visual Basic Standard EXE project and set a reference to the newly created COMDLLDemo.dll. Add a command button on the form and double-click it to open the code window. Then type the code in Listing 4.7.

Listing 4.7 Sample Client Code for Using the Modified SayHi COM Component

```
Private Sub Command1_Click()
    On Error GoTo SayHi_Err
    Dim oHello As New COMDLLDemo.SayHi
    oHello.Name = "Peishu"
    MsgBox oHello.Greeting
    Set oHello = Nothing
    Exit Sub
SayHi_Err:
    MsgBox Err.Description
End Sub
```

Press F5 to run the application. You then see a message similar to Figure 4.9.

Public properties (public variables or public property procedures defined in Visual Basic classes) of COM objects are also called *states*. A object that has state is called a *stateful* object. In contrast, a object without state (that is, without properties) is called a *stateless* object. You'll learn more about stateful and stateless object later in this chapter.

METHODS

Methods define the behavior of a class. In Visual Basic, methods are implemented by `Public Function` or `Public Sub`. Therefore, the `Hello()` and `Greeting()` functions are two methods of the `SayHi.cls` class module.

So far, you have learned about public properties and methods. They can both be accessed from client applications.

EVENTS

Using Visual Basic, you can add event notification functionality to your class. When something interesting happens, your component can raise an event so that the client application can implement an event handler to act accordingly. To implement an event in your class, you need to take two steps. First, you need to declare the event by using the `Event` keyword. The syntax for declaring an event is

```
Event EventName(ParameterList)
```

You define the parameter list as you would in subs or functions.

The second step of implementing an event is to call the `RaiseEvent` method in your procedure and pass parameters, if any, to raise the event so that the client application that implements your event is notified when the event fires.

EXAMPLE

Let's continue using the COMDLLDemo.dll example. For now, define a `HasName` event in the General Declarations section of the SayHi.cls class module:

```
Event HasName(ByVal sMessage As String)
```

In this `HasName` event, you define one string input parameter, `sMessage`. Now insert one line of code inside the `Greeting()` function to raise the event when the client sets the `Name` property (see Listing 4.8).

Listing 4.8   The `Greeting()` Function to Raise an Event

```
Public Function Greeting() As String
    On Error GoTo Greeting_Err
    If Len(m_sName) <> 0 Then
        Greeting = "Hello, " & m_sName & "!"
        'If sName parameter is passed, we rasie HasName event.
        RaiseEvent HasName("A name is passed as " & m_sName & ".")
    Else
        Greeting = "Hello, there!"
    End If
    Exit Function
Greeting_Err:
    MsgBox Err.Description
End Function
```

Here, you simply pass a message to the client application, indicating that a name has been passed in.

Now let's see how to get the event in a client application. To do so, start a new Standard EXE project and name it **UseCOMEvent**. Name the form **frmUseCOMEvent**. Then add a command button to the form and name it **cmdGetEvent**. In the General Declarations section, declare the SayHi object by using the WithEvents keyword:

```
Option Explicit
Dim WithEvents oHello As COMDLLDemo.SayHi
```

This declaration makes the event procedure available to you immediately. By clicking the Object drop-down box of code modules on the form, you can access the oHello_HasName event, as shown in Figure 4.21.

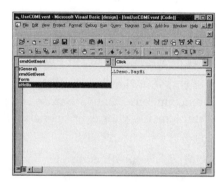

Figure 4.21: *The oHello_HasName event procedure in the code module.*

Next, add some code inside the event procedure so that it looks like this:

```
Private Sub oHello_HasName(ByVal sMessage As String)
    MsgBox sMessage
End Sub
```

Now double-click the command button and add the code in Listing 4.9.

Listing 4.9   Code for the Command Button of the Event Client Application

```
Private Sub cmdGetEvent_Click()
    On Error GoTo GetEvent_Err
    Set oHello = New COMDLLDemo.SayHi
    oHello.Name = "Peishu"
    MsgBox oHello.Greeting
    Set oHello = Nothing
    Exit Sub
GetEvent_Err:
    MsgBox Err.Description
End Sub
```

Press F5 to run the application; then click the Get Event button. You get two message boxes. The first one says A name is passed as Peishu, and the second says Hello, Peishu!. If you comment out the fourth line of code in Listing 4.9, oHello.Name, the event doesn't fire, and you get only one message box containing Hello, there!. This result is exactly what you would expect because you put the RaiseEvent call only in the first part of the If...Else...End If structure (refer to Listing 4.8).

In this section, you learned how to implement events in your COM components and how to handle events in client applications. Here, the events are processed synchronously. Chapter 10, "COM+ Events," discusses how to take advantage of the loosely coupled, asynchronous event services offered by COM+.

Error Handling

So far, I haven't really described error handling for developing Visual Basic COM components. The error handler code in previous examples does nothing more than display a message that describes what's gone wrong when an error happens. Unfortunately, these kinds of error messages are usually nearly useless for the users of your applications. Now I'm going to introduce a couple of useful error handling techniques that can make your COM components more robust and more supportive for troubleshooting when things do go wrong.

RAISING AN ERROR

The first method of handling errors in COM components is raising an error in the error handler of the methods inside your component. You do so by calling the Raise method of the Err object, as illustrated in the following code segment:

```
ErrorHandler:
    Err.Raise Number: = (10000 + vbObjectError), _
    Source:= m_sObjectName, _
    Description: = "Your customized error descriptions"
```

This technique is useful when you want to generate your own error for your component and return a customized error message to the client application that uses the component. Note that the Visual Basic constant vbObjectError is added to the error number to guarantee that your error doesn't conflict with any preserved errors for Visual Basic.

This method of error handling is not suitable, however, for situations in which you want to pass the exact error or errors back to the client application. In this case, you need to use the exact error number in the Raise method, as shown in the following example:

```
Err.Raise Number: = Err.Number, ......
```

If you add the `vbObjectError` constant to the error number, you end up generating completely irrelevant errors to the client application. For example, the error code for OLE DB error `General access denied error` is –2147493639. If you add the `vbObjectError` constant to the error number, you get `Overflow` error (runtime error 6), which has nothing to do with the actual error. Another downside of the raising error strategy is that it is not adequate for returning comprehensive error information, such as the `Errors` collection, back to the client application.

Passing Errors Back to Clients as Output Parameters

EXAMPLE

The second technique is to pass error information back to the client—that is, use the output parameters of the function that causes errors. Listing 4.10 is an error handling example that gathers all the information from the ADO `Errors` collection, pads it into a string variable, and passes this string back to the client application as an output parameter.

TIP

To run the code in Listing 4.10, you need to set a reference to "Microsoft ActiveX Data Access Objects 2.5 Library" in the Visual Basic project.

Listing 4.10   Passing Errors Back to the Client Application as Output Parameters

```
Public Function GetResult(ByVal sConnection As String, _
                          ByVal sSQL As String, _
                          ByRef lRows As Long, _
                          ByRef sErrorMessage As String) As ADODB.Recordset

    Dim oConn       As New ADODB.Connection
    Dim rsGetResult As New ADODB.Recordset
    Dim sErrDesc    As String
    Dim oContext    As ObjectContext

    On Error GoTo GetResult_Err

    'Get hook to the ObjectContext
    Set oContext = GetObjectContext()

    'Connect to the database.
    oConn.Open sConnection

    'Set up the ADO recordset.
    With rsGetResult
        .CursorLocation = adUseClient
        .CursorType = adOpenStatic
```

Listing 4.10   continued

```
                .ActiveConnection = oConn
                .Open sSQL

                lRows = .RecordCount 'rows fetched.
            End With

            'Return the recordset to the client.
            Set GetResult = rsGetResult

            'Up to this point, everybody is happy. So commit.
            If Not oContext Is Nothing Then
                oContext.SetComplete
            End If
            If Not oConn Is Nothing Then Set oConn = Nothing
            Exit Function
GetResult_Err:
            'Something goes wrong, so roll back.
            If Not oContext Is Nothing Then
                oContext.SetAbort
            End If
            If Not oConn Is Nothing Then Set oConn = Nothing

            'Get the error details.
            Dim oError As ADODB.Error
            For Each oError In oConn.Errors
            sErrDesc = sErrDesc & "Error " & CStr(oError.Number) _
                        & ": " & oErrors.Description & vbCrLf
            Next oError

            'Clean up.
            On Error Resume Next
            Set oConn = Nothing
            Set rsGetResult = Nothing
            'Pass error to the client.
            sErrorMessage = sErrDesc

            App.LogEvent m_sObjectName & ".GetResult" & vbCrLf & _
                        sErrDesc, vbLogEventTypeError
End Function
```

Inside the error handler in Listing 4.10, notice that the error information is
also written into the Windows Event Log by calling the LogEvent method of
the App object.

In the client application, you can check the returned error string to decide what to do if any errors occur:

```
If Len(sErrors) > 0 Then 'Some error happens
    'Code for handling errors in client application.
End If
```

Debugging and Testing

Visual Basic allows you to debug and test your COM components by creating a project group. To create a project group, open the COMDLLDemo.vbp project. From the File menu, choose Add Project and select Standard EXE in the Add Project window. This selection adds a project named Project1 and creates a project group named Group1. By default, the COMDLLDemo.vbp project is the startup project. You need to set Project1 as the default project (the client of the COM component) to test the component. To do so, right-click Project1 in the project browser and select Set as Start Up from the pop-up menu (see Figure 4.22).

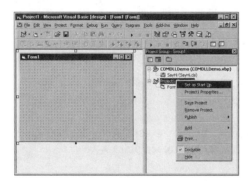

Figure 4.22: *Setting the standard EXE project as the startup project in the project group.*

Notice that Project1 is in bold now, indicating that it's the startup project. Now you need to set a reference to the COM component. To do so, select Project1 from the Project menu, choose References. Check COMDLLDemo from the Available References list. Notice that the Location points to the COMDLLDemo.vbp file instead of the compiled binary file COMDLLDemo.dll. This way, you can debug the code of your component. Also, the name of the project—COMDLLDemo—instead of the description—Visual Basic COM DLL Demo Project—appears in the list. Name the form **frmCOMDLLDemoTest** and set its caption to **COMDLLDemo Test**. Add a text box on the form of the new project you just added and set its `Name` property to **txtName**; then set the `Text` property to `""`. Add a command button, set its name to **cmdTestCOMDLLDemo**, and set its caption to **Test**. Double-click the command button to open the code window. Then add the code in Listing 4.11.

Listing 4.11 Code for the Testing Project

```
Option Explicit

Private Sub cmdTestCOMDLLDemo_Click()
    Dim oHello As New COMDLLDemo.SayHi
    MsgBox oHello.Hello(txtName)
End Sub
```

Listing 4.11 initiates an instance of the COMDLLDemo.SayHi class using the New keyword and calls the Hello message by passing the content of the text box. To test the component, set a stop point in the Hello method of the SayHi class (see Figure 4.23). Press F5 to load the form of the testing client project (Project1). Type a name in the text box and click the command button. You then go to the stop point you set in the Hello method of the SayHi class. Then you can press F8 to step through the code line by line the same way you debug a regular Visual Basic project. At the end of the execution of the Hello method, you go back to the client application, and a message box appears (see Figure 4.24).

Figure 4.23: *Setting a stop point in the* Hello *method of the* SayHi *class.*

Figure 4.24: *Testing the COM component.*

NOTE

You can also debug and test your COM component by starting a separate instance of Visual Basic. Then follow the steps described here to set up a stop point in the code of your component. You need to start the COM component project first by pressing Ctrl ¶ F5. Then you can start the testing project and test your component as you did in the procedures discussed earlier.

In this and previous sections, you learned some basic debugging and error handling techniques for developing COM components. Chapter 12, "More on COM+ Programming," covers more COM+ debugging and error handling issues.

Designing COM Components

So far, this chapter has covered the basic semantics of building COM components, particularly ActiveX DLLs, using Visual Basic. This section teaches you how to design the interfaces, properties, methods, and so on for the classes of your COM components. You'll learn several typical ways for designing your COM components.

COMPONENTS THAT MODEL REAL-WORLD ENTITIES

You can design your COM components to model real-world entities. This task is somewhat similar to data modeling. As a matter of fact, most system designs start with data modeling, especially for Windows DNA applications in which data is usually stored in a relational database management system (RDBMS), such as Microsoft SQL Server. In data modeling, real-world entities are physically implemented as database *tables*. An entity contains attributes that are mapped as columns (or fields) of a table. Figure 4.25 shows the authors table of the pubs database on SQL Server.

Figure 4.25: *The authors table of pubs database.*

As you can see, the authors table has many columns that map the attributes of an author entity. Let's design an Author class from this authors table. Figure 4.26 is a UML class diagram of the Author class.

Figure 4.26: *The* Author *class.*

The Author class in Figure 4.26 has many properties. It also has several methods, such as Add, Delete, Update, and FindByID. Properties are usually implemented by property procedures in combination with private module-level variables. As you learned earlier in this chapter, classes that have many properties are stateful (a property is considered a state of the class). Stateful classes are not scalable. Therefore, you can remodel the Author class as a stateless class, as shown in Figure 4.27.

Figure 4.27: *A stateless* Author *class.*

EXAMPLE

When you're designing a stateless class, you can pass all the information as parameters to the methods. For example, you might design the Add method of the Author class as follows:

```
Public Function Add(ByVal sAuthorID As String, _
                    ByVal sFirstName As String, _
                    ByVal sLastName As String, _
                    ByVal sPhone As String, _
                    ByVal sAddress As String, _
                    ByVal sCity As String, _
                    ByVal sState As String, _
                    ByVal sZip As String, _
                    ByVal bContract As Boolean) As Boolean
```

Now let's look at another example that models a database entity. Figure 4.28 is the table schema for the Orders table in the Northwind database.

Figure 4.28: *The Orders table of Northwind database.*

A stateless Order class might look like the one in Figure 4.29.

Figure 4.29: *A stateless* Order *class.*

The PlaceOrder method can be defined as follows:

```
Public Function Add(ByVal sCustomerID As String, _
                    ByVal sEmployeeID As String, _
                    ByVal dtOrderDate As DateTime, _
                    ByVal dtRequiredDate As DateTime, _
                    ByVal dtShippedDate As DateTime, _
                    ByVal lShipVia As Long, _
                    ByVal cFreight As Currency, _
                    ByVal sShipName As String, _
                    ByVal sShipAddress As String, _
                    ByVal sShipCity As String, _
                    ByVal sShipRegion As String, _
                    ByVal sShipPostalCode As String, _
                    ByVal sShipCountry As String) As Boolean
```

Notice that the OrderID is not part of the input parameters because it is an *identity* column in the database. An identity column in SQL Server is similar to the AutoKey field in an Access database. The value of the column is system-generated.

COMPONENTS THAT PROVIDE SPECIAL SERVICES

In addition to modeling real-world entities, you can also design the classes of your component to provide special services. For example, you can design a File object that provides services for creating, deleting, and manipulating files on your hard drives (see Figure 4.30).

```
        File
┌─────────────────┐
│ ◈ Create()      │
│ ◈ Delete()      │
│ ◈ Save()        │
│ ◈ Update()      │
└─────────────────┘
```

Figure 4.30: *The File class.*

COMPONENTS THAT WRAP PROPRIETARY APIs

You can also use COM components as wrappers that encapsulate proprietary API functions and expose them as the methods of your components. As a result, any client application that can use COM will be able to call the proprietary API functions indirectly through the interfaces of the wrapper components.

A Microsoft ActiveX Data Object (ADO) is an example of a wrapper COM component that encapsulates the native OLE DB function calls and exposes OLE DB functionality through ADO interfaces, such as Connection, Command, and Recordset. Applications that use ADO can enjoy the functionalities provided by the underlying OLE DB providers without explicitly making calls to the OLE DB APIs.

COMPONENTS FOR OTHER PURPOSES

In addition to the methods of designing components described in previous sections, you can design COM components to meet your specific business requirements in a variety of ways. For example, you can wrap the functionalities of existing COM components to simplify the programming for client applications. In the following example, you'll create a COM component that handles interaction with Microsoft Collaboration Data Objects (CDO) (formerly called MAPI or Message Application Programming Interface) interfaces and provides a simple method call for client applications to send email messages.

To begin, start a new ActiveX DLL project and set its properties as shown in Figure 4.31.

EXAMPLE

Change the name of the class (Class1) to **Service**. Add the code in Listing 4.12 to Service.cls and compile the COM DLL component named Email.dll.

Figure 4.31: *The EMail project properties.*

Listing 4.12   Code for the EMail Project

```
Option Explicit

Public Function Send(ByVal sSubject As String, _
                     ByVal sBody As String, _
                     ByVal sProfile As String, _
                     ByVal sRecipient As String) As Boolean

    On Error GoTo Send_Err
    Dim oSession    As Object
    Dim oMessage    As Object
    Dim oRecipent   As Object

    Set oSession = CreateObject("MAPI.Session")
    oSession.logon sProfile

    Set oMessage = oSession.Outbox.Messages.Add
    oMessage.Subject = sSubject
    oMessage.Text = sBody

    Set oRecipant = oMessage.Recipients.Add
    oRecipant.Name = sRecipent
    oRecipant.Resolve

    oMessage.Update
    oMessage.Send showDialog:=False
    oSession.Logoff
    Exit Function
Send_Err:
    App.LogEvent Err.Description
End Function
```

The Service class supports one method, Send. It takes three input parameters and sends an email message through the CDO (MAPI) interface.

NOTE

Notice that instead of setting a reference to the CDO (MAPI) component library and using the New keyword to create an object (an instance of the component) as in previous examples, you declare the variable as an Object data type and use a CreateObject method. The former mechanism of instantiating objects is called *early binding*, whereas the CreateObject method uses *late binding* to create the object. Early binding uses either Vtable binding or dispID binding, depending on whether the component supports dual interfaces. Late binding uses the IDispatch interface, so the performance is relatively slower than early binding. The late binding, however, provides more flexibility.

Now you can create a Standard EXE project to test Email.dll. Figure 4.32 illustrates the design time of the testing project.

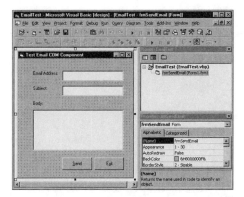

Figure 4.32: *The EmailTest project at design time.*

Listing 4.13 contains the code for the testing client.

Listing 4.13 Code for the EmailTest Project

```
Option Explicit

Private Sub cmdExit_Click()
    Unload Me
End Sub

Private Sub cmdSendEmail_Click()

    On Error GoTo CreateSessionAndLogon_Err

    Dim oMail As Object
    Set oMail = CreateObject("EMail.Service")
    oMail.Send txtSubject, txtBody, _
```

Listing 4.13   continued

```
          "MS Exchange Settings", _
          "pli@wt.net"

     MsgBox "Message sent!"
     Set oMail = Nothing
     Exit Sub

CreateSessionAndLogon_Err:
     MsgBox Err.Description
End Sub
```

Here again, you use the `CreateObject` method (late binding) to create an instance of the `Email.Access` class. Figure 4.33 shows the result of running the testing client application.

Figure 4.33: *The result of the testing application.*

Special Design Considerations

This section discusses several important decisions you need to make when designing the interfaces of your components.

Granularity of Interfaces

When designing an interface, you decide which properties and methods the interface should support. The process of grouping the properties and methods into a particular interface is called *interface factoring*. You can design from a coarse interface that includes many methods and/or properties to a fine interface that contains only a small set of methods and/or properties. In most cases, fine interfaces have several advantages over coarse interfaces and are easier to evolve and maintain.

Stateful Versus Stateless

Earlier in this chapter, you learned about stateful and stateless classes. Whether your class should be stateful or stateless depends on how you are going to use your component. If your components are designed to run in the middle tier, they need to be scalable. Stateless is the choice for this situation. If, on the other hand, you want to use your components on the client side for temporarily cached data so that you don't have to make round trips to the database back end every time you want to look up something, you should design a stateful class.

Passing Parameters

You may have noticed that in previous examples, parameters of methods are declared either using ByVal or ByRef. When a parameter is defined using ByVal, only a copy of the data is passed in the function, but the original data is not affected. If you change the value of the parameter being passed in, the original data inside the calling application is not changed. If you define the parameters using ByRef, the actual memory address pointer of the variable is passed in. Therefore, any changes by the function to the variable are directly made to the original data. For this reason, the parameters defined using ByRef are called *output parameters*. Because of the way ByRef parameters work, you should choose ByVal when possible to avoid unnecessary overhead. Use ByRef only when you need the value to be passed back to clients.

Scripting Clients

When you're designing COM components for scripting clients, such as Active Server Pages, you should take special care to ensure your components behave as expected.

First, scripting languages such as Visual Basic Scripting Edition (or VBScript) support only late binding, so you should design a default interface for the scripting clients. That is, you should use class modules that carry implementation instead of using abstract classes.

Second, scripting languages are not strongly typed; all the variables in VBScripts are of the variant data type. So, when the parameters are declared using ByRef, they should use the variant data type. If you use a specific data type for a parameter that is declared as ByRef, you get a Type mismatch error when calling from scripting languages such as VBScript in ASP. For the parameters declared as ByVal, however, you can use specific data types.

Designing Windows DNA Components

COM components that are designed for Windows DNA applications usually reside in the middle tier, or Business Services tier, of the three-tiered application. These components are better further partitioned into two sublayers: the Business Logic Layer (BLL) and Data Access Layer (DAL). DAL components usually encapsulate data access code that is fine-tuned for specific database back ends, whereas BLL components usually encapsulate business rules that are application-specific. BLL components use the services provided by the DAL components to access data stored in the Data Services tier. This separation of DAL from BLL provides great flexibility for the system to evolve. For example, if you want to migrate your database from one RDBMS to another RDBMS, such as from Oracle to SQL Server, all you need to do is fine-tune your DAL components. No BLL components are affected. On the other hand, should your business rules change, you can simply modify the corresponding BLL components but keep the DAL components unaffected.

COM+ Components

There are several constraints for designing COM+ components such as Queued Components (QC) and components for Loosely Coupled Events (LCE). You'll learn about these limitations later in this book when I discuss these specific COM+ services. Queued Components will be discussed in Chapter 9, "Queued Components." COM+ events will be covered in Chapter 10, "COM+ Events."

What's Next

By now, you have covered enough background to get started building COM+ applications. As the last chapter of Part I of this book, Chapter 5, "Using the Component Services MMC Snap-In," will introduce you to the COM+ world by helping you get familiar with the graphic administration tool for managing and administering COM+ applications.

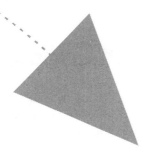

Using the Component Services MMC Snap-In

Windows 2000 provides an administrative tool, the Component Services, that is implemented as a Microsoft Management Console (MMC) snap-in for developers and system administrators to create, configure, and administer COM+ applications.

This chapter teaches you the following:

- What COM+ applications are
- How to create a COM+ application
- How to delete a COM+ application
- How to configure a COM+ application
- How to deploy a COM+ application
- How to convert an existing MTS package into a COM+ application

Introduction to COM+ Applications

A COM+ application is the primary unit of administration and security for Windows 2000 Component Services. It's a group of COM components that usually performs related functions. In Windows 2000, COM+ applications are administered through the Component Services MMC snap-in. Using this Component Services snap-in, you can create new COM+ applications, add components to applications, and set attributes of applications, components, interfaces, and methods. Figure 5.1 shows the Component Services snap-in with the COM+ Applications folder expanded.

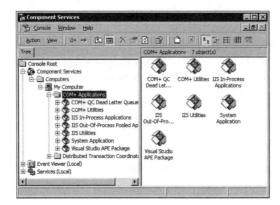

Figure 5.1: *The Component Services MMC snap-in.*

A COM+ application consists of COM components that are compiled as ActiveX DLLs. Components are implementations of one or more interfaces, and interfaces can have methods. A COM+ application defines the deployment scope for the COM components it contains and provides a common configuration scope for the COM components, such as security boundaries and queuing.

NOTE

A COM+ application is roughly equivalent to an MTS package in Windows NT 4.0. A COM+ application allows the COM components it contains (called *configured components*) to receive a richer set of services provided by Windows 2000 Component Services.

Types of COM+ Applications

The following are the four types of COM+ applications:

- Server applications
- Library applications

- Application proxies

- COM+ preinstalled applications

A server application runs in its own process and supports all COM+ services. A library application, on the other hand, runs in the process of its creator (the client). Library applications support only a subset of COM+ services, such as role-based security, but do not support more advanced features, such as remote access or Queued Components (QC).

COM+ allows you to export *application proxies*. An application proxy is a set of files containing registration information that allows a client to remotely access a server application. When these application proxy files are run on a client machine, they write all the information from the COM+ server application to the client machine. When this server-related information, such as CLSIDs, ProgIDs, RemoteServerName, and marshaling information, are written to the client machine, the server application can then be accessed remotely from the client machine.

NOTE

A COM+ application proxy is roughly equivalent to an MTS client executable in Windows NT 4.0. Both are exported from the server machine and run in the client machine to provide proxy information for the server so that the client can access the server remotely.

COM+ also includes a set of preinstalled applications that are used internally by Windows 2000 Component Services. These preinstalled COM+ applications, which include System Application, COM+ Utilities, and IIS Utilities, are located under the COM+ Applications folder in the Component Services snap-in. They are read-only and cannot be modified or deleted. You can see these preinstalled COM+ applications in Figure 5.1.

A Closer Look at a COM+ Application

Each COM+ application contains one or more components. Components in a COM+ application have interfaces, and interfaces have methods. Let's examine the System Application to see what a COM+ application consists of. Figure 5.2 shows a COM+ preinstalled application: System Application. As you can see from the figure, a COM+ application consists of COM components. In this case, the System Application contains four components: `Catsrv.CatalogServer.1`, `COMSVCS.TrackerServer`, `EventPublisher.EventPublisher.1`, and `Mts.MtsGrp.1`. Each COM component has one or more interfaces, and interfaces, in turn, contain methods. As shown in Figure 5.2, the `Mts.MtsGrp.1` component has an interface called `IMtsGrp`. The `IMtsGrp` interface has three methods: `Count`, `Item`, and `Refresh`.

Figure 5.2: *The System Application preinstalled COM+ application.*

Developing a COM+ Application

The process of developing a COM+ application includes designing COM components to encapsulate application logic, compiling the components into an ActiveX DLL and integrating these components into a COM+ application, and administering the application through deployment and maintenance. Designing a COM component involves defining and implementing COM classes and grouping classes into components. After designing the COM components and compiling them into an ActiveX DLL, you can integrate the components into a COM+ application and configure the application.

To take advantage of the COM+ services, a COM component must meet certain specific requirements:

- COM components built for COM+ applications must be in-process server components; that is, they must be compiled as ActiveX DLLs.

- The components must also maintain a type library that describes all classes implemented in the components and defines all the interfaces of the components.

The type library can be embedded in the compiled DLL file or a separate type library file (a TBL file). COM components that are installed in a COM+ application are called *configured components*. Those COM components that are not installed in a COM+ application are called *unconfigured components*. Most unconfigured components can be transformed into configured components by integrating them into a COM+ application, provided that they meet the requirements described previously.

After designing the COM components, you can compile them into ActiveX DLLs and integrate them into a COM+ application and configure the application. You can either create a new COM+ application and install the components into the COM+ application you created, or you can install the components into an existing COM+ application. In the following sections of this chapter you'll learn how to create, configure, and deploy COM+ applications.

Creating a COM+ Application

Before you create COM+ applications, you need to determine how to group your components into these COM+ applications. As I mentioned before, a COM+ application defines a security boundary. The security is checked at the application level, whereas the security between different components inside the same COM+ application is not checked. So, when you design the layout of your COM+ applications, security scope is an important consideration. A COM+ application also decides deployment scope. You can export your components in a COM+ application as a whole. You'll learn about COM+ application deployment later in this chapter. In this section, you'll learn how to use the Component Services snap-in to create a COM+ application and install your COM components into that application.

Creating a New COM+ Application

EXAMPLE

Let's create a new COM+ application. From the Component Services snap-in, right-click the COM+ Application folder and select New, Application (see Figure 5.3).

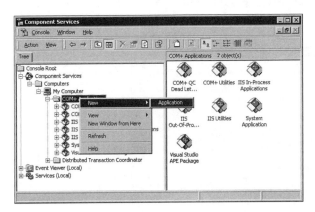

Figure 5.3: *Creating a new COM+ application in the Component Services snap-in.*

Alternatively, you can open the Action menu and then select New, Application.

Click Next on the Welcome screen to go to the Install or Create a New Application screen (see Figure 5.4).

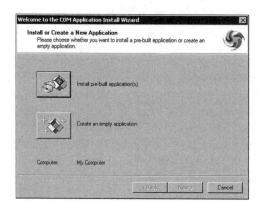

Figure 5.4: *The Install or Create a New Application screen of the COM Application Install Wizard.*

The first button, Install Pre-Built Application(s), allows you to install pre-built applications from an exported COM+ application file (an MSI file) or an MTS package. You'll learn about exporting and importing COM+ applications in the section "Deploying COM+ Applications," and importing MTS packages in the section "Converting MTS Packages into COM+ Applications" later in this chapter. For this example, choose Create an Empty Application, which takes you to the next screen (see Figure 5.5).

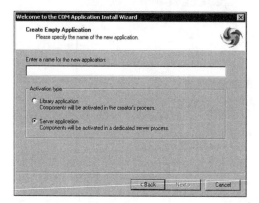

Figure 5.5: *The Create Empty Application screen of the COM Application Install Wizard.*

You can choose to create either a server application, which is the default option, or a library application. I discussed the difference between a server application and a library application earlier in this chapter, which is that a server application runs as a separate process whereas a library application runs at the process of the client application. Here, create a server application. Type **Que's Sample COM+ Application** in the Enter a Name for the New Application text box and click Next. On the next screen (see Figure 5.6), you can set the application identity, in which you specify under which account you want the COM+ application to run.

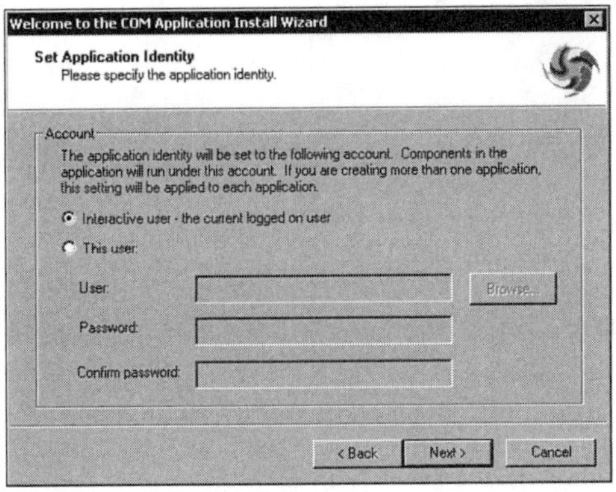

Figure 5.6: *The Set Application Identity screen of the COM Application Install Wizard.*

You can specify Interactive User (the default option) or This User. The Interactive User is whoever is logged on to the server computer. You can set the identity to a specific user account by selecting This User and typing the username and password for the account, which must be a domain user account. Choosing Interactive User makes the Component Services available to applications running on remote computers under any user account, but it requires someone to log on to the server computer. In contrast, This User makes the Component Services available only to the user account you specify, but this option does not require anyone to log on to the server machine. I recommend that you select Interactive User in development environments and choose This User in production environments. In this way, the services will keep running even when no one actually logs on to the server.

TIP

You or the system administrator can reconfigure the Application Identity attribute after the COM+ application is deployed.

NOTE

The Set Application Identity screen is available only for server applications, not for library applications.

For this example, choose the default, Interactive User, and click Next. Click Finish on the last screen of the COM Application Install Wizard. Now you have an empty COM+ application, Que's Sample COM+ Application, as shown in Figure 5.7.

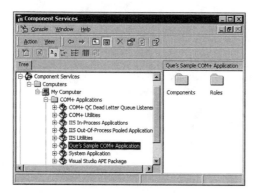

Figure 5.7: *A sample empty COM+ application.*

After you create the empty COM+ application, you are ready to add components into the application either by installing new components or importing existing components.

Installing New Components

EXAMPLE

To install new components to the COM+ application you just created, you can use the COM Component Install Wizard by right-clicking the Components folder under your COM+ application and choosing New, Component (see Figure 5.8).

Select the first option, Install New Component(s), on the Import or Install a Component screen (see 5.9). Then follow the instructions on subsequent screens to install new components into your COM+ application.

Figure 5.8: Installing new components by using the COM Component Install Wizard.

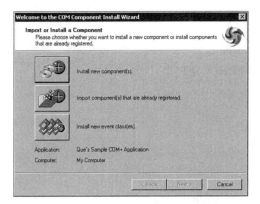

Figure 5.9: The Import or Install a Component screen of the COM Component Install Wizard.

You can also drag the ActiveX DLLs that contain the components you want to install from Windows Explorer and drop them into the right pane of the Component Services under the Components folder. Figure 5.10 shows what the window looks like after COMDLLDemo.dll is dragged from Windows Explorer and dropped into the Component Services.

In this example, the COMDLLDemo.dll has only one class: the SayHi class. Therefore, you have only one component. If you install an ActiveX DLL that has multiple classes, each class creates a corresponding component after you install the ActiveX DLL into a COM+ application.

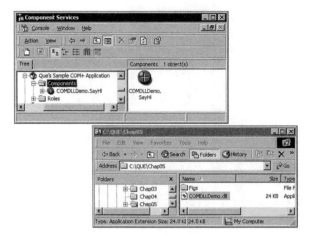

Figure 5.10: *Installing the* COMDLLDemo.SayHi *component by dragging and dropping.*

Deleting Components from a COM+ Application

The easiest way to delete a component from a COM+ application is simply to highlight the component you want to delete and press the Delete key on your keyboard. Then select Yes in the Confirm Item Delete dialog box to delete the component (see Figure 5.11).

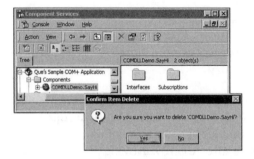

Figure 5.11: *Deleting a component from a COM+ application.*

TIP

For an ActiveX DLL that contains multiple components (classes), you can delete only the specific component and keep the rest of the components in the COM+ application. You can also install two different components from the sample ActiveX DLL into two different COM+ applications by installing both components in both COM+ applications and then deleting unwanted ones from corresponding COM+ applications. In this way, you can install different components of a single ActiveX DLL file into different COM+ applications.

CAUTION

Be careful when you want to delete or reinstall a component from a COM+ application. Make sure you fully understand all its interfaces, methods, classes, attributes, securities, and other settings, as well as the dependencies before you perform this task.

Importing Existing Components

EXAMPLE

Using the Component Services, you can also import components that have already been registered by other means on the computer on which your COM+ application resides. Let's continue to use the COMDLLDemo.dll to see how to import existing components into a COM+ application.

First, manually register COMDLLDemo.dll into the System Registry. To do so, select Start, Run. In the Open text box, type **Regsvr32 /v** followed by the path of the ActiveX DLL, as shown in Figure 5.12, and click OK.

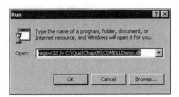

Figure 5.12: Manually registering a COM component.

Click OK on the message box that confirms the ActiveX DLL has been successfully registered.

Now that the component has been registered on the local machine, you can import it into the sample COM+ application. From the Component Services, right-click the Components folder under the COM+ application and select New, Component. In the Import or Install a Component screen (refer to Figure 5.9), click the second button, Import Component(s) That Are Already Registered. On the next screen, Choose Components to Import, highlight the component(s) that you want to import. For this example, highlight the COMDLLDemo.SayHi component (see Figure 5.13). Click Next, and you see a Thank You screen. Click Finish to finish importing COM+ components.

CAUTION

Importing a component into a COM+ application does not populate interfaces, methods, and marshalling information for the component. Therefore, if you plan to distribute the COM+ application later, install rather than import components.

Figure 5.13: *The Choose Components to Import screen of the COM Component Install Wizard.*

Removing COM+ Applications

EXAMPLE

To remove a COM+ application that becomes outdated or is no longer in use, simply highlight the COM+ application in the Component Services and press the Delete key on the keyboard. Then Answer Yes in the Confirm Item Delete dialog box.

If the server application or an application proxy has been installed on the computer using Windows Installer, you can remove the application through the Add/Remove Programs applet from the Control Panel. Alternatively, you can delete it by using the following Windows Installer command-line syntax:

```
Msiexec.exe -x <ApplicationName>.msi
```

You'll learn about Windows Installer in the section "Deploying COM+ Applications" later in this chapter.

Configuring COM+ Applications

In the COM+ programming model, an application is *attribute-based*, or *declarative*. Configuration becomes an essential part of the development process of a COM+ application. How you configure your COM+ application affects the application's behavior and what COM+ services are available for the application.

You can configure four levels of attributes for a COM+ application:

- Application-level
- Component-level (also known as class-level)

- Interface-level
- Method-level

Application-level attributes include Activation, Enforce Access Checks, Security Level, Authentication Level, Impersonation Level, Queuing, Enable CRM, Server Process Shutdown, Permissions, Security Identity, Launch in Debugger, and Enable 3GB Support.

Component-level (or class-level) attributes include Transactions, Synchronization, JIT Activation, Object Pooling, Object Construction, Enforce Component Level Access Checks, Declarative Role Assignments, Queuing Exceptions Class, Activate in Caller's Context, and Instrumentation Events and Statistics.

Interface-level attributes include Declarative Role Assignment and Queued.

Method-level attributes include Declarative Role Assignment and Auto-done.

The following sections briefly discuss some important attribute settings from a functionality perspective.

Configuring Transactions

Chapter 6, "Writing Transactional Components," provides a detailed discussion of COM+ transactions. This section shows you to how to set some important transaction attributes. You can set transaction attributes at the component level. COM+ reads the attributes of your components at run-time to determine the type of transaction service to provide.

EXAMPLE

To set the transaction attributes for the COMDLLDemo.SayHi component, right-click the component in the Component Services and select Properties. Then click the Transactions tab of the Properties sheet (see Figure 5.14).

The five possible transaction attribute values shown in Figure 5.14 are Disabled, Not Supported, Supported, Required, and Requires New. These values correspond to the five possible settings of the MTSTransactionMode property of a class module in a Visual Basic 6.0 ActiveX DLL project, as shown in Table 5.1.

Table 5.1   Transaction Attributes and the **MTSTransactionMode** *Property*

Transaction Attributes	MTSTransactionMode
Disabled	0-NotAnMTSObject
Not Supported	1-NoTransactions
Supported	3-UsesTransactions
Required	4-RequiresTransaction
Requires New	5-RequiresNewTransaction

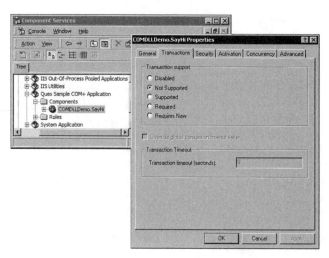

Figure 5.14: *Setting transaction attributes in Component Services.*

NOTE

When a component is created in Visual Basic and installed in a COM+ application, the MTSTransactionMode property is read and converted into the transaction attribute according to Table 5.1. You can always overwrite these predefined transaction attributes of components later by using the Component Services.

The differences between Disabled and Not Supported are subtle. If you set the transaction attribute of a component to Disabled, COM+ preserves the transactional behavior of the component as the unconfigured COM component; the object may or may not participate in the transaction of its caller. If you set the transaction attribute to Not Supported (the default), however, the object never participates in any transaction, regardless of the transactional status of its caller.

When you set the transaction attribute to Supported, the object participates in the transaction of the caller if one exists, but never starts its own transaction.

Setting transaction attributes to Required allows the object to participate in an existing transaction or start a new transaction if there is no transaction of the caller.

If the transaction attribute of a component is marked as Requires New, it always starts a new transaction as the root, regardless of the transactional status of the caller.

NOTE

COM+ does not support nested transactions. Therefore, when the object's transaction attribute is set to Requires New and a transaction exists in the caller, the object always starts an independent, separate transaction.

Configuring Security

COM+ provides a number of security features to protect COM+ applications, including declarative or programmatic role-based security, authentication services, and impersonation/delegation. Chapter 8, "COM+ Securities," covers COM+ security in detail. This section introduces you to setting security attributes for your COM+ applications using the Component Services.

CONFIGURING ROLE-BASED SECURITY

EXAMPLE

Configuring role-based security involves several steps. The first step is to create roles. To create a role in the sample COM+ application, expand the application in the Component Services and right-click the Roles folder. Then select New, Role (see Figure 5.15).

Figure 5.15: *Creating a role using the Component Services.*

Type the name **SayHi Users** in the Role dialog box and click OK. The SayHi Users role is then added to the application (see Figure 5.16).

For the next step, you need to map user accounts to the role you defined. To do so, expand the SayHi Users folder, right-click the Users folder, and then select New, User. In the Select Users or Groups dialog box, select the users or groups that you want to map to the roles defined. For this example, select the Administrator user (see Figure 5.17). Click OK, and Administrator is added to the SayHi Users role (see Figure 5.18).

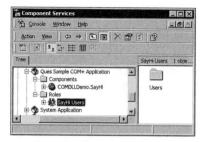

Figure 5.16: *A role has been added to the COM+ application.*

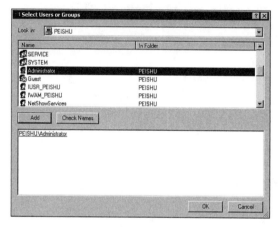

Figure 5.17: *Selecting a user.*

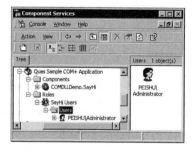

Figure 5.18: *Mapping a user account to a role.*

After the roles have been defined (and optionally, user or group accounts have been mapped to the roles), the next step is to assign the roles to components, interfaces, and methods. To assign a role to your component, right-click the COMDLLDemo.SayHi folder and select Properties. Next, click the Security tab and select SayHi Users from the Roles Explicitly Set for Selected Item(s) box (see Figure 5.19). Finally, click OK to assign the role to the component.

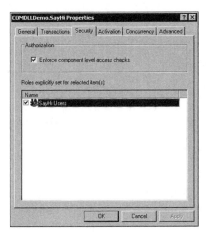

Figure 5.19: *Selecting the SayHi Users role.*

In a similar manner, you can assign roles to the interfaces and their methods.

As the last step for the role-based security to work, you need to enable the authorization at the COM+ application level to let the role-based security take place. To do so, right-click the COM+ application and select Properties. Next, click the Security tab and check Enforce Access Checks for This Application (see Figure 5.20). Then click OK.

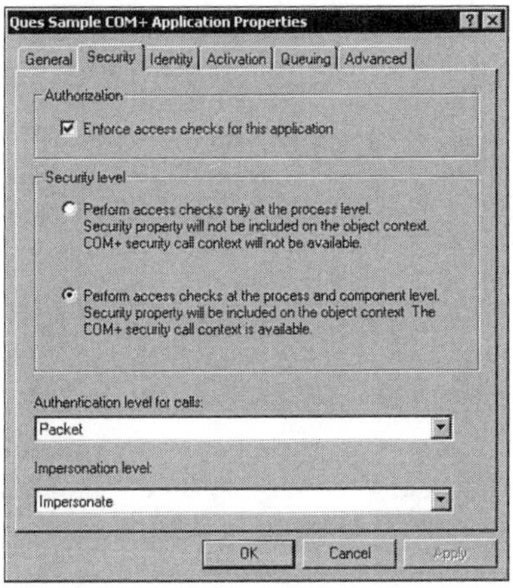

Figure 5.20: *Enabling authorization for a COM+ application.*

As you can see in Figure 5.20, you can further specify the security levels at which to perform access checking, either at the process level or component level.

In addition, you can also specify authentication and impersonation levels. The default authentication and impersonation levels are Packet and Impersonate, respectively.

AUTHENTICATION LEVELS

Authentication is the process of verifying that someone is actually who he or she claims to be. The six authentication levels are described in Table 5.2.

Table 5.2   Authentication Levels

Name	Description
None	No authentication check.
Connect	An authentication check occurs only at connection time.
Call	Authentication occurs at the beginning of every call.
Packet	This level of authentication verifies that all call data is received (the default).
Packet Integrity	This level of authentication also verifies that no call data has been modified in transit.
Packet Privacy	This is the most restrictive level of authentication checking. This level checks authentication and encrypts the packet, including the data and signature.

IMPERSONATION LEVELS

Impersonation is a process that verifies what degree of authority the application grants other applications to use its identity when it calls them. Table 5.3 lists four impersonation levels.

Table 5.3   Impersonation Levels

Name	Description
Anonymous	The server can impersonate the client but without knowledge of the client's identity. The client is anonymous to the server.
Identity	The server can impersonate the client with the client's identity.
Impersonate	The server can impersonate the client while acting on its behavior, with the limitation that the server can access the recources only on the same machine (the default).
Delegate	The server can impersonate the client while acting on its behavior, regardless of whether it is on the same computer as the client.

Configuring JIT Activation

In a distributed computing environment, creating an object and holding a reference to the object usually consume very expensive resources such as memory usage and network traffic. It is desirable for a client to create or activate the object as late as possible and release the reference as soon as it's done with the object. Both MTS and COM+ provide a *Just-in-Time (JIT) activation* mechanism to simplify the programming model and conserve the server resources. The disadvantage of JIT is that there is an overhead each time the object is activated. In most scenarios, however, the benefit of JIT far overweighs the disadvantages.

COM+ also allows you to administratively control the JIT behavior. You can turn on the JIT activation for a component. You can also enable the Auto-done feature at the method level. When the Auto-done feature is enabled for a given method, the object is automatically deactivated on method return.

EXAMPLE

To enable JIT activation for the COMDLLDemo.SayHi component, right-click the component in the Component Services and select Properties. Click the Activation tab and select the Enable Just In Time Activation check box (see Figure 5.21).

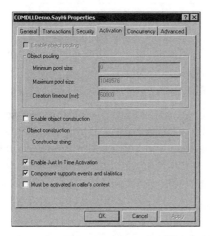

Figure 5.21: *Enabling Just-in-time activation for a component.*

NOTE

If a component is configured to support transaction—that is, its transaction attribute is set to something other than Disabled or Not Supported—JIT activation is automatically enabled, and you cannot disable it.

Now enable the Auto-done feature for the Hello method of the COMDLLDemo.SayHi component. Expand the Interfaces, _SayHi interface and the Methods folder. Then right-click the Hello method and select Properties. On the General tab, select the Automatically Deactivate This Object When This Method Returns check box and click OK (see Figure 5.22).

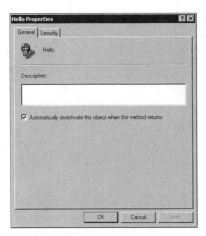

Figure 5.22: *Enabling the Auto-done feature for the* Hello *method.*

CAUTION

When you enable Auto-done for a method, you are actually changing the default behavior of both JIT activation and automation. Exercise this option with care.

Configuring Queuing

COM+ supports Queued Components (QC), which allows activation and interaction with an object in an asynchronous manner. This is achieved by using the Message Queuing services behind the scenes. You'll learn more about QC in Chapter 9, "Queued Components." In this section, you'll learn how to enable queuing for a component.

EXAMPLE

To enable QC for the COMDLLDemo.SayHi component, first you need to set the Queued attribute at the application level. To do so, right-click the sample COM+ application and select Properties. Click the Queuing tab and select the Queued-This Application Can Be Reached by MSMQ Queues check box (see Figure 5.23).

As soon as you click OK after specifying the Queued attribute at the application level, COM+ internally creates several queues to support QC (see Figure 5.24). You'll learn about these queues in Chapter 6.

In addition to setting up the Queued attribute at the application level, you also need to enable the Queuing property at the interface level. For this example, select the _SayHi interface, right-click, and select Properties. Click the Queuing tab and select the Queued check box (see Figure 5.25).

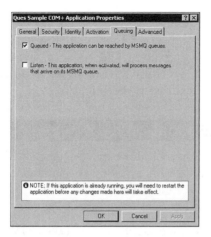

Figure 5.23: *Enabling Queued Components at the COM+ application level.*

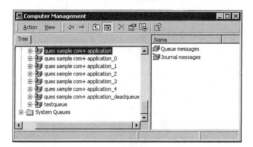

Figure 5.24: *COM+ creates several queues for the application marked Queued.*

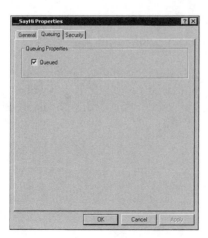

Figure 5.25: *Enable queuing at the interface level.*

Chapter 6 covers more details about QC programming and configuration.

Configuring Other COM+ Attributes

You also can configure other important COM+ attributes, including
Synchronization, Object Queuing, and COM+ events, by using the
Component Services snap-in. I'll cover these configuration attributes in
detail in later chapters that deal with these features.

Deploying COM+ Applications

Deploying a COM+ application includes exporting the COM+ application or
application proxies; you can do both by using the Component Services snap-
in. Let's continue to use the sample COM+ application to see how to deploy
both server applications and application proxies.

EXAMPLE

To export a server application, right-click the sample COM+ application
and choose Export. Click Next in the Welcome screen to open the
Application Export Information screen (see Figure 5.26).

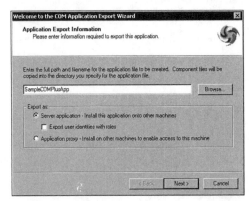

Figure 5.26: *Exporting a COM+ application.*

As you can see in Figure 5.26, you can choose between exporting as a
server application or an application proxy; both generate an MSI file and a
CAB file (see Figure 5.27). You can export an application proxy in a similar
manner.

Figure 5.27: *Exported COM+ application files.*

The exported MSI file is a Windows Installer file. If you select to export as a server application, the Windows Installer file contains all the information about the Registry settings, DLLs, and type libraries describing the interfaces implemented by the COM+ application's classes. If you choose to export as an application proxy, the Windows Installer file contains all the information for a client to access the server remotely.

You can install COM+ server applications or application proxies by using the Component Services snap-in on computers that are running Windows 2000. To install COM+ server applications or application proxies on computers that are not running Windows 2000, you need to make sure that Windows Installer is installed on the target machine. You can download Windows Installer from the Microsoft Web site at

`http://www.microsoft.com/msdownload/platformsdk/instmsi.htm`

Converting MTS Packages into COM+ Applications

If you upgrade a computer from Windows NT 4.0, Windows 95, or Windows 98 with the Windows Option Pack to Windows 2000, the setup process automatically converts all existing MTS packages into COM+ applications.

You can also manually export an MTS package from Windows NT 4.0, Windows 95, or Windows 98 machines and move it to a Windows 2000 machine and then install the MTS package as a COM+ application by using the Component Services.

EXAMPLE

For this example, install an exported MTS package, MTSExportApp.pak, as a COM+ application. To do so, right-click the COM+ Applications folder in the Component Services and select New, Application. Click Next on the Welcome screen and select Install Pre-Built Application(s) on the next screen. In the Files of Type drop-down box on the Install From Application File dialog box, select MTS Package Files(*.PAK) so that the MTS package file becomes available in the dialog box (see Figure 5.28).

Select the MTSExportApp.pak file and follow the instructions on subsequent screens. You can convert the MTS package to a COM+ application, as shown in Figure 5.29.

Figure 5.28: Importing an MTS package to a COM+ application.

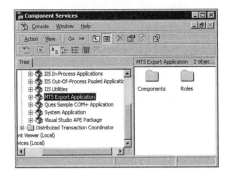

Figure 5.29: Converting an MTS package into a COM+ application.

What's Next

In this chapter, you learned how to use the Component Services snap-in to administer COM+ applications. In Chapter 11, "Administering COM+ Applications Programmatically," you'll learn how to programmatically administer COM+ applications through a scriptable COM interface, the COM+ Catalog. Chapter 6, "Writing Transactional Components," will teach you how to write components that support transactions.

Part II

Developing COM+ Application Components

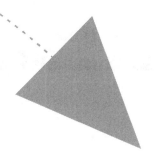

Writing Transactional Components

Transaction support is a basic and important requirement for any serious enterprise or Internet application. COM+ provides a rich set of transaction services that greatly simplify transaction programming. Thus, developers can spend more time solving business problems rather than writing complex code to deal with difficult transaction management scenarios.

This chapter teaches you the following:

- Transaction fundamentals
- Distributed transactions
- COM+ automatic transaction services
- How to write a complete transaction application

Introduction to Transactions

The following sections discuss some basic transaction concepts. You begin with the fundamentals of transactions, and then learn the ACID transaction characteristics. You also learn about transaction managers and transaction monitors, and finally you learn about distributed transactions, 2-pc transaction protocol, and MS DTC.

Transaction Basics

A *transaction* is a series of operations that are considered a unit of work completed as a single, atomic operation. A transaction has only two possible outcomes: either all the work is completed successfully, or none of it is.

Transferring money between two bank accounts is a classic example of a transaction. For instance, you transfer $100 from your checking account to your savings account. Two individual operations are involved in this transaction. The first operation is to take $100 from your checking account. The second operation is to add $100 to your savings account. Each operation is a possible point of failure. If one operation fails, the other cannot succeed either. Otherwise, either you or the bank will be unhappy. You don't want the transaction to succeed in the first operation and fail in the second—that is, $100 be taken from your checking account without being added to your savings account. The bank doesn't want to see the opposite result—that is, $100 added to your savings account without it being removed from your checking account.

ACID Properties

A successful transaction must be *atomic, consistent, isolated*, and *durable*. These attributes are known as the ACID properties of a transaction.

For a transaction to be *atomic,* it must execute exactly once. Either all the operations involved in the unit of work are done, or none of them are done.

The states of data before and after a transaction must be *consistent*. In the money transfer example, the account balances must be consistent, regardless of the output of the transaction. That is, if the transaction succeeds, both accounts should have new balances. Should the transaction fail, none of the account balances should be changed. Maintaining the consistency of data is usually the responsibility of the application developer.

Individual transactions should be *isolated* from one another. None of the transactions should see incomplete results of other transactions. Most transaction managers achieve transaction isolation through *serialization*; that is, individual transactions are are handled one by one in series.

A transaction also must be *durable*. Changes made to the data must be recoverable and survive system failure. Transaction durability is usually achieved by using a transaction log.

Transaction Managers (TMs)

Transaction managers (TMs) are systems designed to manage transaction requirements for applications, ensuring the ACID properties for transactions. Examples of transaction managers include database servers and transaction processing (TP) monitors.

Microsoft Transaction Server (MTS) is Microsoft's implementation of a transaction manager. MTS 1.0 was first introduced in early 1997, and MTS 2.0 was shipped as one of the important services in Windows NT 4.0 Option pack, along with IIS 4.0 and MSMQ 1.0. In Windows 2000, MTS stands for Microsoft Transaction Services and is an integrated part of COM+ component services.

DATABASE SERVERS

Most Relational Database Management Systems (RDBMS), such as Microsoft SQL Server, offer transaction processing capabilities. For example, the following code segment is a Transact SQL (TSQL) statement in Microsoft SQL Server that groups two UPDATE statements into a single transaction, starting with the statement BEGIN TRANSACTION. If everything goes fine—that is, the error number (@@error) is zero—we issue a COMMIT TRANSACTION statement to complete the transaction. Should anything go wrong, we call the ROLLBACK TRANSACTION statement to abort the transaction:

```
/*******************
  Begin transaction
*******************/
BEGIN TRANSACTION
  /*******************
    Update statements
  *******************/
  UPDATE Orders
  SET Status = "Shipped"
  WHERE OrderID = @OrderID
  UPDATE Shipment
  SET ShipDate = getdate()
  WHERE OrderID = @OrderID
  /****************************************************
    In case error occurred, roll back the transaction,
    Otherwise, commit the transaction.
  ****************************************************/
```

```
IF @@error = 0
  COMMIT TRANSACTION
ELSE
  ROLLBACK TRANSACTION
```

As you can see in the preceding code segment, if no error occurs (the @@error global variable is zero), the transaction is committed; otherwise, the transaction is aborted (or rolled back).

TRANSACTION PROCESSING SYSTEMS AND TRANSACTION PROCESSING MONITORS

A transaction processing (TP) system is a complete, end to end system that processes a massive amount of transactions. Such a system can be used to manage sales order entry, airline reservations, payroll, employee records, shipping, and so on.

A typical TP system consists of both software applications and hardware infrastructure and is extremely hard to develop and maintain due to its scope and complexity. To streamline application development, software vendors have produced two product categories that provide transaction-based software specifically designed to manage system-level services. These include database servers, such as Microsoft SQL Server, and transaction processing monitors, or TP monitors.

A TP monitor is a software environment that sits between a transaction processing application and a collection of system services, including database services, operating systems, communications, and user interfaces. When you create COM+ applications to manage transactions, you are using COM+ as a TP monitor. With a TP monitor, you need to write your application to run only as part of the TP monitor environment, whereas the TP monitor itself, in this case, COM+, takes care of managing individual services.

Distributed Transactions

Transactions in which more than one database or machine is involved are called *distributed transactions*. Distributed transactions share the same basic requirements as normal transactions that involve a single database. Managing a distributed application is more complicated than managing a normal transaction because it involves coordinating all the participating databases and resources. The overall output of a distributed transaction must be consistent for all involved parties. The following sections discuss the two-phase commit protocol (2-pc) and how the 2-pc protocol is used to manage distributed transactions. We will also introduce the Microsoft Distributed Transaction Coordinator (MS DTC).

Two-Phase Commit Protocol

The key technology that supports distributed transactions is the *two-phase commit protocol*, sometimes called *2-pc protocol*. This protocol operates in a voting mechanism and has two distinct phases:

- In phase one, each individual TM that participates in a transaction reports to a coordinating TM to indicate its readiness for committing the overall transaction, and also indicates its vote about its own transaction output (success or failure). Therefore, phase one is the preparation phase.

- In phase two, the coordinating TM instructs all the participating TMs to commit the transaction if they all agree to do so, or abort the transaction if at least one TM disagrees.

Microsoft Distributed Transaction Coordinator (MS DTC)

The Microsoft Distributed Transaction Coordinator (MS DTC) is a coordinating transaction manager that implements the 2-pc protocol. MS DTC was originally shipped with Microsoft SQL Server 6.5 and NT Option Pack 4. Now MS DTC is an integrated part of the Windows 2000 operating system.

COM+ and MS DTC work together to make distributed transactions work more seamlessly. When a COM+ application is involved in a transaction that spans multiple databases and/or machines, MS DTC assigns the application a transaction ID, manages all transaction-related communications, and flows the transaction across all the parties involved. In this scenario, COM+ directs MS DTC on behalf of the application.

In the MS DTC architecture, each local computer has a local transaction manager. MS DTC assigns one TM to be the coordinating TM, or *root TM*. The coordinating TM then handles the additional tasks of coordinating all activities among local TMs. Additionally, *resource managers* manage durable data. A Relational Database Management System (RDBMS) is an example of a resource manager. Similarly, *resource dispensers* manage nondurable data, which is data that can be shared. An ODBC driver is an example of a resource dispenser.

All applications and resource managers communicate with their local TMs. The TMs cooperatively manage transactions across machines.

COM+ Automatic Transactions

The following sections discuss automatic transactions supported by COM+ transaction services. As you learned in Chapter 5, "Using the Component

Services MMC Snap-In," in a COM+ application, a component has a transaction attribute, among other declarative attributes. When a component's transaction attribute is appropriately set to something other than Disabled, COM+ uses this transaction attribute to determine its transactional requirement and then provides automatic transaction services accordingly.

Transactional Components

A component whose transactional attribute is configured to support transactions is called a *transactional component*. As you learned in Chapter 5, this means that the transaction attribute for a transactional component must be set to one of the following values: Supported, Required, or Requires New. COM+ checks the transaction attribute of a component before activating an object from the component.

A component that doesn't support transactions usually never participates in a transaction. This type of component does not benefit from the transaction protection provided by COM+ but still incurs the overhead of context creation (a process in which COM+ creates an associated context object when creating initializing your COM object. I will explain the context object in the next section. When you don't want your component to participate in transactions but want to use the COM+ framework, such as location transparency of, you should set the transaction attribute of your component to Disabled to avoid the overhead of context creation. You'll learn why and when to use nontransactional components later in this chapter in the sample application.

Determining the Transaction Output

Before activating a transactional object, COM+ always creates a context object. The context object contains information about its creator and its transaction identifier, as well as *consistent and done bits,* which COM+ uses to determine the commitment and the output of the transaction. The context exposes two interfaces: `IObjectContext` and `IContextState`.

The consistent bit tells the state of an object, whether consistent (`True`) or inconsistent (`False`). Conversely, the done bit indicates the readiness of the component to commit a transaction, regardless of the outcome of the transaction. When COM+ creates an instance of an object, it sets the consistent bit to `True` and the done bit to `False` by default. Until the done bit is set to `True`, indicating it's the time to commit a transaction, you can repeatedly turn the consistent bits on and off. However, only the last change counts.

You can control the granularity of setting the consistent and done bits by using the interfaces provided by COM+. You can set the consistent and done bits at the same time by calling the methods of the IObjectContext interface, as described in Table 6.1.

Table 6.1   *Setting Consistent and Done Bits Through the Methods of the* **IObjectContext** *Interface*

Method	Consistent Bit	Done Bit
SetComplete	True	True
SetAbort	False	True
EnableCommit	True	False
DisableCommit	False	False

Unlike the IObjectContext interface, the IContextState interface offers methods that allow you to set and get consistent and done bits independently of each other. Table 6.2 summaries the IContextState methods and what they do.

Table 6.2   **IContextState** *Methods*

Method	Description
SetDeactivateOnReturn	Sets the done bit
SetMyTransactionVote	Sets the consistent bit
GetDeactivateOnReturn	Returns the Boolean value stored in the done bit
GetMyTransactionVote	Returns the value associated with the consistent bit

A Sample Transaction Application

In this section, you'll learn how to write a complete sample application that uses COM+ transaction services. This section also showcases the process of developing a component-based, multi-tiered application, including developing the case study and architectural design, using the Unified Modeling Language (UML), and defining the transaction scope and attributes for components. The purpose here is to give you a starting point. Most principles you will learn from this sample application are also applicable to writing mission-critical, large-scale applications.

Application Scope

For this example, you'll build an ordering application that utilizes the Northwind sample database that shipped with Microsoft SQL Server 7.0. If the Northwind database has not been installed yet on your system, use the Query Analyzer to run the SQL script file located at *<Your SQL Server root dir>*\MSSQL7\install\instnwnd.sql.

ASSUMPTIONS

For this example, you can make the following assumptions:

- Northwind Trade, Inc., has an order processing center at which its employees take calls or faxes from customers. The employees will use the application you are going to build here to place an order into the system.

- Other applications take care of other aspects of the system, such as adding or modifying customer information and managing products, suppliers, and shippers. So, this application will be solely responsible for placing orders of existing products for existing customers.

- Employees who take calls from customers can order only one product at a time. They can order more than one of that particular product at a time, though.

THE DATABASE SCHEMA

EXAMPLE

In this application, the data modeling is already done. Figure 6.1 illustrates the schema of the Northwind database. The Northwind database has 8 tables, Order, Order Details, Products, Categories, Suppliers, Customers, Shippers and Employees. As shown in Figure 6.1, the database is appropriated normalized. Tables are linked together by a primary key and foreign keys.

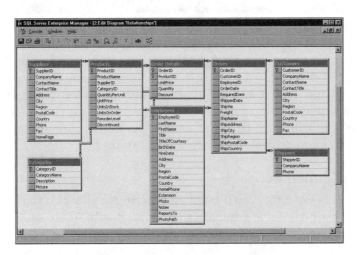

Figure 6.1: *The Northwind database schema.*

This sample application employs a couple of simple business rules:

- The quantity on the order must be less than or equal to the quantity in stock.

- After an order is placed, the quantity in stock (the UnitsInStock column) should be deducted from the Products table (refer to Figure 6.1).

The Workflow of Placing an Order

After an employee receives a call or fax from a customer, he or she typically performs the following tasks:

1. Starts the Northwind ordering application.

2. Selects a product from a list.

3. Fills in the quantity for the product ordered.

4. Selects the customer from a list so that the application can automatically fill in the shipping address information according to the customer's address. The employee can overwrite the default address and enter a different shipping address if necessary.

5. Selects a shipper from a list.

6. Fills in the freight. The application automatically calculates the subtotal and total according to the unit price, quantity, and freight.

7. Selects his or her name from an employee list.

8. Fills in other information as needed and submits the order.

Figure 6.2 illustrates this usage scenario.

Application Architecture

For the purposes of this chapter, you'll design the Northwind ordering application as a three-tiered architecture in which the application is divided into three distinct logic tiers: a *user services* tier, a *business services* tier, and a *data services* tier.

THE USER SERVICES TIER

EXAMPLE

The user services tier, or the presentation tier, is responsible for gathering information from the user and interacting with the business services tier to get information from the data services tier and submit changes back to the data services tier. In this sample application, the user services tier is a simple Visual Basic form, as shown in Figure 6.3.

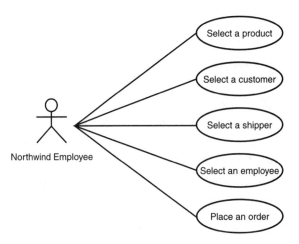

Figure 6.2: *A UML use-case diagram of the Northwind ordering application.*

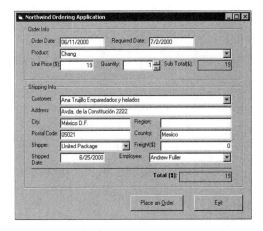

Figure 6.3: *The user services tier of the Northwind ordering application.*

As shown in Figure 6.3, the graphical user interface (GUI) consists of two sections (frames): Order Info and Shipping Info. Most data input is gathered through text boxes. This interface also contains four drop-down combo boxes for the user to select the product, customer, shipper, and employee who processes the order.

THE BUSINESS SERVICES TIER

The business services tier is made up of four COM objects. The Lookup object allows you to get information about the products, customers, shippers, and employees. The Order object lets you place an order. The Product object can be used to update the quantity in stock, and the Access (Data) object is a generic data access wrapper that internally uses ActiveX Data Objects (ADOs) to interact with the database.

Depending on the manner in which data interacts with the COM objects, they may have different transactional requirements or might not participate in the transaction at all.

The Lookup object's primary function is to retrieve data from the database and return a disconnected ADO recordset for the client application for local lookups. These functions do not involve any transactions. Therefore, the Lookup object is better designed as a nontransactional component.

The Order object uses the Access object to place an order in the database and uses the Product object to update the stock quantity. The Product object, in turn, uses the Access object to persist the updates to the database. As you can see, the Order object is the root of the transaction. Its transaction attribute should be set to Required; that way, if the caller of the Order object has a transaction, the Order object is enlisted into the existing transaction. In the sample application, the caller does not have a transaction, so the Order object always starts a new transaction. The Product and Data objects are not the root objects, so their transaction attributes can be set to Supported. If the caller has a transaction, it is enlisted into the existing transaction. In this case, the caller of the Product object is the Order object, and the caller of the Access object is either the Product object or the Order object. All the transactional COM components are hosted by the COM+ runtime environment.

Figure 6.4 defines the transaction boundary and attributes of the sample application.

EXAMPLE

THE DATA SERVICES TIER

The data services tier consists of a data store that is the Northwind database, a Microsoft SQL Server database. You'll also create several stored procedures to facilitate data access and to ensure data integrity. These stored procedures can also be used to implement business rules in conjunction with the COM objects in the business services tier.

Table 6.3 lists the stored procedures you'll use to create the Northwind ordering application.

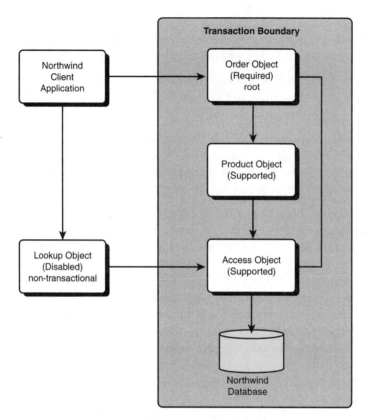

Figure 6.4: *The transaction boundary of the sample application and the transaction attributes of the COM objects.*

Table 6.3   Stored Procedures of the Northwind Ordering Application

Stored Procedure Name	Description
Products_Get	Returns a list of products
Customers_Get	Returns a list of customers
Employees_Get	Returns a list of employees
Shippers_Get	Returns a list of shippers
Orders_Add	Inserts an order into the Orders table, called by the stored procedure Order_Place
OrderDetails_Add	Inserts an order item into the Order Details table, called by stored procedure Order_Place
Products_UpdStock	Deducts the units in stock from the Products table
Order_Place	Places an order

EXAMPLE

Figure 6.5 illustrates the three-tiered architectural design of the sample application. This UML diagram was created in Microsoft Visual Modeler 2.0. Visual Modeler is part of Visual Studio 6.0, Enterprise Edition.

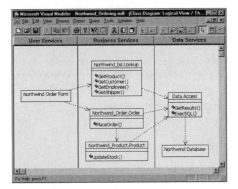

Figure 6.5: *The three-tiered architecture of the sample application.*

Implementation

The following sections will walk you through the code for all the stored procedures, COM objects, and the GUIs of the sample application.

THE STORED PROCEDURES

EXAMPLE

Listing 6.1 shows the `Products_Get` stored procedure, which returns a list of products and other related information.

Listing 6.1   The `Products_Get` Stored Procedure

```
/*****************************************************************
* Name:     Products_Get                                        *
* Purpose: Returns a list of Products and related information *
*****************************************************************/
if exists(select * from sysobjects where id = object_id('Products_Get'))
 drop proc Products_Get
go

create proc Products_Get
as
select      ProductID,
            ProductName,
            UnitPrice
from        Products
where       UnitsInStock > 0
go
```

Listing 6.2 shows the `Customers_Get` stored procedure, which returns a list of customers and their addresses.

Listing 6.2   The `Customers_Get` Stored Procedure

```
/*****************************************************************
* Name:     Customers_Get                                       *
* Purpose: Returns a list of Customers and address information  *
*****************************************************************/

if exists(select * from sysobjects where id =
object_id('Customers_Get'))
 drop proc Customers_Get
go

create proc Customers_Get
as
select     CustomerID,
           CompanyName,
           Address,
           City,
           Region,
           PostalCode,
           Country
from       Customers
go
```

EXAMPLE

Listing 6.3 shows the `Employees_Get` stored procedure, which returns a list of employees.

Listing 6.3   The `Employees_Get` Stored Procedure

```
/**************************************
* Name:     Employees_Get            *
* Purpose: Returns a list of Employees *
**************************************/
if exists(select * from sysobjects where id =
object_id('Employees_Get'))
 drop proc Employees_Get
go

create proc Employees_Get
as
select     EmployeeID,
           FirstName + ' ' + LastName as 'EmployeeName'
from       Employees
go
```

Listing 6.4 shows the `Shippers_Get` stored procedure, which returns a list of shippers.

Listing 6.4 The Shippers_Get Stored Procedure

```
/*************************************
* Name:     Shippers_Get            *
* Purpose: Returns a list of shippers *
*************************************/
if exists(select * from sysobjects where id = object_id('Shippers_Get'))
 drop proc Shippers_Get
go

create proc Shippers_Get
as
select     ShipperID,
           CompanyName
from       Shippers
go
```

Listing 6.5 shows the Orders_Add stored procedure, which inserts a row in the Orders table. This stored procedure is called by another stored procedure, Order_Place.

EXAMPLE

Listing 6.5 The Orders_Add Stored Procedure

```
/***************************************************************
* Name:     Orders_Add                                        *
* Purpose: Add an order to the Orders table.                  *
* Remarks: It is called by stored procedure Order_Place.      *
*          The output parameter @OrderID is returned to the   *
*          caller for subsequent insert to the Order Details  *
***************************************************************/
if exists(select * from sysobjects where id = object_id('Orders_Add'))
  drop proc Orders_Add
go

create proc Orders_Add
 @OrderID int out,
 @CustomerID nchar(5),
 @EmployeeID int,
 @OrderDate datetime,
 @RequiredDate datetime=null,
 @ShippedDate datetime=null,
 @ShipVia int,
 @Freight money =null,
 @ShipName nvarchar(40),
 @ShipAddress nvarchar(60),
 @ShipCity nvarchar(15),
 @ShipRegion nvarchar(15),
```

Listing 6.5 continued

```
 @ShipPostalCode nvarchar(10),
 @ShipCountry nvarchar(15)
as
set nocount on
insert      Orders (
     CustomerID,
     EmployeeID,
     OrderDate,
     RequiredDate,
     ShippedDate,
     ShipVia,
     Freight,
     ShipName,
     ShipAddress,
     ShipCity,
     ShipRegion,
     ShipPostalCode,
     ShipCountry
)
values (
     @CustomerID,
     @EmployeeID,
     @OrderDate,
     @RequiredDate,
     @ShippedDate,
     @ShipVia,
     @Freight,
     @ShipName,
     @ShipAddress,
     @ShipCity,
     @ShipRegion,
     @ShipPostalCode,
     @ShipCountry
)

select @OrderID = @@Identity

set nocount off
go
```

EXAMPLE

Listing 6.6 shows the OrderDetails_Add stored procedure. This stored procedure is also called by the Order_Place stored procedure after inserting a row into the Orders table. The output parameter returned by the Orders_Add stored procedure is used as the input parameter when calling this stored procedure.

Listing 6.6   The `OrderDetails_Add` Stored Procedure

```
/***************************************************************
 * Name:    OrderDetails_Add                                  *
 * Purpose: Add an order item to the Order Details table.     *
 * Remarks: It is called by stored procedure Order_Place.     *
 ***************************************************************/
if exists(select * from sysobjects where id =
object_id('OrderDetails_Add'))
  drop proc OrderDetails_Add
go

create proc OrderDetails_Add
 @OrderID int,
 @ProductID int,
 @UnitPrice money,
 @Quantity smallint,
 @Discount real=0
as
set nocount on
insert  [Order Details] (
     OrderID,
     ProductID,
     UnitPrice,
     Quantity,
     Discount
)
values (
     @OrderID,
     @ProductID,
     @UnitPrice,
     @Quantity,
     @Discount
)
set nocount off
go
```

EXAMPLE

Listing 6.7 shows the `Order_Place` stored procedure, which in turn calls two other stored procedures, `Orders_Add` and `OrderDetails_Add`. This stored procedure uses the transaction to protect data integrity.

Listing 6.7   The `Order_Place` Stored Procedure

```
/***************************************************************
 * Name:    Order_Place                                        *
 * Purpose: Places an order.                                   *
 * Remarks: This stored procedure places an order by calling   *
 *          two stored procedures, Orders_Add and OrderDetails_Add *
 *          The execution of the two stored procedures is wrapped  *
```

Listing 6.7   continued

```
*           into a transaction to ensure the data integrity        *
**********************************************************************/
if exists(select * from sysobjects where id = object_id('Order_Place'))
 drop proc Order_Place
go

create proc Order_Place
 @ProductID int,
 @UnitPrice money,
 @Quantity smallint,
 @Discount real=0,
 @CustomerID nchar(5),
 @EmployeeID int,
 @OrderDate datetime,
 @RequiredDate datetime=null,
 @ShippedDate datetime=null,
 @ShipVia int,
 @Freight money =null,
 @ShipName nvarchar(40),
 @ShipAddress nvarchar(60),
 @ShipCity nvarchar(15),
 @ShipRegion nvarchar(15),
 @ShipPostalCode nvarchar(10),
 @ShipCountry nvarchar(15)
as
set nocount on
declare @OrderID int
begin tranexec Orders_Add @OrderID = @OrderID out,
         @CustomerID = @CustomerID,
         @EmployeeID = @EmployeeID,
         @OrderDate = @OrderDate,
         @RequiredDate = @RequiredDate,
         @ShippedDate = @ShippedDate,
         @ShipVia = @ShipVia,
         @Freight = @Freight,
         @ShipName = @ShipName,
         @ShipAddress = @ShipAddress,
         @ShipCity = @ShipCity,
         @ShipRegion =@ShipRegion,
         @ShipPostalCode =@ShipPostalCode,
         @ShipCountry = @ShipCountry

exec OrderDetails_ADD @OrderID = @OrderID,
         @ProductID = @ProductID,
```

Listing 6.7 continued

```
        @UnitPrice = @UnitPrice,
        @Quantity = @Quantity,
        @Discount = @Discount

set nocount off

if @@error = 0
  commit tran
else
  rollback
go
```

EXAMPLE

Listing 6.8 shows the last stored procedure, Product_UpdStock, which deducts the units in stock from the Products table for the item ordered. This stored procedure implements part of the second business rule: It compares the quantity in stock with the quantity ordered. If the quantity in stock is smaller than the quantity ordered, the stored procedure raises an error that causes the PlaceOrder method of the Product COM object to call SetAbort. Because the Product object is part of the transaction that involves the Order object and the Access object, calling SetAbort causes the entire transaction to abort. Therefore, the order cannot be placed. You'll learn about the implementation of COM objects later in this chapter.

Listing 6.8 The Product_UpdStock Stored Procedure

```
/****************************************************************
 * Name:    Product_UpdStock                                   *
 * Purpose: Deducts the UnitsInStock for the product ordered.  *
 * Remarks: This stored procedure implements the second business *
 *          rule.                                               *
 ****************************************************************/
if exists(select * from sysobjects where id =
object_id('Products_UpdStock'))
 drop proc Products_UpdStock
go

create proc Products_UpdStock
 @ProductID int,
 @Quantity smallint
as

declare    @UnitsInStock smallint
select     @UnitsInStock = UnitsInStock
from       Products
where      ProductID = @ProductID
/****************************************************************
```

Listing 6.8 continued

```
Our business rule #1 states that the quantity you try to order must
not be greater than the units in stock
******************************************************************/
if @UnitsInStock < @Quantity
 raiserror ('You tried to order more items than we have in stock.',16,1)

update   Products
set      UnitsInStock = UnitsInStock - @Quantity
where    ProductID = @ProductID
go
```

COM COMPONENTS

EXAMPLE

As you saw in Figure 6.5 earlier, the Data.Access object (class) is used by all other objects, transactional (such as Northwind_Order.Order and Northwind_Product.Product) and nontransactional (the Northwind_biz. Lookup object). The Data.Access object has two methods: GetResults() and ExecSQL(). The GetResults() method returns a disconnected ADO recordset to the caller, and the ExecSQL() method executes a SQL statement or stored procedure. The transaction attribute of the Data.Access component is set to Supported. From Visual Basic, you set the MTSTransactionMode property to 3-UsesTransaction (see Figure 6.6).

Figure 6.6: Setting the MTSTransactionMode property for the Access class.

In the Visual Basic project, you also need to set a reference to the COM+ Services Type Library, as shown in Figure 6.7.

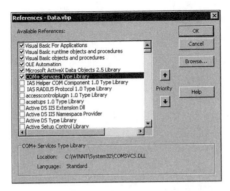

Figure 6.7: *Setting a reference to the COM+ Services Type Library.*

Listing 6.9 shows the code for the `Data.Access` class.

Listing 6.9   The `Data.Access` Class

```
Option Explicit


'**************************************************************************
' File:         Data.vbp
' Object:       Access
' Purpose:      Generic data access object.
' Properties:   ExecSQL() -- Execute SQL statements and/or stored procedures.
'               GetResult() -- Get a recordset from the database.
'**************************************************************************


Private Const m_sObjectName     As String = "Data.Access"


'**************************************************************************
' ExecSQL()
' Purpose: Execute SQL statements and/or stored procedures.
' Inputs:  sConnection      -- ADO connection string.
'          sSQL             -- SQL statement.
' Returns: A boolean variable indicates if the action is successful.
' Modification History
' Date      Initials    Description
' 5/8/00    PLI         Created.
'**************************************************************************


Public Function ExecSQL(ByVal sConnection As String, _
                        ByVal sSQL As String) As Boolean
```

Listing 6.9 continued

```
Dim lErrNo      As Long
Dim sErrDesc    As String
Dim sErrorMsg   As String
Dim oConnection As New ADODB.Connection
Dim oContext    As ObjectContext


On Error GoTo ExecSQL_Err

'Get hook to the ObjectContext
Set oContext = GetObjectContext()

'Connect to the database.
Set oConnection = New ADODB.Connection
With oConnection
    .Open sConnection
    .Execute CommandText:=sSQL
End With

'Up to this point, everybody is happy. So commit.
If Not oContext Is Nothing Then
    oContext.SetComplete
End If

If Not oConnection Is Nothing Then Set oConnection = Nothing
ExecSQL = True
Exit Function
ExecSQL_Err:
    'Something goes wrong, so roll back.
    If Not oContext Is Nothing Then
        oContext.SetAbort
    End If
    ExecSQL = False
    'Get the error details.
    lErrNo = oConnection.Errors(0).Number
    sErrDesc = oConnection.Errors(0).Description

    'Clean up.
    If Not oConnection Is Nothing Then Set oConnection = Nothing

    'Write error details to event log for troubleshooting.
    sErrorMsg = "Error #: " & CStr(lErrNo) & vbCr & _
```

Listing 6.9   continued

```
                    "Description: " & sErrDesc & vbCr & _
                    "Source: " & m_sObjectName & "ExecSQL"

        App.LogEvent m_sObjectName & ".ExecSQL" & vbCrLf & _
                    sErrorMsg, vbLogEventTypeError


    'Raise the error.
    Err.Raise lErrNo

End Function

'*****************************************************************************
' GetResult()
' Purpose: Get an ADO recordset from a SQL action.
' Inputs:   sConnection      -- ADO connection string.
'           sSQL             -- SQL statement.
' Outputs: lRows             -- Rows returned.
' Returns: An ADO Recordset as a result of a SQL action.
' Modification History
' Date       Initials    Description
' 5/8/00     PLI         Created.
'*****************************************************************************

Public Function GetResult(ByVal sConnection As String, _
                          ByVal sSQL As String, _
                          ByRef lRows As Long) As ADODB.Recordset

    Dim oConn      As New ADODB.Connection
    Dim rsGetResult As New ADODB.Recordset
    Dim sErrDesc   As String
    Dim sErrorMsg  As String
    Dim lErrNo     As Long
    Dim oContext   As ObjectContext

    On Error GoTo GetResult_Err

    'Get hook to the ObjectContext
    Set oContext = GetObjectContext()

    'Connect to the database.
    oConn.Open sConnection

    'Set up the ADO recordset properties.
    With rsGetResult
        .CursorLocation = adUseClient
        .CursorType = adOpenStatic
```

Listing 6.9 continued

```
            .LockType = adLockBatchOptimistic
            .ActiveConnection = oConn
            .Open sSQL

            lRows = .RecordCount 'rows fetched.
        End With

        'Return the recordset to the client.
        Set GetResult = rsGetResult

        'Disconnect from the database.
        Set rsGetResult.ActiveConnection = Nothing
        'Up to this point, everybody is happy. So commit.
        If Not oContext Is Nothing Then
            oContext.SetComplete
        End If
        If Not oConn Is Nothing Then Set oConn = Nothing
        Exit Function
GetResult_Err:
        'Something goes wrong, so roll back.
        If Not oContext Is Nothing Then
            oContext.SetAbort
        End If
        If Not oConn Is Nothing Then Set oConn = Nothing

        'Get the error details.
        lErrNo = oConn.Errors(0).Number
        sErrDesc = oConn.Errors(0).Description

        'Clean up.
        On Error Resume Next
        Set oConn = Nothing
        Set rsGetResult = Nothing

        'Write error details to event log for troubleshooting.
        sErrorMsg = "Error #: " & CStr(lErrNo) & vbCr & _
                    "Description: " & sErrDesc & vbCr & _
                    "Source: " & m_sObjectName & "GetInfo"

        App.LogEvent m_sObjectName & ".GetResult" & vbCrLf & _
                    sErrorMsg, vbLogEventTypeError

        'Raise the error.
        Err.Raise lErrNo

End Function
```

The `Northwind_biz.Lookup` object is a nontransactional component. That is, its operation is of type Select; no update is made to the database whatsoever. Therefore, the transaction attribute of the `Northwind_biz.Lookup` is set to Disabled; it can be used as a nonconfigured component. The `Northwind_biz.Lookup` object has four methods: `GetProduct()`, `GetCustomer()`, `GetShipper()`, and `GetEmployee()`. Each `Get` method is implemented similarly. Inside each `Get` method, a `Data.Access` object is created, and its `GetResults()` method is called by passing the appropriate `_Get` stored procedure and returns a list as a disconnected ADO recordset. Listing 6.10 shows the code of the `Northwind_biz.Lookup` class.

EXAMPLE

Listing 6.10 The `Northwind_biz.Lookup` Class

```
Option Explicit


'**************************************************************************
' File:          Northwind_biz.vbp
' Object:        Lookup
' Purpose:       A lookup object that returns a disconnected ADO recordest for
'                local offline lookup.
' Properties:    GetProduct() -- Returns a Product recordset.
'                GetCustomer() -- Returns a Customer recordset.
'                GetShipper() -- Returns a Shipper recordset.
'                GetEmployee() -- Returns an Employee recordset.
'**************************************************************************


'**************************************************************************
' GetProduct()
' Purpose: Calls the GetResult() method of the Data.Access object and returns
'          a disconnected ADO recordset containing products.
' Inputs:  sConnection   -- ADO connection string.
' Returns: A disconnected ADO Recordset.
' Modification History
' Date        Initials    Description
' 6/8/00      PLI         Created.
'**************************************************************************


Public Function GetProduct(ByVal sConnection As String) As ADODB.Recordset
    On Error GoTo GetProduct_Err
```

Listing 6.10   continued

```
    Dim oData      As Object 'Data.Access object.
    Dim rsProduct  As ADODB.Recordset

    Set oData = CreateObject("Data.Access")
    'Calls the stored procedure Products_Get to get a list of products.
    Set rsProduct = oData.GetResult(sConnection, "Products_Get", 0)
    Set GetProduct = rsProduct

    Exit Function
GetProduct_Err:
    'clean up
    If Not rsProduct Is Nothing Then
        Set rsProduct = Nothing
    End If
    Err.Raise Err.Number
End Function


'**********************************************************************
' GetCustomer()
' Purpose: Calls the GetResult() method of the Data.Access object and returns
'          a disconnected ADO recordset containing products.
' Inputs:  sConnection   -- ADO connection string.
' Returns: A disconnected ADO Recordset.
' Modification History
' Date       Initials    Description
' 6/8/00     PLI         Created.
'**********************************************************************

Public Function GetCustomer(ByVal sConnection As String) As ADODB.Recordset
    On Error GoTo GetCustomer_Err
    Dim oData      As Object 'Data.Access object
    Dim rsCustomer As ADODB.Recordset

    Set oData = CreateObject("Data.Access")
    'Calls the stored procedure Customers_Get to get a list of customers.
    Set rsCustomer = oData.GetResult(sConnection, "Customers_Get", 0)
    Set GetCustomer = rsCustomer
    Set oData = Nothing

    Exit Function
GetCustomer_Err:
    'clean up
    If Not rsCustomer Is Nothing Then
```

Listing 6.10   continued

```
            Set rsCustomer = Nothing
        End If
        Err.Raise Err.Number
End Function


'*******************************************************************************
' GetEmployee()
' Purpose: Calls the GetResult() method of the Data.Access object and returns
'          a disconnected ADO recordset containing products.
' Inputs:  sConnection   -- ADO connection string.
' Returns: A disconnected ADO Recordset.
' Modification History
' Date        Initials     Description
' 6/8/00      PLI          Created.
'*******************************************************************************

Public Function GetEmployee(ByVal sConnection As String) As ADODB.Recordset
    On Error GoTo GetEmployee_Err
    Dim oData        As Object 'Data.Access object.
    Dim rsEmployee   As ADODB.Recordset

    Set oData = CreateObject("Data.Access")
    'Calls the stored procedure Employees_Get to get a list of employees.
    Set rsEmployee = oData.GetResult(sConnection, "Employees_Get", 0)
    Set GetEmployee = rsEmployee
    Set oData = Nothing

    Exit Function
GetEmployee_Err:
    'clean up
    If Not rsEmployee Is Nothing Then
        Set rsEmployee = Nothing
    End If
    Err.Raise Err.Number
End Function


'*******************************************************************************
' GetShipper()
' Purpose: Calls the GetResult() method of the Data.Access object and returns
'          a disconnected ADO recordset containing products.
' Inputs:  sConnection   -- ADO connection string.
```

Listing 6.10   continued

```
' Returns: A disconnected ADO Recordset.
' Modification History
' Date       Initials    Description
' 6/8/00     PLI         Created.
'*************************************************************************

Public Function GetShipper(ByVal sConnection As String) As ADODB.Recordset
    On Error GoTo GetShipper_Err
    Dim oData        As Object 'Data.Access object.
    Dim rsShipper    As ADODB.Recordset

    Set oData = CreateObject("Data.Access")
    'Calls the stored procedure Shippers_Get to get a list of shippers.
    Set rsShipper = oData.GetResult(sConnection, "Shippers_Get", 0)
    Set GetShipper = rsShipper
    Set oData = Nothing

    Exit Function
GetShipper_Err:
    'clean up
    If Not rsShipper Is Nothing Then
        Set rsShipper = Nothing
    End If
    Err.Raise Err.Number
End Function
```

Also as shown in Figure 6.5, the Northwind_Product.Product object is called by the Northwind_Order.Order object to update the units in stock. Its one method, UpdateStock(), in turn calls the ExecSQL() method of the Data.Access object to persist the change to the database. The transaction attribute of the Northwind_Product.Product is set to Supported. When an error occurs, such as the violation of the second business rule, the SetAbort() method of the ObjectContext is called and an error raised to cause the root object (the Northwind_Order.Order in this case) to abort the entire transaction. Listing 6.11 shows the code for this Northwind_Product. Product class.

EXAMPLE

Listing 6.11   The Northwind_Product.Product Class

```
Option Explicit

'*************************************************************************
' File:         Northwind_Product.vbp
' Object:       Product
```

Listing 6.11 continued

```
' Purpose:       Used in conjunction with the Northwind_Order.Order object to
'                Update the quantity of units in stock of the Products table.
' Properties:    UpdateStock() -- Updates the units in stock for a given
'                product.
'*************************************************************************


'*************************************************************************
' UpdateStock()
' Purpose: Deducts the units in stock from the quantity ordered.
' Inputs:   iProductID  -- The id of the product ordered.
'           iQuantity -- the quantity of the product ordered.
' Returns: A Boolean value indicating the success or failure of the action.
' Modification History
' Date        Initials    Description
' 6/8/00      PLI         Created.
'*************************************************************************

Public Function UpdateStock(ByVal iProductID As Integer, _
                            ByVal iQuantity As Integer) As Boolean

    On Error GoTo UpdateStock_Err
    Dim oObjectContext As ObjectContext
    Dim odata   As Object 'Data.Access object
    Dim sSQL    As String
    Set oObjectContext = GetObjectContext()
    sSQL = "Exec Products_UpdStock" _
        & " @ProductID = " & iProductID _
        & ", @Quantity = " & iQuantity

    Set odata = CreateObject("Data.Access")
    odata.ExecSQL "Northwind", sSQL
    UpdateStock = True
    If Not oObjectContext Is Nothing Then
        oObjectContext.SetComplete
    End If
    Exit Function
UpdateStock_Err:
    If Not oObjectContext Is Nothing Then
        oObjectContext.SetAbort
    End If
    UpdateStock = False
    Err.Raise Err.Number
End Function
```

The last COM object discussed here is the root object in the entire order-placing transaction: the Northwind_Order.Order object. Because it's the root of the transaction, its transaction attribute is set to Required. The Northwind_Order.Order object has a single method, PlaceOrder(). The PlaceOrder() method calls the ExecSQL() method of the Data.Access method, executing the stored procedure Order_Place to place an order. It then calls the UpdateStock() method of the Northwind_Product.Product object to deduct the quantity in stock. If either method call fails, the entire transaction is aborted. No order is placed, and no quantity in stock is deducted. Listing 6.12 shows the code of the Northwind_Order.Order class.

EXAMPLE

Listing 6.12   The Northwind_Order.Order Class

```
Option Explicit

'*************************************************************************
' File:          Northwind_Order.vbp
' Object:        Order
' Purpose:       Used in conjunction with the Northwind_Product.Product object
'                to Place an order and Update the quantity of units in stock of
'                the Products table.
' Properties:    PlaceOrder() -- Places an order and updates the units in stock
'                for the product ordered.
'*************************************************************************


'*************************************************************************
' PlaceOrder()
' Purpose: Places an order and deducts the units in stock from the quantity
' ordered.
' Inputs:  iProductID   -- The id of the product ordered.
'          cUnitPrice -- the unit price of the product ordered.
'          iQuantity -- the quantity of the product ordered.
'          sCustomerID -- the id of the customer who placed the order.
'          iEmployeeID -- the id of the employee who processed the order.
'          dOrderDate -- the date when the product is ordered.
'          dRequiredDate -- the date when the product is required.
'          dShippedDate -- the data when the product is shipped.
'          iShipVia -- the id of the shipper.
'          cFreight -- the freight.
'          sShipName -- the shipping name.
'          sAddress -- the shipping address.
'          sCity -- the shipping city.
```

Listing 6.12 continued

```
'          sRegion -- the shipping region.
'          sPostalCode -- the shipping postal code.
'          sCountry -- the shipping country.
' Returns: A Boolean value indicating the success or failure of the action.
' Modification History
' Date       Initials    Description
' 6/8/00     PLI         Created.
'****************************************************************************

Public Function PlaceOrder(ByVal iProductID As Integer, _
                           ByVal cUnitPrice As Currency, _
                           ByVal iQuantity As Integer, _
                           ByVal sCustomerID As String, _
                           ByVal iEmployeeID As Integer, _
                           ByVal dOrderDate As Date, _
                           ByVal dRequiredDate As Date, _
                           ByVal dShippedDate As Date, _
                           ByVal iShipVia As Integer, _
                           ByVal cFreight As Currency, _
                           ByVal sShipName As String, _
                           ByVal sAddress As String, _
                           ByVal sCity As String, _
                           ByVal sRegion As String, _
                           ByVal sPostalCode As String, _
                           ByVal sCountry As String) As Boolean

        On Error GoTo PlaceOrder_Err
        Dim oData          As Object 'Data.Access object.
        Dim oProduct       As Object 'Northwind_Product.Product object.
        Dim sSQL           As String
        Dim oObjectContext As ObjectContext

        Set oObjectContext = GetObjectContext()

        sSQL = "Exec Order_Place" & _
               "  @ProductID = " & iProductID & _
               ", @UnitPrice = " & cUnitPrice & _
               ", @Quantity = " & iQuantity & _
               ", @CustomerID = '" & sCustomerID & "'" & _
               ", @EmployeeID = " & iEmployeeID & _
               ", @OrderDate = '" & dOrderDate & "'" & _
               ", @RequiredDate = '" & dRequiredDate & "'" & _
               ", @ShippedDate = '" & dShippedDate & "'" & _
               ", @ShipVia = " & iShipVia & _
```

Listing 6.12   continued

```
              ", @Freight = " & cFreight & _
              ", @ShipName = '" & sShipName & "'" & _
              ", @ShipAddress = '" & sAddress & "'" & _
              ", @ShipCity = '" & sCity & "'" & _
              ", @ShipRegion = '" & sRegion & "'" & _
              ", @ShipPostalCode = '" & sPostalCode & "'" & _
              ", @ShipCountry = '" & sCountry & "'"

        'Place the order.
        Set oData = CreateObject("Data.Access")
        oData.ExecSQL "Northwind", sSQL
        Set oData = Nothing

        'Update quantity in stock.
        Set oProduct = CreateObject("Northwind_Product.Product")
        oProduct.UpdateStock iProductID, iQuantity
        Set oProduct = Nothing

        If Not oObjectContext Is Nothing Then
            oObjectContext.SetComplete
        End If
        PlaceOrder = True
        Exit Function
PlaceOrder_Err:
    PlaceOrder = False
    If Not oObjectContext Is Nothing Then
        oObjectContext.SetAbort
    End If
    Err.Raise Err.Number
End Function
```

Now you can create an empty COM+ application called **Northwind** and install the three components that support transactions: Data.Access, Northwind_Order.Order, and Northwind_Product.Product. The results are shown in Figure 6.8.

Notice that the transaction attributes you set in Visual Basic are automatically picked up by the COM+ application after you install the components.

THE ORDER FORM

Earlier in Figure 6.3, you saw the order form used in this example. This section walks you through the code behind the scenes.

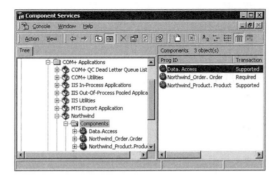

Figure 6.8: *The Northwind COM+ application and its components.*

EXAMPLE

Listing 6.13 shows the general declaration section of the form. Two groups of module-level variables are declared. The four ADO recordset objects hold the disconnected recordset by the methods of the `Northwind_biz.Lookup` object. The second group of module-level variables tracks the IDs behind the scenes.

Listing 6.13   The General Declaration Section of the Order Form

```
Option Explicit
'Module level variables for holding disconnected
'ADO recordsets as local data cache for lookups.
Private m_rsProduct  As New ADOR.Recordset
Private m_rsCustomer As New ADOR.Recordset
Private m_rsEmployee As New ADOR.Recordset
Private m_rsShipper  As New ADOR.Recordset


'Module level variables for tracking lookup IDs.
Private iProductID   As Integer
Private sCustomerID  As String
Private iEmployeeID  As Integer
Private iShipperID   As Integer
```

The `Load` event procedure of the form initializes the module-level recordset objects, populates the combo boxes on the form, and provides other basic information (see Listing 6.14).

Listing 6.14   The `Load` Event of the Order Form

```
Private Sub Form_Load()
    On Error GoTo Load_Err

    'Set disconnected recordsets.
    Dim oLookup    As New Northwind_Biz.Lookup
    Set m_rsProduct = oLookup.GetProduct("Northwind")
    Set m_rsCustomer = oLookup.GetCustomer("Northwind")
    Set m_rsEmployee = oLookup.GetEmployee("Northwind")
```

Listing 6.14 continued

```
Set m_rsShipper = oLookup.GetShipper("Northwind")
Set oLookup = Nothing

'Populate the Product combo box and set the productid.
Do Until m_rsProduct.EOF
    cbProduct.AddItem m_rsProduct!ProductName
    m_rsProduct.MoveNext
Loop
cbProduct.ListIndex = 1
m_rsProduct.MoveFirst
m_rsProduct.Find "ProductName = '" & cbProduct.Text & "'"
iProductID = m_rsProduct!ProductID
txtUnitPrice = m_rsProduct!UnitPrice

'Populate the Customer combo box and set the customerid
'and address info.
Do Until m_rsCustomer.EOF
    cbCustomer.AddItem m_rsCustomer!CompanyName
    m_rsCustomer.MoveNext
Loop
cbCustomer.ListIndex = 1
m_rsCustomer.MoveFirst
m_rsCustomer.Find "CompanyName = '" & cbCustomer.Text & "'"
sCustomerID = m_rsCustomer!CustomerID
txtAddress = m_rsCustomer!Address & vbNullString
txtCity = m_rsCustomer!City & vbNullString
txtRegion = m_rsCustomer!Region & vbNullString
txtPostalCode = m_rsCustomer!PostalCode & vbNullString
txtCountry = m_rsCustomer!Country & vbNullString

'Populate the Employee combo box and set the employeeid.
Do Until m_rsEmployee.EOF
    cbEmployee.AddItem m_rsEmployee!EmployeeName
    m_rsEmployee.MoveNext
Loop
cbEmployee.ListIndex = 1
m_rsEmployee.MoveFirst
m_rsEmployee.Find "EmployeeName = '" & cbEmployee.Text & "'"
iEmployeeID = m_rsEmployee!EmployeeID

'Populate the Shipper combo box and set the shipperid.
Do Until m_rsShipper.EOF
    cbShipper.AddItem m_rsShipper!CompanyName
    m_rsShipper.MoveNext
Loop
cbShipper.ListIndex = 1
```

Listing 6.14   continued

```
    m_rsShipper.MoveFirst
    m_rsShipper.Find "CompanyName = '" & cbShipper.Text & "'"
    iShipperID = m_rsShipper!ShipperID

    'Set the default order date to today.
    txtOrderDate.Text = Format(Date, "mm/dd/yyyy")
    Exit Sub
Load_Err:
    MsgBox Err.Description
End Sub
```

The GUI behavior is managed by the Change events of the text boxes, the Click events of the combo boxes, and so on. It is worthwhile to mention the code behind the Click event of the four combo boxes. These combo boxes hold lists of products, customers, shippers, and employees for fast lookups. Disconnected ADO recordsets are used for this purpose. The Clickevents of the combo boxes use the Find method of the ADO recordsets to navigate the disconnected recordsets and populate other text boxes and so on. Listing 6.15 shows the code of the events that maintain the GUI behavior.

EXAMPLE

Listing 6.15   Control Events That Maintain the GUI Behavior

```
Private Sub txtFreight_Change()
    txtTotal = Val(txtSubTotal) + Val(txtFreight)
End Sub

Private Sub txtOrderDate_Change()
    txtRequiredDate = DateAdd("d", 21, txtOrderDate)
    txtShippedDate = DateAdd("d", 14, txtOrderDate)
End Sub

Private Sub txtSubTotal_Change()
    txtTotal = Val(txtSubTotal) + Val(txtFreight)
End Sub

Private Sub txtUnitPrice_Change()
    txtSubTotal = Val(txtUnitPrice) * Val(txtQuantity)
End Sub

Private Sub udQuantity_DownClick()
    If Val(txtQuantity) = 1 Then Exit Sub
    txtQuantity = Val(txtQuantity) - 1
    txtSubTotal = Val(txtUnitPrice) * Val(txtQuantity)
End Sub

Private Sub udQuantity_UpClick()
    txtQuantity = Val(txtQuantity) + 1
```

Listing 6.15   continued

```
        txtSubTotal = Val(txtUnitPrice) * Val(txtQuantity)
End Sub

Private Sub cbProduct_Click()
    m_rsProduct.MoveFirst
    m_rsProduct.Find "ProductName ='" & ConvertQuote(cbProduct.Text) &
 "'"
    iProductID = m_rsProduct!ProductID
    txtUnitPrice = m_rsProduct!UnitPrice
End Sub

Private Sub cbCustomer_Click()
    With m_rsCustomer
        .MoveFirst
        .Find "CompanyName ='" & ConvertQuote(cbCustomer.Text) & "'"
        sCustomerID = !CustomerID
        txtAddress = !Address & vbNullString
        txtCity = !City & vbNullString
        txtRegion = !Region & vbNullString
        txtPostalCode = !PostalCode & vbNullString
        txtCountry = !Country & vbNullString
    End With
End Sub

Private Sub cbShipper_Click()
    With m_rsShipper
        .MoveFirst
        .Find "CompanyName ='" & ConvertQuote(cbShipper.Text) & "'"
        iShipperID = !ShipperID
    End With
End Sub

Private Sub cbemployee_Click()
    With m_rsEmployee
        .MoveFirst
        .Find "EmployeeName ='" & ConvertQuote(cbEmployee.Text) & "'"
        iEmployeeID = !EmployeeID
    End With
End Sub

Private Sub cmdExit_Click()
    Unload Me
End Sub
```

Notice that the Click events of the combo boxes call a ConvertQuote() function. This helper function handles the embedded single quote in the search criteria. Listing 6.16 shows the ConvertQuote() function.

EXAMPLE

Listing 6.16   The `ConvertQuote()` Helper Function

```
Public Function ConvertQuote(ByVal sQuoteString As String) As String
    'Helper function that deals with embedded single quote in the
string
    Dim iQuotePos
    'Find the single quote in the string
    iQuotePos = InStr(sQuoteString, Chr(39))
    If iQuotePos = 0 Then
        ConvertQuote = sQuoteString
    Else
        ConvertQuote = Left(sQuoteString, iQuotePos - 1) & _
                       Chr(39) & Mid(sQuoteString, iQuotePos)
    End If
End Function
```

The `Click` event of the Place an Order command button, shown in Listing 6.17, triggers the ordering process. It calls the `PlaceOrder()` method of the `Northwind_Order.Order` object to place the order.

Listing 6.17   The `Click` Event of the Place an Order Command Button

```
Private Sub cmdOrder_Click()
    On Error GoTo cmdOrder_Err
    Screen.MousePointer = vbHourglass
    Dim oOrder As Object 'Northwind_Order.Order object
    Set oOrder = CreateObject("Northwind_Order.Order")
    oOrder.PlaceOrder iProductID, CCur(txtUnitPrice.Text), CInt(txtQuantity.Text),
                      sCustomerID, iEmployeeID, CDate(txtOrderDate.Text), _
                      CDate(txtRequiredDate.Text), CDate(txtShippedDate.Text), _
                      iShipperID, CCur(txtFreight.Text), cbCustomer.Text, _
                      txtAddress.Text, txtCity.Text, txtRegion.Text, _
                      txtPostalCode.Text, txtCountry.Text

    Set oOrder = Nothing
    Screen.MousePointer = vbDefault
    MsgBox "Order has been processed!"

    Exit Sub
cmdOrder_Err:
    Screen.MousePointer = vbDefault
    MsgBox Err.Description
End Sub
```

Taking the Application for a Test Drive

Now you're ready to run the sample application to see how COM+ manages the transactions in action. To do so, open the NorthwindOrder.vbp Visual Basic application (the front end) and press F5 start it. The order form is then loaded; it looks similar to the form in Figure 6.3.

Before you start placing an order, check the database and set up some baselines so that you know what's happening to your order later. To do so, open the SQL Server Query Analyzer, select the Northwind database, and then type and run the following SQL statement to figure out the maximum order ID in the database:

```
select max(OrderID) from Orders
```

In my case, the Query Analyzer returns 11077 as the maximum order ID. Your case may vary, depending on your database, but that's not important. Now check one more thing before getting started. Type the SQL statements shown in Figure 6.9 and press Ctrl+D and then Ctrl+E. The first key combination configures the Query Analyzer so that the results will be displayed in a grid view, as shown in Figure 6.9.

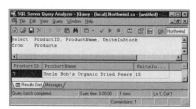

Figure 6.9: *Checking the product information for ID 7.*

The query returns the product name as "Uncle Bob's Organic Dried Pears" and shows that 15 units are in stock.

Now that you've set your baseline, you're ready to take an order. For this example, select Uncle Bob's Pears as the product and order 10 units. Then select Consolidated Holdings as your customer. Notice that as soon as you select a new customer from the drop-down list, the address information is automatically changed to reflect the correct address for the customer selected. This process is done entirely offline by searching the disconnected recordset, as you learned earlier. Next, pick Speedy Express as the shipper and assume Andrew Fuller is the Northwind employee who is going to place the order. Charge $15 for the freight, so this brings the total price of the order to $315. Now click the Place an Order button, and a confirmation message box will appear shortly, indicating that the order has been processed (see Figure 6.10).

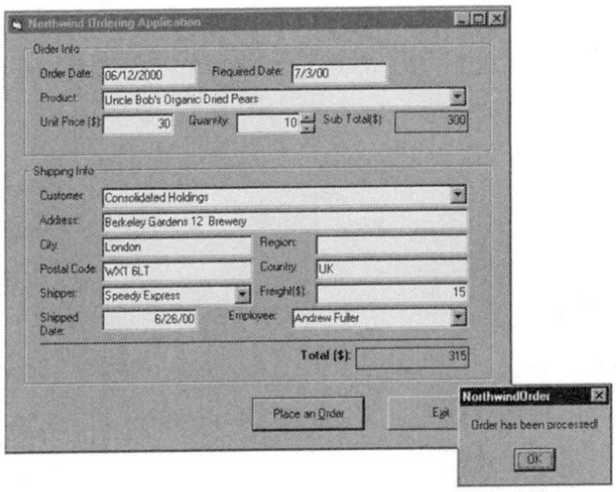

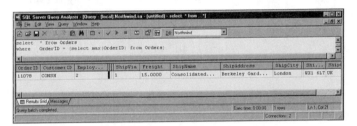

Figure 6.10: Placing an order.

Now check the database to make sure the order is processed as you expected. Run the SQL statement with a subquery like the one in Figure 6.11. When you do, the lower part of the Query Analyzer window displays the results that confirm the order was processed correctly.

Figure 6.11: Checking the order being processed.

You also need to make sure that the second business rule is followed; that is, the 10 units of Uncle Bob's pears should be deducted from the Products table. To do so, run the query in Figure 6.9 again, and this time it shows that 5 units are left in stock (see Figure 6.12). Everything is going fine so far.

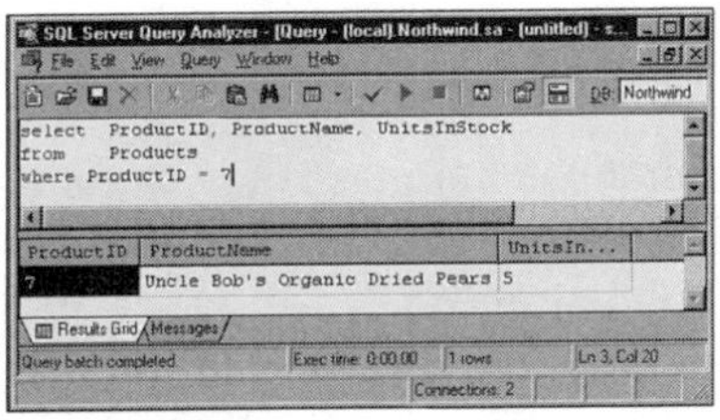

Figure 6.12: Verifying the number of units left in stock.

Now keep everything the same on the ordering form and click the Place an Order button again. This time, you get an error message saying that you tried to order more items than are available in stock (see Figure 6.13).

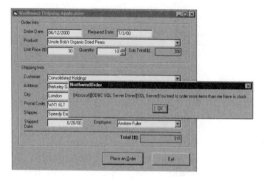

Figure 6.13: *A message box indicates that you can't order more items than the number of units in stock.*

So what happened? You tried to order 10 units again, but only 5 units were left, so this is a violation of the first business rule. In this case, the stored procedure raises an error and causes the COM object to call SetAbort to terminate the transaction. If you check the Orders table at this point, you will notice that the maximum order ID is still 11078. No new orders are placed.

Conclusions

The preceding sections demonstrated a complete sample application that uses COM+ automatic transaction services. You first learned about the three-tiered architectural design, which is the foundation of Windows DNA, as introduced in Chapter 2, "Windows DNA 2000 and COM+." Keep in mind that this is a *logical* architecture. You can physically deploy the application in a single machine (as you did in the sample) or distribute different tiers and components to multiple machines across the network, which is usually the case in a real-world scenario. You should always test, benchmark, and stress-test different deployment options to achieve the maximum possible performance as well as scalability.

You also learned how to implement business rules by using both SQL stored procedures and COM objects. Stored procedures can also implement transactions, as you learned by using the Order_Place stored procedure. This approach can sometimes simplify transaction management. The bottom line is that there are always different solutions to a problem domain. Which solution you use depends on a variety of factors. You have to balance the pros and cons of available options to make a final decision.

You also need to partition the COM objects into two distinct categories: transactional and nontransactional. Objects that don't modify any data should be designated as nontransactional.

Also, take a few minutes to review the syntax used to create the COM objects from the transaction root object. You used the CreateObject() function instead of the CreateInstance() function of the ObjectContext object. Actually, COM+ supports both syntaxes. If you want to run the application under MTS, however, you need to change CreateObject() to CreateInstance to enlist the object being created into the existing transaction of the creator.

Finally, you should keep in mind the way errors are handled in transactional COM objects. For this example, you used the raising error strategy, which has something to do with the way COM+ ends a transaction. When a COM object encounters an error and calls SetAbort, the transaction may still continue until the root object of the transaction calls SetAbort. By raising an error to the root object, you can speed up the ending of the transaction should an error occur.

What's Next

This chapter covered the transaction services provided by COM+ and guided you through the entire process of building a complete COM+ transaction application based on a three-tiered architecture. Chapter 7, "Compensating Resource Manager (CRM)," will introduce you to CRM, a new COM+ service. There, you'll learn how to use CRM to extend the MS DTC's transactional support to some traditionally nontransactional resources, such as file systems.

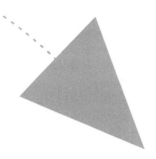

Compensating Resource Manager (CRM)

In the preceding chapter, you learned about COM+ transaction services and how to write transactional components and use them in your applications. In this chapter, you'll learn how to extend COM+ transaction services to nontransactional resources by using a new feature provided by COM+: the Compensating Resource Manager (CRM) framework.

This chapter teaches you the following:

- What resource dispensers and resource managers are
- The fundamentals of the Compensating Resource Manager (CRM)
- How to write your own CRM
- Issues involved in developing a CRM

Resource Dispensers Versus Resource Managers

COM+ internally works with Microsoft Distributed Transaction Coordinator (MS DTC). It uses other system resources to provide automatic transaction services to the components that are configured to support transaction (that is, the transaction attribute is set to Required, Requires New, or Supported, as described in Chapter 5, "Using the Component Services MMC Snap-In"). Resource managers and resource dispensers are two important system services for COM+ to utilize system resources.

Resource managers are system services that manage durable data. They ensure that the data will survive a system failure. Relational database management systems (such as SQL Server, Sybase, and Oracle) and other data stores such as Microsoft Exchange Server and persistent message queues are examples of resource managers. This chapter discusses the Compensating Resource Manager (CRM), which is a special type of resource manager. CRM allows you to extend the COM+ transaction service to other resources that don't participate in MS DTC transactions.

Resource dispensers are system services that manage nondurable, shared-state data. They also manage the connections to resource managers. Examples of resource dispensers include ODBC drivers, OLE DB providers, and transient message queues.

The Compensating Resource Manager (CRM)

In this section, I will discuss the lack of resource manager development tools in the Software Development Kit (SDK) that are shipped with MTS. I will then teach you the COM+ Compensating Resource Manager (CRM) and the added values CRM provided to Visual Basic developers. Then I discuss how to develop a CRM using the CRM architecture, interfaces and their methods in great detail. In a latter section of this chapter, "A Sample CRM Application," I will show you how to leverage the CRM architecture to add extended transaction support to the Northwind Application we developed in last chapter.

Limitation of the MTS SDK

Microsoft Transaction Server (MTS) ships with a Software Development Kit (SDK) that provides a toolkit for developing resource managers. These resource managers can then be used to expand the transaction services provided by MTS to nontransactional resources. Some examples of nontransactional resources include file systems, email systems, or desktop databases such as Microsoft Access. These resources do not support the transaction protocols such as the OLE Transactions protocol and the X/Open XA protocol, so they cannot participate in MS DTC transactions. With the help of the SDK, developers can implement the transaction protocols mentioned earlier in the form of resource managers. This allows traditionally non-transactional resources to utilize the transaction protection provided by MTS and MS DTC. The SDK is designed for programmers who want to implement resource managers in C++. It is not practical to implement resource managers in Visual Basic. Therefore, you need to have skills in C++ if you want to create resource managers.

TIP

In the context of this chapter, *non-transactional resources* refers to those resources that don't participate in MS DTC distributed transactions (and thus MTS or COM+ transactions). Even though these resources might implement some form of transactional functionality themselves, as far as MS DTC is concerned, they are non-transactional resources. For example, even though Microsoft Access has its own transaction support, it is considered a non-transactional resource because Access does not participate in MS DTC distributed transactions.

What Is the CRM?

Now that you are completely disheartened by the fact that you cannot write resource managers using Visual Basic, I will tell you there is a light at the end of the tunnel. Microsoft created a way for you to leverage your VB skills and still achieve the same functionality. In addition to the SDK that targets C++, Microsoft built into COM+ the Compensating Resource Manager (CRM) as an alternative and easier way to write resource managers. The CRM supports multiple interfaces that are each optimized to support specific languages, such as C++, Visual Basic, and Visual J++.

Unlike MTS, however, the CRM is not a product. Rather, it is a framework that provides an infrastructure and toolkit for developers to integrate non-transactional resources with MS DTC.

The CRM Architecture

Figure 7.1 illustrates the CRM architecture. As you can see in the figure, the CRM architecture is made up of several components. Some of these components (in white with the rounded corners) are internal components provided by the CRM infrastructure. The other components (in gray with rounded corners) are the responsibility of application developers. These components work together with the CRM infrastructure to make nontransactional resources appear to be transactional.

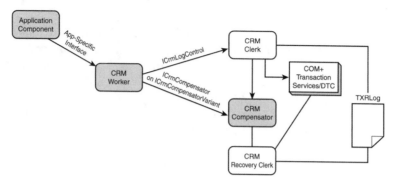

Figure 7.1: *The CRM architecture.*

Developing a CRM

Developing a CRM involves writing two specific components: namely, the CRM Worker and the CRM Compensator. You also need to write an application component that interacts with the CRM Worker component through an application-specific interface (see Figure 7.1).

THE CRM WORKER AND CRM COMPENSATOR

The CRM Worker component needs to initialize an instance of the CRM Clerk component. This needs to be done only once. The CRM Worker implements the ICrmLogControl interface so that the CRM Worker can write log records to a durable log file for later compensating actions.

The CRM Compensator component needs to implement either the ICrmCompensator interface or the ICrmCompensatorVariants interface. The ICrmCompensator interface delivers unstructured log records as BLOBs (Binary Large Object datatypes) of bytes and is suitable for languages such as Visual C++ or Visual J++. The ICrmCompensatorVariants interface delivers structured log records as variant arrays and is optimized for languages such as Visual Basic. These interfaces allow the CRM Compensator to receive transaction outcome notification of both the prepare and commit phases of a two-phase commit (2-pc) transaction.

THE ICrmLogControl INTERFACE

The ICrmLogControl interface provides a means for the CRM Worker and CRM Compensator to write records to the durable log file. Table 7.1 lists some important methods defined in the ICrmLogControl interface.

Table 7.1   Important Methods of the `ICrmLogControl` *Interface*

Methods	Description
RegisterCompensator	Called by the CRM Worker to specify the CRM Compensator so that the CRM infrastructure knows which CRM component to create upon the completion of the transaction to perform compensating actions.
WriteLogRecordVariants	Used by the CRM Worker and CRM Compensator to write structured records in the form of variant arrays to the durable log file.
ForceLog	Called by the CRM to force all log records to be durable on disk.
ForgetLogRecord	Called by the CRM Worker to forget the last log record.
ForceTransactionToAbort	Called by the CRM Worker to perform an immediate abort call on the transaction.
TransactionUOW	Allows CRMs to obtain the transaction Unit Of Work (UOW), a GUID, without having to log the transaction UOW in the log record.

After an instance of the CRM Clerk is initiated, the CRM Worker first needs to notify the CRM infrastructure which CRM Compensator to use to receive transaction outcome notifications and perform compensating actions. It does so by calling the `RegisterCompensator()` method, passing the ProgID of the CRM Compensator, a description, and a flag constant that controls which phases of transaction completion should be received by the CRM Compensator, and whether recovery should fail in-doubt transactions remain after recovery has been attempted. This is an *asynchronous method call*. So, if the CRM Worker receives a "recovery in progress" error code, it will continuously keep trying until it succeeds.

TIP

An *in-doubt transaction* is a transaction that has been prepared but hasn't received a decision to commit or abort because the server coordinating the transaction is unavailable.

Before performing the actual work that involves transactions, the CRM Worker needs to write information to the durable log file in the form of variant arrays by calling the `WriteLogRecordVariants()` method. This process is known as *write-ahead*. The information that must be written into the log is application-specific. The CRM Compensator relies on this information to perform compensating actions later, at which time it will either abort or commit the transactions. For the log to be durable, the CRM Worker also needs to call the `ForceLog()` method of the `ICrmLogControl` interface through the CRM Clerk object.

In case of an error during the normal operation, the CRM Worker must abort the transaction immediately by calling the `ForceTransactionToAbort()` method. After the CRM Worker is done with its actions, it must persist the records to the log, and it must release the `ICrmLogControl`.

NOTE

The CRM Worker must run under an MS DTC transaction. Therefore, the transaction attribute of the CRM Worker component (the class) should be configured as Supported; that is, you should set the `MTSTransactionMode` property to `4-RequiresTransaction`.

THE `ICrmCompensatorVariants` INTERFACE

When a transaction is completed because the application component calls `SetComplete` or `SetAbort`, the CRM infrastructure creates the CRM Compensator. The `ICrmCompensatorVariants` interface provides a mechanism for the CRM infrastructure to deliver structured log records to the CRM Compensator component developed in Visual Basic. Table 7.2 describes the 10 methods supported by the `ICrmCompensatorVariants` interface.

Table 7.2   Methods of the `ICrmCompensatorVariants` *Interface*

Methods	Description
SetLogControl	Passes an `ICrmLogControl` interface to the CRM Compensator. You can use the `ICrmLogControl` interface to write further log records as needed. This method is the first one called on the CRM Compensator after it is created.
BeginPrepareVariants	Notifies the CRM Compensator about the prepare phase of the transaction completion and that records are about to be delivered. Prepare notifications are never received during recovery, only during normal processing.
PrepareRecordVariants	Passes a log record to the CRM Compensator during the prepare phase. Log records are passed in the order they were originally written. This method may be received by the CRM Compensator multiple times, once for each log record that was written.
EndPrepareVariants	Notifies the CRM Compensator that it has received all the log records available during the prepare phase.
BeginCommitVariants	Notifies the CRM Compensator about the commit phase of the transaction completion and that records are about to be passed.
CommitRecordVariants	Passes a log record to the CRM Compensator during the commit phase.

Table 7.2   continued

Methods	Description
`EndCommitVariants`	Notifies the CRM Compensator that it has passed all the records available during the commit phase.
`BeginAbortVariants`	Notifies the CRM Compensator about the abort phase of the transaction completion and that records are about to be passed.
`AbortRecordVariants`	Passes a log record to the CRM Compensator during the abort phase.
`EndAbortVariants`	Notifies the CRM Compensator that it has received all the log records available during the abort phase.

The CRM Compensator may first be notified of the prepare phase of the transaction completion. It can vote either Yes or No to the prepare request. If its vote is No, the CRM Compensator will no longer receive any further abort notifications. In case of a client abort, the CRM Compensator will only receive abort notifications, not prepare notifications. The majority of the compensating action is done in two methods: `BeginCommitVariants()` and `AbortRecordVariants()`. You write code in the `BeginCommitVariants()` method to commit the transaction and implement the logic in the `AbortRecordVariants()` method to perform any compensating actions. The CRM Compensator can log new records to the durable log if necessary.

NOTE

You should not assume that the same CRM Compensator instance will receive notification during both phases (that is, phase 1, the prepare phase, and phase 2, the commit or abort phase) because they could be interrupted by recovery.

NOTE

The CRM Compensator does not run under an MS DTC transaction. Therefore, the transaction attribute of the component (the class) that implements the `ICrmCompensatorVariants` interface must be configured as Disabled; that is, you should set the `MTSTransactionMode` property to `0-NotAnMTSObject`.

INSTALLATION OF CRM COMPONENTS

CRM components (the CRM Worker and CRM Compensator) can be installed either into a COM+ server application or a COM+ library application. They must always run in a server application, however. When they are installed under a library application, the client process cannot get the services of CRM. The advantage of installing the CRM components into a library application is that the CRM services are available to more than one server application. If the CRM components are installed into a server application, their services are available only to that specific server application.

Table 7.3 summarizes the recommended COM+ configurations for the CRM Worker and CRM Compensator that are developed in Visual Basic.

Table 7.3 Recommended COM+ Configurations for the CRM Worker and CRM Compensator

Components	Transaction	JIT	Threading Model
CRM Worker	Required	Yes	Apartment
CRM Compensator	Disabled	No	Apartment

You also need to develop an application component that creates a CRM Worker instance to perform the work. Installing the application component into the sample COM+ application as the CRM Worker and CRM Compensator is recommended. Its transaction attribute should be configured as Supported.

You also need to enable the CRM services at the COM+ application level to use the CRM. Otherwise, if you attempt to use a CRM within the server application, the CRM will fail. To enable the CRM for use in an application, in Component Services, right-click the COM+ application for which you want to enable CRM and then select Properties. Click the Advanced tab and check the Enable Compensating Resource Managers check box (see Figure 7.2).

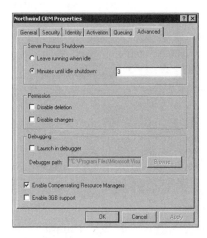

Figure 7.2: *Enabling CRM for a COM+ application.*

A Sample CRM Application

Now that you've learned enough background about CRM, it's time to develop a sample CRM application. You will expand the Northwind ordering application you worked with in Chapter 6, "Writing Transactional

Components," by including some actions involving resources in the Microsoft Access database and enlisting Microsoft Access resources into the existing transaction scope. You are going to leverage the power of the COM+ CRM infrastructure. Before you start building the sample application, though, take a look at a small example to see that resources in Microsoft Access are not transactional, from an MS DTC perspective.

EXAMPLE

Using Microsoft Access Resources

For this example, first create an Access database called **CRM** with a single table also called **CRM**, as shown in Figure 7.3.

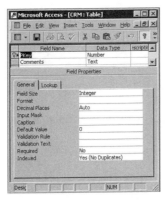

Figure 7.3: *The CRM table in an Access CRM database.*

Next, create a SQL Server database called **COMPlus** with a single table, again called **CRM** (see Figure 7.4).

Figure 7.4: *The CRM table in the SQL Server COMPlus database.*

Notice that the two CRM tables are virtually identical in structure. Now insert one row into the CRM table on the SQL Server database by running the following script from the SQL Server Query Analyzer:

```
Insert into CRM values(1,'Testing Access Transaction')
```

Now create two Data Source Names (DSNs), CRM and COMPlus, pointing to the Access database and SQL Server database created earlier, respectively.

Next, build a COM component that tests the transaction behavior of Microsoft Access. To do so, start a new ActiveX DLL project, "AccessTx," and set the rest of its properties as shown in Figure 7.5.

Figure 7.5: *The project properties of the AccessTx component.*

Add a class module into the AccessTx project and set its properties as shown in Figure 7.6.

Figure 7.6: *The properties of the CAccessTx class module.*

In this component, implement a single method called TestAccessTrans() by adding a public function to the CAccessTx class module, as in Listing 7.1.

Listing 7.1 The TestAccessTrans() Method

```
Public Function TestAccessTrans() As Boolean

    Dim oObjectContext As ObjectContext
    Dim oConn1 As New ADODB.Connection
    Dim oConn2 As New ADODB.Connection
    Dim sSQL As String

    On Error GoTo TestAccessTrans_Err
    Set oObjectContext = GetObjectContext()
```

Listing 7.1 continued

```
    sSQL = "Insert into CRM values(1,'Testing Access Transaction')"

    'Attempt to insert a row in Access CRM table.
    With oConn1
        .Open "CRM"
        .Execute sSQL
        .Close
    End With
    Set oConn1 = Nothing

    'Attempt to insert a row in SQL Server CRM table.
    'This will fail due to the primary key violation.
    With oConn2
        .Open "COMPlus"
        .Execute sSQL
        .Close
    End With
    Set oConn2 = Nothing

    If Not oObjectContext Is Nothing Then
        oObjectContext.SetComplete
    End If
    Exit Function
TestAccessTrans_Err:
    If Not oObjectContext Is Nothing Then
        oObjectContext.SetAbort
    End If
    Err.Raise Err.Number, "TestAccessTrans", Err.Description
End Function
```

In the TestAccessTx function, you declare two ADO Connection objects to hold two connections: one to the Access database and another to the SQL Server database. After creating an ObjectContext object, you try to execute the same SQL statement that is designed to insert one row in each of the CRM tables. Recall that the CRM table in Access is empty, whereas the SQL Server CRM table already has a row with the same primary key value, 1. Therefore, the first insert (to the Access database) should succeed, whereas the second (to the SQL Server database) will fail because of the violation of the primary key constraint. Because you call SetAbort in the error handler, if these two actions are protected by the COM+ transaction (through MS DTC), both actions should be rolled back. That is, after the method call, nothing should happen. The Access CRM table should not have a row inserted, and the SQL Server CRM table should still have only one row. Now check to see whether this is the case.

Compile the project to create the AccessTx.dll. Create an empty COM+ server application and install the AccessTx.dll component (see Figure 7.7).

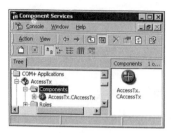

Figure 7.7: *The* AccessTx *component in the* AccessTx *COM+ application.*

Now start a new Visual Basic Standard EXE project and create a reference to AccessTx.dll. Place a command button (Command1) on the form. Double-click the command button and type the code shown in Listing 7.2.

Listing 7.2   Code for Testing the AccessTx Component

```
Private Sub Command1_Click()
    On Error GoTo Test_Err
    Dim oAccessTx As New AccessTx.CAccessTx
    oAccessTx.TestAccessTrans
    Exit Sub
Test_Err:
    MsgBox Err.Description
End Sub
```

Press F5 to run the application. Clicking the command button on the form opens a message box that indicates you have a primary key constraint violation on the SQL Server (see Figure 7.8). This is the result you expected.

Figure 7.8: *A primary key constraint violation error.*

Now open the CRM table in the Access database. In this case, a record does make it to the CRM table (see Figure 7.9).

So what happened? The problem is that even though you call the SetAbort method, the insert action to the Access database is not protected under the transaction. Therefore, you have proved that Microsoft Access is a non-transactional resource. In the following sections, you'll build a sample CRM application that makes Access data sources to participate in the COM+/DTC transaction.

Figure 7.9: The row made its way to the Access database.

EXAMPLE

The Northwind CRM Sample Application

In this sample application, you'll expand the Northwind ordering application you built in the preceding chapter. You'll add some functionalities to learn how to use the CRM infrastructure to extend the reach of MS DTC to enlist Microsoft Access database as part of the entire order processing transaction.

You'll modify the order processing workflow by adding two more sub-processes. After the order is processed, you'll send an invoice to the invoice system, which uses Microsoft Access as its data store. At the end of the ordering process, you'll check the credit history of the customer to decide whether the order should be processed or canceled.

DATABASE PREPARATION

For purposes of this chapter, create a Northwind_Invoice Access database that contains a single table, Invoice, as shown in Figure 7.10.

Figure 7.10: The Invoice table on the Access Invoice database.

You also need to create a DSN for the Northwind_Invoice database and name it **Invoice**.

Another process is to perform a credit check before ending the transaction. If the customer has a bad credit history, then the entire transaction will be aborted. To implement the credit function, add a Credits table in the Northwind database by running the script in Listing 7.3.

Listing 7.3   SQL Script for Creating the Credits Table

```
if exists(select * from sysobjects
     where type='u'
     and id = object_id('Credits'))
 drop table Credits
go


--This will create a new table "Credits"
Select CustomerID, 'Standing' =1 into Credits
from Customers
go


--Add a primary key to CustomerID column
alter table Credits add constraint PKey_Credits primary key
(CustomerID)
go
--Change the data type of Standing form int(default) to bit
alter table Credits alter column Standing bitgo
--Let the companies whose names start with letter "B" to have bad
credit.
update Credits
set Standing = 0
where customerid like 'B%'
```

The last thing you do in Listing 7.3 is to change the Standing of all the customers whose names start with the letter *B* to 0. For this example, assume those customers have bad credit histories (in reality, most of them might be innocent, though).

APPLICATION DESIGN

To make the data manipulation of the Microsoft Access database transactional, you need to create a pair of CRM components: a CRM Worker and CRM Compensator. You also need to create an application component whose transaction attribute should be set to support transactions. This component needs to create a CRM Worker that, in turn, will register a CRM Compensator to the CRM infrastructure to ensure that the action is reversible.

Figure 7.11 is a Unified Modeling Language (UML) diagram that illustrates the system architecture of the sample Northwind CRM application.

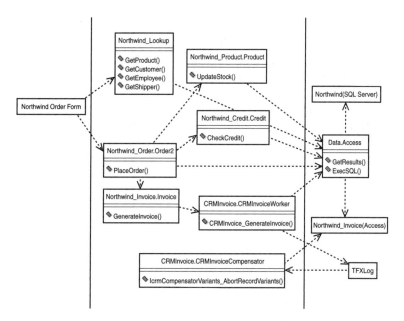

Figure 7.11: *The system architecture of the sample Northwind CRM application.*

Figure 7.12 defines the transaction scope of the sample application. As you can see, the Access database, Invoice, is also included in the transaction boundary.

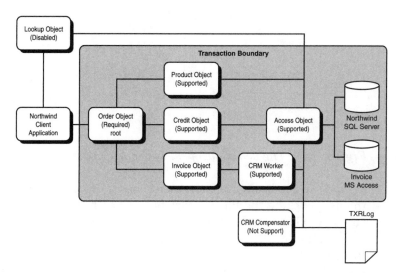

Figure 7.12: *The transaction scope of the sample Northwind CRM application.*

THE WORKFLOW

Figure 7.13 illustrates the modified workflow of the ordering process in the sample application, presented as a UML sequence diagram. The UML sequence diagram is a very powerful means by which you can document and verify your design logic. A sequence diagram displays the interactions between objects and resources. It also describes the sequences in which different events occur during the application's lifetime. The vertical rectangle boxes in a sequence diagram represent the lifetime of individual objects.

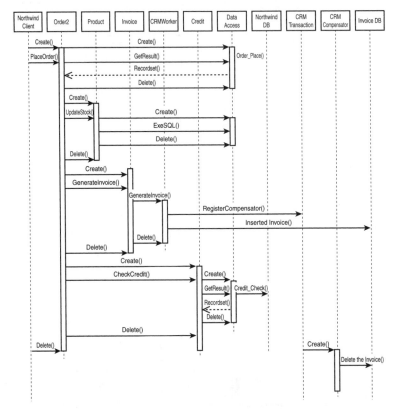

Figure 7.13: *The workflow of the ordering process.*

As you can see in Figure 7.13, the ordering process starts (as the result of the user clicking the Place Order button) with the creation of an Order2 object (you'll learn about the Order2 object versus the Order object later) and a call to its PlaceOrder() method. The Order2 object, in turn, creates three objects, invoking appropriate methods in one after the other. As happened in the sample application you created in the preceding chapter, the Order2 object inserts an order to the Northwind database and updates the quantity in stock through the `Data.Access` object and the `Northwind_Product.Product` object. Then the `Order2` object creates an `Invoice` object and calls the `GenerateInvoice()` method. To ensure that the action of generating the invoice is also transactional, the `Invoice` object creates a CRM Worker object and calls its `GenerateInvoice()` method. The first thing the CRM Worker object does in the `GenerateInvoice()` method is to register a CRM Compensator object with the CRM infrastructure. Then the CRM Worker object inserts an invoice into the Invoice database. After generating the invoice, the `Order2` object then creates a `Credit` object and calls the `CheckCredit()` method to verify the credit history of the customer.

After finishing the credit check, the `Order2` object (the transaction root) commits the transaction if everything is in order. Should anything go wrong, the entire transaction will be aborted. This means that the order should not be entered into the Northwind database (both the Orders and Order Details table), and the quantity of the specific product should not be deducted. And, of course, the invoice should not be inserted in the Invoice database. Although the actions of placing the order and updating the stock are protected by the COM+ automatic transaction service, the Invoice action is protected through the CRM infrastructure.

After the completion of the transaction, the CRM infrastructure consults with MS DTC for the final outcome of the transaction. If the transaction is aborted, the CRM infrastructure starts an instance of the CRM Compensator object registered earlier by the CRM Worker object and gets information from the log file (not shown in the illustration). It also performs a compensating action (in this case, deletes the invoice from the Invoice database).

In the following sections, I'll walk you through code examples to see how to implement CRM support in the sample application.

THE Order2 OBJECT

If you compare Figure 7.11 with Figure 6.5 in Chapter 6, "Writing Transactional Components," you'll notice that the `Order2` object in Figure 7.11 interacts with two more objects than the `Order` object in Figure 6.5. This is a significant change. For example, to generate an invoice, the client application needs to pass more parameters to the `Order2` object. In Chapter 4, "Introduction to Visual Basic COM Programming," you learned that COM requires that the interface of a COM object should be immutable after it is published. Otherwise, the older client applications that use the COM object will crash. For this reason, instead of changing the signature of the `PlaceOrder` method of the `Order` class, you add a new class named Order2.cls to the Northwind_Order.vbp project (see Figure 7.14).

Figure 7.14: *The Order2.cls class in the Northwind_Order.vbp project.*

NOTE

To ensure that older client applications don't crash, you need to keep the binary compatibility set to the existing Northwind_Order.dll before you compile the project with the new class.

Listing 7.4 shows the new `PlaceOrder()` function in Order2.cls.

Listing 7.4   The `PlaceOrder()` Function of Order2.cls

```
Public Function PlaceOrder(ByVal iProductID As Integer, _
                           ByVal cUnitPrice As Currency, _
                           ByVal iQuantity As Integer, _
                           ByVal sCustomerID As String, _
                           ByVal iEmployeeID As Integer, _
                           ByVal dOrderDate As Date, _
                           ByVal dRequiredDate As Date, _
                           ByVal dShippedDate As Date, _
                           ByVal iShipVia As Integer, _
                           ByVal cFreight As Currency, _
                           ByVal sShipName As String, _
                           ByVal sAddress As String, _
                           ByVal sCity As String, _
                           ByVal sRegion As String, _
                           ByVal sPostalCode As String, _
                           ByVal sCountry As String, _
                           ByVal sCustomer As String, _
                           ByVal sSalesPerson As String, _
                           ByVal sShipper As String, _
                           ByVal sProductName As String, _
                           ByVal cSubtotal As Currency, _
                           ByVal cTotal As Currency) As Boolean

            On Error GoTo PlaceOrder_Err
            Dim oData          As Object 'Data.Access object.
            Dim oProduct       As Object 'Northwind_Product.Product object.
            Dim oInvoice       As Object 'Northwind_Invoice.Invoice object.
            Dim oCredit        As Object 'Northwind_Credit.Credit object.
            Dim sSQL           As String
            Dim oObjectContext As ObjectContext
```

Listing 7.4   continued

```
Dim rsOrder        As New ADOR.Recordset
Dim iOrderID       As Integer
Dim lRows          As Long


Set oObjectContext = GetObjectContext()

'Place the order.
sSQL = "Exec Order_Place" & _
        "  @ProductID = " & iProductID & _
        ", @UnitPrice = " & cUnitPrice & _
        ", @Quantity = " & iQuantity & _
        ", @CustomerID = '" & sCustomerID & "'" & _
        ", @EmployeeID = " & iEmployeeID & _
        ", @OrderDate = '" & dOrderDate & "'" & _
        ", @RequiredDate = '" & dRequiredDate & "'" & _
        ", @ShippedDate = '" & dShippedDate & "'" & _
        ", @ShipVia = " & iShipVia & _
        ", @Freight = " & cFreight & _
        ", @ShipName = '" & sShipName & "'" & _
        ", @ShipAddress = '" & sAddress & "'" & _
        ", @ShipCity = '" & sCity & "'" & _
        ", @ShipRegion = '" & sRegion & "'" & _
        ", @ShipPostalCode = '" & sPostalCode & "'" & _
        ", @ShipCountry = '" & sCountry & "'"

Set oData = CreateObject("Data.Access")
'oData.ExecSQL "Northwind", sSQL
Set rsOrder = oData.GetResult("Northwind", sSQL, lRows)
If lRows <> 0 Then
    iOrderID = rsOrder!OrderID
End If
Set oData = Nothing


'Update quantity in stock.
Set oProduct = CreateObject("Northwind_Product.Product")
oProduct.UpdateStock iProductID, iQuantity
Set oProduct = Nothing


'Process the invoice.
Set oInvoice = CreateObject("Northwind_Invoice.Invoice")
oInvoice.GenerateInvoice iOrderID, _
                          sCustomerID, _
                          sSalesPerson, _
                          dOrderDate, _
```

Listing 7.4   continued

```
                                        dRequiredDate, _
                                        dShippedDate, _
                                        sShipper, _
                                        iProductID, _
                                        sProductName, _
                                        iQuantity, _
                                        cUnitPrice, _
                                        cSubtotal, _
                                        cFreight, _
                                        cTotal, _
                                        sCustomer, _
                                        sAddress, _
                                        sCity, _
                                        sRegion, _
                                        sPostalCode, _
                                        sCountry

            Set oInvoice = Nothing

            'Check the credit.
            Set oCredit = CreateObject("Northwind_Credit.Credit")
            oCredit.CheckCredit sCustomerID
            Set oCredit = Nothing

            If Not oObjectContext Is Nothing Then
                oObjectContext.SetComplete
            End If
            PlaceOrder = True
            Exit Function
PlaceOrder_Err:
        PlaceOrder = False
        If Not oObjectContext Is Nothing Then
            oObjectContext.SetAbort
        End If
        Err.Raise Err.Number
End Function
```

In Listing 7.4, you change the call to the stored procedure by calling the
GetResult method of the Data.Access object instead of ExecSQL as you did in
the PlaceOrder method in Order.cls in the preceding chapter. You do so
because you modify the Order_Place stored procedure to return the Order
ID by using a SELECT statement near the end of the stored procedure.
Listing 7.5 shows the modified stored procedure.

Listing 7.5 The Modified `Order_Place` Stored Procedure

```
/********************************************************************
* Name:     Order_Place                                          *
* Purpose: Places an order.                                      *
* Remarks: We modified the original stored procedure by adding   *
*          a SELECT statement to return the Order ID             *
********************************************************************/
if exists(select * from sysobjects where id = object_id('Order_Place'))
 drop proc Order_Place
go

create proc Order_Place
 @ProductID int,
 @UnitPrice money,
 @Quantity smallint,
 @Discount real=0,
 @CustomerID nchar(5),
 @EmployeeID int,
 @OrderDate datetime,
 @RequiredDate datetime=null,
 @ShippedDate datetime=null,
 @ShipVia int,
 @Freight money =null,
 @ShipName nvarchar(40),
 @ShipAddress nvarchar(60),
 @ShipCity nvarchar(15),
 @ShipRegion nvarchar(15),
 @ShipPostalCode nvarchar(10),
 @ShipCountry nvarchar(15)
as
set nocount on
declare @OrderID int
begin tranexec Orders_Add @OrderID = @OrderID out,
            @CustomerID = @CustomerID,
            @EmployeeID = @EmployeeID,
            @OrderDate = @OrderDate,
            @RequiredDate = @RequiredDate,
            @ShippedDate = @ShippedDate,
            @ShipVia = @ShipVia,
            @Freight = @Freight,
            @ShipName = @ShipName,
            @ShipAddress = @ShipAddress,
            @ShipCity = @ShipCity,
            @ShipRegion =@ShipRegion,
```

Listing 7.5 continued

```
                  @ShipPostalCode =@ShipPostalCode,
                  @ShipCountry = @ShipCountry

exec OrderDetails_ADD @OrderID = @OrderID,
                  @ProductID = @ProductID,
                  @UnitPrice = @UnitPrice,
                  @Quantity = @Quantity,
                  @Discount = @Discount

set nocount off

select 'OrderID' = @OrderID

if @@error = 0
  commit tran
else
  rollback

go
```

The Order ID is returned as a single-row, single-column ADO recordset. After it is returned, the Order ID value is then used in the call to generate an invoice. You could modify the `Order_Place` stored procedure to make the Order ID an output parameter instead. However, this approach would involve adding a new method to the `Data.Access` object for handling the output parameter of a stored procedure in ADO, as discussed in Chapter 2, "Windows DNA 2000 and COM+." By using the approach shown here, you can minimize changes to the existing application.

THE Credit OBJECT

Now create a Northwind_Credit.vbp project with a single class named Credit.cls (see Figure 7.15) to simplify the credit-checking process. The Credit.cls implements a single method named `CheckCredit`, which calls a stored procedure named `Credit_Check`.

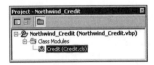

Figure 7.15: *The Northwind_Credit.vbp project.*

Listings 7.6 and 7.7 show the `CheckCredit` method and the `Credit_Check` stored procedure, respectively.

Listing 7.6 The `CheckCredit` Method of the Credit.cls

```
Public Function CheckCredit(ByVal sCustomerID As String) As Boolean
    On Error GoTo CheckCredit_Err
    Dim oObjectContext  As ObjectContext
    Dim oData           As Object 'Data.Access object.
    Dim sSQL            As String
    Dim rsResult        As ADOR.Recordset
    Dim lRows           As Long


    Set oObjectContext = GetObjectContext()

    sSQL = "Exec Credit_Check @CustomerID = '" & sCustomerID & "'"

    Set oData = CreateObject("Data.Access")
    Set rsResult = oData.GetResult("Northwind", sSQL, lRows)
    Set oData = Nothing

    If rsResult!Standing = True Then
        CheckCredit = True
    Else
        Err.Raise vbObjectError + 512 + 1, _
                  "Northwind_Credit", _
                  "Bad credit history. Order has been canceled!"
    End If


    If Not oObjectContext Is Nothing Then
        oObjectContext.SetComplete
    End If
    Exit Function
CheckCredit_Err:
    CheckCredit = False
    If Not oObjectContext Is Nothing Then
        oObjectContext.SetAbort
    End If
    Err.Raise Number:=Err.Number, Description:=Err.Description
End Function
```

Listing 7.7 The `Credit_Check` Stored Procedure

```
if exists(select * from sysobjects
      where id = object_id('Credit_Check'))
  drop proc Credit_Check
go

create proc Credit_Check
 @CustomerID nchar(5)
as
```

Listing 7.7 continued

```
select      Standing
from        Credits
where       CustomerID = @CustomerID

if @@rowcount = 0
 raiserror ('This customer does not exist.',16,1)
go
```

The Credit_Check stored procedure returns information about the customer's credit status (see Listing 7.7). The CheckCredit method verifies the Standing. If the customer's credit is not in good standing, this method raises a customized error to abort the transaction.

THE CRM OBJECTS AND THE Invoice OBJECT

The most important objects discussed in this chapter are the CRM Worker and the CRM Compensator objects. To implement a pair of CRM objects, you first must create an interface that specifies the methods the CRM Worker needs to implement. So, for this example, create a CRMInvoiceLib.vbp project with an abstract interface named ICRMInvoice, as shown in Figure 7.16.

Figure 7.16: *The CRM interface named* ICRMInvoice.

This abstract interface defines a single method, GenerateInvoice, without a concrete implementation (see Listing 7.8).

Listing 7.8 The GenerateInvoice Method Definition

```
Public Function GenerateInvoice(ByVal sOrderID As String, _
                                ByVal sSQL As String) As Boolean

    'This is a method definition in an interface.
    'It is up to the classes that implement ICRMInvoice
    'interface to provide specific implementations.


End Function
```

With this ICRMInvoice interface in place, you are now ready to create the CRM Worker and CRM Compensator components. To do so, start a new ActiveX DLL project, name the project **CRMInvoice**, and set the rest of its properties as shown in Figure 7.17.

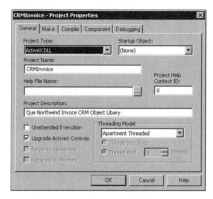

Figure 7.17: *The CRMInvoice.vbp project.*

In the project, set references to the COM+ Services Type Library, Que's Data Access Object Library, and Que Northwind Invoice CRM Interface, as shown in Figure 7.18.

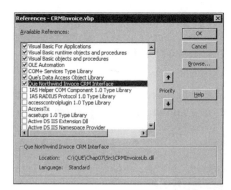

Figure 7.18: *Setting references for the CRMInovice.vbp project.*

Next, open the code window of CRMInvoiceWorker.cls.

In the CRMInvoice.vbp project, add two class modules named CRMInvoiceWorker.cls and CRMInvoiceCompensator.cls. Set the MTSTransactionMode property of CRMInvoiceWorker.cls to 2-RequiresTransaction and CRMInvoiceCompensator.cls to 0-NotAnMTSObject.

Listing 7.9 shows the code in the General Declaration section of CRMInvoiceWorker.cls.

Listing 7.9 The General Declaration Section of CRMInvoice.cls

```
Option Explicit

Dim m_oCRMClerk        As CRMClerk
Dim m_oCrmLogControl   As ICrmLogControl

Private Const XACT_E_RECOVERYINPROGRESS = -2147799170#

Implements ICRMInvoice
```

Here, you declare two module-level object variables: `CRMClerk` and `ICrmLogControl`. The CRM Worker uses `CRMClerk` to write records to a durable log through the `ICrmLogControl` interface.

Then you define a constant, `XACT_E_RECOVERYINPROGRESS`, to hold the return value (error code) of the `RegisterCompensator()` method of the `ICrmLogControl` interface. You use this constant to check against this return value to see whether the Compensator is registered and to decide whether you need to continue calling the `RegisterCompensator()` method.

The last line of code in Listing 7.9 implements the `ICRMInvoice` discussed in the preceding section. The `Implements` keyword makes the `GenerateInvoice` function defined in the `ICRMInvoice` interface available in the `CRMInvoiceWorker` class.

Click the Object drop-down box on the upper-left side of the code window to see `ICRMInvoice` in the drop-down list (see Figure 7.19).

Figure 7.19: *The* `ICRMInvoice` *interface in the Object drop-down box.*

Selecting `ICRMInvoice` from the drop-down list generates the skeleton code for the `ICRMInvoice_GenerateInvoice` method. By default, the function is Private, so change it to Public. This way, the client can call the `GenerateInvoice` method as normal. Finally, type the code in Listing 7.10 to implement the logic of generating an invoice.

Listing 7.10   The `ICRMInvoice_GenerateInvoice` Method

```
Public Function ICRMInvoice_GenerateInvoice(ByVal sOrderID As String, _
                                    ByVal sSQL As String) As
Boolean
'=======================================================================
'Note: After the "Implements", the function will default to private,
'      Change it to Public so that the client can directly call this
'      method by conventional means.
'=======================================================================
    On Error GoTo GenerateInvoice_Err

    Dim aLogRecord(0)   As Variant
    Dim oData           As Object 'Data.Access object

    'Create an instance of the CRM clerk if none exists yet.
    If m_oCrmLogControl Is Nothing Then
        Call GetCrmLogControl
    End If

    'Register the Compensator
    Call RegisterCRMInvoiceCompensator

    'Write Ahead--write the where clause into the log for
    'possible rollback.

    aLogRecord(0) = "Where OrderID = " & sOrderID
    m_oCrmLogControl.WriteLogRecordVariants aLogRecord
    'Force the log to ensure this log record is durable in the log
    m_oCrmLogControl.ForceLog

    'Now we are ready for generating the invoice.
    Set oData = CreateObject("Data.Access")
    oData.ExecSQL "Invoice", sSQL
    Set oData = Nothing

    ICRMInvoice_GenerateInvoice = True
    Exit Function
GenerateInvoice_Err:
    ICRMInvoice_GenerateInvoice = False
    'Abort the transaction.
    m_oCrmLogControl.ForceTransactionToAbort
    'Raise the error.
    Err.Raise Number:=Err.Number, Description:=Err.Description
End Function
```

The CRM Worker is responsible for normal operation. It first creates an instance of the CRM Clerk. The CRM Clerk implements an `ICRMLogControl` interface and is responsible for registering the CRM Compensator to the

CRM infrastructure to receive the outcome notification upon transaction completion.

Listing 7.11 shows the `GetCrmLogControl()` method.

Listing 7.11   The `GetCrmLogControl()` Method

```
Private Sub GetCrmLogControl()

    On Error GoTo GetCrmLogControl_Err

    Set m_oCRMClerk = New CRMClerk
    Set m_oCrmLogControl = m_oCRMClerk

    Exit Sub


GetCrmLogControl_Err:
    Err.Raise Number:=Err.Number, Description:=Err.Description
End Sub
```

In Listing 7.11, notice that you use the syntax to create a custom interface. See Chapter 4, "Introduction to Visual Basic COM Programming," for details about default and custom interfaces.

A one-to-one relationship exists between a CRM Worker instance and a CRM Clerk instance. So, this `GetCrmLogControl()` method should be called only once for the entire lifetime of the CRM Worker instance. This is done by checking whether the module-level variable `m_oCrmLogControl` is set yet. Only if the `m_oCrmLogControl` object is not set yet should you create an instance of the CRM Clerk (see Listing 7.10).

After making sure the CRM Clerk is created, the CRM Worker then calls the `RegisterCRMInvoiceCompensator` method to register the CRM Compensator (see Listing 7.12).

Listing 7.12   The `RegisterCRMInvoiceCompensator` Method

```
Private Sub RegisterCRMInvoiceCompensator()

    On Error GoTo RegisterCrmInvoiceCompensator_Err

    Dim sProgId        As String
    Dim sDescription   As String

    sProgId = "CRMInvoice.CRMInvoiceCompensator"
    sDescription = "Que Northwind Invoice CRM Sample"

    On Error Resume Next
    m_oCrmLogControl.RegisterCompensator sProgId, _
```

Listing 7.12 continued

```
                                    sDescription, _
                                    CRMREGFLAG_ALLPHASES


    ' may have to wait while recovery is in progress
    Do While Err.Number = XACT_E_RECOVERYINPROGRESS
        DoEvents
        m_oCrmLogControl.RegisterCompensator sProgId, _
                                    sDescription, _
                                    CRMREGFLAG_ABORTPHASE


    Loop


    On Error GoTo RegisterCrmInvoiceCompensator_Err


    Exit Sub

RegisterCrmInvoiceCompensator_Err:
    Err.Raise Number:=Err.Number, Description:=Err.Description
End Sub
```

As you can see in Listing 7.12, the CRM Worker registers the CRM Compensator by calling the RegisterCompensator() method of the CRM Clerk through the ICRMLogControl object, passing in the ProgID, a description, and a flag.

The ProgID in the example is CRMInvoice.CRMInvoiceCompensator. The last parameter of the RegisterCompensator() method is a flag that gives you fine granular control over which phases of transaction completion you are interested in so that the CRM Compensator will receive the notification. In this example, you should be especially interested in the abort phase of the transaction completion, so set the flag to CRMREGFLAG_ABORTPHASE.

Due to the timing issue, you use a Do...While loop to check the return value of the RegisterCompensator() method call to make sure the CRM Compensator is eventually registered.

Now go back to Listing 7.10, which shows the ICRMInvoice_GenerateInvoice function. After the CRM has been instantiated and the CRM Compensator is registered, the CRM needs to write a record to the durable log before it performs the actual action so that later the CRM infrastructure can perform a compensating action if needed. This is known as *write-ahead*.

The write-ahead is performed by calling the WriteLogRecordVariants() method of the CRM Clerk object, passing a variant array. This record will be used by the CRM Compensator to perform a compensating action later if something goes wrong. In the sample application, the normal action is to insert a row into the Invoice table in a Microsoft Access database. So, the reverse action would be to delete the row you inserted if the whole ordering process fails to keep the system in a consistent state. The trick you are going to use here is to pass a Where clause that includes the primary key. So later, the CRM Compensator will know exactly which row in the Invoice table to delete if something goes wrong.

The WriteLogRecordVariants() method call is followed by a ForceLog() call to ensure that the log record is durable, so the system can be recovered should it experience a possible failure during the process.

Now that you've written a durable log record, you are ready to do the action insert. To do so, create the Data.Access object and call its ExecSQL method to perform the insert. If something goes wrong, call the ForceTransactionToAbort() method before raising an error. Calling this method notifies MS DTC that you vote to abort the transaction.

Now you can turn your attention to another important part of the show: the CRMInvoiceCompensator class.

In the General Declaration section of the class module, insert these two lines of code:

```
Implements ICrmCompensatorVariants
Dim m_oCrmLogControl As ICrmLogControl
```

This first line exposes all the methods in the ICrmCompensatorVariants interface so that they become available to the CRMInvoiceCompensator object.

The second line declares a module-level object variable of the ICrmLogControl interface: m_oCrmLogControl. This variable can be used to hold the ICrmLogControl interface delivered by the CRM infrastructure through the SetLogControlVariants() method call (see Listing 7.13) so that the CRM Compensator can also write additional log records if necessary.

Listing 7.13   The SetLogControlVariants() Method

```
Private Sub ICrmCompensatorVariants_SetLogControlVariants(ByVal _
            pLogControl As ICrmLogControl)
    Set m_oCrmLogControl = pLogControl
End Sub
```

In this example, the most important method of the ICrmCompensatorVariants interface is AbortRecordVariants(). This method performs the reverse action using the log record. Listing 7.14 shows the code implemented for the AbortRecordVariants() method.

Listing 7.14 The `AbortRecordVariants()` Method

```
Private Function ICrmCompensatorVariants_AbortRecordVariants(pLogRecord) _
                As Boolean

    On Error GoTo AbortRecordVariants_Err

    Dim sWhereClause    As String
    Dim sSQL            As String
    Dim oData           As Object 'Data.Access object

    sWhereClause = pLogRecord(0)
    sSQL = "Delete * from Invoice " & sWhereClause

    Set oData = CreateObject("Data.Access")
    oData.ExecSQL "Invoice", sSQL
    Set oData = Nothing

    ICrmCompensatorVariants_AbortRecordVariants = True
    Exit Function

AbortRecordVariants_Err:
    ICrmCompensatorVariants_AbortRecordVariants = False
    Err.Raise Number:=Err.Number, Description:=Err.Description
End Function
```

You wrote a `Where` clause as the log record, so in the `AbortRecordVariants()` method, you can easily build a SQL statement that deletes the specific row identified by the primary key.

In the `CommitRecordVariants` method, you simply set the return type of the function to `True`. If everything goes well, no further action is required, as in the Abort action (see Listing 7.15).

Listing 7.15 The `CommitRecordVariants` Method

```
Private Function ICrmCompensatorVariants_CommitRecordVariants(pLogRecord)_
                As Boolean

    On Error GoTo CommitRecordVariants_Err

    'No clean up required in our situation.
    ICrmCompensatorVariants_CommitRecordVariants = True
    Exit Function

CommitRecordVariants_Err:
    Err.Raise Number:=Err.Number, Description:=Err.Description
End Function
```

Listing 7.16 shows the rest of the methods for the CRM Compensator object.

Listing 7.16   The Rest of the Methods for the CRM Compensator Object

```
Private Sub ICrmCompensatorVariants_EndAbortVariants()
    'Do nothing.
    Exit Sub
End Sub

Private Sub ICrmCompensatorVariants_EndCommitVariants()
    'Do nothing.
    Exit Sub
End Sub

Private Function ICrmCompensatorVariants_EndPrepareVariants() As Boolean

    ICrmCompensatorVariants_EndPrepareVariants = True

End Function

Private Function ICrmCompensatorVariants_PrepareRecordVariants(pLogRecord) _
                   As Boolean

    ICrmCompensatorVariants_PrepareRecordVariants = False

End Function
```

After developing the CRM Worker and CRM Compensator, you also need an application component that uses the CRM objects you just created. This application component in the example is the Northwind_Invoice.Invoice object. To create this object, create an ActiveX DLL project named **Northwind_Invoice.vbp** and change the name of the class module from Class1 to **Invoice**. Set the MTSTransactionMode to 2-RequiresTransaction. This Invoice class has only one method, GenerateInvoice(), as shown in Listing 7.17.

Listing 7.17   The GenerateInvoice() Method of the Invoice Class

```
Public Function GenerateInvoice(ByRef iOrderID As Integer, _
                                ByVal sCustomerID As String, _
                                ByVal sSalesPerson As String, _
                                ByVal dOrderDate As Date, _
                                ByVal dRequiredDate As Date, _
                                ByVal dShippedDate As Date, _
                                ByVal sShipVia As String, _
                                ByVal iProductID As Integer, _
                                ByVal sProductName As String, _
                                ByVal iQuantity As Integer, _
```

Listing 7.17 continued

```
                                ByVal cUnitPrice As Currency, _
                                ByVal cSubTotal As Currency, _
                                ByVal cFreight As Currency, _
                                ByVal cTotal As Currency, _
                                ByVal sShipTo As String, _
                                ByVal sAddress As String, _
                                ByVal sCity As String, _
                                ByVal sRegion As String, _
                                ByVal sPostalCode As String, _
                                ByVal sCountry As String) As Boolean


    On Error GoTo GenerateInvoice_Err

    Dim oObjectContext  As ObjectContext
    Dim oCRMInvoice     As Object 'CRMInvoice.CRMInvoiceWorker object.
    Dim sSQL            As String

    Set oObjectContext = GetObjectContext()

    sSQL = "Insert into Invoice Values(" _
        & iOrderID & ",'" & sCustomerID & "','" & sSalesPerson & "',#" _
        & dOrderDate & "#,#" & dRequiredDate & "#,#" & dShippedDate & "#,'" _
        & sShipVia & "'," & iProductID & ",'" & sProductName & "'," _
        & iQuantity & "," & cUnitPrice & "," & cSubTotal & "," _
        & cFreight & "," & cTotal & ",'" & sShipTo & "','" _
        & sAddress & "','" & sCity & "','" & sRegion & "','" & sPostalCode _
        & "','" & sCountry & "')"

    Set oCRMInvoice = CreateObject("CRMInvoice.CRMInvoiceWorker")
    oCRMInvoice.ICRMInvoice_GenerateInvoice CStr(iOrderID), sSQL
    Set oCRMInvoice = Nothing

    If Not oObjectContext Is Nothing Then
        oObjectContext.SetComplete
    End If
    Exit Function

GenerateInvoice_Err:
    If Not oObjectContext Is Nothing Then
        oObjectContext.SetAbort
    End If
    Err.Raise Number:=Err.Number, Description:=Err.Description
End Function
```

The GenerateInvoice() method of the Invoice class simply builds an Insert SQL statement, creates an instance of the CRMInvoice.CRMInvoiceWorker object, and calls its ICRMInvoice_GenerateInvoice method.

CHANGES MADE TO THE FRONT END

Because you are going to use the new Order2 object as described earlier in this chapter, you need to make some changes to the front end, the Northwind Order form. Listing 7.18 shows the modified code for the Click event of the Place an Order command button.

Listing 7.18   The Modified cmdOrder_Click Event Procedure

```
Private Sub cmdOrder_Click()
    On Error GoTo cmdOrder_Err
    Screen.MousePointer = vbHourglass

    Dim oOrder      As Object   'The Northwind_Order.Order2 object
    Dim iOrderID    As Integer 'Used to hold the output parameter.

    'Process the order.
    Set oOrder = CreateObject("Northwind_Order.Order2")
    oOrder.PlaceOrder iProductID, _
                    CCur(txtUnitPrice.Text), _
                    CInt(txtQuantity.Text), _
                    sCustomerID, _
                    iEmployeeID, _
                    CDate(txtOrderDate.Text), _
                    CDate(txtRequiredDate.Text), _
                    CDate(txtShippedDate.Text), _
                    iShipperID, _
                    CCur(txtFreight.Text), _
                    cbCustomer.Text, _
                    txtAddress.Text, _
                    txtCity.Text, _
                    txtRegion.Text, _
                    txtPostalCode.Text, _
                    txtCountry.Text, _
                    cbCustomer.Text, _
                    cbEmployee.Text, _
                    m_rsShipper!CompanyName, _
                    m_rsProduct!ProductName, _
                    CCur(txtSubTotal.Text), _
                    CCur(txtTotal.Text)

    Set oOrder = Nothing

    Screen.MousePointer = vbDefault
```

Listing 7.18   continued

```
    MsgBox "Order has been processed!"

    Exit Sub
cmdOrder_Err:
    Screen.MousePointer = vbDefault
    MsgBox Err.Description, vbCritical
End Sub
```

EXAMPLE

SETTING UP THE COM+ CRM APPLICATION

Now it's time to compile or recompile all the ActiveX DLLs you just built or rebuilt. You need to create a COM+ application for the CRM sample application.

To get started, create an empty COM+ server application called Northwind CRM. Install the components from the DLLs you compiled, including CRMInvoice.dll, Northwind_Invoice.dll, Northwind_Credit.dll, and Northwind_Order.dll. After you install the Northwind_Order.dll, notice that it generates two components in the Northwind CRM COM+ application: Northwind_Order.Order and Northwind_Order.Order2. Because the Northwind_Order.Order component already exists in the Northwind COM+ application you built in the preceding chapter, delete it from the Northwind CRM COM+ application. Figure 7.20 shows the two COM+ applications along with the components in each application.

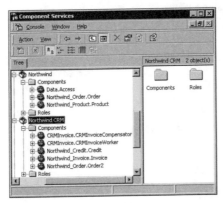

Figure 7.20: *The Northwind and Northwind CRM COM+ applications.*

Next, you need to enable the CRM for the Northwind CRM COM+ application. To do so, right-click the Northwind CRM application in Component Services, choose Properties, click the Advanced tab, and then select the Enable Compensating Resource Managers check box (see Figure 7.2).

As soon as you check this option and close the Properties page, COM+ automatically creates a CRM log file and places it in the same directory as the DTC log file (see Figure 7.21). The CRM log filename is the Application ID of the CRM COM+ application with the extension .crmlog.

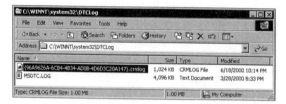

Figure 7.21: A CRM log file is created.

NOTE

If your application uses CRM, make certain that the Enable Compensating Resource Manager option is checked. Otherwise, the calls to CRM will fail.

Earlier in this chapter, you learned that you need to disable the JIT (Just-in-time activation) for the CRM Compensator. To do so, right-click the CRMInvoice.CRMInvoiceCompensator component in Component Services, choose Properties, click the Activation tab, and deselect the Enable Just In Time Activation check box (see Figure 7.22).

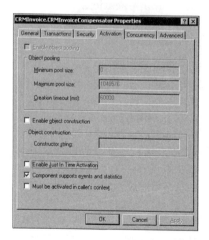

Figure 7.22: Disabling JIT for the CRMInvoice.CRMInvoiceCompensator component.

Now everything is set, and you're ready for a test drive.

Running the Sample CRM Application

To run your completed CRM application, open the modified NorthwindOrder.vbp Visual Basic project and press F5 to launch the application. Before you process an order, take a snapshot of the system to set up a baseline for the test as you did for the original Northwind ordering application in Chapter 6. In this example, the maximum Order ID is 11099. For this example, order 10 Teatime Chocolate Biscuits (ProductID 19) for customer Bólido Comidas preparadas. Before you place the order, check that you have 25 Teatime Chocolate Biscuits in stock. You choose customer Bólido Comidas preparadas because you know that the order is supposed to be canceled. Remember that when you populated the Credits table, you intentionally set bad credit for all customers whose names start with *B*. Last, make sure that the Invoice table is empty because you haven't ordered anything yet. Therefore, there is no invoice at this point.

Now let the show start. Charge $25 for the freight. Click the Place an Order button and guess what? An error message is returned, indicating that the customer has bad credit, and the order is canceled (see Figure 7.23).

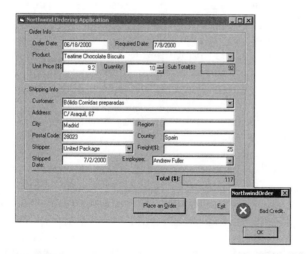

Figure 7.23: *The application returns an error that indicates Customer Bólido Comidas preparadas has bad credit.*

Now check the databases to verify that the system is in a consistent state. The maximum Order ID is still 11099, so no order has been placed. The UnitsInStock for product Teatime Chocolate Biscuits is still 25. Finally, you can see that no entry appears in the Invoice table of the Northwind_Invoice database. So, everything is in order.

Now keep everything on the order form the same but switch to another customer, Ernst Handel. Try to place the order again. This time, you get a confirmation message box that says the order has been processed. Again, check the databases. This time, you'll find a new order with Order ID 11101 in the orders table and that ProductID 19 now has 15 items in stock. Most importantly, the Invoice table in the Access database, Northwind_Invoice, also has an invoice with Order ID 11101 (see Figure 7.24).

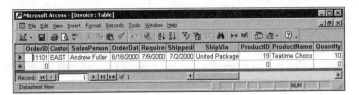

Figure 7.24: *An invoice with Order ID 11101 in the Invoice table of the Northwind_Invoice database.*

As you can see, the order made it all the way through the process. Something interesting happened, though. Notice that the Order ID is 11101. The maximum Order ID before processing the order was 11099. So, the Order ID skipped one. What happened to Order ID 11100? Well, the Order ID column in the orders table is an Identity column. It is an autoincremental number that is maintained by the system. The workflow of processing an order is as follows: creating an order, updating the stock, generating an invoice, and checking the credit. If anything goes wrong in the process, the entire thing is rolled back. The Invoice is rolled back by the CRM Compensator—it is deleted from the table by the `AbortRecordVariants()` method (see Listing 7.14). However, the orders and the products tables are reversed by the SQL Server and MS DTC. It is obvious that the order was originally entered into the orders table. When MS DTC is notified to abort the entire transaction, it deletes the orders record as the CRM did to the invoice. The DTC does not, however, reset the identity value to 11100, thus leaving a gap in the Order ID.

CRM Development Issues

In the sample application you just built, the scenario of using CRM is greatly simplified. You must be aware of several practical issues, however, when developing a real-world CRM solution.

Isolation

Unlike a normal COM+ transaction that supports all the ACID properties, CRM supports only atomicity, consistency, and durability of the transactions but does not support isolation. It is the CRM developer's responsibility to provide isolation support. For example, in the Microsoft Access database scenario, during the transaction, the Access table is not locked by default and can be accessed by any other processes. Therefore, the developer of the CRM must manage the isolation by himself.

Recovery

Recovery is the process of completing any interrupted transactions due to abnormalities such as a system failure. When a server process with CRM enabled restarts, the CRM infrastructure locates the CRM log file using the Application ID of the COM+ application. If it detects any uncompleted transactions, it consults the MS DTC for the transaction outcome. It then creates a CRM Compensator to commit or abort the transaction. The CRM Worker must handle the "Recovery in progress" situation by checking the XACT_E_RECOVERYINPROGRESS return code.

The CRM Compensator should also be designed to keep the recovery time as short as possible so that the CRM server application is not blocked out for too long to start a new CRMWorker.

Idempotence

A CRM Compensator might receive the same log record more than once. Therefore, the action the CRM Compensator performs, either undo or redo, must be *idempotent*. This means no matter how many times a specific action is repeated, the result should stay the same.

Other Considerations

You also should take care of some other issues. For example, the CRM Compensator must deal with a situation in which the CRM Worker writes a record to the log without actually performing the action for any reason. The CRM Compensator must also handle cases in which the client aborts the transaction; in this situation, the MS DTC is not notified, nor is the CRM Compensator.

When developing a CRM application, you should carefully consider all the potential issues before you start building it. Beware that not all situations are suitable for a CRM solution.

Applications that can take advantage of CRM include file systems, the Windows Registry, desktop databases, and some legacy applications.

What's Next

In this chapter, you learned that CRM provides an easier way to build a resource manager and to make traditionally nontransactional resources participate in the 2-pc transaction of MS DTC. Chapter 8, "COM+ Security," will teach you how to build highly secured applications using the security services provided by COM+.

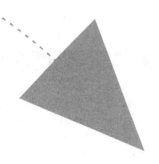

COM+ Security

Chapter 5, "Using the Component Services MMC Snap-In," briefly introduced how to configure COM+ security. In this chapter, you'll explore a rich set of security features of COM+ in great detail.

This chapter teaches you the following:

- How the COM+ security architecture works

- What role-based security is

- What authorization and authentication are

- How impersonation works

- How to implement security in three-tiered applications

- Other security issues such as audit trails, library applications security, and QC security

COM+ Security Architecture

At a high level, COM+ security requirements can be simplified into one sentence: "Who can do what to what?" Here, the *who* is referred to as the *principal*. It can be a user, a client application, or whoever makes a request for some system resources. The first *what* in the sentence means what kinds of actions the principal is allowed to perform. The second *what* is a system resource, such as data in a Relational Database Management System (RDBMS). The governing mechanism as to "Who can do what to what" is referred to as a *security policy*. A facility that ensures a security policy is enforced is referred to as a *reference monitor*.

Figure 8.1 illustrates a high level of the COM+ security architecture.

EXAMPLE

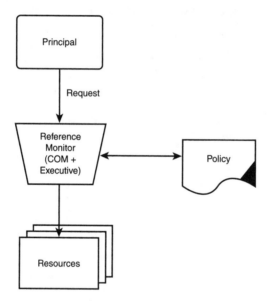

Figure 8.1: *COM+ security architecture.*

In Figure 8.1, a principal requests to do something to the resources through the reference monitor. The reference monitor, the COM+ Executive in this case, checks against a security policy to see whether the request is allowed (a process called *authorization* that will be discussed later in this chapter).

In this chapter, you'll explore how COM+ implements this security architecture to provide a declarative, automatic security service. You'll also learn how to programmatically customize and extend the COM+ security infrastructure to meet the specific security needs of your applications.

Role-Based Security

The automatic security services provided by COM+, which are based on the successful security model introduced in Microsoft Transaction Server (MTS), greatly simplify the otherwise daunting task of implementing sophisticated security mechanisms for distributed applications. At the core of the COM+ security model is role-based security.

A *role* is a logical grouping of users who share the same security privilege. A role is usually mapped to a specific type of user of your application. For example, a banking application might have bank clerks, tellers, and managers. So, you can create three corresponding roles—Clerks, Tellers, and Managers—that map to these three groups of users. Each individual user account can then be assigned to a specific role. For example, you might assign user Joe to the Clerks role, user Mark to the Managers role, and users Jennifer and Mary to the Tellers role.

In MTS, you can define roles for an MTS package and then associate them with the components inside the MTS package. In COM+, you can associate roles to a COM+ application, the components, the interfaces, all the way down to the methods of each interface.

Designing Roles

The process of defining and categorizing users is a very important step in the design and analysis of an application (or a project), especially when security is one of the major concerns. Let's look at the security requirement/user profile part of a design document for a *commission tracking system* to see how to fulfill the security requirements of the application. This commission tracking system tracks information on consultants for an IT staffing company. This information includes their pay rates, billable hours, and so on and applies some business rules to the data to calculate commissions for recruiters and account managers. It also supports flexible reporting that will facilitate the statistic commission analysis and tracking.

The following statements are abstracted from the design document. They describe the users and their privileges in this commission tracking system:

1. *Recruiters* can enter, modify, and review the basic information of the consultants.

2. *Account Managers* can enter, modify, and review the billing information of the consultants.

3. *Time Sheet Data Entry Personnel* can enter, modify, and review billable-hour information.

4. *Human Resource Personnel* can run *Headcount Reports* for all recruiters and account managers.

5. *Financial Personnel* can run *Commission Reports* for all recruiters and account managers.

6. A Recruiter can run *Commission Reports* only for his or her own commission.

7. An Account Manager can run *Commission Reports* only for his or her commission.

Statements 1 through 5 are suitable for using roles because they clearly define the users and what kinds of actions they can perform in the commission tracking system. You can directly map these users into corresponding roles.

The last two statements, however, are not suitable for using role-based security because the access decision relies on the characteristics of a particular piece of data. In this case, security checking must often be performed at the database level or using other mechanisms, such as parameterized stored procedures, that you'll learn about later in this chapter.

Using Roles to Authorize Clients

You can use role-based security to provide an *authorization* mechanism that enforces a specific security policy. That is, you can define which role can perform what kinds of operations to what resources. When the application runs, COM+ will enforce the security policy by conducting role checks.

CREATING ROLES

You can create roles administratively by using the Component Services snap-in or programmatically by using the scriptable COM+ administration object model. You'll learn how to declare roles in Visual Basic code in Chapter 11, "Administering COM+ Applications Programmatically." This section demonstrates how you can declare roles by using the Components Services snap-in.

EXAMPLE

From the Component Services snap-in, create an empty COM+ server application called **Commission Tracking**. Expand the Commission Tracking COM+ application you just created, right-click the Roles folder, and choose New, Role, as shown in Figure 8.2.

Enter **Recruiters** as the name of the new role; then click OK. In the same manner, create four other roles—Account Managers, Time Sheet Clerks, HR Personnel, and Financial Personnel—as shown in Figure 8.3.

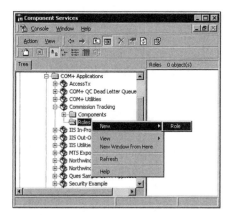

Figure 8.2: Declaring a new role in Component Services.

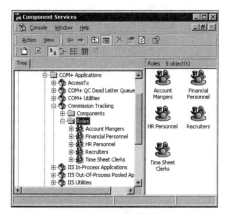

Figure 8.3: Different roles in the Commission Tracking application.

After creating the roles, you can assign user accounts to appropriate roles. For this example, assign user pli to the Financial Personnel role. To assign accounts, expand the Financial Personnel folder under the Roles folder, right-click the Users folder, and choose New, User, as shown in Figure 8.4.

When the Select Users or Groups dialog box appears, select pli from the users list at the top of the dialog box and click the Add button. The user pli then appears at the bottom of the dialog box (see Figure 8.5).

Click OK to close the dialog box, and you will notice that the user pli has been added to the Financial Personnel role (see Figure 8.6).

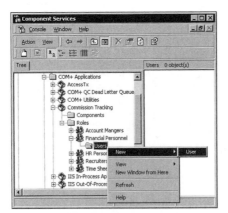

Figure 8.4: *Adding a new user to a role.*

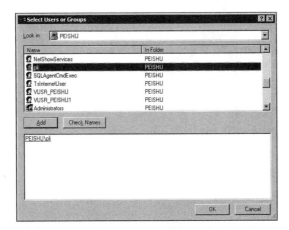

Figure 8.5: *Selecting a user from the list.*

Figure 8.6: *User pli has been assigned to the Financial Personnel role.*

ASSIGNING ROLES

EXAMPLE

In COM+, you can assign roles at three different levels: component, interface, and method. To see how to assign a role to an appropriate level, create three business objects (components) for your commission tracking system. Figures 8.7 through 8.9 show the interface and methods of these components.

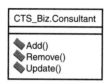

Figure 8.7: *The* `CTS_Biz.Consultant` *component has three methods:* `Add()`, `Remove()`, *and* `Update()`.

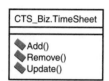

Figure 8.8: *The* `CTS_Biz.TimeSheet` *component has three methods:* `Add()`, `Remove()`, *and* `Update()`.

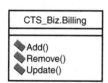

Figure 8.9: *The* `CTS_Biz.Billing` *component has three methods:* `Add()`, `Remove()`, *and* `Update()`.

These business components are responsible for adding, deleting, or updating the consultants, time sheets, and billing information.

Now install these components into the Commission Tracking COM+ application, as shown in Figure 8.10.

Now you can assign different roles to the appropriate components. Recruiters can access consultants' information, so you can assign the Recruiter role to the `CTS_Biz.Consultant` component. In this case, assigning the role at the component level is enough. But you can assign the role all the way to the method level to see the capabilities of the COM+ role-based security service.

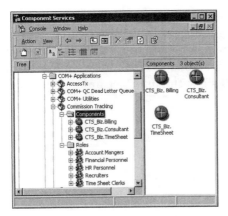

Figure 8.10: The `CTS_Biz` *components in the Commission Tracking COM+ application.*

NOTE

Role assignments are inherited down the natural chain of inclusion. That is, if you assign a role to a component, it is implicitly assigned to every interface and method exposed by that component. In this example, you explicitly assign a role to a component, an interface, and methods solely for the purpose of demonstration.

NOTE

Before you assign roles, make sure that you enable access checking at the COM+ application level (see Figure 8.11).

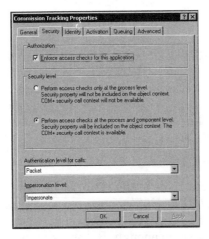

Figure 8.11: Enabling access checking for the Commission Tracking COM+ application.

To assign the Recruiter role to the CTS_Biz.Consultant component, right-click the CTS_Biz.Consultant component folder in the Component Services snap-in and select Properties. Click the Security tab on the Properties page and select Recruiters from the Roles Explicitly Set for Selected Item(s) list, as shown in Figure 8.12.

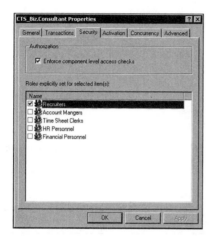

Figure 8.12: *Assigning the Recruiters role to the* CTS_Biz.Consultant *component.*

In a similar fashion, you can assign the Recruiter role to the _Consultant interface or any of its methods (Add, Remove, or Update), as shown in Figures 8.13 and 8.14.

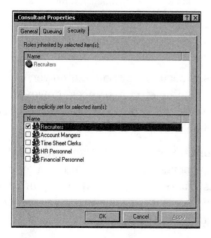

Figure 8.13: *Assigning the Recruiters role to the* _Consultant *interface.*

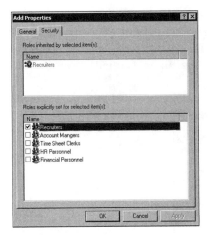

Figure 8.14: *Assigning the Recruiters role to the* `Add()` *method.*

NOTE

In Figures 8.13 and 8.14, the Recruiters role appears in the Roles Inherited by Selected Item(s) section, as explained earlier.

TIP

When you compile your COM component to an ActiveX DLL (or ActiveX EXE), Visual Basic will append an underscore "_" to the default interfaces. For example, the Consultant interface becomes _Consultant in OLE Viewer or in COM+ Component Services snap-in. Strictly speaking, a default interface (such as the Consultant interface) is not an "interface" because it carries implementation. This is not allowed in other programming languages, such as C++, in which you must separate the interface from the implementation.

PROGRAMMING ROLE-BASED SECURITY

COM+ declarative role-based security provides a powerful means for implementing security policies. In some circumstances, however, you may want to implement more flexible and yet more powerful security solutions in code based on COM+ role-based security.

EXAMPLE

For example, in the commission tracking system, the HR Personnel are permitted to run Head Count reports, and the Financial Personnel are allowed to run Commission reports. To examine the capability of programmatically controlled COM+ role-based security, create the three components shown in Figure 8.15 to implement the reporting functionality.

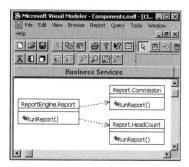

Figure 8.15: *The COM components that implemented the reporting functionality in the commission tracking system.*

As you can see from Figure 8.15, one report engine component, ReportEngine.Report, supports a single method, RunReport(). The report engine interacts with two other reporting components to process different reports. The Report.Commission and Report.HeadCount components are responsible for processing Commission reports and HeadCount reports, respectively. Each reporting component also supports a RunReport() method. In this example, the implementations of RunReport at each reporting component (Report.Commission or Report.HeadCount) are similar. They simply write a message to the event log, indicating a specific type of report has been generated (see Listing 8.1).

Listing 8.1 The RunReport() Methods of Report.Commission and Report.HeadCount

```
'=========================================================
'The RunReport() method of the Report.HeadCount object
'=========================================================
Public Function RunReport() As Boolean
    'You can implement the actual code here
    'to process the Commission reports

    'Here we simply write to the event log,
    'indicating that we have generated a HeadCount report.

    App.LogEvent "A HeadCount Report is created!"
End Function


'=========================================================
'The RunReport() method of the Report.Commission object
'=========================================================
Public Function RunReport() As Boolean
```

Listing 8.1 continued

```
'You can implement the actual code here
'to process the Commission reports

'Here we simply write to the event log,
'indicating that we have generated a Commission report.

App.LogEvent "A Commission Report is created!"
End Function
```

EXAMPLE

The responsibility of the report engine, `ReportEngine.Report`, is to see whether the caller is in a specific role that is permitted to run a specific report. If the caller belongs to one of the two roles—either HR Personnel or Financial Personnel, for example—the `RunReport()` method initializes an appropriate reporting component to process the report the caller is granted to run. Listing 8.2 shows the `RunReport()` method of the `ReportEngine.Report` component.

Listing 8.2 The `RunReport()` Method of `ReportEngine.Report`

```
Public Function RunReport() As Boolean
    On Error GoTo RunReport_Err
    Dim oSecCallContext As SecurityCallContext
    Dim oReport As Object

    'Create an instance of SecurityCallContext.
    Set oSecCallContext = GetSecurityCallContext()

    If oSecCallContext.IsCallerInRole("HR Personnel") Then
        'If the caller is in HR Personnel role, she
        'should be able to run the HeadCount reports.
        Set oReport = CreateObject("Report.HeadCount")
        'Process the report.
        oReport.RunReport
        Set oReport = Nothing
    ElseIf oSecCallContext.IsCallerInRole("Financial Personnel") Then
        'If the caller is in Financial Personnel role, he
        'should be able to run the Commission reports.
        Set oReport = CreateObject("Report.Commission")
        'Process the report.
        oReport.RunReport
        Set oReport = Nothing
    Else
        'Otherwise we raise an error, indicating the caller is
        'in neither roles that is permitted to run reports
        Err.Raise Number:=vbObjectError + 512 + 1, _
                Source:="ReportEngine.RunReport", _
```

Listing 8.2 continued

```
                Description:="You are not permitted to run reports!"
        Exit Function
    End If

    Exit Function
RunReport_Err:
    Err.Raise Err.Number
End Function
```

You then can install the three components into the Commission Tracking
COM+ application (see Figure 8.16).

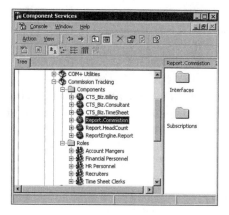

Figure 8.16: *Installing the three reporting components into the Commission
Tracking COM+ application.*

Now it's time to test the code. Start a standard Visual Basic EXE project,
name it **TestingSecurity**, and name the form **frmTestingSecurity**. Then set
a reference to the report engine, as shown in Figure 8.17.

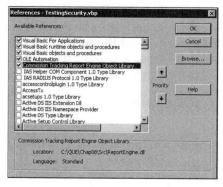

Figure 8.17: *Setting a reference to the report engine in the testing project.*

Place a command button on the form and name it **cmdRunReport**. Then add the code in Listing 8.3 in the Click event procedure of the command button.

Listing 8.3 The Click Event Procedure of the Command Button

```
Private Sub cmdRunReport_Click()
    On Error GoTo Report_Err
    Screen.MousePointer = vbHourglass
    Dim oReport As Object ' ReportEngine.Report object
    Set oReport = CreateObject("ReportEngine.Report")
    oReport.RunReport
    Set oReport = Nothing
    Screen.MousePointer = vbDefault
    MsgBox "Report has been generated!"
    Exit Sub
Report_Err:
    Screen.MousePointer = vbDefault
    MsgBox Err.Description
End Function
```

Now press F5 to start the testing application and then click the command button. You get the error message Permission denied (see Figure 8.18).

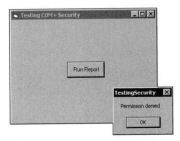

Figure 8.18: *Permission denied error message.*

So what happened? Well, you haven't assigned an appropriate role to the report engine component yet. Remember that you assigned user pli to the Financial Personnel role, which is permitted to run Commission reports. Now assign both the HR Personnel and Financial Personnel roles to the ReportEngine.Report component (see Figure 8.19) and try to run the testing application again.

This time, you get a Report has been generated confirmation message (see Figure 8.20).

Now you can verify this report by checking the event log. Figure 8.21 shows the result.

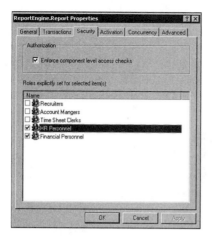

Figure 8.19: *Assigning roles to the* ReportEngine.Report *component.*

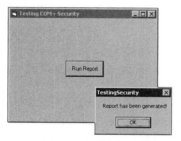

Figure 8.20: *A message box indicates that the report has been generated.*

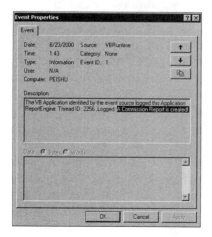

Figure 8.21: *A message in the event log confirms the result.*

Now remove the user pli (which is the account you logged in earlier) from the Financial Personnel role, add it to the HR Personnel role, and try the testing application. Again, you get a confirmation message like the one in Figure 8.20. If you check the event log, however, you will find that this time a HeadCount report has been generated instead of the Commission report (see Figure 8.22).

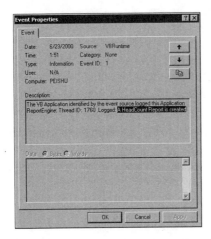

Figure 8.22: *After you reassign the user pli to the HR Personnel role, a HeadCount report is generated instead.*

Now go to the extreme by reassigning the user pli to the Recruiters role and add the Recruiters role to the ReportEngine.Report component (see Figure 8.23). Then try the testing application again.

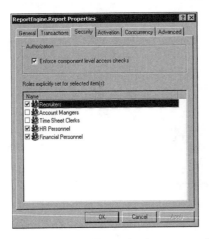

Figure 8.23: *Reassigning user pli to the Recruiters role and adding the Recruiters role to the ReportEngine.Report component.*

This time, you get a customized error message (see Figure 8.24), as defined in Listing 8.2, because the Recruiters role falls into the `Else` part of the `If...ElseIF...Else...End If` structure of the listing and the error is raised.

Figure 8.24: *A customized error is returned.*

Authorization Versus Authentication

In the preceding sections, you learned how to use the COM+ role-based security model to authorize clients. The process that controls what actions a client can perform on which server resources is known as *authorization*. Before you can authorize clients, however, you should be able to verify that a client is actually who he claims he is. This process of verifying the authenticity of a claim of identity is referred as *authentication*. In COM+, authentication is an automatic service provided by Windows 2000, and it is completely transparent to the application. As a developer, you just need to set the authentication level of the COM+ application. Authentication can be done by both the server and client. The server and client authenticate each other. Server authentication is more important than client authentication, however. Refer to Table 5.2 in Chapter 5 for an explanation of the different authentication levels.

EXAMPLE

To configure the authentication level for the server (the COM+ application, in this case), right-click the COM+ application and select Properties. Click the Security tab of the Properties page and select an authentication level from the drop-down list. The default authentication level for the COM+ application is Packet (see Figure 8.25).

To set the authentication level for a client, you need to run the DCOM configuration utility, Dcomcnfg.exe, by choosing Start, Run. Click the Default Properties tab. The default authentication level for a client is Connect (see Figure 8.26).

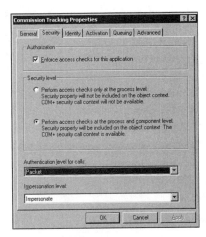

Figure 8.25: Configuring the authentication level for a COM+ application.

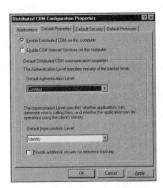

Figure 8.26: Configuring the authentication level for a client using the DCOM configuration utility, Dcomcnfg.exe.

If the client and the server are set to different authentication levels, COM+ negotiates the two authentication levels based on the following formula:

Final Authentication Level = Maximum(Client, Server)

Impersonation

Impersonation is the ability of a thread to execute in a security context that is different from the context of the process that owns the thread. Impersonation across the network is called *delegation*. The server uses an access token that represents the client's credentials so that it can access exactly the same resources as the client.

Impersonating Clients

EXAMPLE

In some scenarios, a server application may try to access resources under the identity of its client. The access check is thus performed against the client's identity instead of the server's. This action is known as *impersonating the client*. Figure 8.27 illustrates impersonation and delegation.

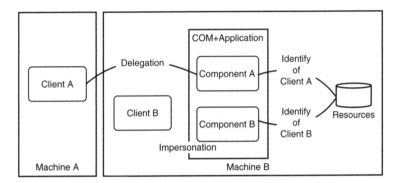

Figure 8.27: *An example of impersonation and delegation.*

In Figure 8.27, when Client A calls Component A in the COM+ application whose impersonation level is set to Impersonate (the default—refer to Figure 8.11), delegation is used because this is a cross machine call. The call to Component B from Client B is impersonation because they are on the same machine. To the resource (a relational database, for example), Component A has Client A's identity, whereas Component B becomes Client B.

Cloaking

During impersonation/delegation, the server can mask its own identity when making calls on the client's behalf; this capability is known as *cloaking*.

Cloaking can be either static or dynamic. In static cloaking, the original client identity, realized as the server access token, can be presented once to a downstream server on the first call, and the same thread token will be used on all subsequent method calls. In dynamic cloaking, on the other hand, the original client identity is resolved as the server thread token on a per-call basis to the downstream server. Whereas this "late resolving" feature of dynamic cloaking offers more flexibility than static cloaking, it also results in considerable performance overhead.

Security in Three-Tiered Applications

Implementing a sound security mechanism in a three-tiered application becomes a little tricky. Due to the distributed nature of such an application, you can enforce security in the middle tier, the database, or both places. The choice you make can have significant implications on the complexity, performance, and scalability of the three-tiered application. The following sections compare and contrast the pros and cons of each strategy and present you with several typical security scenarios for three-tiered applications.

Security at the Middle Tier

Generally speaking, the middle tier is a good place to enforce security. By enforcing it here, you can leverage the automatic security services provided by COM+. When you set securities at the middle tier, you can simplify the authentication at the database level. To the database, the COM+ application that hosts your components in the middle tier becomes the sole identity it needs to authenticate. Because user credentials are unified in this case, resources such as database connections can be pooled to improve scalability. This approach can often optimize data access as well, thus improving performance. Using COM+ role-based security also greatly simplifies the implementation and administration of security, making the solution more durable.

The downside of enforcing security at the middle tier, though, is that in some circumstances role-based security mechanisms alone are not sufficient. In these situations, you should consider other alternatives.

Applications using this security strategy fall into the *trusted server scenario*.

Security at the Database

Enforcing security at the database level has become standard for legacy two-tiered client/server applications. This strategy works only in situations in which the data is intricately bound to very small classes of users, and those relationships must be somehow reflected within the data itself. For example, security requirements 6 and 7 of the Commission Tracking application you saw earlier in this chapter tie the user and the data together in the security policy.

Enforcing security at the database level presents many drawbacks. Impersonating clients at the database is usually a very slow process, and because each client (user) logs on under its own security credential, there is no way to preserve server resources such as database connections; they cannot be pooled. Therefore, enforcing security at the database level has a significant impact on the performance and scalability of the application.

Applications using this security strategy belong to the *impersonation scenario*.

Mixed Security Scenarios

Both trusted server scenarios are usually preferable to the impersonation scenario in most cases. In reality, however, you will often find that you need to implement both strategies in your application, depending on the specific security requirements of the application.

Let's go back to the Commission Tracking example. In previous sections, you learned how to fulfill most security requirements of the commission tracking system—namely, requirements 1 through 5, as you saw earlier. Security requirements 6 and 7, however, cannot be met by role-based security alone. One of the solutions is to impersonate individual users at the database back end and use stored procedures at the database to selectively return the filtered data according to user credentials, such as user IDs. An alternative to impersonating individual users is to use the application logic to authorize users. For example, you can create a Users table in the database and store application-specific user accounts in it to handle user logins. This way, you can implement specific security features by using stored procedures and application-specific logic yet leverage the role-based security service provided by COM+.

Other Security Considerations

So far, you've learned about the basic security features provided by COM+. The following sections briefly discuss other security issues of COM+ applications.

Audit Trails

Listing 8.2 used the `SecurityCallContext` object of the COM+ Services Type Library to check whether a user was in a specific role and, based on the results, to decide whether the user should perform certain activities.

EXAMPLE

In addition to `SecurityCallContext`, COM+ provides a few more security-related objects and interfaces that allow you to perform several security functions programmatically. For example, you can use the `Security` property of the current object's `ObjectContext` to identify the direct caller and original callers of the method call. This way, you can track all the upstream callers down the entire calling chain, providing a great way to implement audit trails in your application. The code fragments in Listing 8.4 show

how to retrieve the direct caller and original caller information by using `ObjectContext`.

Listing 8.4   Retrieving Caller Information Using `ObjectContext`

```
Public Function ComponentDirectCaller() As String
    Dim oObjectContext As ObjectContext

    Set oObjectContext = GetObjectContext()
    ComponentDirectCaller =
oObjectContext.Security.GetDirectCallerName()

End Function

Public Function ComponentOriginalCaller() As String

    Dim oObjectContext As ObjectContext

    Set oObjectContext = GetObjectContext()
    ComponentOriginalCaller =
oObjectContext.Security.GetOriginalCallerName()

End Function
```

Security for Library Applications

Because library applications run in the client's process, which may have its own security settings, security for library applications requires special considerations.

Library applications use the security access token of the client process; they don't have their own user identity. Therefore, a library application has the same privileges as the client. Library applications do not perform process-level security checking. They can use only component-level access checking. You can not impersonate library applications; you can impersonate only the client that hosts library applications.

Security for Queued Components (QC)

Queued Components (QC) have particular security issues that will be discussed in the next chapter.

What's Next

This chapter discussed the automatic security services provided by COM+. Chapter 9, "Queued Components," will introduce you to one of the most exciting new features of COM+. By using the Queued Component architecture, you can develop powerful asynchronous processing applications in much the same way as you do in DCOM.

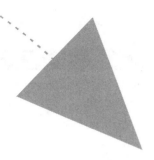

Queued Components

Chapter 3, "Introduction to Microsoft Message Queuing Services (MSMQ)," showed you how to use the asynchronous programming model of MSMQ to improve the availability and robustness of distributed applications. In this chapter, you'll learn about one of the key features provided by COM+: Queued Components, or QC.

This chapter teaches you the following:

- The basics of Queued Components
- How to develop Queued Components
- How to handle exceptions in Queued Components
- Security in Queued Components

Introduction to Queued Components

To better understand Queued Components (QC), let's take a moment to review some limitations of DCOM and MSMQ technologies.

DCOM Limitations

Using DCOM, a client can transparently invoke a method of a COM object that resides on a remote machine. The client doesn't care about exactly where the COM object resides. The client will treat the remote COM object as if it resides at the same process. DCOM takes care of this. Although the location transparency offered by the DCOM protocol greatly simplifies the programming model from the client perspective, it has its own limitations. The biggest problem with the DCOM programming paradigm is its synchronous processing model. When using DCOM, all the parties involved in a process must be available at the same time. The lifetime of the server (the COM object in this case) is completely controlled by the client. The server is tied up for the entire duration between the first line and last line of the client code. As you can see, the DCOM programming model offers poor availability, reliability, and scalability.

What About MSMQ?

As you learned in Chapter 3, MSMQ resolves the availability, reliability, and scalability issues of the DCOM programming model and improves the robustness and fault tolerance of distributed applications. A typical MSMQ scenario is illustrated in Figure 3.6 of Chapter 3. To use MSMQ (or any message queuing product for that matter) in your application, however, you have a lot of responsibilities as a developer. Typically, you need to take care of all the following:

- Understanding the underlying message queuing software as well as the appropriate APIs that allow you to send, receive, and manipulate the messages processed by the message queuing software

- Sending the message to the queue

- Designing the format of the message being passed

- Developing a receiver that will listen to the queue for incoming messages, dequeue the message, and invoke appropriate components to process the messages

- Handling bad message processing

Is it possible for the underlying infrastructure, such as COM+, to take care of most of the responsibilities listed here so that, as a developer, you need only focus on resolving business problems instead of plumbing code? That's exactly what the Queued Components services of COM+ are designed to do.

Queued Components Architecture

Figure 9.1 illustrates the Queued Components architecture.

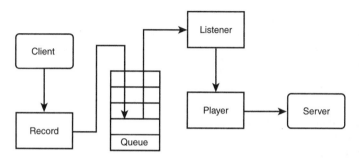

Figure 9.1: *The Queued Components architecture.*

In a Queued Components environment, when a client makes a call to the server (a Queued Component), the call is actually made to a QC recorder. The recorder records the call from the client and marshals the data along with the information about the queueable interfaces of the server component, the client's security context, and so on into an MSMQ message and sends it to a queue. On the server side, COM+ provides a queue listener and a message player. The listener watches the queue for any incoming messages, receives the messages from the queue, and passes them to the player. The player then invokes the server component, unmarshals the message, and makes the method call to the server component. In this architecture, the server component is decoupled from the client, and the processing is completely asynchronous.

However, all the complex activities such as call recording, data marshaling and unmarshaling, message passing, and object invoking are handled by the QC services of COM+ behind the scenes and are transparent to both the client and server component. As an application developer, you are responsible for building the server component and configuring its interface and the COM+ application that hosts the component as queueable. That's pretty much all you need to do. You need to use a specific syntax in the client to instantiate the server component. And there are some constraints for building the server components. You'll learn about these issues later in this chapter.

The Benefits of Queued Components

The Queued Components architecture provides the asynchronous processing advantages of message queuing, the simplicity of DCOM, and the declarative features of COM+. It offers a number of benefits, such as availability, scalability, reliability, robustness, and server scheduling.

AVAILABILITY

The asynchronous capability of the underlying message queuing system of Queued Components improves the server component availability. The client can now continuously take requests without having to ensure that the server component is running. All the calls to the server component are queued for processing as soon as the server component is available. For example, an online ordering system can take orders from customers even though the server that processes the orders may or may not be available immediately.

SCALABILITY

In the Queued Components system, the server component is decoupled from the client. After making a call, the client no longer has to wait until the server finishes processing; it can immediately turn around to serve other requests. Therefore, scalability is greatly improved. This capability is especially important for Web-based applications. The Internet Information Server (IIS) supports only a limited number of client threads that can be executed simultaneously, somewhere between 20 to 50. Consider the online ordering application; there can be a maximum of only 50 instances of the Order object (the server component) running at a given time. Therefore, shortening the lifetime of a server component means it can serve more requests in a given time period.

NOTE

IIS implemented a thread pooling mechanism to support a maximum number of concurrent clients. The size of the thread pool is configurable through a registry setting. In IIS 4.0, the default thread pool size is 10; you can finely tune this default pool size between 5 and 20. In IIS 5.0, the default thread pool size is 25 and the recommended maximum thread pool size is 100.

For information about thread pooling of IIS 4.0, please refer to Ted Pattison's article, "IIS Threading and State Management," available at http://www.microsoft.com/Mind/0299/basics/basics0299.htm. For information about threading pooling of IIS 5.0, see the Microsoft Knowledge Base article, "How to Tune the ASPProcessorThreadMax," Q238583, available from Microsoft Support at http://support.microsoft.com/support/kb/articles/Q238/5/83.ASP.

RELIABILITY AND ROBUSTNESS

When the message queuing services are used, the delivery of the message (the call in this case) is guaranteed. In case of a server failure, the transactions are automatically rolled back, so the message doesn't get lost.

OFFLINE SUPPORT

Queued Components can support disconnect scenarios in which sales representatives use mobile computing devices, such as laptops, notebooks, and palm computers, to take orders offline and later connect to the server to process the orders.

SERVER SCHEDULING

In a Queued Components environment, the server component operates independently of the client. This architecture separates time-critical tasks from non–time-critical ones and allows the non–time-critical tasks to be completed at a later, off-peak period. In the online ordering scenario, taking order requests is a time-critical operation, whereas processing the order is not. On the other hand, processing orders usually takes longer than taking the order requests. For a Web-based online ordering application, the actual time of taking the order request usually starts when a customer clicks the Submit button. If the application is designed using Queued Components, as far as the customer is concerned, the order is complete as soon as the Web server receives the request. However, processing orders may involve several processes, such as checking inventory, verifying customers' credit, generating invoices, and arranging shipping. So processing orders could be a very time-consuming process compared to taking orders. By separating the order taking and order processing into two independent processes, you can allow the order requests to build up (queue) so that the server component can process them at its own pace.

Queued Components and Transactions

In the loosely coupled, asynchronous environment of Queued Components, transactions are handled differently from the real-time scenarios of COM and DCOM. When you design a Queued-Components–enabled application with transaction requirements, you need to change your mindset a little bit. Let's look at an ordering/shipping application to see how the transactions are used in both the DCOM and Queued Components scenarios.

Say that the ordering/shipping application has two components, an Order object and a Shipping object, running on two different machines. A client sends a request to the Order object, which inserts a row in the Order database, and then sends a shipping request to the Shipping object. The

Shipping object then processes the shipping and updates the Shipping database. Figures 9.2 and 9.3 illustrate the transaction boundaries of this ordering/shipping application in both the DCOM and QC scenarios.

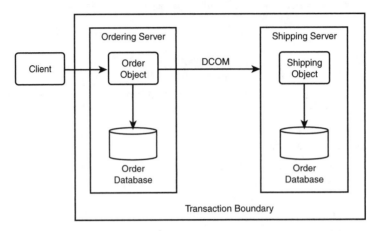

Figure 9.2: *Transaction boundary of the ordering/shipping application in DCOM.*

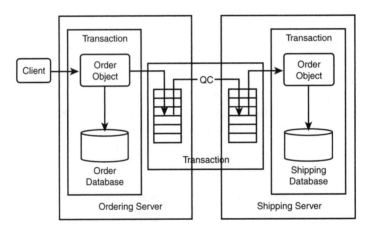

Figure 9.3: *Transaction boundaries of the ordering/shipping application in QC.*

In the DCOM scenario shown in Figure 9.2, both ordering and shipping processes are wrapped into a single transaction. Each subprocess, including the network connection, is a possible point of failure. So, DCOM is not a very robust solution in this scenario.

In the QC scenario shown in Figure 9.3, however, the single transaction in DCOM is split into three individual transactions. The first transaction involves the Order object and the Order database. MSMQ moves the message from one queue to another queue, using its transacted capabilities to guarantee delivery only once. If the order request is successfully taken, the Order database is updated, and the message is sent to the input queue. If the message does not reach the queue, it is aborted and the database update is rolled back. The second transaction in the QC scenario happens when the queue manager discovers that the server is available, perhaps at a later time. A messaging mover moves the message from the client queue manager to the server queue manager. The third transaction involves the Shipping object and the Shipping database. If the shipper component fails in the middle of the transaction, the database update is rolled back, and the message is not lost. Therefore, the data integrity is protected. These three transactions are independent of one another. In this scenario, the Shipping object is a Queued Component, and the Order object is its client.

NOTE

If the transaction attribute of the Queued Component is set to Required or Supported, the MSMQ queue is transacted. In this case, MSMQ accepts delivery of the message only if the client-side transaction commits. If the transaction attribute of the Queued Component is configured as Requires New, MSMQ accepts the message even if the client-side transaction aborts.

Poison Messages

Sometimes a message cannot be processed for some reason, such as a problem with the server or queuing system. This unprocessed message is called a *poison message*. When a poison message is discovered, the transaction is rolled back, and the message is put back on the top of the queue. It is dequeued again if the same condition is repeated. This message can continue looping for some time until the problem is corrected. Queued Components handle poison messages by a series of retries. If all the retries are exhausted, the message is moved to a final resting queue. At that point, the Queued Components search for an exception class; if they find an exception class, they invoke the FinalServerRetry() or FinalClientRetry() method of the IPlayBackControl interface that the exception class implements, depending on whether the problem is on the client side or on the server side. The exception handling mechanism of Queued Components provides a powerful means by which you can be quickly notified about a poison message, and it allows you to implement creative solutions to correct problems. You'll learn about exception handling and exception classes later in this chapter.

Developing Queued Components

Developing Queued Components is actually a straightforward process. You construct a Queued Component that is basically an ActiveX DLL with some constraints, which you'll learn about later. Then you configure the appropriate interfaces of the component so that it can be queued. You also need to configure the COM+ application that hosts your Queued Components so that it can be queued and enable the listing to MSMQ for incoming Queued Components messages. You can use either the Component Services snap-in or the scriptable COM+ Administrative object model to perform configuration tasks. Finally, you activate the Queued Component from the client by using a special syntax of the GetObject() function.

This section walks you through the process of building a simple Queued Component and demonstrates how to invoke its method from a client. Later in this chapter, you'll enhance the Northwind ordering application you developed in Chapter 6, "Writing Transactional Components," and Chapter 7, "Compensating Resource Manager (CRM)," by adding Queued Components capability to improve the robustness and availability of the application.

Queued Components Development Constraints

Messages are delivered in one way only in Queued Components. This mechanism provides a loosely coupled relationship between the client and server component. As a result of this one-way communication, you need to follow several design constraints so that your component can be queued.

The first constraint is that to cope with the one-way communication paradigm, all the methods in your queue must have no output parameters and return values. This means that the methods have to be implemented as subroutines instead of functions, and the parameters must be declared as ByVal rather than ByRef.

In addition, restrictions are placed on the types of input parameters that can be passed to a Queued Component. The Queued Component marshals the input arguments from the client and passes them to the server component through MSMQ. This process limits the data types that can be marshaled. Simple data types, such as integers, strings, and booleans, can be marshaled easily, whereas more complex data types need special help to be marshaled.

For example, when you pass an object to a Queued Component as an input parameter, the client passes the object to the QC recorder. The recorder has to marshal the object into an MSMQ message and pass it to the listener. The listener, in turn, picks up the message and passes it to the player. The player then has to unmarshal the message and re-instantiate the object to dispatch it to the method call specified by the client. Because all the input parameters must be passed by value in Queued Components, but COM+ does not support pass-by-value semantics for standard COM objects, the object being passed must support the `IPersistStream` interface in order for the player to re-instantiate it. Because the lifetime of the server component in Queued Components is independent of the client, the object must not make assumptions about when it will be re-instantiated.

ADO recordsets and OLE DB rowsets both support the `IPersistStream` interface, so they can be passed to Queued Components. Because server-side recordsets or rowsets cannot be marshaled using `IPersistStream`, you must use client-side recordsets or rowsets. For ADO recordsets, you need to specify the `Cursorlocation` property of the recordset to `adUseClient`.

Using Visual Basic 6.0, you can build persistable objects by specifying the `Persistable` property of a class module as `1-Persistable` (see Figure 9.4).

Figure 9.4: *Setting the `Persistable` property of a class module.*

TIP

MSDN knowledge base article Q246627, "Pass Objects as Parameters to COM+ Queued Components," demonstrates how to create a persistable object in Visual Basic and pass it to a Queued Component. Search MSDN for Q246627 to obtain this article.

Building a Simple Queued Component

Now let's build a simple Queued Component to examine the process of using COM+ Queued Components. To do so, start a new ActiveX DLL project in Visual Basic and set the properties of the project as shown in Figure 9.5.

EXAMPLE

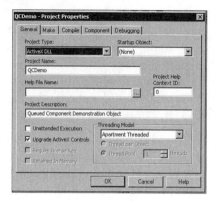

Figure 9.5: *The properties of the* QCDemo *Queued Component project.*

Rename the Class1 class module to **QC1** and add the simple RunQC() method shown in Listing 9.1.

Listing 9.1   The RunQC() Method of the QCDemo.QC1 Component

```
Public Sub RunQC()
    App.LogEvent "QC Request Received @" & Now() & "."
End Sub
```

As you can see, only one line of code in the RunQC() method of this QCDemo.QC1 component is implemented as a Public Sub. It just writes a string to the event log, indicating a QC request has been received and posting a timestamp that denotes when it was received.

Now compile the component into QCDemo.dll, and you are ready to configure your new Queued Component.

Configuring a Queued Component

To configure a Queued Component, start by invoking the Component Services snap-in and creating a new empty COM+ application called **QC Demo** (see Figure 9.6).

Right-click the QC Demo COM+ application you just created and select Properties. Click the Queuing tab of the Properties page. Then select the "Queued - This Application Can Be Reached by MSMQ Queues" check box and the "Listen - This Application, When Activated, Will Process Messages That Arrive on Its MSMQ Queue" check box, as shown in Figure 9.7.

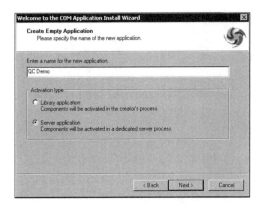

Figure 9.6: *Creating an empty COM+ application called QC Demo.*

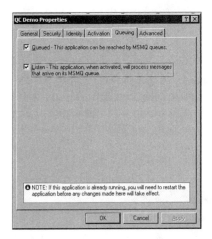

Figure 9.7: *Ensuring that the QC Demo COM+ application can be queued.*

NOTE

The MSMQ Workgroup configuration does not permit Queued Components to support application security. If you have Windows 2000 installed with the Workgroup configuration (i.e., not installed as a Domain Controller), you must disable security on each Queued Application accessed in this configuration. This includes disabling security on both the client and server applications if the application proxy has already been exported. Otherwise, you get a `Permission denied` error. To disable security for your COM+ application, right-click the application, select Properties, and then select the Security tab. Finally, change the Authentication Level for Calls setting to None (see Figure 9.8).

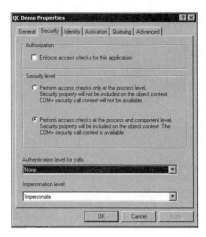

Figure 9.8: *Disabling security of the application in the Workgroup configuration.*

Now you have an empty, queueable COM+ application. It's time to install the component and configure it as queueable. To do so, expand the QC Demo COM+ application, right-click the Components folder, and then select New, Component. Next, install QCDemo.dll as a new component. Expand the QCDemo.QC1 component you just installed and select the Interfaces folder. Then right-click the _QC1 interface on the right pane and select Properties (see Figure 9.9).

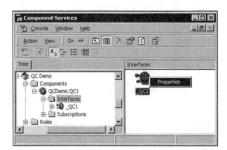

Figure 9.9: *Accessing the properties of the _QC1 interface.*

On the Properties page of the _QC1 interface, click the Queuing tab and select the Queued check box in the Queuing Properties group, as shown in Figure 9.10.

And that's it! Now you have a fully functional COM+ application that utilizes a Queued Component.

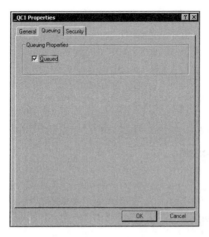

Figure 9.10: *Making the _QC1 interface queueable.*

Activating a Queued Component

To activate a Queued Component from the client, you use a pair of *monikers,* queue and new, to call the GetObject() function in Visual Basic. To create an instance of the sample QCDemo.QC1 object, you use the following syntax:

```
Dim oQC As Object
Set oQC = GetObject("queue:/new:QCDemo.QC1")
```

A *moniker* is an object that implements the IMoniker interface. It acts as a name that uniquely identifies a COM object. In the same way that a path identifies a file in the file system, a moniker identifies a COM object in the directory namespace.

THE new MONIKER

You can directly activate a component by using the GetObject() method with the new moniker. The new moniker accepts a ProgID or a CLSID (with or without braces) for the component to be activated. The new moniker can be used with any COM components that support the IClassFactory interface, not just a Queued Component. The syntax for using the new moniker is

```
Dim oQC As Object
Set oQC = GetObject("new:QCDemo.QC1")
```

or

```
Dim oQC As Object
Set oQC = GetObject("new:{73A0803F-D06F-465E-822E-24BEB7AB0735}")
```

or

```
Dim oQC As Object
Set oQC = GetObject("new:73A0803F-D06F-465E-822E-24BEB7AB0735")
```

The queue Moniker

The queue moniker is specifically used to activate a Queued Component. It accepts optional parameters that alter the properties of the message sent to MSMQ. You can also specify the destination queue for the message to be sent. Tables 9.1 and 9.2 list parameters that affect the destination queue and the MSMQ messages, respectively.

Table 9.1 **queue** *Moniker Parameters That Affect the Destination Queue*

Parameter	Description
ComputerName	Specifies the computer name portion of an MSMQ queue pathname. If this parameter is not specified, the computer name associated with the configured application is used. Refer to Chapter 3 for the syntax of the PathName property of MSMQQueueInfo.
QueueName	Specifies the queue name portion of an MSMQ queue pathname. If this parameter is not specified, the queue name associated with the configured application is used. Refer to Chapter 3 for the syntax of the PathName property of MSMQQueueInfo.
PathName	Specifies the MSMQ queue pathname. If this parameter is not specified, the MSMQ queue pathname associated with the configured application is used. Refer to Chapter 3 for the syntax of the PathName property of MSMQQueueInfo.
FormatName	Specifies the MSMQ format name—for example, DIRECT=OS:peishu\PRIVATE$\QC Demo. Refer to Chapter 3 for the syntax of the FormatName property of MSMQQueueInfo.

Table 9.2 **queue** *Moniker Parameters That Affect the MSMQ Message*

Parameter	Description
AppSpecifc	Specifies an integer that can be used to identify the message so that the receiver can filter out only the messages from a specific application.
AuthLevel	Specifies the message authentication level. An authenticated message is digitally signed and requires a certificate for the user sending the message. You can specify the AuthLevel to either MQMSG_AUTH_LEVEL_NONE(0) or MQMSG_AUTH_LEVEL_ALWAYS(1). For a Workgroup configuration, you should always use MQMSG_AUTH_LEVEL_NONE.
Delivery	Specifies the message delivery option, whether you want the message to be persistent and survive system failures and machine reboots. This value is ignored for transacted queues. Acceptable values include MQMSG_DELIVERY_EXPRESS(0) and MQMSG_DELIVERY_RECOVERABLE(1).

Table 9.2   continued

Parameter	Description
EncryptAlgorithm	Specifies the encryption algorithm to be used by MSMQ. Acceptable values include `CALG_RC2` and `CALG_RC4`.
HashAlgorithm	Specifies a cryptographic hash function. Acceptable values include `CALG_MD2`, `CALG_MD4`, `CALG_MD5`, `CALG_SHA1`, `CALG_MAC`, `CALG_SSL3_SHAMD5`, `CALG_HMAC`, and `CALG_TLS1PRF`.
Journal	Specifies the MSMQ message journal option. Acceptable values include `MQMSG_JOURNAL_NONE(0)`, `MQMSG_DEALETTER(1)`, and `MQMSG_JOURNAL (2)`.
Label	Specifies a message label string up to `MQ_MAX_MSG_LABEL_LEN` characters.
MaxTimeToReachQueue	Specifies a maximum time, in seconds, for the message to reach the queue. Acceptable values include `INFINITE` and `LONG_LIVED`.
MaxTimeToReceive	Specifies a maximum time, in seconds, for the message to be received by the target application. Acceptable values include `INFINITE` and `LONG_LIVED`.
Priority	Specifies a message priority level. Acceptable values include `MQ_MIN_PRIORITY(0)`, `MQ_MAX_PRIORITY(7)`, and `MQ_DEFAULT_PRIORITY(7)`.
PrivLevel	Specifies a privacy level used to encrypt messages. Acceptable values include `MQMSG_PRIV_LEVEL_NONE(0)`, `MQMSG_PRIV_LEVEL_BODY(2)`, `MQMSG_PRIV_LEVEL_BODY_BASE(1)`, and `MQMSG_PRIV_LEVEL_BODY_ENHANCED(3)`.
Trace	Specifies trace options used in tracing MSMQ routing. Acceptable values include `MQMSG_TRACE_NONE(0)` and `MQMSG_SEND_ROUTE_TO_REPORT_QUEUE(1)`.

For example, you can create a Queued Component by specifying an AppSpecific attribute of a message through a queue moniker parameter:

```
Dim oQC As Object
Set oQC = GetObject("queue:AppSpecific=12345/new:QCDemo.QC1")
```

Building a Client to Test the Queued Component

EXAMPLE

Now it's time to build a client application to test the QCDemo.QC1 Queued Component. First, create a standard EXE Visual Basic project and place a command button (Command1) on the form. Then add the code in Listing 9.2 to the Click event of Command1.

Listing 9.2   The Click Event Procedure of the Client Application

```
Private Sub Command1_Click()
    On Error GoTo ErrHandler
    Dim oQC As Object
    Set oQC = GetObject("queue:/new:QCDemo.QC1")
    oQC.RunQC
    Set oQC = Nothing
    MsgBox "QC request sent!"
    Exit Sub
ErrHandler:
    MsgBox Err.Description
End Sub
```

Remember that the Queued Component named QCDemo.QC1 will write a message to the event log when its RunQC() method is called. So, clean the event log before you start your testing to establish a baseline. To do so, open the Event Viewer from Start, Programs, Administrative Tools. Then select the Application folder from the left pane of the Event Viewer. Click the Action menu and select Clear All Events (see Figure 9.11).

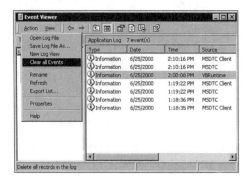

Figure 9.11: Clearing the event log.

Answer No to the dialog that asks whether you want to save the Application log before clearing it.

Now go back to the client project and press F5 to start it. When you click the command button, you get a confirmation message that says the QC request has been sent (see Figure 9.12).

Now switch back to the Event Viewer. You'll find no message appears in the event log at this point. So what's wrong?

Well, the problem has something to do with the way in which the Queued Component starts. Making method calls on a Queued Component does not execute the method immediately. Instead, the call is recorded by the QC recorder, marshaled, and sent to MSMQ. Unlike when you activate a remote component using DCOM, the Queued Component is not instantiated when the client calls a particular method. The call is converted into an MSMQ message and will stay in the application-specific queue created by the Queued Component when you configure your COM+ application to be queuedable. In this case, the Queued Component creates a queue named QC Demo, which can be viewed through the Computer Management snap-in. If you look at the queue at this point, you will see a message there (see Figure 9.13). The message is actually the marshaled method call to the Queued Component, the RunQC() of QCDemo.QC1.

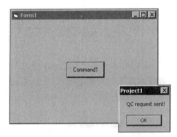

Figure 9.12: *Testing the client application.*

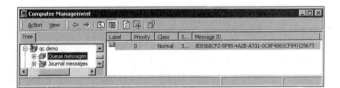

Figure 9.13: *The method call is converted into an MSMQ message and temporarily stored in the application-specific queue.*

You can activate a COM+ application containing Queued Components in several ways, including manually starting it in the Component Services snap-in, starting it by using scripting and the Windows Task Scheduler, or programmatically starting it through the COM+ Administrative SDK functions.

You'll learn about the use of scripting and programming COM+ Administrative object models in Chapter 11, "Administering COM+ Applications Programmatically." For now, start the QC Demo COM+ application by right-clicking the application in Component Services and selecting Start, as shown in Figure 9.14.

After you start the QC Demo application, notice that the message in the queue is gone. If you look at the event log now, you'll find that an information message is logged by the QDDemo.QC1 Queued Component (see Figure 9.15).

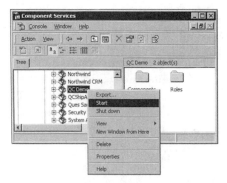

Figure 9.14: Starting the QC Demo COM+ application in Component Services.

Figure 9.15: A message has been written to the event log.

Double-click the message on the right pane of the Event Viewer to open the message. You'll see that it is the message you're looking for (see Figure 9.16).

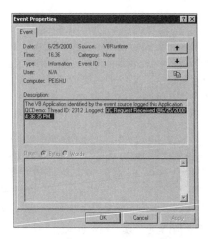

Figure 9.16: The description of the event message.

Other Considerations About Queued Components

In addition to the development constraints on Queued Components you've learned about, you need to pay attention to some other design issues, such as whether to use QC in your application, how to handle the responses to the client, whether your complete should maintain states, and so on.

QC OR NOT QC

Although using Queued Components offers a number of benefits to distributed application development, under some circumstances Queued Components may not be a durable solution. When considering whether your application can take advantage of Queued Components, you need to think in terms of *critical path* and *time-independence*. A critical path is an activity that is critical to a business. In the online ordering application, the activity of taking orders is a critical path. Activities that can be taken out of the critical path are good candidates for using Queued Components. For example, the credit card checking and shipping arrangement in an online ordering system are not part of the critical path and can take advantage of Queued Components.

Another important consideration is time-independence. If some processes can be identified as time-independent of other processes, these processes usually lend themselves to being Queued Components. For example, shipping and order processing can be processed in a time-independent manner, so you can enable queuing for the shipping component.

HANDLING RESPONSES

In some situations, a client may request a response from a server component. For example, the client placing an order may want to know the status of that order. The requests for responses are handled differently in asynchronous processing models such as Queued Components and synchronous processing systems such as DCOM. In a Queued Components application, the communication is one-way only. This means that when the server sends a response upon a request from the client, there is no guarantee that the same instance of the client will be receiving the response because the client and server components have different and usually un-overlapped lifetimes. When the server sends back the response, sometimes the original requestor is gone (being terminated, for example). Therefore, the responses from the server component are usually handled as another one-way messaging, as opposite to the requests. The server can create a response object. You'll see an example of using a `Notify` object, a Queued Component, as a response from the server later in this chapter when you look at the queueable Northwind ordering application.

Statelessness of the Components

Statelessness in Queued Components is as important as in DCOM applications. Because every method call involves message recording, data marshaling and unmarshaling, call reassembling, and so on, you should keep Queued Components as stateless as possible. That is, you should pass every piece of data as input parameters to the function call instead of using public properties. Statelessness can also improve scalability because it requires less time from the server component, thus releasing the server component to respond to more requests.

Exception Handling

If, for some reason, a message cannot be successfully delivered to its intended destination, a poison message is generated, as you learned earlier in this chapter. Queued Components handle poison messages by a series of retries. As soon as you enable queuing in your COM+ application (refer to Figure 9.7), the Queued Components generate a set of queues for your Queued Components application. In the QC Demo example, the Queued Components generated seven queues, as shown in Figure 9.17.

Figure 9.17: *Seven queues are created for the QC Demo sample application.*

The seven queues generated by the Queued Components fall into three categories:

- An application queue, also referred to as an *input queue,* for storing messages from the recorder—the qc demo queue

- Five intermediate queues used for possible retries—qc_demo_0 to qc_demo_4

- A final resting queue to place the undeliverable messages after exhausting all the retry efforts—the qc_demo_deadqueue

NOTE

The queue names are case sensitive. The name of the application-specific queue is actually *QC Demo* instead of *qc demo*. In the Computer Management snap-in, the queue names are displayed in all lowercase, so lowercase is used to refer to queue names for the sake of consistency.

Server-Side Error Handling

When a poison message is detected, the listener and player work together to handle the situation. If a transaction being played back aborts, MSMQ moves the message back to the top of the input queue. If the problem persists, the listener loops continuously through in the following pattern:

1. Dequeue the message from the queue.

2. Instantiate the object.

3. Roll back the transaction if it fails again.

4. Put the message back on top of the queue.

By default, the Queued Components create five retry queues AppName_0 to AppName_5; each retry queue allows three retries with different retry intervals, as described in Table 9.3.

Table 9.3   Retry Intervals of Each Retry Queue

Retry Queue	Retry Interval
First retry queue	1 minute
Second retry queue	2 minutes
Third retry queue	4 minutes
Fourth retry queue	8 minutes
Fifth retry queue	16 minutes

When the listener fails three retry efforts in a particular retry queue, COM+ moves the message to the next retry queue. If all the retry queues are exhausted and the problem still persists, COM+ moves the message to the final resting queue. At this point, the player issues a COM+ event to notify interested parties that the message cannot be played. If an exception class was specified for the Queued Component, the player calls the FinalServerRetry function of the IPlaybackControl interface implemented by the exception class. Exception classes will be discussed shortly.

TIP

You can selectively delete any or all the retry queues from the Computer Management snap-in to customize the retry times and intervals to fit your specific needs.

Client-Side Error Handling

Client-side failures are handled similarly to server-side failures. MSMQ can move a message to its destination queue if, for some reason, the message cannot be moved from the client to the server. Under these circumstances, the message is moved to the client-side queue manager's Xact Dead Letter queue (the "Transactional Dead-Letter Messages" system queue). The Queued Components monitor the dead letter queue. If a message has been moved, the Queued Components create an instance of the exception class, if one exists, and call the `FinalClientRetry` method of the `IPlaybackControl` interface that is implemented by the exception class.

The Exception Class

EXAMPLE

The *exception class* is an ActiveX DLL that implements the `IPlaybackControl` interface. Let's create an exception class for the QC Demo example to demonstrate how to associate the exception class to a Queued Component. Start a new ActiveX DLL project in Visual Basic, name the project **QCDemoException**, name the class module **Exception**, and then set a reference to the COM+ Services Type Library, as shown in Figure 9.18.

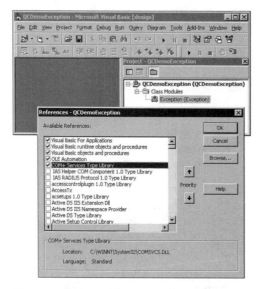

Figure 9.18: *Creating an Exception class.*

In the General Declaration section of the class module, enter the following line of code:

```
Implements IPlaybackControl
```

Click the Object drop-down list of the code window and select the `IPlaybackControl interface` to generate the skeleton of the `IPlaybackControl_FinalClientRetry()` subroutine. Select `FinalServerRetry` from the Procedure drop-down list on the top-right corner of the code window to generate the skeleton of the `IPlaybackControl_FinalServerRetry()` subroutine, as shown in Figure 9.19.

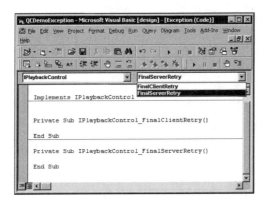

Figure 9.19: *Implementing the `IPlaybackControl` interface in the exception class.*

Now you are ready to add code to the subroutines that implements specific business logic for handling exceptions. This example simply displays a message box, indicating that either a client or a server final retry has failed. Listing 9.3 illustrates the complete code in the Exception.cls.

Listing 9.3 Functions in Exception.cls

```
Option Explicit

Implements IPlaybackControl


Private Sub IPlaybackControl_FinalClientRetry()
    MsgBox "Client retry failed for QCDemo.QC1"
End Sub

Private Sub IPlaybackControl_FinalServerRetry()
    MsgBox "Server retry failed for QCDemo.QC1"
End Sub
```

Save the project and make QCDemoException.dll. Doing so also registers the exception class into the System Registry. Now you can associate this exception class to the QC Demo Queued Component by expanding the QC Demo COM+ application folder in the Component Servers snap-in to expose the QCDemo.QC1 component. Right-click the component and select Properties. Click the Advanced tab of the Properties page, type **QCDemoException.Exception** in the Queuing Exception Class text box (see Figure 9.20), and click OK.

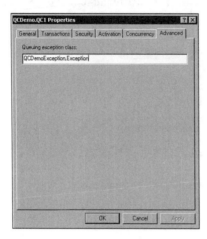

Figure 9.20: *Specifying the exception class of the* QCDemo.QC1 *component.*

You can specify either the ProgID or the CLSID of the exception class in this box.

Queued Components Security

Queued Components support role-based security and can check the role membership of their caller programmatically by calling the IsCallerInRole() or IsUserInRole() method of the SecurityCallContext object discussed in Chapter 8, "COM+ Security."

Due to the disconnected nature of the Queued Components architecture, however, the impersonation-style security, which allows a server to obtain an access token of the client, is not supported. The actual caller is not available for the server because it didn't call the server directly; the calls were marshaled by the recorder and sent to the queue as messages.

When designing security for applications that use Queued Components, you should keep this asynchronous, indirect processing mode in mind.

Making the Northwind Ordering Application Queueable

In the following sections, you'll continue to improve the Northwind Ordering application introduced in Chapter 6, "Writing Transactional Components," and enhanced in Chapter 7, "Compensating Resource

Manager (CRM)." Here, you'll add the Queued Components capability to this application.

The System Architecture

Figure 9.21 illustrates the modified architecture in which Queued Components will be used.

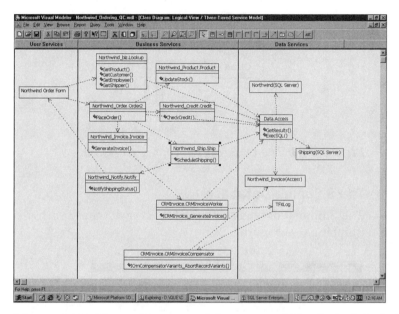

Figure 9.21: *The architecture of the proposed Northwind Ordering application with Queued Components capability.*

As you can see in Figure 9.21, you will add a couple of COM components, `Northwind_Ship.Ship` (in the center of the illustration) and `Northwind_ Notify.Notify` (on the bottom-left side of the `Northwind_Ship.Ship` component). Both are designed as Queued Components. You'll also add a SQL Server database named Shipping.

Figure 9.22 shows a simplified workflow focusing on the Queued Components.

After the `Order2` object finishes placing an order, including updating the stock and checking the credit, it calls the `ScheduleShipping()` method Queued Component, the `Ship` object. The `Ship` object is responsible for inserting a shipping record into the Shipping table of the Shipping database. Then the `Ship` object invokes a `Notify()` method of another Queued Component, the `Notify` object. The `Notify` object displays a confirmation message, indicating the shipping for a specific order has been arranged.

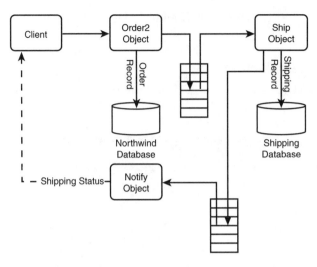

Figure 9.22: *The Ordering/Shipping workflow.*

The Shipping Database

EXAMPLE

The Shipping database is a SQL Server database with a single table named Shipping (see Figure 9.23).

Column Name	Datatype	Length	Precision	Scale	Allow Nulls	Identity	Identity Seed	Identity
ShippingID	int	4	10	0		✓	10000	1
OrderID	int	4	10	0	✓			
ProductName	varchar	80	0	0	✓			
Quantity	int	4	10	0	✓			
Shipper	varchar	40	0	0	✓			
ShippingDate	datetime	8	0	0	✓			
Customer	varchar	40	0	0	✓			
Address	varchar	60	0	0	✓			
City	varchar	15	0	0	✓			
Region	varchar	15	0	0	✓			
PostalCode	varchar	10	0	0	✓			
Country	varchar	15	0	0	✓			

Figure 9.23: *The Shipping table schema.*

Next, you need to create a stored procedure called Shipping_Schedule to facilitate the shipping scheduling. This stored procedure inserts a shipping record into the Shipping table and returns a single row and single column rowset, the ShippingID. Listing 9.4 illustrates the code of this stored procedure.

Listing 9.4 The `Shipping_Schedule` Stored Procedure

```
if exists(select * from sysobjects
        where id = object_id('Shipping_Schedule'))
 drop proc Shipping_Schedule
go

create proc Shipping_Schedule
 @OrderID int,
 @ProductName varchar(80),
 @Quantity int,
 @Shipper varchar(40),
 @ShippingDate datetime,
 @Customer varchar(40),
 @Address varchar(60),
 @City varchar(15),
 @Region varchar(15),
 @PostalCode varchar(10)=null,
 @Country varchar(15)
as
 insert Shipping
        (OrderID,
         ProductName,
         Quantity,
         Shipper,
         ShippingDate,
         Customer,
         Address,
         City,
         Region,
         PostalCode,
         Country
         )
        values
        (@OrderID,
         @ProductName,
         @Quantity,
         @Shipper,
         @ShippingDate,
         @Customer,
         @Address,
         @City,
         @Region,
         @PostalCode,
         @Country
         )

select 'ShippingID'=@@identity
go
```

You also create a DSN named Shipping that points to the Shipping database.

The Queued Components

EXAMPLE

The next step is to create an ActiveX DLL project named **Northwind_Notify** and name the class module **Notify**. Then add the NotifyShippingStatus() method in Listing 9.5.

Listing 9.5   The NotifyShippingStatus() Method of the Northwind_Notify.Notify Component

```
Public Sub NotifyShippingStatus(ByVal sShipStatus As String)
    MsgBox Prompt:=sShipStatus, Title:="Northwind_Notify.Notify"
End Sub
```

The NotifyShippingStatus() method simply displays a message about the shipping status. Now make the Northwind_Notify.dll. Create another ActiveX DLL project named **Northwind_Ship** and name the class module **Ship**. Then add the ScheduleShipping() method in Listing 9.6.

Listing 9.6   The ScheduleShipping Method of the Northwind_Ship.Ship Component

```
Public Sub ScheduleShipping(ByVal iOrderID As Integer, _
                            ByVal sProductName As String, _
                            ByVal iQuantity As Integer, _
                            ByVal sShipper As String, _
                            ByVal dShippingDate As Date, _
                            ByVal sCustomer As String, _
                            ByVal sAddress As String, _
                            ByVal sCity As String, _
                            ByVal sRegion As String, _
                            ByVal sPostalCode As String, _
                            ByVal sCountry As String)

    On Error GoTo ScheduleShipping_Err

    Dim oData      As Object 'Data.Access object.
    Dim sSQL       As String
    Dim lRows      As Long
    Dim rsShipping As New ADOR.Recordset
    Dim iShippingID As Integer
    Dim oNotify    As Object 'Northwind_Notify.Notify object
    Dim sShipStatus As String

    'Process Shipping
    sSQL = "Exec Shipping_Schedule @OrderID =" & iOrderID _
            & ", @ProductName = '" & sProductName & "'" _
            & ", @Quantity = " & iQuantity _
            & ", @Shipper = '" & sShipper & "'" _
```

Listing 9.6   continued

```
            & ", @ShippingDate = '" & dShippingDate & "'" _
            & ", @Customer = '" & sCustomer & "'" _
            & ", @Address = '" & sAddress & "'" _
            & ", @City = '" & sCity & "'" _
            & ", @Region = '" & sRegion & "'" _
            & ", @PostalCode = '" & sPostalCode & "'" _
            & ", @Country ='" & sCountry & "'"

    Set oData = CreateObject("Data.Access")

    Set rsShipping = oData.GetResult("Shipping", sSQL, lRows)
        If lRows <> 0 Then
            iShippingID = rsShipping!ShippingID
        End If
        Set oData = Nothing

    'Send Notification
    sShipStatus = "Shipping has been scheduled for OrderID " _
                & CStr(iOrderID) & vbCrLf _
                & "Shipping ID: " & CStr(iShippingID) & "."

    Set oNotify = GetObject("queue:/new:Northwind_Notify.Notify")
    oNotify.NotifyShippingStatus sShipStatus

    Exit Sub
ScheduleShipping_Err:
    App.LogEvent "Northwind_Ship.Ship Error #: " _
                & CStr(Err.Number) & vbCrLf _
                & Err.Description & "."
End Sub
```

The ScheduleShipping() method calls the stored procedure named
Shipping_Schedule to insert a shipping record into the Shipping database
and returns a shipping ID. Then it builds a message about the shipping
status and passes this message to another Queued Component,
Northwind_Notify.Notify.

Now you're ready to compile the project to make Northwind_Ship.dll.

Creating and Configuring the Queueable COM+ Application

The next step is to create an empty COM+ application, name it **Northwind
Shipping,** and mark the application, as described earlier in this chapter.
Now install the two Queued Components you built: Northwind_Notify.dll
and Northwind_Ship.dll. Enable queuing for the _Notify and _Ship interfaces, as you did earlier for the _QC1 interface in the QC Demo example.

The completed COM+ Queued Components application looks like the one in Figure 9.24.

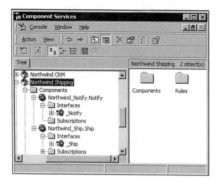

Figure 9.24: *The Northwind shipping COM+ QC application.*

Modifying Order2 Components

EXAMPLE

Now you need to modify the `PlaceOrder()` method of the `Northwind_Order.Order2` component to use the Queued Components. Listing 9.7 shows the modified code with the changes highlighted.

Listing 9.7 The Modified `PlaceOrder()` Method of `Northwind_Order.Order2` Component

```
Public Function PlaceOrder(ByVal iProductID As Integer, _
                           ByVal cUnitPrice As Currency, _
                           ByVal iQuantity As Integer, _
                           ByVal sCustomerID As String, _
                           ByVal iEmployeeID As Integer, _
                           ByVal dOrderDate As Date, _
                           ByVal dRequiredDate As Date, _
                           ByVal dShippedDate As Date, _
                           ByVal iShipVia As Integer, _
                           ByVal cFreight As Currency, _
                           ByVal sShipName As String, _
                           ByVal sAddress As String, _
                           ByVal sCity As String, _
                           ByVal sRegion As String, _
                           ByVal sPostalCode As String, _
                           ByVal sCountry As String, _
                           ByVal sCustomer As String, _
                           ByVal sSalesPerson As String, _
                           ByVal sShipper As String, _
                           ByVal sProductName As String, _
```

Listing 9.7   continued

```
                                ByVal cSubtotal As Currency, _
                                ByVal cTotal As Currency) As Boolean

    On Error GoTo PlaceOrder_Err
    Dim oData          As Object 'Data.Access object.
    Dim oProduct       As Object 'Northwind_Product.Product object.
    Dim oInvoice       As Object 'Northwind_Invoice.Invoice object.
    Dim oCredit        As Object 'Northwind_Credit.Credit object.
    Dim oShip          As Object 'Northwind_Ship.Ship object.
    Dim sSQL           As String
    Dim oObjectContext As ObjectContext
    Dim rsOrder        As New ADOR.Recordset
    Dim iOrderID       As Integer
    Dim lRows          As Long


    Set oObjectContext = GetObjectContext()

    'Place the order.
    sSQL = "Exec Order_Place" & _
          "  @ProductID = " & iProductID & _
          ", @UnitPrice = " & cUnitPrice & _
          ", @Quantity = " & iQuantity & _
          ", @CustomerID = '" & sCustomerID & "'" & _
          ", @EmployeeID = " & iEmployeeID & _
          ", @OrderDate = '" & dOrderDate & "'" & _
          ", @RequiredDate = '" & dRequiredDate & "'" & _
          ", @ShippedDate = '" & dShippedDate & "'" & _
          ", @ShipVia = " & iShipVia & _
          ", @Freight = " & cFreight & _
          ", @ShipName = '" & sShipName & "'" & _
          ", @ShipAddress = '" & sAddress & "'" & _
          ", @ShipCity = '" & sCity & "'" & _
          ", @ShipRegion = '" & sRegion & "'" & _
          ", @ShipPostalCode = '" & sPostalCode & "'" & _
          ", @ShipCountry = '" & sCountry & "'"

    Set oData = CreateObject("Data.Access")
    'oData.ExecSQL "Northwind", sSQL
    Set rsOrder = oData.GetResult("Northwind", sSQL, lRows)
    If lRows <> 0 Then
        iOrderID = rsOrder!OrderID
```

Listing 9.7 continued

```
End If
Set oData = Nothing

'Update quantity in stock.
Set oProduct = CreateObject("Northwind_Product.Product")
oProduct.UpdateStock iProductID, iQuantity
Set oProduct = Nothing

'Process the invoice.
Set oInvoice = CreateObject("Northwind_Invoice.Invoice")
oInvoice.GenerateInvoice iOrderID, _
                         sCustomerID, _
                         sSalesPerson, _
                         dOrderDate, _
                         dRequiredDate, _
                         dShippedDate, _
                         sShipper, _
                         iProductID, _
                         sProductName, _
                         iQuantity, _
                         cUnitPrice, _
                         cSubtotal, _
                         cFreight, _
                         cTotal, _
                         sCustomer, _
                         sAddress, _
                         sCity, _
                         sRegion, _
                         sPostalCode, _
                         sCountry

Set oInvoice = Nothing

'Check the credit.
Set oCredit = CreateObject("Northwind_Credit.Credit")
oCredit.CheckCredit sCustomerID
Set oCredit = Nothing

If Not oObjectContext Is Nothing Then
    oObjectContext.SetComplete
End If

'Arrange Shipping.
Set oShip = GetObject("queue:/new:Northwind_Ship.Ship")
oShip.ScheduleShipping iOrderID, _
                       sProductName, _
```

Listing 9.7 continued

```
                                        iQuantity, _
                                        sShipper, _
                                        dShippedDate, _
                                        sCustomer, _
                                        sAddress, _
                                        sCity, _
                                        sRegion, _
                                        sPostalCode, _
                                        sCountry


        Set oShip = Nothing

        PlaceOrder = True
        Exit Function
PlaceOrder_Err:
    PlaceOrder = False
    If Not oObjectContext Is Nothing Then
        oObjectContext.SetAbort
    End If
    Err.Raise Err.Number
End Function
```

Save the modified code and recompile Northwind_Order.dll. After recompiling, you need to notify COM+ that you have modified and recompiled the component. To do so, click the Add-Ins menu from the Visual Basic IDE and then select Component Services, Refresh All Components Now (see Figure 9.25).

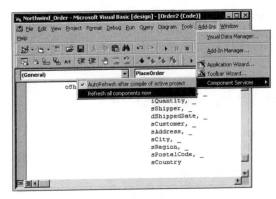

Figure 9.25: *Refreshing COM+ components after recompiling.*

Taking the Application for a Test Drive

Now you're ready to test the queueable Northwind Ordering application. Note that you made all the changes in the middle tier and the database back end. You did not change any interfaces (although you did introduce some new interfaces). As a result, all these changes are transparent to the front-end application, the order form. Therefore, you can use the VB order form you built in Chapter 7.

Now start the Northwind Ordering application, select a product, and click the Place an Order button. A confirmation box appears, indicating that the order has been processed (see Figure 9.26).

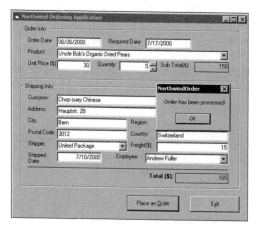

Figure 9.26: *The order has been confirmed.*

If you check the shipping database, you will find that the shipping record has been added to the Shipping table with Shipping ID 10002 and Order ID 11113 (see Figure 9.27).

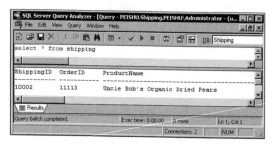

Figure 9.27: *A shipping record has been inserted into the Shipping table.*

Now start the Northwind Shipping COM+ application from the Component Services by right-clicking the application and selecting Start. A notification message from Northwind_Notify.Notify indicates that the shipping has been scheduled (see Figure 9.28).

Figure 9.28: *Shipping has been confirmed.*

What's Next

In this chapter, you learned about one of the most important features of COM+: Queued Components. You also learned how easily you can add QCs into an existing application. In Chapter 10, "COM+ Events," you'll learn about another key feature of COM+: Loosely Coupled Events (LCEs).

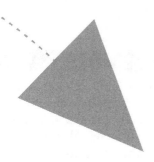

COM+ Events

This chapter introduces another important feature of COM+: Loosely Coupled Events, or LCE. COM+ events differ from traditional Tightly Coupled Events (TCE) in that they extend the COM+ programming model to support late bound events. COM+ Events service allows you to build extensible event-driven applications in a configurable way.

This chapter teaches you the following:

- COM+ event basics
- How to build a simple LCE program
- How to incorporate LCE with the Northwind application
- Some advanced COM+ event topics
- When not to use LCE

Introduction to COM+ Events

Distributed enterprise applications often need to be notified whenever specific events happen. For example, an order application might need to be notified if the inventory of a specific item is below a threshold so that a back order can be placed. Usually, another application, or subsystem, would be responsible for notifying the order application that a specific event had just happened. The application that sends the notification is called an *event publisher,* and an application that receives notification is referred to as an *event subscriber*. Traditionally, subscribers frequently check with the publisher to see whether something they need has happened. This process is known as *pooling*. There are a couple of drawbacks to this model. First, the subscribers must check with the publisher at a predefined time interval to see whether something has happened, even though nothing has changed yet. Checking this often is a waste of time for both the publisher and subscribers. Second, even if something did happen, a time lag occurs between the moment the event actually happened and the time the subscriber polled. For this reason, event notification models provide a better solution than the pooling model.

Event Notification Models

In event notification models, instead of letting the subscriber frequently check (*pool*) for specific changes, the publisher automatically notifies all the subscribers whenever specific events have occurred. The two types of event notification models are the *Tightly Coupled Event (TCE)* model and the *Loosely Coupled Event (LCE)* model.

TIGHTLY COUPLED EVENT (TCE) MODEL

EXAMPLE

Traditional event notifications fall into the Tightly Coupled Event (TCE) category. In a TCE model, the publisher is provided with an interface so that when something a subscriber needs happens, the publisher can call a method of the interface (see Figure 10.1).

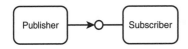

Figure 10.1: The Tightly Coupled Event (TCE) model.

In a TCE system, the publisher and subscriber must have great knowledge of each other. The publisher and subscriber have overlapping lifetimes; they both have to be up and running at the same time. The mechanism used in the communication must be known in advance. In addition, TCE cannot filter events from either the publisher end nor the subscriber end. The events implemented in Visual Basic COM components introduced in Chapter 4, "Introduction to Visual Basic COM Programming," are examples of TCEs.

LOOSELY COUPLED EVENT (LCE) MODEL

EXAMPLE

In contrast, COM+ events provide a Loosely Coupled Event notification model. In the LCE model of COM+, the publisher and the subscriber are no longer tied to each other. They are loosely connected by the COM+ event system (see Figure 10.2).

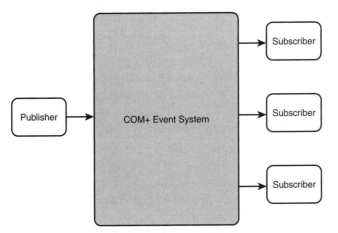

Figure 10.2: *The COM+ Loosely Coupled Event (LCE) model.*

In the COM+ LCE model, the contact information (called a *subscription*) is separated from both the publisher and the subscribers and is stored in the COM+ catalog, called the *event store*. The event subscription is managed by the COM+ event system. Subscribers can inquire into the event store to find the subscriptions they need and subscribe to them. This can be done both declaratively through the Component Services snap-in or programmatically through the COM+ Administration object model (or API). The COM+ event system is responsible for notifying event subscribers should specific events they need occur.

NOTE

This chapter demonstrates how to use the Component Services snap-in to create a COM+ event application, install and configure components, subscribe to events, and so on. Chapter 11, "Administering COM+ Applications Programmatically," discusses how to manage COM+ events programmatically through the COM+ Administration object model.

This layer of abstraction decouples the tight relationship between the publisher and the subscriber in a TCE model and results in a number of advantages. First, the event publisher and subscriber no longer need to be aware of each other as long as both agree to a special event interface that is registered and managed by the COM+ event system. As such, the publisher and the subscriber can be developed independently.

Second, the publisher and the subscriber can have totally different lifetimes. A publisher can fire an event without having the subscriber up and running and vice versa.

Finally, the communication and notification semantics are taken care of by the COM+ event system, which greatly simplifies the event programming model. The COM+ event system allows you to "configure" the event (such as specify the event class, associate the event publishers and event subscribers, and so on). In traditional event programming models (TCEs), everything has to be predefined, more or less hard coded. In addition, COM+ events also support *event filtering*, a way to designate event notification only when certain events happen or when certain criteria are reached.

The COM+ Event Architecture

Figure 10.3 illustrates the COM+ event architecture. In the COM+ event model, the interface (IYourEvent in the figure) is defined by an abstract class, EventClass. Subscribers implement this interface defined by EventClass. EventClass is registered in the COM+ event system, either declaratively or programmatically, and its information is stored in the COM+ event store. Subscribers query the event store, find the events they are need, and subscribe to them. The subscription is also stored in the COM+ event store. Subscription can also be done either declaratively or programmatically. To fire an event, the publisher creates an instance of the EventClass object and calls one of the event methods defined in the interfaces of EventClass. The COM+ event system service looks at the event store for subscriptions and creates instances of subscribers to deliver the events.

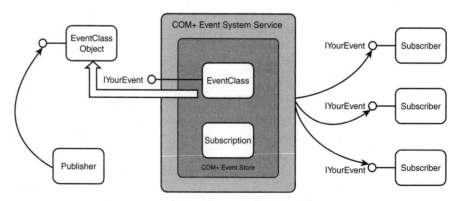

Figure 10.3: The COM+ event architecture.

THE EventClass OBJECT

The EventClass object is a COM component that defines the interfaces of events. It is a persistent object that is stored in the COM+ event store and managed by the COM+ event system service. EventClass is an abstract class that only defines interfaces and carries no implementations.

EventClass contains metadata, including EventCLSID, EventClassName, TypeLibrary, and other *publication attributes*. EventCLSID and EventClassName are unique identifiers that can be used by the subscribers to request the events offered by a particular EventClass. EventCLSID is the CLSID of the EventClass component, and EventClassName is the ProgID of the component. TypeLibrary stores a list of interfaces defined by EventClass, and the publication attributes define how the events are going to be published through EventClass.

EventClass is an ActiveX DLL that must be self-registering. This requirement is automatically met when you develop the EventClass object and compile it in Visual Basic.

EVENTS

An *event* is a specific method defined in one of the interfaces of EventClass. The same constraints as in Queued Components (QC) apply here as well. That is, the event, or method, must have only input parameters and no return values. In Visual Basic, this means you have to declare the arguments of the event method as ByVal. The method has to be defined as a Public Sub.

EVENT SUBSCRIBERS

A event subscriber is a normal COM component that implements the interfaces defined in EventClass. You write code in the corresponding event procedures that are responsible for processing the events according to specific business requirements. The subscribers need to be installed into a COM+ application so that they can subscribe to appropriate events, either declaratively or programmatically.

SUBSCRIPTIONS

A subscription is stored in the COM+ event store. Subscribers create subscriptions so that the COM+ event system can manage and deliver events. Subscriptions contain information about the identity (SubscriptionID) and location (MachineName) of subscribers, delivery method, event method (MethodName), EventClass, and PublisherID property of an event class so that the subscriber can receive events.

Subscriptions exist independently from EventClass. You can disable a subscription either declaratively through the Component Services snap-in or programmatically by using the COM+ Administration object model.

Subscriptions fall into three types: *persistent*, *transient*, and *per-user*. The first type of subscription, the persistent subscription, resides in the COM+ event store and is independent from the subscriber's lifetime. Persistent subscriptions are written to disk so that they survive system reboots. When a persistent subscription is created, the COM+ event system activates the subscriber it needs to deliver an event to. The subscriber object can be created either directly or through a moniker if the subscriber is a Queued Component. After each event call, the subscriber object is destroyed. The repeated creation and destruction of a subscriber object can incur significant performance overheads. A persistent subscription can be created through the Component Services or the COM+ Administration object model.

The second type of subscription, the transient subscription, is also stored in the COM+ event store. Because it is not written to the disk, a transient subscription is deleted if the event system or operating system is shut down. A transient subscription contains an interface pointer to an already-created instance of a subscriber. If the instance of the subscriber is destroyed or if a problem occurs in the event system or operating system, the subscription disappears. However, a transient subscription is usually more efficient than a persistent subscription because it avoids frequent object creation and destruction.

NOTE

Transient subscription cannot be created through the Component Services snap-in. You have to use the COM+ Administration object model, which is described in Chapter 11, "Administering COM+ Applications Programmatically."

The third type of subscription, the per-user subscription, can deliver events only for subscribers logged in to the machine where the event system resides. When a subscriber logs on, the event system enables all the subscriptions whose PerUser property is set to True and whose UserName property is set to the name of the user who logged on. When the subscriber logs off, the subscription is disabled.

NOTE

Per-user subscriptions work only in scenarios in which the publisher and subscribers are on the same machine. The event system can detect logon and logoff only at the publisher's machine, not on the machine where the subscribers reside.

EVENT PUBLISHERS

An event publisher can be any application that is capable of interacting with COM objects. Applications developed using Visual Studio tools, such as Visual Basic, Visual C++, and Visual InterDev, can publish events. Other examples of event publishers are Microsoft SQL Server and Microsoft Exchange Server. To publish an event (sometimes called *fire an event*), all the publisher needs to do is create an instance of the `EventClass` object and call one of its methods.

A Sample LCE Application

Now that you've read enough theory about COM+ LCE, this section introduces a simple example to demonstrate how to create an LCE application. For this example, a Stock Watcher application frequently checks three fictitious stocks: CPLS (COMPlus), VIBS (Visual Basic), and EXMP (By Example). If any stock exceeds a threshold of 190, the Stock Watcher will fire a `StockHigh` event. Similarly, if any stock falls below a threshold of 10, the Stock Watcher will fire another event, `StockLow`. The COM+ event system will be responsible for delivering these events to the subscribers.

The `EventClass` Object

EXAMPLE

To build a COM+ event application, you first need to create an `EventClass` object. As you learned earlier, `EventClass` is an abstract component that defines the interfaces of events. So, you are going to create an ActiveX DLL project in Visual Basic that contains an abstract class. Name the project **EventStock** and the class module **IEvent**. This follows the naming convention of prefixing the letter I on the class name to indicate that it's an interface, which is an abstract class in Visual Basic. The `EventStock` project is illustrated in Figure 10.4.

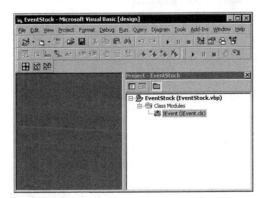

Figure 10.4: The `EventStock` project.

This IEvent interface implements two events: StockHigh and StockLow. Listing 10.1 contains the code that defines these two events.

Listing 10.1   The Events of the EventStock EventClass

```
Public Sub StockHigh(ByVal StockSymbol As String, _
                     ByVal StockValue As Single)
    'The EventClass only defines the interface,
    'so on implementation here.
End Sub

Public Sub StockLow(ByVal StockSymbol As String, _
                    ByVal StockValue As Single)
    'The EventClass only defines the interface,
    'so on implementation here.
End Sub
```

These two events are similar. Both require two arguments: a string variable for the stock symbol and a single variable for the stock value. Because IEvent is an interface, an abstract class, you don't have any implementation for both events.

Next, compile the project to create the EventStock.dll. Now that you have EventClass in place, you can register it with the COM+ event system. First, in the Component Services snap-in, create an empty server COM+ application and name it **Stock EventClass**.

Next, you need to register the EventClass object you just created. To do so, expand the Stock EventClass COM+ application, right-click the Components folder, and choose New, Components. After you view the Welcome screen of the COM Component Install Wizard, click the Install New Event Class(es) button (see Figure 10.5) and select EventStock.dll.

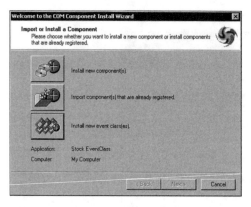

Figure 10.5: _Install the EventClass, EventStock in Component Services snap-in._

That's basically all you need to do to get an event class registered with the COM+ event system.

Now expand the Components folder; right-click the EventStock.IEvent component, and select Properties. When you click the Advanced tab of the Properties page, you will notice that a new section, LCE, has been added (see Figure 10.6).

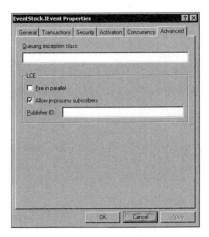

Figure 10.6: *If a component is installed as a COM+ event class, an LCE section is added to the Properties page.*

The Subscriber

EXAMPLE

With EventClass in place, you are now ready to build the subscriber. A subscriber is an ActiveX DLL that implements the interfaces defined in EventClass. Start a new ActiveX DLL project in Visual Basic, name it **StockSubscriber**, and name the class module **Subscriber**, as shown in Figure 10.7.

Then set a reference to the EventClass object you created and registered earlier (see Figure 10.8).

In the General Declaration section, add this one line of code:

```
Implements IEvent
```

This line allows you to expose the events defined in the interface in the subscriber.

Listing 10.2 illustrates the implementation of the StockHigh and StockLow events.

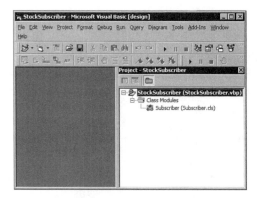

Figure 10.7: *The StockSubscriber project.*

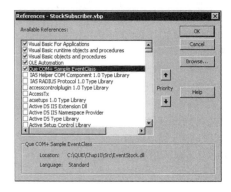

Figure 10.8: *Setting a reference to EventClass, EventStock.dll.*

Listing 10.2   The Implementation of Events in StockSubscriber

```
Private Sub IEvent_StockHigh(ByVal StockSymbol As String, _
                             ByVal StockValue As Single)

    MsgBox "Stock " & StockSymbol _
           & " is now above 190 and reaches " & StockValue & "!"

    App.LogEvent "Stock " & StockSymbol & " is now above 190 and
reaches " _
           & StockValue & "!"
End Sub

Private Sub IEvent_StockLow(ByVal StockSymbol As String, _
                            ByVal StockValue As Single)

    MsgBox "Stock " & StockSymbol & _
           " is now below 10 with a market value of " _
           & StockValue & "."
```

Listing 10.2   continued

```
    App.LogEvent "Stock " & StockSymbol _
            & " is now below 10 with a market value of " & StockValue &
"!"
End Sub
```

This listing simply displays a message box and also writes the event log for debugging and troubleshooting purposes.

Now compile the project to make StockSubscriber.dll. Then you are ready to subscribe to the event. To do so, create an empty server application in the Component Services snap-in and name it **Stock Event Subscriber**. After installing StockSubscriber.dll into this COM+ application, expand the Components folder, right-click the Subscriptions folder, and choose New, Subscription, as shown in Figure 10.9.

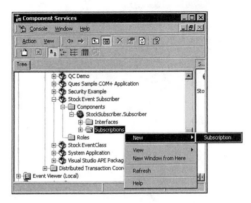

Figure 10.9: *Subscribing an event in the Component Services.*

On the Select Subscription Method(s) screen of the COM New Subscription Wizard, you can specify which events you are interested in from the available interfaces (see Figure 10.10). You can specify individual events or simply select the interface that contains all the events you want to subscribe to. Because you are interested in both StockHigh and StockLow events, choose the _IEvent interface.

On the next wizard screen, you can select the EventClass object that implements the events. For this example, pick up the EventClass object you built earlier, EventStock.IEvent (see Figure 10.11).

Then you need to name your subscription. On the next wizard screen, enter **StockWatch** as the name of the subscription (see Figure 10.12).

Figure 10.10: Selecting events you want to subscribe to.

Figure 10.11: Selecting the event class.

Figure 10.12: Naming the subscription.

By checking the Enable This Subscription Immediately check box in Figure 10.12, you can enable the subscription as soon as it is created. You can also leave it unchecked and later enable it from the Properties page of the subscription. At this point, click Next and then Finish. Figure 10.13 shows the StockWatch subscription you just created in the Component Services snap-in.

Figure 10.13: The StockWatch event subscription.

The Publisher

EXAMPLE

The event publisher in this example, the Stock Watcher program, is a Standard EXE Visual Basic project. It has only one form with a timer control, as shown in Figure 10.14.

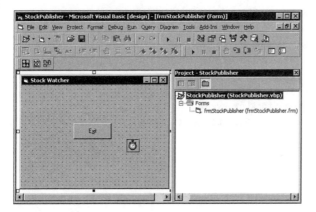

Figure 10.14: The StockSubscriber project.

Set the Interval property of the timer to 2000 (2 seconds) and add the code in the Timer event as in Listing 10.3.

Listing 10.3 The `Timer` Event Procedure of `StockPublisher`

```
Private Sub Timer1_Timer()
    On Error GoTo Stock_Err
    Dim oEventStock      As Object 'the EventStock.IEvent
    Dim sngStockValue    As Single
    Dim sStockSymbol     As String
    Static i             As Integer 'declared as static to preserve
value
                                    'after firing the timer

    i = i + 1 'increment the counter by 1 every time

    'Assign different stock symbols in turn
    Select Case i
        Case 1
            sStockSymbol = "CPLS" 'COM+
        Case 2
            sStockSymbol = "VIBS" 'Visual Basic
        Case 3
            sStockSymbol = "EXMP" 'By Example
            i = 0 'if counter reaches 3, reset it to 0 to start over
    End Select

    'Create an instance of the EventClass
    Set oEventStock = CreateObject("EventStock.IEvent")

    'Simulate the stock changes.
    sngStockValue = CSng((Rnd * 1000) / 5)

    'If the stock value is greater than 190,
    'we fire a StockHigh event.
    If sngStockValue > 190 Then
        oEventStock.StockHigh sStockSymbol, sngStockValue
    ElseIf sngStockValue < 10 Then
    'If the stock value is less than 10,
    'we fire a StockLow event.
        oEventStock.StockLow sStockSymbol, sngStockValue
    End If
    Set oEventStock = Nothing
    Exit Sub
Stock_Err:
    MsgBox Err.Description
End Sub
```

This listing uses the timer control along with the Visual Basic Rnd function to simulate three fictitious stock changes. It also declares a static counter (an integer) to persist its value. Each time the Timer event fires, the counter is incremented by 1. When the counter reaches 3, it is reset to 0 so that you can repeatedly watch the three stocks in turn.

After creating an instance of `EventClass`, `EventStock.IEvent`, you can check the random stock value to see whether it meets one of the watch criteria and decide whether you want to publish an event and which event you want to publish.

Running the Sample Application

EXAMPLE

Press F5 to start the Stock Watcher application. After a while, you see a message box from the StockSubscriber, indicating that one of the events you're interested in watching has just happened. In this case, the message says that the CPLS stock is lower than 10 (see Figure 10.15).

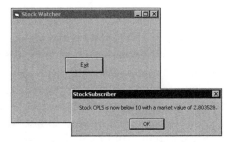

Figure 10.15: *A* `StockLow` *event is fired.*

You can open the event log to see a confirmation event, as shown in Figure 10.16.

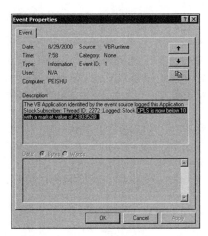

Figure 10.16: *The* `StockLow` *event in the event log.*

If you keep the Stock Watcher application running, it continually fires events whenever one of the predefined criteria is met. Figure 10.17 shows that a StockHigh event has been fired.

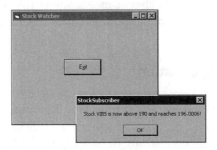

Figure 10.17: *A* StockHigh *event has been fired.*

Adding LCE to the Northwind Application

This section demonstrates how to add the LCE functionality to the Northwind Application you've developed over the preceding chapters. You'll add another business rule to this application that states whenever a specific item falls to a quantity 10 or below, you need to notify somebody to place a back order for that item. To simplify the discussion, this section doesn't deal with a situation in which the quantity of the item is already lower than 10 before you place the order. Another business rule introduced in Chapter 6, "Writing Transactional Components," still applies, though; that is, if quantity of the item you try to order exceeds the number of that item in stock, the order will be canceled.

What you need here is an inventory monitoring system, or inventory watcher. The inventory watcher will keep an eye on the UnitsInStock column of the Products table in the Northwind database. If some item falls lower than 10, the inventory watcher will fire an event so that the appropriate party will be notified and the back order will be taken care of. You will leverage the COM+ LCE for event notification. In addition to the inventory watcher, you need two more components for this inventory monitoring system. You need an EventClass to define the event and register it to the COM+ event system. You also need a subscriber that can subscribe to the event and take appropriate actions in response to that event.

The Northwind Inventory EventClass

The first thing you need to build is the EventClass. To do so, create a Northwind_Inventory project with a class module, Inventory.cls (see Figure 10.18).

EXAMPLE

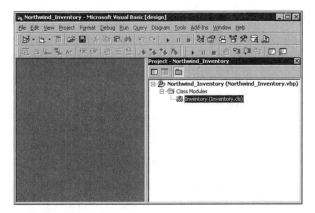

Figure 10.18: *The* `Northwind_Inventory.Inventory` *EventClass.*

Now add the event definition, `InventoryLow`, in the class module, as in Listing 10.4.

Listing 10.4   The `InventoryLow` Event Definition in the `Northwind_Inventory.Inventory` EventClass

```
Public Sub InventoryLow(ByVal BackOrder As String)
    'EventClass, no implementation here.
End Sub
```

Compile `EventClass` and register it to the COM+ event system by creating an empty COM+ server application named **Northwind Inventory EventClass.** Then install the Northwind_Inventory.dll as an event class. Figure 10.19 shows the registered `EventClass` in the Component Services snap-in.

Figure 10.19: *The* `Northwind_Inventory.Inventory` *EventClass registered in the COM+ event system.*

The Northwind Inventory Event Subscriber

EXAMPLE

The subscriber here is even simpler than the one you built earlier for the Stock Watcher application. Name this project **Northwind_InvSubscriber** and give it one class module named **InvSubscriber** (see Figure 10.20).

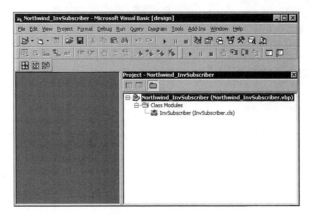

Figure 10.20: The Northwind_InvSubscriber project.

Listing 10.5 contains the code for the subscriber; it simply displays a message passed to use through the event. Of course, you need to set a reference to the event you're trying to implement (see Figure 10.21).

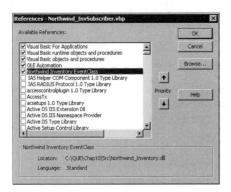

Figure 10.21: Setting a reference to EventClass in the subscriber.

Listing 10.5   The Implementation of the InventoryLow Event in the Subscriber

```
Implements Inventory

Private Sub Inventory_InventoryLow(ByVal BackOrder As Variant)
    MsgBox BackOrder
End Sub
```

Now install the subscriber and subscribe to the `LowInventory` event. Compile the Northwind_InvSubscriber.dll and install it in a COM+ server application named **Northwind Inventory Subscriber**. Then create a subscription, name it **InventoryWatch**, and subscribe to the `LowInventory` event as you did for the `StockWatch` subscription. Figure 10.22 shows this subscription.

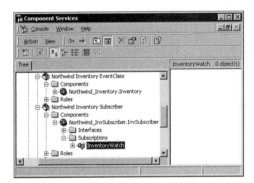

Figure 10.22: *The* `InventoryWatch` *event subscription.*

The Event Publisher

EXAMPLE

The event publisher is getting a little tricky here. In this scenario, it is the inventory monitor described earlier. Where should you put this inventory monitor anyhow? Because you want to monitor the inventory, the UnitsInStock column of the Products table, writing an update trigger on the Products table seems to be a natural choice. SQL Server provides an OLE automation mechanism that allows you to create COM objects and invoke their methods from within the stored procedures and triggers. The tricky part is that the event defined in `EventClass` is a *sub* that has no return values. When you make a method call from SQL Server (in a stored procedure and/or trigger), you use the extended stored procedure `sp_OAMthod`, which expects the method to have return values. You need to work around this problem. To do so, you create a wrapper component that implements a function which can be called by SQL Server. The wrapper object, in turn, creates an instance of `EventClass` and invokes its method. Here, you create a wrapper project named **Northwind_InvPublisher** with a class named **Publisher** (see Figure 10.23).

This wrapper implements a `BackOrder()` method as a Boolean function, which fires the event on behalf of the SQL Server stored procedure. Listing 10.6 illustrates this `BackOrder()` method.

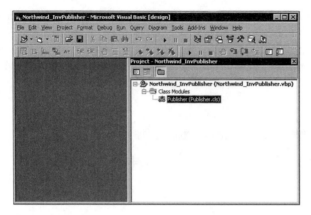

Figure 10.23: *The* `Publisher` *wrapper project.*

Listing 10.6   The `BackOrder()` Method of the Wrapper Component

```
Public Function BackOrder(ByVal sBackOrder As String) As Boolean
    On Error GoTo BackOrder_Err
    Dim oInventory As Object 'Northwind_Inventory.Inventory object
    Set oInventory = CreateObject("Northwind_Inventory.Inventory")
    oInventory.InventoryLow sBackOrder
    Set oInventory = Nothing
    Exit Function
BackOrder_Err:
    App.LogEvent Err.Description, 1
End Sub
```

Now compile the wrapper project into the Northwind_InvPublisher.dll.
With the help of this wrapper object, you can write the trigger and stored
procedure. You could directly put the code that interacts with the wrapper
COM object inside the trigger itself. Doing so, however, may inhibit your
flexibility in implementing the logic of dealing with the wrapper component. For example, if you need to invoke the wrapper component somewhere else in the SQL Server database later, from other triggers or stored
procedures, you end up repeating the code elsewhere. So you can extract
this logic out of the trigger and put it in a stored procedure. In this way,
should a need arise in the future to use the wrapper object elsewhere in
the database, you simply can use this stored procedure instead of writing
the same code again. Listing 10.7 illustrates the stored procedure
`Inventory_BackOrder`, which takes a character input parameter.

Listing 10.7   The `Inventory_BackOrder` Stored Procedure

```
if exists(select 1 from sysobjects where id =
object_id('Inventory_BackOrder'))
  drop proc Inventory_BackOrder
go

create proc Inventory_BackOrder
 @BackOrder varchar(255)
as

set nocount on

declare @oInventory int,
      @hr int,
      @Retval int

exec @hr = sp_OACreate 'Northwind_InvPublisher.Publisher', @oInventory
out

if @hr <> 0
  begin
    exec sp_displayoaerrorinfo @oInventory, @hr
    return
  end

exec @hr = sp_OAMethod @oInventory, 'BackOrder', @retval out, @BackOrder
if @hr <> 0
  begin
    exec sp_OAGetErrorInfo
    EXEC sp_displayoaerrorinfo @oInventory, @hr

    return
  end

exec @hr = sp_OADestroy @oInventory
if @hr <> 0
  begin
    exec sp_displayoaerrorinfo @oInventory, @hr
    return
  end
go
```

This listing uses several SQL Server extended stored procedures for OLE automation. `sp_OACreate()` allows you to create an instance of a COM object; its function is similar to the `CreateObject()` function in Visual Basic. `sp_OAMethod` lets you invoke the method of the COM object, using the object token returned by `sp_OACreate`. The `sp_OADestroy` extended stored procedure allows you to release the COM object; it works the same way as you set the object to Nothing in Visual Basic. Due to the scope of this book, I will not cover the details of how this OLE automation extended stored procedure works. You can refer to SQL Server Books Online for more information.

TIP

If you study the OLE automation examples in the SQL Server documentation, you will find that the extended stored procedure sp_OAGetErrorInfo is used to report errors that occur during the OLE automation calls. Unfortunately, the information regarding the errors returned by this stored procedure is too generic to be useful. Therefore, in this stored procedure, you use another stored procedure for reporting errors, sp_displayoaerrorinfo. This stored procedure, in turn, calls another stored procedure, sp_hexadecimal, for converting the error code to hex values. You can find a detailed explanation of these two stored procedures in the Microsoft SQL Server Programmer's Toolkit in the Microsoft Platform SDK documentation, which is available on the MSDN Web site. The code for these two stored procedures appears in Listings 10.8 and 10.9. You need to compile the code in these listings before you can compile the code in Listing 10.7.

Listing 10.8 The sp_displayoaerrorinfo Stored Procedure

```
CREATE PROCEDURE sp_displayoaerrorinfo
     @object int,
     @hresult int
AS
DECLARE @output varchar(255)
DECLARE @hrhex char(10)
DECLARE @hr int
DECLARE @source varchar(255)
DECLARE @description varchar(255)
PRINT 'OLE Automation Error Information'
EXEC sp_hexadecimal @hresult, @hrhex OUT
SELECT @output = '  HRESULT: ' + @hrhex
PRINT @output
EXEC @hr = sp_OAGetErrorInfo @object, @source OUT, @description OUT
IF @hr = 0
BEGIN
SELECT @output = '  Source: ' + @source
PRINT @output
SELECT @output = '  Description: ' + @description
PRINT @output
END
ELSE
BEGIN
    PRINT "  sp_OAGetErrorInfo failed."
    RETURN
END
GO
```

Listing 10.9 The sp_hexadecimal Stored Procedure

```
CREATE PROCEDURE sp_hexadecimal
    @binvalue varbinary(255),
    @hexvalue varchar(255) OUTPUT
AS
DECLARE @charvalue varchar(255)
DECLARE @i int
DECLARE @length int
DECLARE @hexstring char(16)
SELECT @charvalue = '0x'
SELECT @i = 1
SELECT @length = DATALENGTH(@binvalue)
SELECT @hexstring = '0123456789abcdef'
WHILE (@i <= @length)
BEGIN
DECLARE @tempint int
DECLARE @firstint int
DECLARE @secondint int
SELECT @tempint = CONVERT(int, SUBSTRING(@binvalue,@i,1))
SELECT @firstint = FLOOR(@tempint/16)
SELECT @secondint = @tempint - (@firstint*16)
SELECT @charvalue = @charvalue +
SUBSTRING(@hexstring, @firstint+1, 1) +
SUBSTRING(@hexstring, @secondint+1, 1)
SELECT @i = @i + 1
END

SELECT @hexvalue = @charvalue
GO
```

Now you're ready to create the trigger that actually monitors the units in stock for the Products table. Name the trigger **tr_Products_U**. Listing 10.10 contains the code of the trigger.

Listing 10.10 The tr_Products_U Trigger

```
if exists(select * from sysobjects where id =
object_id('tr_Products_U'))
 drop trigger tr_Products_U
go

create trigger tr_Products_U
on Products
for update
as
declare @ProductID int,
    @UnitsInStock smallint,
```

Listing 10.10 *continued*

```
      @BackOrder varchar(255),
      @ProductName varchar(40)

/*******************************************************
Note: This trigger only takes care of single row
      update. For multiple-row updates, we need to
      use other techniques such as cursor to handle
      each product.
*******************************************************/
select      @ProductID = i.ProductID,
      @UnitsInStock = i.UnitsInStock
from   inserted i

if @UnitsInStock < 10
  begin
    select @ProductName = ProductName from Products
    where ProductID = @ProductID
    select @BackOrder = 'Product ID# ' +
    convert(varchar(10),@ProductID) + ': ' + char(34)
      + @ProductName + char(34) + ' has only ' +
convert(char(1),@UnitsInStock)
      + ' units on stock, back order requested.'
    exec Inventory_BackOrder @BackOrder = @BackOrder
  end
go
```

To simplify the discussion, this listing deals only with single row updates in the trigger. You may notice that an *inserted* table is referenced in this trigger. This logic table is available only from triggers. An update in SQL Server is treated by a delete followed by an insert. Before the update is permanently committed to the database, SQL Server keeps both copies of the data in its transaction log and exposes the old data as a *deleted* table (another logic table) and the new data as the inserted table. These two logic tables, inserted and deleted, are available only from the triggers so that you can check their values to decide whether you want to commit the update or abort the change (called *roll back* in SQL Server). In this trigger, you compare the new data with the lowest threshold, which is 10. If the value after the update is lower than 10, the trigger fires an event by calling the stored procedure Inventory_BackOrder.

A Test Drive

Figure 10.24 illustrates the results of the test of the Northwind application with LCE enabled.

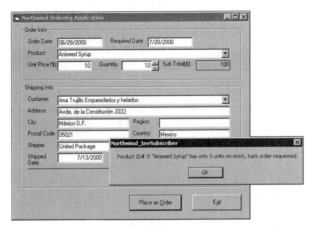

Figure 10.24: *A fired event returns a message indicating that a product is low in stock.*

Advanced COM+ Events Topics

The following sections introduce several advanced COM+ events features, including event filtering and parallel event firing. You can also combine the LCE with QC to provide asynchronous event notifications.

Event Filtering

COM+ provides event filtering capabilities, including publisher-side event filtering and parameter filtering, which are explained in the following sections.

PUBLISHER FILTERING

A publisher can decide which subscriber should receive a specific event by filtering the order and firing off an event method defined in an `EventClass`. COM+ provides publisher filtering with a filter component that supports one of the two publisher filtering interfaces.

If you want `EventClass` to be queueable, you must implement the `IMultiInterfacePublisherFilter` interface by specifying the `MultiInterfacePublisherFilterCLSID` property of the `EventClass`.

Otherwise, you can implement the `IPublisherFilter` interface and specify the `PublisherFilterID` property to the filter object. Because Visual Basic supports only the `IPublisherFilter` interface, I'll only discuss how to implement the `IPublisherFilterCLSID` interface in a filter component to provide publisher filtering.

When the publisher creates an instance of `EventClass`, the COM+ event system checks the event store to see whether the `PublisherFilterID` attribute is specified. If this attribute is set, the COM+ event system creates an instance of the filter component and calls the `Initialize()` and `PrepareToFire()` methods.

EXAMPLE

Let's look at an example of an event filter component to see how publisher filtering works. First, create an ActiveX DLL project in Visual Basic named **EventFilter** and name the class module **Filter** (see Figure 10.25).

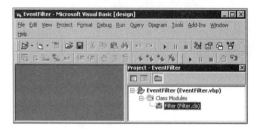

Figure 10.25: The `EventFilter` project.

Next, set a reference in the project to the COM+ event system type library, as shown in Figure 10.26.

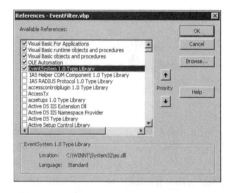

Figure 10.26: Set a reference to the COM+ Event System Type Library in the `EventFilter` project.

In the General Declaration section of the class module, enter the following lines of code:

```
Private m_oEventControl    As IEventControl
Private m_oSubscriptions    As IEventObjectCollection

Implements IPublisherFilter
```

The first two lines in this code segment declare two module-level variables to hold references to the `IEventControl` and `IEventObjectCollection` objects. The last line implements the `IPublisherFilter` interface.

Listing 10.11 illustrates the implementation of the `Initialize()` and `PrepareToFire()` methods.

Listing 10.11   The `Initialize()` and `PrepareToFire()` Methods of the Filter Component

```
Private Sub IPublisherFilter_Initialize(ByVal methodName As String, _
                                    ByVal dispUserDefined As
Object)


    Set m_oEventControl = dispUserDefined
    Set m_oSubscriptions = m_oEventControl.GetSubscriptions(methodName,
"", 0)

End Sub


Private Sub IPublisherFilter_PrepareToFire(ByVal methodName As String, _
                        ByVal firingControl As
                        EventSystemLib.IFiringControl)

    Dim i As Integer
    For i = 0 To m_oSubscriptions.Count - 1
        If m_oSubscriptions.Item(i).Name = "StockWatch" Then
            firingControl.FireSubscription m_oSubscriptions(i)
        End If
    Next i
End Sub
```

After an instance of the filter component is created, COM+ calls the `Initialize()` and `PrepareToFire()` methods. When COM+ calls the `Initialize()` method, it passes the method name and an `IEventControl` object. This method call retrieves the subscription collection of `IEventClass` by calling the `GetSubscription` method and assigning this collection to one of the module-level variables.

The `PrepareToFire()` method is passed a `firingControl` object that supports a `FireSubscriptions` method. You loop through the module-level subscription collection created by the `Initialize()` method and select the `StockWatch` subscription to fire an event.

You can not use the Component Services to specify the `PublisherFilterCLSID`. You must use the COM+ Administration object model to do so. Listing 10.12 demonstrates how to specify the `PublisherFilterID` property by using the COM+ Administration object model.

Listing 10.12   Associating the `PublisherFilterID` to the Filter Component

```
Dim oCatalog As New COMAdmin.COMAdminCatalog
Dim oApps As COMAdmin.COMAdminCatalogCollection
Dim oApp As COMAdmin.COMAdminCatalogObject
Dim oComps As COMAdmin.COMAdminCatalogCollection
Dim oEvent As COMAdmin.COMAdminCatalogObject
Dim i As Integer

Set oApps = oCatalog.GetCollection("Applications")
oApps.Populate

For i = 0 To oApps.Count - 1
    Debug.Print oApps.Item(i).Name
    If oApps.Item(i).Name = "Stock EventClass" Then
        Set oComps = oApps.GetCollection("Components",
oApps.Item(i).Key)
        oComps.Populate
        Exit For
    End If
Next

For i = 0 To oComps.Count - 1
    If oComps.Item(i).Name = "EventStock.dll" Then
        Set oEvent = oComps.Item(i)
        oEvent.Value("MultiInterfacePublisherFilterCLSID") _
                    = "EventFilter.Filter"
        oComps.SaveChanges
        Exit For
    End If
Next

oApps.SaveChanges
```

The line of code specifying the event filter component is highlighted in Listing 10.12. You'll learn about the COM+ Administration object model in Chapter 11, "Administering COM+ Applications Programmatically."

PARAMETER FILTERING

The parameter setting can be set on the subscription side. To add filter criteria, right-click the subscription and select Properties. Select the Options tab and enter the Filter criteria, as shown in Figure 10.27.

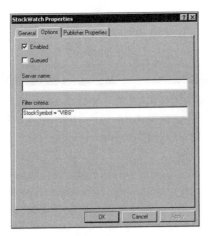

Figure 10.27: Setting Filter criteria for a subscription.

Parallel Event Filtering

When multiple subscribers are subscribed to a single event, the COM+ event system delivers the events one at a time in an unpredictable manner. You can configure the EventClass component, however, to request that the event system uses multiple threads to deliver an event to multiple subscribers at the same time. To do so, you simply set the FireInParallel property of EventClass to True. You can do so by using the Component Services snap-in or the COM+ Administration object model. To set this property in Component Services, simply select the Fire in Parallel check box on the Advanced tab of the EventClass's Properties page, as shown previously in Figure 10.6.

NOTE

Setting the FireInParallel property of EventClass to True does not necessarily guarantee that the event will be delivered at the same time to multiple subscribers. It simply gives the COM+ event system the permission to do so.

LCE and Queued Components (QC)

You can combine COM+ LCE and QC in a variety of ways to provide asynchronous event notifications. For example, you can set EventClass to make the publisher queueable or specify the subscriber as a queueable component. You can also set both EventClass and the subscriber as queued components.

If you configure a subscriber as a queueable component, the COM+ event system automatically initializes it by using the "queue" moniker. If you configure EventClass as a queueable component, however, the publisher has to use the new/queue monikers syntax, as discussed in Chapter 9, "Queued Components," to create an instance of EventClass.

Other Considerations

Although COM+ events provide a powerful means and simplified programming model for developers to incorporate LCE into applications, you need to be aware of a number of performance implications before you decide to use LCE in these applications.

One of the major limitations of LCE is that calls from EventClass to subscribers are synchronous. As a result, EventClass may be blocked from other subscribers at a given time until it is done with a specific subscriber. This blocking can propagate all the way back to the publisher, blocking the event firing itself. Therefore, LCE is not suitable for multicast event notification scenarios.

Another performance issue involved in LCE is that as long as EventClass creates an instance of the subscriber, the subscriber will reside in memory until the event system is shut down. Because the initiation of subscribers is controlled internally by the COM+ event system, you cannot easily change this behavior in code.

What's Next

So far, you have learned about most of the COM+ features, including Transaction Services in Chapter 6, the Compensating Resource Manager (CRM) in Chapter 7, Queued Components (QC) in Chapter 9, and the Loosely Coupled Events (LCE) in this chapter. Chapter 11, "Administering COM+ Applications Programmatically," introduces you to the COM+ Administration object model and teaches you how to perform administrative tasks that may or may not be possible through the Component Services snap-in.

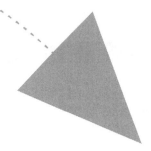

Administering COM+ Applications Programmatically

In Chapter 5, "Using the Component Services MMC Snap-In," you learned how to create and configure COM+ applications by using the Component Services snap-in. In this chapter, you'll learn how to programmatically administer COM+ applications through the COM+ Administration object model (or COMAdmin object model).

This chapter teaches you the following:

- How to use the COM+ catalog
- How the COMAdmin objects work
- How to perform basic administrative tasks by using the COMAdmin objects
- How to create and configure COM+ applications for the Northwind sample application
- How to use the Windows Scripting Host (WSH) to automate COM+ administration

The COM+ Catalog

The *COM+ catalog* is the underlying data store that holds all COM+ configuration data. Whenever you perform any administration tasks either through the Component Services snap-in or through the COMAdmin objects that will be introduced shortly, you are actually reading and writing data stored in the catalog.

The Registration Database and the COM+ Catalog

Internally, COM+ stores all configuration data in the COM+ class *registration database*, or *RegDB*. The RegDB holds data for all configured components installed in COM+ applications. The COM+ runtime uses the data stored in the RegDB to properly activate the objects in an appropriate context and determine what kinds of services should be provided according to its declarative attributes. All the changes you make to the configurations are transactional because the RegDB is a consumer of the Compensating Resource Manager (CRM). It can participate in DTC transactions.

The COM+ catalog is a logical abstraction of the physical data store in the RegDB. It presents COM+ data in a hierarchical way similar to what you saw in the Component Services snap-in. The COM+ catalog provides the only means by which you can access the RegDB. To access the COM+ catalog, you must either use the Component Services snap-in or the COMAdmin objects.

The Catalog Server

Every machine running under Windows 2000 has a COM+ *catalog server,* which is a query engine. Its job is to control the access to the catalog data stored on the machine. When you use COMAdmin objects to perform programmatic administration, you first instantiate a top-level COMAdmin object to implicitly open a session with the local catalog server.

Authority Concerns

You need to have Administrator's privileges on any machine for which you want to change any data to the COM+ catalog. This applies to using both the Component Services snap-in and the COMAdmin objects.

The COM+ Admin Objects Model

COM+ provides a programming model, the COMAdmin Objects model, to allow you to administer COM+ applications programmatically. Through this programming model, you can perform any tasks that you would perform using the Component Services snap-in. In addition, using the COMAdmin objects, you can also set some configurations that you cannot do by using the Component Services snap-in, such as creating a transient event subscription.

Most programming object models you are familiar with offer a hierarchical representation of the entities they map to. For example, in the Jet Data Access Objects (DAO), you specify a Workspace object through the top-level DBEngine object. Then you call a CreateDatabase() method of the Workspace object to instantiate an instance of the Database object. From there, you can access the table objects, query objects, and so on by calling the appropriate methods of the Database objects. In the Remote Data Access Objects (RDO), you use the Environment, Connection, and Resultset objects to access database objects in a hierarchical manner, using a specific object at a specific hierarchical level. Other examples include ActiveX Data Objects (ADO) and SQL Server Distributed Management Objects (SQL-DMO).

The COMAdmin Objects

Unlike the programming object models mentioned in the preceding section, however, the COMAdmin library, which resides in the Comadmin.dll, provides three generic objects. These objects are COMAdminCatalog, COMAdminCatalogCollection, and COMAdminCatalogObject. The top-level object, the COMAdminCatalog object that represents the COM+ catalog itself. The COMAdminCatalogCollection is a generic object that can represent *any collection at any level* on the catalog. Similarly, the COMAdminCatalogObject is a generic object that can represent any item that is contained within a collection.

You use COMAdminCatalog to establish a basic connection to the catalog server when you instantiate it. You use COMAdminCatalogCollection and COMAdminCatalogObject repeatedly to traverse the hierarchy of the catalog.

NOTE

The COMAdminCatalogCollection and COMAdminCatalogObject objects are "generic" objects, meaning that they can be used to represent any objects in the COMAdmin object model hierarchy (except for the root object, COMAdminCatalog) in a recursive manner.

THE COMAdminCatalog OBJECT

The COMAdminCatalog object is the top-level object in the COMAdmin object model. It represents the COM+ catalog itself. You use this object to initiate a session to the catalog server. You can also use the COMAdminCatalog object to perform tasks such as accessing the collections on the catalog, creating COM+ applications, installing components, starting and stopping services, or connecting and administering remote servers.

The COMAdminCatalogCollection Object

The COMAdminCatalogCollection object is a generic object that represents *any* collection on the COM+ catalog. You can use this object to enumerate, add, remove, and retrieve items in a collection or access related collections.

The COMAdminCatalogObject Object

The COMAdminCatalogObject object is also a generic object that represents items in a collection on the COM+ catalog. You can use this object to get and set properties of the item it represents.

COM+ Administration Collections

COM+ Administration collections provide a way of holding and organizing configuration data stored on the COM+ catalog. Figure 11.1 illustrates the COM+ Administration collections.

As shown in Figure 11.1, COM+ collections are organized in a hierarchical manner, with the COM+ catalog (represented by the COMAdminCatalog object) as the root of the hierarchy. The collections correspond to the folders appearing in the Component Services snap-in, as shown in Figure 11.2.

These collections are represented by the COMAdminCatalogCollection objects. You can access these collections from either the COMAdminCatalog object, if it is a top-level collection, or from the parent COMAdminCatalogCollection, if it is a subcollection of another collection. As you will see in the examples later, understanding the hierarchical relationships in Figure 11.1 is very important because all the collections are represented by a single object, the COMAdminCatalogCollection object.

In addition, three other collections are related to every collection listed in Figure 11.1. The PropertyInfo collection allows you to retrieve information about the properties that a specified collection supports. The RelatedCollectionInfo collection can be used to retrieve information about other collections related to the collection from which it is called. The ErrorInfo collection provides you with additional error details that are not available through the standard Visual Basic Err object.

Important Methods and Properties

Microsoft COM+ Platform SDK documentation (see Appendix A for the resources)lists the methods, properties, and syntax of COMAdmin objects as well as Administration collections. The following sections introduce several basic yet very important methods and/or properties that you must understand to be able to work with the examples in this chapter.

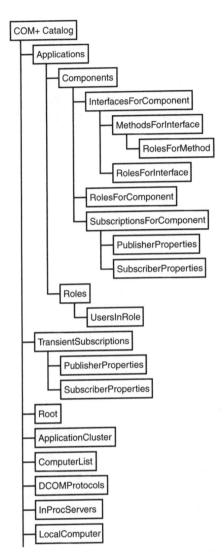

Figure 11.1: *COM+ Administration collections.*

Methods of the COMAdminCatalog Object

You'll use the following methods for the COMAdminCatalog object:

- The GetCollection method returns one of the top-level collections, such as the Applications collection. It takes the name of the collection as the only input parameter.

- The InstallComponent method allows you to install a component to the COM+ application you specified.

- The `InstallEventClass` method is similar to the `InstallComponent` method, except that the component it tries to install is actually an EventClass.

- The `StartApplication` method starts a COM+ application you specified. This capability can be very helpful if you're administering a COM+ application for Queued Components (QC).

Figure 11.2: *Folders and items in the Component Services snap-in.*

METHODS OF THE COMAdminCatalogCollection OBJECT

All five methods of the `COMAdminCatalogCollection` object are important. These methods are `GetCollection`, `Add`, `Remove`, `Populate`, and `SaveChanges`.

Unlike the `GetCollection` method of the `COMAdminCatalog` object, which returns a top-level collection, the `GetCollection` method of the `COMAdminCatalogCollection` object returns a collection of another parent collection. When you call the `GetCollection` method of a collection, you specify the collection name that is a subcollection of the collection object you are calling and a *key* value of the parent item to which this collection belongs.

You can add an item to or remove it from the collection by calling the `Add` or `Remove` method, respectively, passing the index of the item in the collection.

The `Populate` and `SaveChanges` methods deserve a little extra explanation here. When you retrieve data from the COM+ catalog data store, the data is stored in a memory cache. All the changes you made through the COMAdmin objects do not persist to the COM+ catalog data store until you call the SaveChanges method of the collection. The Populate method retrieves the data from the COM+ catalog data store and *refreshes* the data stored in the cache. The effect of the Populate method is similar to the Requery method of the ADO Recordset object. That is, if the collection is created the first time, a call to Populate "populates" the cache with the data retrieved from the catalog data store. After you manipulate the data in the cache and call the Populate method before calling the SaveChanges method, all the changes to the cache are lost, and the data retrieved from the catalog data store overwrites the data you changed in the cache. On the other hand, this result can be useful if you want to discard the changes. You can simply call Populate before calling SaveChanges.

CAUTION

One mistake developers often make is forgetting to call the Populate method after retrieving a collection. The collection remains empty unless you call Populate. The problem is that this mistake is very difficult to detect. Any attempt to enumerate the collection doesn't generate an error. You don't get reliable results either.

PROPERTIES OF THE COMAdminCatalogObject OBJECT

The two important properties of the COMAdminCatalogObject object are Value and Key. You use the Value property to get or set properties of a specific item. The Key property represents the key value of an item that uniquely identifies the item. You need to specify the key value of a parent item when you want to retrieve a collection of this item; you do so by calling the GetCollection method of the collection that contains this parent item.

Basic COM+ Administration with the COMAdmin Objects

The following sections provide some Visual Basic samples to demonstrate how you can use the COMAdmin objects to perform some basic COM+ administration tasks.

Retrieving Information from COM+ Applications

EXAMPLE

Listing 11.1 repeatedly uses the COMAdminCatalogCollection and COMAdminCatalogObject objects and the administration collections (shown in Figure 11.1) to enumerate all the COM+ applications, components, interfaces, methods, roles, users, and event subscriptions in the computer where the code is running.

Listing 11.1   Enumerating the COM+ Applications, Components, Interfaces, Methods, Roles, Users, and Event Subscriptions in a Computer

```
Private Sub DisplayCOMPlusInfo()
    Dim oCatalog    As COMAdminCatalog
    Dim oApps       As COMAdminCatalogCollection
    Dim oApp        As COMAdminCatalogObject
    Dim oComps      As COMAdminCatalogCollection
    Dim oComp       As COMAdminCatalogObject
    Dim oIFs        As COMAdminCatalogCollection
    Dim oIF         As COMAdminCatalogObject
    Dim oMethods    As COMAdminCatalogCollection
    Dim oMethod     As COMAdminCatalogObject
    Dim oRoles      As COMAdminCatalogCollection
    Dim oRole       As COMAdminCatalogObject
    Dim oUsers      As COMAdminCatalogCollection
    Dim oUser       As COMAdminCatalogObject
    Dim oSubs       As COMAdminCatalogCollection
    Dim oSub        As COMAdminCatalogObject
    Dim sComplus    As String

    Screen.MousePointer = vbHourglass
    'Get connect to the COM+ Catalog Server.
    Set oCatalog = New COMAdmin.COMAdminCatalog

    'Get the Applications collection.
    Set oApps = oCatalog.GetCollection("Applications")
    'Populate the Applications collection.
    oApps.Populate
    'Loop through the Applications collection to access individual
    'applications.
    For Each oApp In oApps
        sComplus = sComplus & vbCrLf & "Application: " _
                & oApp.Name & vbCrLf
        'For each application, get its Components collection.
        Set oComps = oApps.GetCollection("Components", oApp.Key)
        'Populate the Components collection so we can access them.
        oComps.Populate
        'Loop through the Components collection of a given
        'application to access individual components
        For Each oComp In oComps
            sComplus = sComplus & vbTab & "Component: " _
                    & oComp.Name & vbCrLf
            'Get the Interfaces under each component.
            Set oIFs = oComps.GetCollection("InterfacesForComponent", _
                                            oComp.Key)
            'Populate the interface collection in order to access the items.
            oIFs.Populate
```

Listing 11.1   continued

```
'Loop through each interface.
For Each oIF In oIFs
    sComplus = sComplus & vbTab & vbTab _
            & "Interface: " & oIF.Name & vbCrLf
    'Get the methods for each interface.
    Set oMethods = oIFs.GetCollection("MethodsForInterface", _
                                        oIF.Key)
    oMethods.Populate
    For Each oMethod In oMethods
        sComplus = sComplus & vbTab & vbTab & vbTab _
                & "Method: " & oMethod.Name & vbCrLf
        'Get the roles for each method.
        Set oRoles = oMethods.GetCollection("RolesForMethod", _
                                            oMethod.Key)
        'Populate the roles.
        oRoles.Populate
        'Loop through the roles collection.
        For Each oRole In oRoles
            sComplus = sComplus & vbTab & vbTab & vbTab & vbTab _
                    & "Role: " & oRole.Name & vbCrLf
        Next
    Next
    'Get the Roles for each interface,
    'we reuse the oRoles and oRole objects
    Set oRoles = oIFs.GetCollection("RolesForInterface", oIF.Key)
    'Populate the roles.
    oRoles.Populate
    'Loop through the roles collection.
    For Each oRole In oRoles
        sComplus = sComplus & vbTab & vbTab & vbTab _
                & "Role: " & oRole.Name & vbCrLf
    Next
Next

'Get the roles for each component.
Set oRoles = oComps.GetCollection("RolesForComponent", oComp.Key)
'Populate the roles.
oRoles.Populate
'Loop through the roles collection.
For Each oRole In oRoles
    sComplus = sComplus & vbTab & vbTab _
            & "Role: " & oRole.Name & vbCrLf
Next

'Get the Subscriptions for each component.
Set oSubs = oComps.GetCollection("SubscriptionsForComponent", _
```

Listing 11.1   continued

```
                                                      oComp.Key)
            'Populate the subscriptions.
            oSubs.Populate
            'Loop through the subscriptions.
            For Each oSub In oSubs
                sComplus = sComplus & vbTab & vbTab _
                        & "Subscription: " & oSub.Name & vbCrLf
            Next
        Next

        Set oRoles = oApps.GetCollection("Roles", oApp.Key)
        oRoles.Populate
        'Loop through the roles collection.
        For Each oRole In oRoles
            sComplus = sComplus & vbTab & "Role: " & oRole.Name & vbCrLf
            Set oUsers = oRoles.GetCollection("UsersInRole", oRole.Key)
            oUsers.Populate
            For Each oUser In oUsers
                sComplus = sComplus & vbTab & vbTab & _
                        "User: " & oUser.Name & vbCrLf
            Next
        Next
    Next
    On Error Resume Next
    Dim sFile As String
    sFile = "C:\QUE\Chap11\Src\ComplusApps.txt"
    Kill sFile
    Open sFile For Output As #1
    Print #1, sComplus
    Close #1

    Screen.MousePointer = vbDefault
    MsgBox "COM+ Applications information in this machine is saved in " _
        & sFile & "."
End Sub
```

The output of the code in Listing 11.1 is written to an external text file named ComplusApps.txt. Figure 11.3 shows a portion of the ComplusApps.txt file that lists the components, interfaces, methods, and event subscriptions in the Northwind Inventory Subscriber COM+ application you created in Chapter 10, "COM+ Events."

Figure 11.4 shows what the same COM+ application looks like in the Component Services snap-in.

Figure 11.3: *Part of the file generated by the code in Listing 11.1 that lists information about the Northwind Inventory Subscriber COM+ application.*

Figure 11.4: *The Northwind Inventory Subscriber COM+ application in the Component Services snap-in.*

Let's see how it works. The first part of Listing 11.1 declares local variables used in this routine:

```
Dim oCatalog    As COMAdminCatalog
Dim oApps       As COMAdminCatalogCollection
Dim oApp        As COMAdminCatalogObject
Dim oComps      As COMAdminCatalogCollection
Dim oComp       As COMAdminCatalogObject
Dim oIFs        As COMAdminCatalogCollection
Dim oIF         As COMAdminCatalogObject
Dim oMethods    As COMAdminCatalogCollection
Dim oMethod     As COMAdminCatalogObject
Dim oRoles      As COMAdminCatalogCollection
Dim oRole       As COMAdminCatalogObject
Dim oUsers      As COMAdminCatalogCollection
Dim oUser       As COMAdminCatalogObject
Dim oSubs       As COMAdminCatalogCollection
Dim oSub        As COMAdminCatalogObject
Dim sComplus    As String
```

You can see that except for the oCatalog object that is declared as the COMAdminCatalog object and the sComplus string variable that is used to store the content of the COM+ catalog returned by this routine, most of the variables are pairs of COMAdminCatalogCollection and COMAdminCatalogObject objects. These same types of objects are used in this routine over and over to traverse the COM+ catalog hierarchical structure to retrieve information at different levels.

After the variable declaration, the following line of code creates an instance of the COMAdminCatalog object and establishes a session with the catalog server:

```
Set oCatalog = New COMAdmin.COMAdminCatalog
```

Then the following code returns the Applications collection by calling the GetCollection method of the COMAdminCatalog object:

```
Set oApps = oCatalog.GetCollection("Applications")
    oApps.Populate
```

Notice that the Populate method is called to guarantee that the oApps collection isn't empty. The oApps collection is the top-most collection in this sample routine; it represents all the COM+ applications installed in the machine where this routine is running.

Then you start this top-most loop to enumerate all the COM+ applications installed in this machine:

```
For Each oApp In oApps
        sComplus = sComplus & vbCrLf & "Application: " _
                & oApp.Name & vbCrLf
```

Inside the top-most loop, you return Components for each application by calling the GetCollection method of the Applications collection of that application:

```
Set oComps = oApps.GetCollection("Components", oApp.Key)
oComps.Populate
```

Here, you pass the name of the collection as Components and a key value of the application. Again, you called the Populate method right after the collection is returned.

Then you loop through each component and append the information about components to the string variable:

```
For Each oComp In oComps
    sComplus = sComplus & vbTab & "Component: " _
            & oComp.Name & vbCrLf
```

In a similar manner, you repeat this pattern to retrieve information about interfaces, methods, and subscriptions.

Then you call the GetCollection method of the Applications collection again, but this time you pass Roles as the Name parameter and loop through the Roles collection to retrieve information about roles and users in each role:

```
Set oRoles = oApps.GetCollection("Roles", oApp.Key)
oRoles.Populate
'Loop through the roles collection.
For Each oRole In oRoles
```

```
    sComplus = sComplus & vbTab & "Role: " & oRole.Name & vbCrLf
    Set oUsers = oRoles.GetCollection("UsersInRole", oRole.Key)
    oUsers.Populate
    For Each oUser In oUsers
        sComplus = sComplus & vbTab & vbTab & "User: " & oUser.Name & vbCrLf
    Next
Next
```

Notice that you reuse the `oRole` and `oRoles` variables in this routine three times.

After you finish enumerating collections and items for the COM+ applications, you write the contents to an external text file like this:

```
Open sFile For Output As #1
Print #1, sComplus
Close #1
```

Figure 11.3 displays only a partial list of the contents of the output file, with one COM+ application shown in the figure.

NOTE

If you use early binding to create the `COMAdminCatalog` object (by using the `New` keyword), you need to set a reference to the COM+ 1.0 Admin Type Library, as shown in Figure 11.5, in your project.

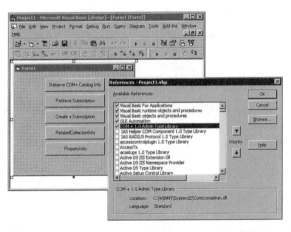

Figure 11.5: *Setting a reference to the COM+ 1.0 Admin Type Library in the project.*

EXAMPLE

Retrieving Subscription Information

Listing 11.2 demonstrates how to retrieve detailed subscription information for the `StockWatch` subscription you created in Chapter 10.

Listing 11.2   Displaying the Detailed Subscription Information for the StockWatch Subscription

```
Private Sub GetStockWatchSubscription()
    On Error GoTo COMAdmin_Err

    Dim oCatalog    As COMAdmin.COMAdminCatalog
    Dim oApps       As COMAdmin.COMAdminCatalogCollection
    Dim oApp        As COMAdmin.COMAdminCatalogObject
    Dim oComps      As COMAdmin.COMAdminCatalogCollection
    Dim oComp       As COMAdmin.COMAdminCatalogObject
    Dim oSubs       As COMAdmin.COMAdminCatalogCollection
    Dim oSub        As COMAdmin.COMAdminCatalogObject
    Dim oProps      As COMAdmin.COMAdminCatalogCollection
    Dim oProp       As COMAdmin.COMAdminCatalogObject
    Dim sProp       As String

    Set oCatalog = New COMAdmin.COMAdminCatalog
    Set oApps = oCatalog.GetCollection("Applications")
    oApps.Populate
    For Each oApp In oApps
        If oApp.Name = "Stock Event Subscriber" Then
            Exit For
        End If
    Next
    Set oComps = oApps.GetCollection("Components", oApp.Key)
    oComps.Populate
    For Each oComp In oComps
        If oComp.Name = "StockSubscriber.Subscriber" Then
            Exit For
        End If
    Next

    Set oSubs = oComps.GetCollection("SubscriptionsForComponent", oComp.Key)
    oSubs.Populate
    For Each oSub In oSubs
        If oSub.Name = "StockWatch" Then
            Exit For
        End If
    Next

    Set oProps = oSubs.GetCollection("PropertyInfo", oSub.Key)
    oProps.Populate
    For Each oProp In oProps
        Debug.Print oProp.Name & ": " & oSub.Value(oProp.Name)
    Next
    MsgBox "Subscription information retrieved!"
    Exit Sub
```

```
COMAdmin_Err:
    MsgBox Err.Description
End Sub
```

Here, you return a `PropertyInfo` collection of the Subscriptions collection and write the contents about the `StockWatch` subscription to the debug window:

```
Set oSubs = oComps.GetCollection("SubscriptionsForComponent", oComp.Key)
oSubs.Populate
For Each oSub In oSubs
    If oSub.Name = "StockWatch" Then
        Exit For
    End If
Next

Set oProps = oSubs.GetCollection("PropertyInfo", oSub.Key)
oProps.Populate
For Each oProp In oProps
    Debug.Print oProp.Name & ": " & oSub.Value(oProp.Name)
Next
```

Figure 11.6 shows the contents of the debug window after the execution of the routine in Listing 11.2.

Figure 11.6: *The debug window displays the properties of the* `StockWatch` *subscription.*

EXAMPLE

Registering a Subscription

Listing 11.3 demonstrates how you can create the `StockWatch` subscription by using the COM+ 1.0 Admin Type library. In Chapter 10, you used the Component Services snap-in.

Listing 11.3 Creating a `StockWatch` Subscription

```
Private Sub CreateStockWatchSubscription()
    On Error GoTo COMAdmin_Err

    Dim oCatalog    As COMAdmin.COMAdminCatalog
    Dim oApps       As COMAdmin.COMAdminCatalogCollection
```

Listing 11.3 continued

```
    Dim oApp         As COMAdmin.COMAdminCatalogObject
    Dim oComps       As COMAdmin.COMAdminCatalogCollection
    Dim oComp        As COMAdmin.COMAdminCatalogObject
    Dim oSubs        As COMAdmin.COMAdminCatalogCollection
    Dim oSub         As COMAdmin.COMAdminCatalogObject
    Dim oProps       As COMAdmin.COMAdminCatalogCollection
    Dim oProp        As COMAdmin.COMAdminCatalogObject
    Dim sProp        As String

    Set oCatalog = New COMAdmin.COMAdminCatalog
    Set oApps = oCatalog.GetCollection("Applications")
    oApps.Populate
    For Each oApp In oApps
        If oApp.Name = "Stock Event Subscriber" Then
            Exit For
        End If
    Next
    Set oComps = oApps.GetCollection("Components", oApp.Key)
    oComps.Populate
    For Each oComp In oComps
        If oComp.Name = "StockSubscriber.Subscriber" Then
            Exit For
        End If
    Next

    Set oSubs = oComps.GetCollection("SubscriptionsForComponent", oComp.Key)

    Set oSub = oSubs.Add
    oSub.Value("Name") = "StockWatch"
    oSub.Value("EventCLSID") = "EventStock.IEvent"
    oSub.Value("Enabled") = True

    oSubs.SaveChanges
    MsgBox "The StockWatch subscription is created!"
    Exit Sub
COMAdmin_Err:
    MsgBox Err.Description
End Sub
```

Here, you first loop through the Applications collection to find the Stock Event Subscriber COM+ application and then search the Components collection to get the StockSubscriber.Subscriber component. Then you call the GetCollection method against the Components collection and ask to return a Subscriptions collection by specifying the name of the collection as SubscriptionsForComponent:

```
Set oSubs = oComps.GetCollection("SubscriptionsForComponent", oComp.Key)
```

After the Subscriptions collection is returned, instead of calling the `Populate` method as you did in the preceding two examples and earlier in this example, you call the `Add` method to add the subscription item to the Subscriptions collection and set the `Name`, `EventCLSID`, and `Enabled` properties:

```
Set oSub = oSubs.Add
oSub.Value("Name") = "StockWatch"
oSub.Value("EventCLSID") = "EventStock.IEvent"
oSub.Value("Enabled") = True
```

After setting the properties for the subscription, you persist the change back to the COM+ catalog data store by calling the `SaveChange` method against the Subscriptions collection:

```
oSubs.SaveChanges
```

CAUTION

Before you run the code in Listing 11.3, I recommend that you back up the existing COM+ application by exporting the Stock Event Subscriber, as I described in Chapter 5.

Using the `RelatedCollectionInfo` Collection

Listing 11.4 demonstrates how to use the `RelatedCollectionInfo` collection to query the collections related to the Applications collection.

Listing 11.4   Listing All the Collections Related to the Applications Collection

```
Private Sub GetRelatedColsForApplications()
    Dim oCatalog    As COMAdminCatalog
    Dim oApps       As COMAdminCatalogCollection
    Dim oApp        As COMAdminCatalogObject
    Dim oComps      As COMAdminCatalogCollection
    Dim oComp       As COMAdminCatalogObject
    Dim oColInfos   As COMAdminCatalogCollection
    Dim oColInfo    As COMAdminCatalogObject


    'Get connected to the COM+ Catalog Server.
    Set oCatalog = New COMAdmin.COMAdminCatalog

    Set oApps = oCatalog.GetCollection("Applications")
    oApps.Populate

    Set oColInfos = oApps.GetCollection("RelatedCollectionInfo", "")
    oColInfos.Populate
    For Each oColInfo In oColInfos
```

Listing 11.4 continued

```
      Debug.Print oColInfo.Name
   Next

End Sub
```

As I mentioned earlier, you can use the `RelatedCollectionInfo` collection in all the collections to figure out what collections are related to the collection you're interested in. To return the `RelatedCollectionInfo` collection, call the `GetCollection` method against the collection you're querying by using an empty string as the second argument like this:

```
Set oColInfos = oApps.GetCollection("RelatedCollectionInfo", "")
```

Figure 11.7 shows the results in the debug window. You can see that the Applications collection has five related collections: `Components`, `Roles`, `RelatedCollectionInfo`, `PropertyInfo`, and `ErrorInfo`.

Figure 11.7: *The debug window displays the results of the code in Listing 11.4.*

Creating and Configuring COM+ Applications for Northwind

In the preceding sections, you examined several simple examples to see how you can use the COMAdmin objects to perform some basic administration tasks. The following sections show you how to use the COMAdmin objects exclusively as an alternative to the Component Services snap-in; you can use it to create and configure COM+ applications for the Northwind example developed in previous chapters, including creating and configuring COM+ applications for transactions, CRM, QC, and COM+ Events.

To follow the examples here, create a Standard EXE project in Visual Basic and set a reference to the COM+ 1.0 Admin Type Library. Add five command buttons on the form so that the project looks like the one in Figure 11.8.

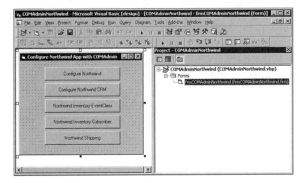

Figure 11.8: *The COMAdminNorthwind project.*

You are going to create and configure five COM+ applications for the Northwind application by using the COMAdmin objects. Figure 11.9 shows the COM+ applications you created in previous chapters by using the Component Services snap-in.

Figure 11.9: *Five COM+ applications of the Northwind sample application.*

CAUTION

Before you test the code here, back up all five Northwind COM+ applications by exporting the Stock Event Subscriber as described in Chapter 5, "Using the Component Services MMC Snap-In." Preserving the existing configuration for the Northwind application is critical because you will use all the COM+ services you built for the Northwind application in Chapter 13, "Northwind Traders Online: A COM+ Enabled Windows DNA 2000 Application."

EXAMPLE

Configuring Transactions

For this example, you are going to create a COM+ application named Northwind and install several transactional components in it. Configuring transactional components is straightforward. If you design your components appropriately, COM+ automatically picks up the transactional attributes you set at design time which is the MTSTransactionMode property of the Visual Basic class module.

The code in Listing 11.5 shows how to create a COM+ application and install components into it.

Listing 11.5 Creating the Northwind COM+ Application and Installing Transactional Components

```
Private Sub cmdNorthwind_Click()
    Dim oCatalog        As COMAdminCatalog
    Dim oApplications   As COMAdminCatalogCollection
    Dim oApplication    As COMAdminCatalogObject
    Dim sApplication    As String
    Dim i               As Integer

    On Error GoTo COMAdminNorthwind_Err
    Screen.MousePointer = vbHourglass
    sApplication = "Northwind"

    Set oCatalog = New COMAdminCatalog
    Set oApplications = oCatalog.GetCollection("Applications")
    'Don't forget to populate the collection!
    oApplications.Populate

    'search for existing one, if found, remove it.
    For i = 0 To oApplications.Count - 1
        If oApplications.Item(i).Name = sApplication Then
            oApplications.Remove i
            Exit For
        End If
    Next
    oApplications.SaveChanges

    'Add a new COM+ application
    Set oApplication = oApplications.Add
    oApplication.Value("Name") = sApplication
    oApplications.SaveChanges

    'Install the Data.Access component.
    oCatalog.InstallComponent sApplication, _
                        "C:\QUE\Chap06\Src\Data.dll", _
                        "", _
                        ""

    'Install the Northwind_Order.Order and Northwind_Order.Order2 components.
    oCatalog.InstallComponent sApplication, _
                        "C:\QUE\Chap07\Src\Northwind_Order.dll", _
                        "", _
                        ""

    'Install the Northwind_Product.Product component.
    oCatalog.InstallComponent sApplication, _
```

Listing 11.5   continued

```
                                        "C:\QUE\Chap06\Src\Northwind_Product.dll", _
                                        "", _
                                        ""


    oApplications.SaveChanges
    Screen.MousePointer = vbDefault
    MsgBox "Components Installed"
    Exit Sub
COMAdminNorthwind_Err:
    Dim oErrors As COMAdminCatalogCollection
    Dim oError  As COMAdminCatalogObject
    Dim sError  As String
    Set oErrors = oApplications.GetCollection("ErrorInfo", "")
    oErrors.Populate
    sError = Err.Description & vbCrLf
    For Each oError In oErrors
        sError = sError & oError.Name & vbCrLf
    Next
    Screen.MousePointer = vbDefault
    MsgBox sError
End Sub
```

In the first part of the code in Listing 11.5, you check for the existence of the application you're trying to create. If one is found, you delete it by calling the remove method of the Applications collection, passing the index of the application in the collection. Then you save the changes back to the COM+ catalog data store:

```
sApplication = "Northwind"

Set oCatalog = New COMAdminCatalog
Set oApplications = oCatalog.GetCollection("Applications")
'Don't forget to populate the collection!
oApplications.Populate

'search for existing one, if found, remove it.
For i = 0 To oApplications.Count - 1
    If oApplications.Item(i).Name = sApplication Then
        oApplications.Remove i
        Exit For
    End If
Next
oApplications.SaveChanges
```

Then you add the application to the Applications collection returned earlier by calling the Add method, specifying the name of the application, and saving the changes:

```
'Add a new COM+ application
Set oApplication = oApplications.Add
oApplication.Value("Name") = sApplication
oApplications.SaveChanges
```

After the COM+ application is created, you install three ActiveX DLLs into the COM+ application:

```
'Install the Data.Access component.
oCatalog.InstallComponent sApplication, _
                          "C:\QUE\Chap06\Src\Data.dll", _
                          "", _
                          ""


'Install the Northwind_Order.Order and Northwind_Order.Order2 components.
oCatalog.InstallComponent sApplication, _
                          "C:\QUE\Chap07\Src\Northwind_Order.dll", _
                          "", _
                          ""


'Install the Northwind_Product.Product component.
oCatalog.InstallComponent sApplication, _
                          "C:\QUE\Chap06\Src\Northwind_Product.dll", _
                          "", _
                          ""
```

Northwind_Order.dll contains two class modules: Order.cls and Order2.cls. So, it generates two components after being installed in the COM+ application: Northwind_Order.Order and Northwind_Order.Order2.

The last thing you do is save the changes:

```
oApplications.SaveChanges
```

Because COM+ can pick up the transactional attributes set up for components at design time, you do not explicitly specify these transaction attributes for the components in code. If you want to set the transaction attributes to something different than the design-time settings, you need to specify them in code by setting the Transaction property of the components. For example, the following code segment sets the transaction attribute for the Northwind_Order.Order component to Requires New:

```
Set oComponents = oApplications.GetCollection("Components", oApplication.Key)
For Each oComponent In oComponents
    If oComponent.Name = "Northwind_Order.Order" Then
```

```
            oComponent.Value("Transaction") = COMAdminTransactionRequiresNew
            Exit For
        End If
Next
```

One more thing I want to mention about this example is its error handler. The following segment demonstrates how you can use the `ErrorInfo` collection:

```
COMAdminNorthwind_Err:
    Dim oErrors As COMAdminCatalogCollection
    Dim oError  As COMAdminCatalogObject
    Dim sError  As String
    Set oErrors = oApplications.GetCollection("ErrorInfo", "")
    oErrors.Populate
    sError = Err.Description & vbCrLf
    For Each oError In oErrors
        sError = sError & oError.Name & vbCrLf
    Next
    Screen.MousePointer = vbDefault
    MsgBox sError
```

If you want to get the `ErrorInfo` collection, you call the `GetCollection` method of the collection for which you want to collect errors; then you specify `ErrorInfo` as the name of the collection and an empty string (`""`) as the key value. The error handler appends any error in the `ErrorInfo` collection to the standard error to give you a comprehensive error report when the error occurs.

After executing the code in Listing 11.5, you can check the results in the Component Services snap-in.

EXAMPLE

Configuring Compensating Resource Manger

For the example shown in Listing 11.6, you are going to create the Northwind CRM COM+ application that hosts four components: two transaction components and a pair of CRM Worker and CRM Compensator components.

Listing 11.6 Creating the Northwind CRM COM+ Application and Installing Two Transactional Components and a Pair of CRM Worker and CRM Compensator Components

```
Private Sub cmdNorthwindCRM_Click()
    Dim oCatalog        As COMAdminCatalog
    Dim oApplications   As COMAdminCatalogCollection
    Dim oApplication    As COMAdminCatalogObject
```

Listing 11.6 continued

```
Dim sApplication     As String
Dim i                As Integer

On Error GoTo COMAdminNorthwindCRM_Err
Screen.MousePointer = vbHourglass
sApplication = "Northwind CRM"

Set oCatalog = New COMAdminCatalog
Set oApplications = oCatalog.GetCollection("Applications")
'Don't forget to populate the collection!
oApplications.Populate

'search for existing one, if found, remove it.
For i = 0 To oApplications.Count - 1
    If oApplications.Item(i).Name = sApplication Then
        oApplications.Remove i
        Exit For
    End If
Next
oApplications.SaveChanges

'Add a new COM+ application
Set oApplication = oApplications.Add
oApplication.Value("Name") = sApplication
'Enable the CRM
oApplication.Value("CRMEnabled") = True
oApplications.SaveChanges

'Install the CRMInvoice.CRMWorker and CRMInvoice.CRMCompensator components.
oCatalog.InstallComponent sApplication, _
                    "C:\QUE\Chap07\Src\CRMInvoice.dll", _
                    "", _
                    ""

'Install the Northwind_Credit.Credit component.
oCatalog.InstallComponent sApplication, _
                    "C:\QUE\Chap07\Src\Northwind_Credit.dll", _
                    "", _
                    ""

'Install the Northwind_Invoice.Invoice component.
oCatalog.InstallComponent sApplication, _
                    "C:\QUE\Chap07\Src\Northwind_Invoice.dll", _
```

Listing 11.6   continued

```
      "", _
      ""
```

```
      oApplications.SaveChanges
      Screen.MousePointer = vbDefault
      MsgBox "CRM Components Installed"
      Exit Sub
COMAdminNorthwindCRM_Err:
      Dim oErrors As COMAdminCatalogCollection
      Dim oError  As COMAdminCatalogObject
      Dim sError  As String
      Set oErrors = oApplications.GetCollection("ErrorInfo", "")
      oErrors.Populate
      sError = Err.Description & vbCrLf
      For Each oError In oErrors
          sError = sError & oError.Name & vbCrLf
      Next
      Screen.MousePointer = vbDefault
      MsgBox sError
End Sub
```

The code in Listing 11.6 is similar to the code in Listing 11.5 with one exception—it specifies that the COM+ application is CRM-enabled:

```
oApplication.Value("CRMEnabled") = True
```

You can verify the results by checking the Northwind CRM COM+ application in the Component Services snap-in.

Installing an EventClass

EXAMPLE

For the example shown in Listing 11.7, you are going to create a COM+ application named Northwind Inventory EventClass and install an EventClass named `Northwind_Inventory.Inventory` in the COM+ application.

Listing 11.7   Creating the Northwind Inventory EventClass COM+ Application and installing the `Northwind_Inventory.Inventory` EventClass

```
Private Sub cmdNorthwindInvEvent_Click()
    Dim oCatalog       As COMAdminCatalog
    Dim oApplications  As COMAdminCatalogCollection
    Dim oApplication   As COMAdminCatalogObject
```

Listing 11.7 continued

```
Dim sApplication      As String
Dim i                 As Integer

On Error GoTo COMAdminNorthwindInvEvent_Err
Screen.MousePointer = vbHourglass
sApplication = "Northwind Inventory EventClass"

Set oCatalog = New COMAdminCatalog
Set oApplications = oCatalog.GetCollection("Applications")
'Don't forget to populate the collection!
oApplications.Populate

'search for existing one, if found, remove it.
For i = 0 To oApplications.Count - 1
    If oApplications.Item(i).Name = sApplication Then
        oApplications.Remove i
        Exit For
    End If
Next
oApplications.SaveChanges

'Add a new COM+ application
Set oApplication = oApplications.Add
oApplication.Value("Name") = sApplication
oApplications.SaveChanges

'Install the Northwind_Inventory.Inventory as an event class.
oCatalog.InstallEventClass sApplication, _
                           "C:\QUE\Chap10\Src\Northwind_Inventory.dll", _
                           "", _
                           ""

oApplications.SaveChanges
Screen.MousePointer = vbDefault
MsgBox "Inventory EventClass Installed"
Exit Sub
COMAdminNorthwindInvEvent_Err:
Dim oErrors As COMAdminCatalogCollection
Dim oError  As COMAdminCatalogObject
Dim sError  As String
Set oErrors = oApplications.GetCollection("ErrorInfo", "")
oErrors.Populate
sError = Err.Description & vbCrLf
For Each oError In oErrors
    sError = sError & oError.Name & vbCrLf
Next
```

Listing 11.7 continued

```
    Screen.MousePointer = vbDefault
    MsgBox sError
End Sub
```

Again, the code here is straightforward and similar to the two examples you saw earlier. The only exception is that this time you call the `InstallEventClass` method instead of the `InstallComponent` method of the `COMAdminCatalog` object:

```
oCatalog.InstallEventClass sApplication, _
                    "C:\QUE\Chap10\Src\Northwind_Inventory.dll", _
                    "", _
                    ""
```

After running the code in Listing 11.7, you can verify that the component is actually installed as an EventClass by checking the Advanced tab of its Properties page in the Component Services snap-in. You should see the LCE group on the Advanced tab, as shown in Figure 11.10.

Figure 11.10: *The Advanced tab of the EventClass' Properties page.*

EXAMPLE

Subscribe to the Event

For the example in Listing 11.8, you are going to create the Northwind Inventory Subscriber COM+ application, install a subscriber component named `Northwind_InvSubscriber.InvSubscriber`, and add a subscription named `InventoryWatch`.

Listing 11.8 Creating the Northwind Inventory Subscriber COM+ Application, Installing a Subscriber Component, and Adding a Subscription

```
Private Sub cmdNorthwindInvSubscriber_Click()
    Dim oCatalog        As COMAdminCatalog
    Dim oApplications   As COMAdminCatalogCollection
```

Listing 11.8 continued

```
Dim oApplication      As COMAdminCatalogObject
Dim oComponents       As COMAdminCatalogCollection
Dim oComponent        As COMAdminCatalogObject
Dim oSubscriptions    As COMAdminCatalogCollection
Dim oSubscription     As COMAdminCatalogObject
Dim sApplication      As String
Dim i                 As Integer

On Error GoTo COMAdminNorthwindSubscriber_Err
Screen.MousePointer = vbHourglass
sApplication = "Northwind Inventory Subscriber"

Set oCatalog = New COMAdminCatalog
Set oApplications = oCatalog.GetCollection("Applications")
'Don't forget to populate the collection!
oApplications.Populate

'search for existing one, if found, remove it.
For i = 0 To oApplications.Count - 1
    If oApplications.Item(i).Name = sApplication Then
        oApplications.Remove i
        Exit For
    End If
Next
oApplications.SaveChanges
'Add a new COM+ application
Set oApplication = oApplications.Add
oApplication.Value("Name") = sApplication
oApplications.SaveChanges

'Install the Northwind_InvSubscriber.InvSubscriber component.
oCatalog.InstallComponent sApplication, _
                "C:\QUE\Chap10\Src\Northwind_InvSubscriber.dll", _

                ""
                    , _
                ""

'Get the components collection.
Set oComponents = oApplications.GetCollection("Components", _
                oApplication.Key)
'Loop through the components collection to find the subscriber.
'populate the components collection first.
oComponents.Populate
For Each oComponent In oComponents
    If oComponent.Name = "Northwind_InvSubscriber.InvSubscriber" Then
        Exit For
```

Listing 11.8   continued

```
        End If
    Next

    'Retrieve the subscriptions collection and add our subscription.
    Set oSubscriptions = oComponents.GetCollection("SubscriptionsForComponent",
-
                        oComponent.Key)
    Set oSubscription = oSubscriptions.Add
    'Set up the properties for the subscription and save the changes.
    oSubscription.Value("Name") = "InventoryWatch"
    oSubscription.Value("EventCLSID") = "Northwind_Inventory.Inventory"
    oSubscription.Value("MethodName") = "InventoryLow"
    oSubscription.Value("Enabled") = True
    oSubscriptions.SaveChanges

    Screen.MousePointer = vbDefault
    MsgBox "Subscriber Component Installed"
    Exit Sub
COMAdminNorthwindSubscriber_Err:
    Dim oErrors As COMAdminCatalogCollection
    Dim oError  As COMAdminCatalogObject
    Dim sError  As String
    Set oErrors = oApplications.GetCollection("ErrorInfo", "")
    oErrors.Populate
    sError = Err.Description & vbCrLf
    For Each oError In oErrors
        sError = sError & oError.Name & vbCrLf
    Next
    Screen.MousePointer = vbDefault
    MsgBox sError
End Sub
```

The first half of this example is again straightforward; you should be able
to understand it without requiring any further explanation. The second half
adds an event subscription. It is similar to the earlier example of adding
the StockWatch event subscription. The difference is that in the StockWatch
example you added an event subscription for an existing component. Here,
you install the component first and then add the subscription.

Notice that you also add the following line of code:

```
oSubscription.Value("MethodName") = "InventoryLow"
```

This line names the specific method (or event) you're interested in. Naming
the method is not necessary in this example because the EventClass has
only one event: InventoryLow. If the EventClass has multiple events, as in
the StockWatch example, and you don't specify MethodName, you end up

subscribing to all the events the EventClass supports. Therefore, the MethodName property gives you fine-grained control over which individual event you want to subscribe to.

You can check the result of the event subscription in the Component Services snap-in.

EXAMPLE

Configuring Queued Components

For the example in Listing 11.9, you are going to create a COM+ application named Northwind Shipping, install two queued components, and enable the Queued Components functionality.

Listing 11.9   Creating the Northwind Shipping COM+ Application, Installing Two Queued Components, and Enabling the Queued Components Functionality

```
Private Sub cmdNorthwindShipping_Click()
    Dim oCatalog        As COMAdminCatalog
    Dim oApplications   As COMAdminCatalogCollection
    Dim oApplication    As COMAdminCatalogObject
    Dim sApplication    As String
    Dim oComponents     As COMAdminCatalogCollection
    Dim oComponent      As COMAdminCatalogObject
    Dim oInterfaces     As COMAdminCatalogCollection
    Dim oInterface      As COMAdminCatalogObject
    Dim i               As Integer

    On Error GoTo COMAdminNorthwindShipping_Err
    Screen.MousePointer = vbHourglass
    sApplication = "Northwind Shipping"

    Set oCatalog = New COMAdminCatalog
    Set oApplications = oCatalog.GetCollection("Applications")
    'Don't forget to populate the collection!
    oApplications.Populate

    'search for existing one, if found, remove it.
    For i = 0 To oApplications.Count - 1
        If oApplications.Item(i).Name = sApplication Then
            oApplications.Remove i
            Exit For
        End If
    Next
    oApplications.SaveChanges
    'Add a new COM+ application
```

Listing 11.9   continued

```
Set oApplication = oApplications.Add
oApplication.Value("Name") = sApplication
oApplication.Value("QueuingEnabled") = True
oApplication.Value("QueueListenerEnabled") = True

'For WorkGroups Windows 2000 installation, you need to remove
'the comment of the next line to avoid a "Permission denied" error.
'oApplication.Value("Authentication") = COMAdminAuthenticationNone

'Save the changes at the application level before moving on.
oApplications.SaveChanges

'Install the Northwind_Ship.Ship component.
oCatalog.InstallComponent sApplication, _
                          "C:\QUE\Chap09\Src\Northwind_Ship.dll", _
                          "", _
                          ""
'Get the Northwind_Ship.Ship component we just installed.
Set oComponents = oApplications.GetCollection("Components", _
                oApplication.Key)
oComponents.Populate

For Each oComponent In oComponents
    If oComponent.Name = "Northwind_Ship.Ship" Then
        Exit For
    End If
Next

'Get the _Ship interface.
Set oInterfaces = oComponents.GetCollection("InterfacesForComponent", _
                oComponent.Key)
oInterfaces.Populate
For Each oInterface In oInterfaces
    If oInterface.Name = "_Ship" Then
        Exit For
    End If
Next
'Enable queuing for the _Ship interface.
oInterface.Value("QueuingEnabled") = True
'Save the changes at the interface level before continuing.
oInterfaces.SaveChanges

'Install the Northwind_Notify.Notify component.
oCatalog.InstallComponent sApplication, _
```

Listing 11.9   continued

```
                                      "C:\QUE\Chap09\Src\Northwind_Notify.dll", _
                                      "", _
                                      ""
    'Get the Northwind_Notify.Notify component we just installed.
    Set oComponents = oApplications.GetCollection("Components", _
                    oApplication.Key)
    oComponents.Populate

    For Each oComponent In oComponents
        If oComponent.Name = "Northwind_Notify.Notify" Then
            Exit For
        End If
    Next

    'Get the _Notify interface.
    Set oInterfaces = oComponents.GetCollection("InterfacesForComponent", _
                    oComponent.Key)
    oInterfaces.Populate
    For Each oInterface In oInterfaces
        If oInterface.Name = "_Notify" Then
            Exit For
        End If
    Next

    'Enable queuing for the _Notify interface.
    oInterface.Value("QueuingEnabled") = True
    'You still need to call the SaveChanges method at the
    'interface level, even though you will call the SaveChanges
    'method at the application right after.
    oInterfaces.SaveChanges
    oApplications.SaveChanges

    'you can start the COM+ application to enable
    'Queued Components right away.
    oCatalog.StartApplication sApplication

    Screen.MousePointer = vbDefault
    MsgBox "QC Components Installed"
    Exit Sub
COMAdminNorthwindShipping_Err:
    Dim oErrors As COMAdminCatalogCollection
    Dim oError  As COMAdminCatalogObject
```

Listing 11.9   continued

```
    Dim sError  As String
    Set oErrors = oApplications.GetCollection("ErrorInfo", "")
    oErrors.Populate
    sError = Err.Description & vbCrLf
    For Each oError In oErrors
        sError = sError & oError.Name & vbCrLf
    Next
    Screen.MousePointer = vbDefault
    MsgBox sError
End Sub
```

To enable the Queued Components functionality, you need to do two things. First, you need to specify the `QueuingEnabled` and `QueueListenerEnabled` properties to `True` at the application level:

```
oApplication.Value("Name") = sApplication
oApplication.Value("QueuingEnabled") = True
oApplication.Value("QueueListenerEnabled") = True
```

Second, you need to set the `QueuingEnabled` property for the interface to `True`:

```
oInterface.Value("QueuingEnabled") = True
```

To verify the result of the code, open the Component Services snap-in. Locate and right-click the Northwind Shipping application you just created; then select the Queuing tab. Both the Queued and Listen check boxes should be checked, as shown in Figure 11.11.

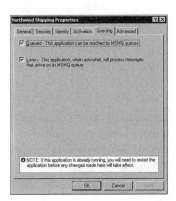

Figure 11.11: *The QC is enabled at the COM+ application level.*

You can also verify that the `Queued` property of the `_Ship` and `_Notify` interfaces are also set, as shown in Figure 11.12.

Figure 11.12: *Verifying that queuing is enabled for the interfaces.*

Using the Windows Scripting Host to Automate COM+ Administration

Before finishing this chapter, I want to introduce you to the Windows Scripting Host (WSH) and show you how to use it along with a scripting language such as VBScript to automate COM+ administration.

What Is the Windows Scripting Host?

The Microsoft Windows Scripting Host, or WSH, is a scripting host for 32-bit Windows platforms. In Windows NT 4.0, the WSH comes in the Windows NT 4.0 Option Pack. In Windows 2000, however, it is an integrated part of the operating system. You don't have to do any special installation to get the WSH in Windows 2000.

WSH supports both VBScript and Jscript (the Microsoft version of JavaScript). It allows you to write scripting code and save it as a script file (with a .vbs file extension for VBScript code and a .js extension for Jscript code). You can execute this script file just as you do a DOS batch file to automate administrative tasks such as installing and configuring COM components. You can either double-click it from Windows Explorer or run the command-line version of the WSH from the DOS prompt.

EXAMPLE

Using the WSH to Configure Northwind Event Subscription

For this example, you'll convert the code in Listing 11.8 to a scripting code, save it as a .vbs file, and execute it at a DOS prompt.

Listing 11.10 shows the scripting code, which is a VBScript version of Listing 11.8 with a little modification.

Listing 11.10   The VBScript Version of Listing 11.8

```
Dim oCatalog
Dim oApplications
Dim oApplication
Dim oComponents
Dim oComponent
Dim oSubscriptions
Dim oSubscription
Dim sApplication
Dim i

WScript.Echo "Starting Northwind COM+ Application Installation..."

sApplication = "Northwind Inventory Subscriber"

'Set oCatalog = New COMAdminCatalog
set oCatalog = CreateObject("COMAdmin.ComAdminCatalog")
Set oApplications = oCatalog.GetCollection("Applications")
'Don't forget to populate the collection!
oApplications.Populate

'search for existing one, if found, remove it.
For i = 0 To oApplications.Count - 1
    If oApplications.Item(i).Name = sApplication Then
        oApplications.Remove i
        Exit For
    End If
Next
oApplications.SaveChanges
'Add a new COM+ application
Set oApplication = oApplications.Add
oApplication.Value("Name") = sApplication
oApplications.SaveChanges

'Install the Northwind_InvSubscriber.InvSubscriber component.
oCatalog.InstallComponent sApplication, _
                          "C:\QUE\Chap10\Src\Northwind_InvSubscriber.dll", _
                          "", _
                          ""

'Get the components collection.
Set oComponents = oApplications.GetCollection("Components", _
                  oApplication.Key)
'Loop through the components collection to find the subscriber.
'populate the components collection first.
oComponents.Populate
```

Listing 11.10   continued

```
For Each oComponent In oComponents
    If oComponent.Name = "Northwind_InvSubscriber.InvSubscriber" Then
        Exit For
    End If
Next

'Retrieve the subscriptions collection and add our subscription.
Set oSubscriptions = oComponents.GetCollection("SubscriptionsForComponent", _
                        oComponent.Key)
Set oSubscription = oSubscriptions.Add
'Set up the properties for the subscription and save the changes.
oSubscription.Value("Name") = "StockWatch"
oSubscription.Value("EventCLSID") = "Northwind_Inventory.Inventory"
oSubscription.Value("MethodName") = "InventoryLow"
oSubscription.Value("Enabled") = True
oSubscriptions.SaveChanges

    WScript.Echo "Subscriber Component Installed!"
```

The conversion is straightforward here. In VBScript, all the variables are the variant type, so your first task is to remove the types for the variable declaration—that is, remove the ...AS Type part. Second, you can't use the error handler with the On Error Goto syntax, so you remove this syntax as well. Third, the Screen object is no longer available, so you must get rid of the two lines of code that refer to the Screen object. Last, you optionally replace the Msgbox with the WScript.Echo method. The difference is that Msgbox will show VBScript in the message title, whereas WScript.Echo will display WScript. Finally, save the code in Listing 11.10 to a file as **InstallNorthwindInvSubscriber.vbs**.

To execute the scripting file, you can simply double-click it from the Windows Explorer. Alternatively, you can execute the following command from the DOS prompt:

```
Cscript //i \C:\Que\Chap11\Src\InstallNorthwindInvSubscriber.vbs
```

The DOS prompt window in Figure 11.13 shows the results of the script upon execution.

Figure 11.13: *The result of executing the script.*

What's Next

Chapter 12, "More on COM+ Programming", will introduce some more COM+ features. Visual Basic 6.0 does not support some of these COM+ features. The next chapter will also explain what happens to some other features introduced in the beta version of COM+ specification. You'll also learn about some other issues involved in COM+ programming.

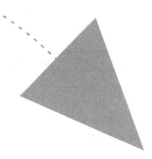

More on COM+ Programming

This last chapter in Part II, "Developing COM+ Application Components," will introduce you to some other COM+ features, including something that has already been introduced in the Microsoft Transaction Server (MTS). It also covers material that was originally available in the beta release of COM+ 1.0 but has either been redeployed or simply been removed from the final release.

This chapter teaches you the following:

- The basics of the object constructor string
- The basics of the Shared Property Manager (SPM)
- How to debug in COM+
- How object pooling works
- Some missing pieces from COM+ 1.0 beta release

Object Constructor Strings

An object constructor string is another declarative configuration feature of COM+. The COM+ 1.0 Services Type Library provides an IObjectConstruct interface for you to control the object construction process by passing in parameters from other methods or objects. This mechanism allows you to implement the IObjectConstruct interface in your component and adminis-tratively enable and set an object constructor string either by using the Component Services snap-in or the COM+ Admin object models. When COM+ instantiates the component, it checks the configuration of that com-ponent. If the constructor is enabled and the constructor string is set, COM+ first calls the Construct method of the IObjectConstruct interface and passes the construction to the component as an input parameter. Your component can then use this dynamic constructor string to perform specific actions at a given time. For example, you can set the object constructor string to define a database connection string and pass it to the component at runtime instead of using a file Data Source Name (DSN). This approach has some performance advantages because using the constructor string is faster than using a file DSN.

EXAMPLE

Let's look at an example to see how it works. For this example, use the Data.Access component you created in Chapter 6, "Writing Transactional Components." Here, you'll learn how to use the object constructor string to administratively define a data connection string and pass it to the compo-nent at runtime.

To get started, open the Data.Access project and add the following two lines of code in the General Declaration section of the class module, Access.cls, right below the constant declaration of m_sObjectName:

```
Private m_sConnection As String
Implements IObjectConstruct
```

When you press Enter, the IObjectConstruct_Construct method becomes available, as shown in Figure 12.1.

Now add the following code in the Construct method:

```
Private Sub IObjectConstruct_Construct(ByVal pCtorObj As Object)
    m_sConnection = pCtorObj.ConstructString
End Sub
```

If object construction is enabled and the construction string is set for the component in the COM+ application, the Construct method is called when an instance of the Data.Access component is created. When the Construct method is called, it stores the construction string in the module-level vari-able m_sConnection so that it becomes available for other methods that will use the connection string to connect to the database.

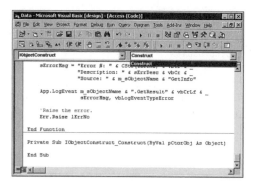

Figure 12.1: Implementing the IObjectConstruct interface.

Now you need to modify the two methods of the Data.Access component. Listing 12.1 shows the modified methods, with the newly added code highlighted.

Listing 12.1   The Modified ExecSQL Method and the GetResult Method of the Data.Access Component

```
'*****************************************************************************
' ExecSQL()
' Purpose: Execute SQL statements and/or stored procedures.
' Inputs:   sConnection        -- ADO connection string.
'           sSQL               -- SQL statement.
' Outputs: sErrorMessage      -- Error details.
' Returns: A boolean variable indicates if the action is successful.
' Modification History
' Date        Initials    Description
' 05/08/00   PLI          Created.
' 07/10/00   PLI          Added Object Constructor String
'*****************************************************************************

Public Function ExecSQL(ByVal sConnection As String, _
                        ByVal sSQL As String) As Boolean

    Dim lErrNo      As Long
    Dim sErrDesc    As String
    Dim sErrorMsg   As String
    Dim oConnection As New ADODB.Connection
    Dim oContext    As ObjectContext


    On Error GoTo ExecSQL_Err
```

Listing 12.1 continued

```
'Get hook to the ObjectContext
Set oContext = GetObjectContext()

'Check to see if the object constructor string is set.
'If it is, use it to overwrite the sConnection variable.
If Len(m_sConnection) <> 0 Then
    sConnection = m_sConnection
End If

'Connect to the database.
Set oConnection = New ADODB.Connection
With oConnection
    .Open sConnection
    .Execute CommandText:=sSQL
End With

'Up to this point, everybody is happy. So commit.
If Not oContext Is Nothing Then
    oContext.SetComplete
End If

If Not oConnection Is Nothing Then Set oConnection = Nothing
ExecSQL = True
Exit Function
ExecSQL_Err:
    'Something goes wrong, so roll back.
    If Not oContext Is Nothing Then
        oContext.SetAbort
    End If
    ExecSQL = False
    'Get the error details.
    lErrNo = oConnection.Errors(0).Number
    sErrDesc = oConnection.Errors(0).Description

    'Clean up.
    If Not oConnection Is Nothing Then Set oConnection = Nothing

    'Write error details to event log for troubleshooting.
    sErrorMsg = "Error #: " & CStr(lErrNo) & vbCr & _
                "Description: " & sErrDesc & vbCr & _
                "Source: " & m_sObjectName & "ExecSQL"

    App.LogEvent m_sObjectName & ".ExecSQL" & vbCrLf & _
                sErrorMsg, vbLogEventTypeError
```

Listing 12.1 continued

```
        'Raise the error.
        Err.Raise lErrNo

End Function

'*******************************************************************************
' GetResult()
' Purpose: Get an ADO recordset from a SQL action.
' Inputs:   sConnection        -- ADO connection string.
'           sSQL               -- SQL statement.
' Outputs: lRows               -- Rows returned.
'           sErrorMessage      -- Error details.
' Returns: An ADO Recordset as a result of a SQL action.
' Modification History
' Date       Initials    Description
' 05/08/00   PLI         Created.
' 07/10/00   PLI         Added Object Constructor String
'*******************************************************************************

Public Function GetResult(ByVal sConnection As String, _
                          ByVal sSQL As String, _
                          ByRef lRows As Long) As ADODB.Recordset

    Dim oConn       As New ADODB.Connection
    Dim rsGetResult As New ADODB.Recordset
    Dim sErrDesc    As String
    Dim sErrorMsg   As String
    Dim lErrNo      As Long
    Dim oContext    As ObjectContext

    On Error GoTo GetResult_Err

    'Get hook to the ObjectContext
    Set oContext = GetObjectContext()

    'Check to see if the object constructor string is set.
    'If it is, use it to overwrite the sConnection variable.
    If Len(m_sConnection) <> 0 Then
        sConnection = m_sConnection
    End If

    'Connect to the database.
    oConn.Open sConnection

    'Set up the ADO recordset properties.
    With rsGetResult
```

Listing 12.1   continued

```
            .CursorLocation = adUseClient
            .CursorType = adOpenStatic
            .LockType = adLockBatchOptimistic
            .ActiveConnection = oConn
            .Open sSQL

            lRows = .RecordCount 'rows fetched.
        End With

        'Return the recordset to the client.
        Set GetResult = rsGetResult

        'Disconnect from the database.
        Set rsGetResult.ActiveConnection = Nothing
        'Up to this point, everybody is happy. So commit.
        If Not oContext Is Nothing Then
            oContext.SetComplete
        End If
        If Not oConn Is Nothing Then Set oConn = Nothing
        Exit Function
GetResult_Err:
        'Something goes wrong, so roll back.
        If Not oContext Is Nothing Then
            oContext.SetAbort
        End If
        If Not oConn Is Nothing Then Set oConn = Nothing

        'Get the error details.
        lErrNo = oConn.Errors(0).Number
        sErrDesc = oConn.Errors(0).Description

        'Clean up.
        On Error Resume Next
        Set oConn = Nothing
        Set rsGetResult = Nothing

        'Write error details to event log for troubleshooting.
        sErrorMsg = "Error #: " & CStr(lErrNo) & vbCr & _
                    "Description: " & sErrDesc & vbCr & _
                    "Source: " & m_sObjectName & "GetInfo"

        App.LogEvent m_sObjectName & ".GetResult" & vbCrLf & _
                    sErrorMsg, vbLogEventTypeError
```

Listing 12.1   continued

```
    'Raise the error.
    Err.Raise lErrNo

End Function
```

As you can see, both methods work in the same way in respect to using the constructor string. If the module-level connection string variable is set, the methods use it to overwrite the input parameter named sConnection.

Now you can save the project, recompile Data.dll, and refresh the Data.Access component in the COM+ application named Northwind. The most reliable way of refreshing an object in a COM+ application is to delete it from the COM+ application and reinstall it (you'll learn about this task later in this chapter).

Next, you need to enable object construction and set the constructor string for the Data.Access component in the Northwind COM+ application. To do so using the Component Services, expand the Northwind COM+ application, right-click the Data.Access component, and select Properties. Click the Activation tab, select the Enable Object Construction check box, and enter a ADO connection string, as shown in Figure 12.2.

Figure 12.2: *Enabling object construction and setting the constructor string on the Properties page.*

EXAMPLE

Alternatively, you can enable object construction and set a constructor string by using the COM+ Admin objects. In this example, you can modify the code from Listing 11.5 in the preceding chapter so that it becomes the code in Listing 12.2; the new code is highlighted for you here.

Listing 12.2 Creating the Northwind COM+ Application and Installing Transactional Components with Object Construction Enabled and the Constructor String Set

```
Private Sub cmdNorthwind_Click()
    Dim oCatalog        As COMAdminCatalog
    Dim oApplications   As COMAdminCatalogCollection
    Dim oApplication    As COMAdminCatalogObject
    Dim sApplication    As String
    Dim i               As Integer

    On Error GoTo COMAdminNorthwind_Err
    Screen.MousePointer = vbHourglass
    sApplication = "Northwind"

    Set oCatalog = New COMAdminCatalog
    Set oApplications = oCatalog.GetCollection("Applications")
    'Don't forget to populate the collection!
    oApplications.Populate

    'search for existing one, if found, remove it.
    For i = 0 To oApplications.Count - 1
        If oApplications.Item(i).Name = sApplication Then
            oApplications.Remove i
            Exit For
        End If
    Next
    oApplications.SaveChanges

    'Add a new COM+ application
    Set oApplication = oApplications.Add
    oApplication.Value("Name") = sApplication
    oApplications.SaveChanges

    'Install the Data.Access component.
    oCatalog.InstallComponent sApplication, _
                              "C:\QUE\Chap06\Src\Data.dll", _
                              "", _
                              ""

    'Install the Northwind_Order.Order and Northwind_Order.Order2 components.
    oCatalog.InstallComponent sApplication, _
                              "C:\QUE\Chap07\Src\Northwind_Order.dll", _
                              "", _
                              ""

    'Install the Northwind_Product.Product component.
    oCatalog.InstallComponent sApplication, _
```

Listing 12.2 continued

```
                                 "C:\QUE\Chap06\Src\Northwind_Product.dll", _
                                 "", _
                                 ""


    'To set up transaction attributes for the components.
    Dim oComponents As COMAdmin.COMAdminCatalogCollection
    Dim oComponent  As COMAdmin.COMAdminCatalogObject

    'Enable object construction and set the constructor string.
    Set oComponents = oApplications.GetCollection("Components", _
                                            oApplication.Key)
    oComponents.Populate
    For Each oComponent In oComponents
        If oComponent.Name = "Data.Access" Then
            Exit For
        End If
        If oComponent.Name = "Data.Access" Then
            oComponent.Value("ConstructionEnabled") = True
            oComponent.Value("ConstructorString") = _
            "DSN=Northwind;UID=sa;PWD=;"
        End If
    Next
    oComponents.SaveChanges

    oApplications.SaveChanges
    Screen.MousePointer = vbDefault
    MsgBox "Components Installed"
    Exit Sub
COMAdminNorthwind_Err:
    Dim oErrors As COMAdminCatalogCollection
    Dim oError  As COMAdminCatalogObject
    Dim sError  As String
    Set oErrors = oApplications.GetCollection("ErrorInfo", "")
    oErrors.Populate
    sError = Err.Description & vbCrLf
    For Each oError In oErrors
        sError = sError & oError.Name & vbCrLf
    Next
    Screen.MousePointer = vbDefault
    MsgBox sError
End Sub
```

TIP

Prior to COM+, storing and retrieving the database connection string in a three-tiered application could be a little tricky. You can store the connection string in many places. For example, you can store it in the System Registry or in a system DSN or a file DSN. The clients or other components then can retrieve the connection information from either the System Registry or from a DSN and pass it to the data object. Using the object construction feature of COM+, however, you can remove the responsibility of storing the connection string from the component developer. At deployment time, the system administrator can dynamically decide the connection string and administratively set it up for the data access component using object construction. This capability offers better performance and flexibility.

Shared Property Manager

Chapter 4, "Introduction to Visual Basic COM Programming," discussed stateless versus stateful objects and explained their impact on the scalability of multitiered, distributed applications. To make your application scalable, you should keep your components stateless. Under certain circumstances, however, you may still want to store some shared transient data to be utilized by multiple components. Using global variables is not an option in a distributed environment due to concurrency and name collision issues. To solve this problem, originally MTS and now COM+ provides a solution for stored shared transient data called the Shared Property Manager (SPM, pronounced *spam*).

The SPM is implemented as a resource dispenser that stores shared transient data in memory. It also provides shared property groups that establish unique namespaces for the shared properties they contain to avoid name collisions. The SPM also implements a locking and serialization mechanism to support multiple, concurrent updates and prevent data from being lost.

Using the SPM is pretty straightforward. The SPM provides a hierarchical object model with three objects, as illustrated in Figure 12.3.

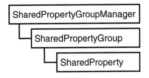

Figure 12.3: The Shared Property Manager object model.

The SharedPropertyGroupManager object lets you create shared property groups or obtain access to existing shared property groups. The

SharePropertyGroup object allows you to create and access shared properties in a shared property group. You use the SharedProperty object to set and retrieve the value of a shared property.

EXAMPLE

A typical example of using the SPM is a component that automatically generates a transaction number in a bank transaction scenario. To see how this works, create a sample component named BankTrans.TransNumber by creating a BankTrans Visual Basic ActiveX DLL project with a single class module named TransNumber.cls, as shown in Figure 12.4.

Figure 12.4: The BankTrans.TransNumber *component in Visual Basic.*

First, set a reference to the COM+ Services Type Library in the Visual Basic project and set the MTSTransactionMode property of the class module to 4-RequriesNewTransaction.

Add code in the class module to implement a method named GetNextTransNo() for the component, as shown in Listing 12.3.

Listing 12.3   Implementing a GetNextTransNo() Method for the BankTrans.TransNumber Component

```
Option Explicit

Private Const m_sObjectName = "BankTrans.TransNumber"

Public Function GetNextTransNo() As Long


    On Error GoTo ErrorHandler

    Dim oObjectContext As ObjectContext
    Set oObjectContext = GetObjectContext()

    Dim oSPM          As New COMSVCSLib.SharedPropertyGroupManager
    Dim oSPMGroup     As COMSVCSLib.SharedPropertyGroup
    Dim oSPMProperty  As COMSVCSLib.SharedProperty
    Dim bResult       As Boolean


    Set oSPMGroup = oSPM.CreatePropertyGroup("TransNo", _
                                        LockMethod, _
```

Listing 12.3 continued

```
                                                Process, _
                                                bResult)

    Set oSPMProperty = oSPMGroup.CreateProperty("NextTransNo", bResult)
    If bResult = False Then
        oSPMProperty.Value = 10000
    End If


    oSPMProperty.Value = oSPMProperty.Value + 1
    If Not oObjectContext Is Nothing Then
        oObjectContext.SetComplete
    End If

    GetNextTransNo = oSPMProperty.Value
    Exit Function


ErrorHandler:
    If Not oObjectContext Is Nothing Then
        oObjectContext.SetAbort
    End If
    GetNextTransNo = -1
    Err.Raise Err.Number, m_sObjectName, Err.Description
End Function
```

The code first creates an instance of the shared property group manager, oSMP, using the New keyword. It then creates a shared property group named TransNo by calling the CreatePropertyGroup method of the Shared Property Manager.

The CreatePropertyGroup method takes four parameters. The first parameter defines the name of the shared property group.

The second parameter defines the locking behavior of the Shared Property Manager. You can set it to either LockSetGet (0, the default) or LockMethod. LockSetGet locks a property during a Value call (get_Value or put_Value), ensuring that every get or set operation is atomic. This guarantees that no two clients can access the same property at the same time but still allows other clients to concurrently access other properties in the same group. The LockMethod locks all the properties in the shared property group for exclusive use by the caller as long as the caller's current method is executing.

The third parameter specifies the effective release mode for a shared property group, either Standard (0, the default), which automatically destroys the property group after all clients have released their references on the property group; or Process (1), which doesn't destroy the property group until the process that creates it has terminated.

The fourth parameter is an output parameter, a Boolean type that indicates whether the property group you tried to create already exists. It returns True if the property group already exists and False if it does not.

After creating the property group, you then create a shared property named TransNo by calling the CreateProperty method of the shared property group. The CreateProperty method takes two parameters: an input parameter that specifies the name of the property you want to create and an output parameter that indicates whether the property already exists. If the TransNo property does not exist prior to the call, you set the initial transaction number to 10000.

The next line of code increments the TransNo by one each time the method is called.

Now you're ready to compile BankTrans.dll and test it. To do so, start another Visual Basic Standard EXE, place a command button on the form, and put some code in the Click event of the command button like this:

```
Private Sub Command1_Click()
    Dim oSPM As Object
    Dim lRetVal As Long

    Set oSPM = CreateObject("BankTrans.TransNumber")

    lRetVal = oSPM.GetNextTransNo()

    MsgBox "Current Transaction No: " & lRetVal
End Sub
```

Name both the project and the form **TestSPM** and make an executable named **TestSPM.exe**.

COM+ greatly enhanced the debugging capability for Visual Basic, even letting you test the SPM behavior without installing the component into a COM+ application. To test it, go back to the BankTrans.vbp project and press Ctrl+F5 to start the component. Now start two instances of TestSPM.exe and click the command buttons on each form in turn. You will notice that the transaction number keeps increasing with every click of the command button, no matter which command button you click.

Figure 12.5: *Testing the SPM without running a Visual Basic instance of the component and installing it into a COM+ application will result in an error.*

After fully testing the component, you can install it in a COM+ application. You can create an empty server application named SPM and installed the BankTrans.TransNumber component there (see Figure 12.6).

Figure 12.6: *The BankTrans.TransNumber component is installed in the SPM COM+ application.*

Figure 12.7: Changing the default server process shutdown behavior.

Debugging COM+ Components

If you developed many MTS components in Visual Basic prior to COM+, you will appreciate the enhanced debugging capabilities that COM+ has added to the Visual Basic IDE.

EXAMPLE

For example, to run a component in debug mode without installing it in an MTS package, you have to disable all the references and calls to the IObjectContext interface. A common workaround is to check the existence of ObjectContext and then decide whether you should call its methods such as SetComplete or SetAbort, as shown in the following code segment:

```
'declare a ObjectContext variable
Dim oObjectContext As ObjectContext

'get a handle of the ObjectContext.
Set oObjectContext = GetObjectContext()

'............
'do some work here
'............

'if everything is ok, commit the transaction.
'before doing that, make sure the ObjectContext exists.
If Not oObjectContext Is Nothing Then
    oObjectContext.SetComplete
End If
Exit Function

ErrorHandler:
'if something is wrong, rollback the transaction.
'check to make sure the Object exists first.
```

```
If Not oObjectContext Is Nothing Then
    oObjectContext.SetComplete
End If
'............
'other error handling code
'............
End Function
```

This workaround is no longer necessary for the COM+ component. You can directly call the SetComplete or SetAbort method by using the following shortcut syntax, even though the component has not been installed into a COM+ application yet:

```
GetObjectContext.SetComplete
```

or

```
GetObjectContext.SetAbort
```

Another noticeable debugging enhancement is the availability of the ObjectContext object in the Class_Initialize and Class_Terminate events. In MTS, the ObjectContext object is not available in these two events. Any code that attempts to access the ObjectContext object (that is, trying to create an instance of the ObjectContext and call its methods) inside the Class_Initialize and Class_Terminate events will fail. You have to implement the IObjectControl interface and use its Activate and Deactivate methods to perform startup and shutdown tasks, as shown in the following code segment:

```
Implements ObjectControl

Private Sub ObjectControl_Activate()
    'Startup code goes here...
End Sub

Private Sub ObjectControl_Deactivate()
    'Shutdown code goes here...
End Sub

Private Function ObjectControl_CanBePooled() As Boolean
    ObjectControl_CanBePooled = False
End Function
```

In COM+, this is no longer the case. You can directly put your startup code inside the Class_Initialize event and the shutdown code inside the Class_Terminate event. You can also set breakpoints inside these events and use other Visual Basic IDE debugger facilities such as watches.

COM+ also allows you to debug multiple components. A client can call any number of DLLs running in the same project group or in separate project groups. The objects in the grouped DLL projects can call each other arbitrarily, flowing context as needed. This was not possible in the MTS world.

In addition, as I mentioned earlier, COM+ also supports debugging for the SPM components.

NOTE

When the components are running under debug mode, COM+ treats them as if they were running inside a COM+ library application. All limitations related to library applications apply.

NOTE

If you have the Visual Basic IDE and COM+ installed on the same machine, a Component Services add-in shows up under the Visual Basic IDE's Add-Ins menu, as shown in Figure 12.8. It replaces the Microsoft Transaction Service add-in for MTS under Windows NT 4.0. The purpose of this add-in is to update the Registry each time you recompile a component that is installed in an MTS package or a COM+ application. This add-in facility is no longer reliable for COM+ components, however, because COM+ may store configuration information in both the System Registry and COM+ registration database (RegDB). It is strongly recommended that you manually uninstall and reinstall the components after each recompilation.

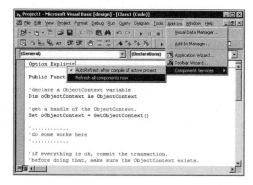

***Figure 12.8:** The Component Services add-in in the Visual Basic IDE.*

In spite of the great enhancements of COM+, the Visual Basic IDE still has some debugging limitations, including multithreading, component tracking, remote calls, and process isolation. Under these circumstances, you may need to use other tools to overcome the limitations of the Visual Basic debugger. One of these tools is Visual C++ 6.0, another member of the Visual Studio 6.0 suite.

You can also leverage the debugging capability of Visual C++ 6.0 to debug the compiled components—that is, the DLLs.

Let's use the Data.Access example again to see how to debug a compiled Visual Basic component using the Visual C++ debugger. First, you need to set up several properties for the component in the Visual Basic project. To get started, open the BankTrans.vbp project in Visual Basic, select File, and click Make Data.dll.... In the Make Project dialog, click the Options button and then select the Compile tab. Select Compile to Native Code, No Optimization, and Create Symbolic Debug Info, as shown in Figure 12.9.

Figure 12.9: *Setting up the compilation properties for a component in order to debug the compiled component in Visual C++ IDE.*

Click OK to close the Project Properties dialog box. Click OK again to make BankTrans.dll; overwrite the old one when prompted. Next, close the Visual Basic project. Then delete the original Data.Access component from the Northwind COM+ application and reinstall it from Data.dll.

Now open a new Visual Basic Standard EXE project, name it **VCDebuggerTest**, and name the form **frmVBDebuggerTest**. Place a command button on the form and type the code in the Click event of the command button as shown in Listing 12.4.

Listing 12.4   The Click Event of the Testing Client

```
Private Sub Command1_Click()
    Dim oData    As Object 'Data.Access
    Dim oRS      As Object 'ADO Recordset.
    Dim sSQL     As String
    Dim lRows    As Long

    Set oData = CreateObject("Data.Access")
    Set oRS = oData.GetResult("Pubs", sSQL, lRows)

    MsgBox oRS("au_fname") & " " & oRS("au_lname")

End Function
```

Set the same compilation configurations as you did for Data.dll (Compile to Native Code, No Optimization, and Create Symbolic Debug Info) and compile the VCDebuggerTest.exe. Then close the Visual Basic project.

Now you are ready to debug Data.dll by using the Visual C++ IDE. To do so, start the Visual C++ 6.0 IDE from the Visual Studio 6.0 groups and select File, Open Workspace. Then specify All Files (*.*) as the Files of type, browse to Data.dll, and click Open. A workspace is created, as shown in Figure 12.10.

Figure 12.10: The Data.dll Visual C++ workspace.

Select File, Open and specify All Files(*.*). Browse to the Access.cls file and click Open. The source code of the Access.cls class module then becomes available in the Visual C++ IDE. You can set the breakpoint by placing the cursor in the line where you want to set it and pressing F9 (see Figure 12.11).

Figure 12.11: Setting the breakpoint in Visual C++ IDE.

Select Project, Settings. Next, select the Debug tab and specify the fully qualified path for Dllhost.exe, followed by the ProcessID, as in the following syntax:

```
C:\WINNT\System32\Dllhost.exe /ProcessID:{ProcessID}
```

You can obtain the ProcessID from the Component Services snap-in. To do so, expand the Northwind COM+ application and right-click the

Data.Access component. On the General tab, highlight the GUID labeled Application and right-click. Select Copy to copy the ProcessID to the Clipboard (see Figure 12.12).

Figure 12.12: *Copying the ProcessID to the Clipboard.*

Then switch back to the Visual C++ IDE and paste the ProcessID as part of the parameters for Dllhost.exe, as shown in Figure 12.13.

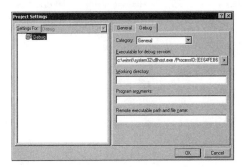

Figure 12.13: *Specifying the path for Dllhost.exe in the Executable for Debug Session box.*

Now you can start debugging the compiled Data.dll by pressing F5. All the Visual C++ debugging features become available, such as multithreading debugging.

Object Pooling

Object pooling is also a new feature of COM+. It is used to improve performance by creating a pool of objects (instances of components). Instead of physically destroying an object after the last client releases a reference to the object, COM+ places the object in a pool. The next time another client (or the same client) wants to use the object, COM+ hands it one of the unused objects from the pool. This process is completely transparent from the client. The client still has the illusion that it created a new instance of the object.

By reusing existing live objects instead of reinstantiating them from scratch, you can reduce overhead to a certain extent (it is not completely eliminated, though, because getting an object from the pool also involves some overhead).

The pool size is adjustable. You can specify the minimum and maximum number of objects in a pool.

Unfortunately, object pooling is out of the reach of Visual Basic 6.0 based on the limitations of the threading model supported by VB. In Chapter 1, "What COM+ Is All About," and Chapter 4, "Introduction to Visual Basic COM Programming," I described the different threading models and mentioned that Visual Basic supports only the Single-threaded Apartment (STA) model. The STA model requires that all the calls to the object must be made through a single thread in the main apartment (see Chapter 1). This is called *thread affinity*. In contrast, if you want to enable object pooling, the object itself must not be tied to any specific threads. The object should be accessible by any threads. This requires that the object must be a free-threaded model, a threading model that is not supported in Visual Basic 6.0.

NOTE

According to a recent Microsoft announcement, the next version of Visual Basic, as part of VisualStudio.NET, will support free-threaded models, among other exciting features. So, the ability to create poolable components in Visual Basic is almost a certainty in the near future.

In addition, keep in mind that using object pooling makes sense only in certain circumstances, such as when construction of an object is computationally intensive, construction of an object fetches initialization information from a file or a database, or construction of an object involves establishing a non-COM connection to another process or computer. Even under these situations, object pooling may or may not be the optimal solution. For example, using a dedicated local SQL Server database as a data cache usually offers higher performance over other approaches. You should always perform some benchmark testing to evaluate different alternatives.

Missing Pieces of COM+ 1.0 Beta Release

If you ever get a chance to play with the COM+ 1.0 beta version (available in Windows 2000 Beta 3 Release Candidate 1) or read some COM+ resources based on the beta versions of COM+, you may discover terms such as *Component Load Balancing (CLB)*, *In-Memory Database (IMDB)*, and *Transactional Shared Property Manager (TSPM)*. In the final release of COM+ (and Windows 2000), they are all gone. So what are CLB, IMDB, or TSPM, and what happened to them?

Component Load Balancing (CLB) is a technology that dynamically identifies the least busy server in a cluster of servers to evenly redirect the workload for all the servers in the cluster. The CLB architecture uses a dedicated server as a CLB server on which a CLB service is running. Redundant components are deployed among all the servers in the cluster. The CLB service frequently queries all the servers in the cluster to see which one has the smallest workload and dynamically distributes the requests to that server.

Microsoft decided to redeploy the CLB from Windows 2000 to the Microsoft Application Center (or AppCenter) 2000. Although Microsoft seemed to have a good reason of doing this, one thing is for sure: This feature is no longer free (as the rest of the COM+ features are); you have to pay for it. At least, you have to purchase the AppCenter 2000.

What about the IMDB and TSPM? IMDB was originally designed as a mechanism for cache transient, transactional database-style data that resides in RAM, as its name implies, to provide high-speed database lookup capabilities to applications. Applications can access IMDB through either OLE DB or ADO.

TSPM is a programming interface that creates a cache for a client to use for transactional, synchronized access to application-defined shared properties across multiple processes. TSMP is built on top of IMDB. TSMP uses IMDB to persist data.

Unfortunately, the feedback Microsoft collected on the use of the IMDB indicated that it did not perform as the developers had expected in most customer scenarios. Besides, IMDB has other shortcomings, such as no query processor and no support for stored procedures. As a result, Microsoft decided to remove IMDB and TSPM entirely from the final release of COM+ 1.0.

As I mentioned earlier, for transient data caching, using a dedicated local SQL Server database turns out to be a very appealing option.

What's Next

This chapter ends Part II of this book. In Part III, "Building Real-World COM+ Services Applications," you will push the Northwind Traders application to the Internet and build an Enterprise Application Integration (EAI) solution by using COM+ and XML.

Part III

Building Real World COM+ Services Applications

Northwind Traders Online: A COM+ Enabled Windows DNA 2000 Application

In previous chapters, you learned about all the services provided by COM+. You saw the Northwind Ordering System evolving into a fully COM+ enabled application, including automatic Transaction Services, the Compensating Resource Manager (CRM), Queued Components (QC), and Loosely Coupled Events (LCE). In this chapter, you'll learn how to make Northwind a Web-enabled Windows DNA 2000 application.

This chapter teaches you the following:

- The Northwind Traders Online system architecture

- All the COM+ applications and components used in Northwind Traders Online

- How to build the Northwind Traders Online Web site

Northwind Traders Online: Welcome to the Web

The Internet revolution has completely changed the way people conduct business. Today, companies realize that getting on the Web late could result in losing business or even losing the company itself. Northwind Traders is no exception. For purposes of this book, you have built a Web site that allows the Northwind Traders customers to order products directly over the Internet. Whereas Northwind Traders may still take orders by telephone calls and faxes, the Web site allows customers to order products over the Internet 24 hours a day, 7 days a week.

The Purpose of the Web Application

The purpose here is to demonstrate how easily you can build a fully functional Web application by leveraging the elegant design architecture of Windows DNA and the powerful, rich services of COM+. I do not intend, though, to fully cover the techniques of Active Server Pages (ASP) or Web development because those topics are completely beyond the scope of this book. Besides, you can find tremendous resources and books about ASP out there. Here, you will build a simple Web site with four ASP pages. The ASP techniques you will use here are basic, with an emphasis on interacting with and using COM and COM+ components and services.

A Brief Tour

The Northwind Traders Online Web application is designed to allow Northwind customers to order products from the Northwind Web site, reducing the cost of the call center. The Web site you will build duplicates the basic functionality of the Visual Basic ordering application built in previous chapters. This duplication of functionality is only at a conceptual level because Web interface behaviors are completely different from a Win32 GUI interface, such as a Visual Basic application. The Northwind Traders Online Web application contains four Web pages although you created only one form in the Visual Basic application.

A Web application should be secured, so you need a login page. Figure 13.1 shows the first page, the login page, of the Northwind Traders Online Web site.

After a customer types a customer ID and password, the Product Selection page opens, as shown in Figure 13.2.

The product IDs in the Product Selection list are hyperlinks. When the customer clicks the product ID of his or her choice, the Place an Order page opens, displaying the ID, name, and unit price of the product the customer chose (see Figure 13.3).

Figure 13.1: *The login page of Northwind Traders Online Web site.*

Figure 13.2: *The Product Selection page, from which the customer can select a product he or she wants to order.*

After specifying the quantity he or she wants to order, the customer clicks the Check Out button to submit the order. If everything goes fine, a confirmation page is displayed to the customer, summarizing customer, order, and shipping/billing information and indicating that the order has been processed (see Figure 13.4.)

As you can see, a single Visual Basic form is converted into several Web pages as a result of the different GUI behavior between the Web interface and the Win32 interface.

Figure 13.3: *The Place an Order page.*

Figure 13.4: *The confirmation page summarizes order information.*

Putting It All Together

The Northwind application has evolved over the course of the previous chapters. In each chapter, you added a new COM+ feature. Additionally, you added Web functionality in this chapter. Now let's look at the big picture, the application architecture. Later, you'll drill down to individual service layers to take a closer look at the application.

The N-Tiered Application Architecture

Figure 13.5 is a Unified Modeling Language (UML) diagram that illustrates the N-tiered, Windows DNA architecture of the Northwind Traders Online application.

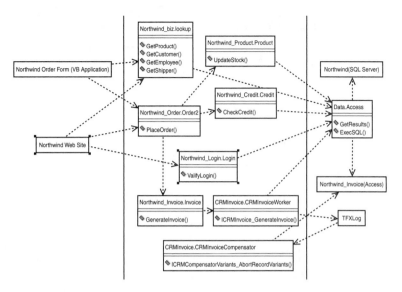

Figure 13.5: *The architecture of the Northwind Traders Online Windows DNA application.*

Compare this diagram with Figure 7.11 of Chapter 7, "Compensating Resource Manager (CRM)," to see the two new components added to the application. The first new component is the Web site front end, and the second is the new COM component that helps provide security for the Web application.

The Workflow

Figure 13.6 illustrates the workflow of the Northwind Traders Online Web application.

The following are the steps of the workflow:

1. A customer enters customer ID and password information and clicks the Login button. This login page initiates the Login object and calls the VerifyLogin() method. The Login object, in turn, creates an instance of the Data.Access object and executes a stored procedure through the Data.Access object to verify the customer ID and password. If the customer successfully logged in, the product list page is displayed for the customer.

2. The product list page creates an instance of the Lookup object, which, in turn, submits a stored procedure call to the Data.Access object to return a list of products. The customer can click one of the hyperlinks on the product list page to display the Place an Order page.

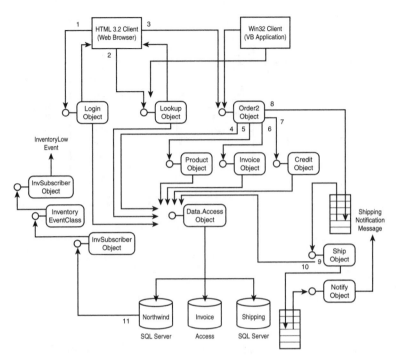

Figure 13.6: *The workflow of the Northwind Traders Online Web application.*

3. After the customer specifies the quantity he or she wants to order and clicks the Check Out button, the order Web page initiates an Order2 object to process the order. (For a description of the Order2 object, read Chapter 7). This action starts a transaction. The Order2 object is the root of the transaction.

4. The Order2 object inserts an order (populating both Orders and Order Details tables) by calling a stored procedure through the Data.Access object.

5. After inserting an order into the database, the Order2 object needs to update the units in stock of the Products table. It does so by creating a Product object, which, in turn, calls a stored procedure through the Data.Access object. At this point, the stored procedure compares the quantity being ordered to the number of units in stock. If the quantity is greater than the number of units in stock, an error is raised and the transaction is aborted.

6. The Order2 object then creates an instance of the Invoice object to add an invoice to the Invoice database through the Data.Access object. Because the Invoice database is a Microsoft Access database, the

transaction of the inserting-invoice process is protected through the Compensating Resource Manager of COM+, as described in Chapter 7.

7. The Order2 object initializes the Credit object to verify the customer's credit. The Credit object calls a stored procedure through the Data.Access object to check the customer's credit history.

8. If the customer passes the credit verification, the Order2 object creates a Queued Component, the Ship object, through the Queued Components service of COM+ to send a shipping request. At this point, if everything goes well, the Order2 object commits the transaction and makes all the changes permanent.

9. The Ship Queued Component inserts a shipping record to the Shipping database through the Data.Access object.

10. The Ship object creates another Queued Component, the Notify object, to send a shipping notification.

11. An update trigger in the Products table of the Northwind database watches the changes of the inventory. If the number of units in stock for a specific product is lower than 10 as the result of an update, the trigger calls a stored procedure, which creates an instance of a publisher object through OLE automation (InvPublisher). The publisher object, in turn, initializes an instance of the EventClass and fires a COM+ LCE event. The COM+ event system locates the subscriber object (InvSubscriber) to deliver the event.

Now that you've walked through the entire order processing workflow, you can see that the Northwind Traders Online application is a multitiered, highly distributed application. The application takes advantage of all the important COM+ services, including Transaction Services, the Compensating Resource Manager, Queued Components, and Loosely Coupled Events.

You should also notice that, because Northwind Traders Online is a Windows DNA application, every request from the client to the database is handled by middle-tier COM or COM+ components. The front ends (either the HTML 3.2 client or the Win32 client) never directly interact with databases. The database schemas and physical locations are totally transparent to the clients.

In addition, the middle tier is further partitioned as two subtiers. The business logic tier contains business objects such as Login, Lookup, Order2, Product, Invoice, and Credit. The data access tier contains one generic data access object, the Data.Access object, which encapsulates all the intricate details of dealing with database back ends. In this Data.Access object, you use the Microsoft ActiveX Data Objects (ADO) object model as the database-accessing mechanism to all the databases—either SQL Server databases or Microsoft Access databases. The business logic tier objects access databases through the Data.Access object.

The Presentation Tier: User Services

As in any typical Windows DNA application, the presentation layer of the Northwind application contains both a Win32 client built in Visual Basic and an HTML 3.2 client built in Active Server Pages. The Win32 client application is used by the Northwind employees at their corporate call centers, whereas the HTML 3.2 Web client is used directly by customers 24 hours a day, 7 days a week through the Internet.

Due to the differences in their GUI behaviors, the HTML 3.2 Web client contains four Web pages, whereas the Win32 application has only one Visual Basic form.

The Northwind Traders Online Web site uses Microsoft Active Server Pages technology. As you learned in Chapter 2, "Windows DNA 2000 and COM+," an ASP page is server-side scripting code saved in a .asp file and stored on the Internet Information Services (IIS) Web server. An .asp file can contain both scripting code and standard HTML code. The scripting code executes on the server side and sends back pure HTML pages to the Web browser.

The Northwind Traders Online application has four ASP pages, as shown in Figure 13.7. These ASP pages were developed in Microsoft Visual InterDev 6.0.

Figure 13.7: *Northwind Traders Online ASP pages in a Visual InterDev project.*

Table 13.1 summarizes these ASP pages and their functions.

Table 13.1   ASP Pages in the Northwind Traders Online Web Application

ASP Page	Description
Login.asp	Handles user logins, checks the customer ID and password, and generates an HTML page as in Figure 13.1
Products.asp	Displays a list of available products, generates an HTML page as in Figure 13.2, and allows the customer to select a product from the list
Order.asp	Handles online orders and generates an HTML page as in Figure 13.3
Confirmation.asp	Displays a confirmation page to the customer about his or her order by generating an HTML page as in Figure 13.4

You'll learn about these ASP pages in detail later in this chapter as you build your Web site.

The Middle Tier: Business Services

The middle tier of the Northwind Traders Online application contains both nonconfigured components and COM+ configured components, depending on whether the components need transaction or other COM+ services.

NONCONFIGURED COMPONENTS

The Northwind Traders Online application has two nonconfigured components: Northwind_Login.Login and Northwind_Biz.Lookup. The methods of these components simply query the databases and get results returned from databases. No database updating is involved in these components, so you don't need transactions here. Besides, these two components do not need any other COM+ services, such as CRM, QC, and LCE. Therefore, they are designed as nonconfigurable, regular COM components.

Tables 13.2 and 13.3 describe the methods supported in the Northwind_Login.Login and Northwind_Biz.Lookup components, respectively.

*Table 13.2   Method of the **Northwind_Login.Login** Component*

Method	Description
VerifyLogin	Checks customer credentials based on the customer ID and password

*Table 13.3   Methods of the **Northwind_Biz.Lookup** Component*

Methods	Description
GetProduct	Returns a list of products
GetCustomer	Returns a list of customers
GetEmployee	Returns a list of employees
GetShipper	Returns a list of shippers

The HTML 3.2 Web client uses only the GetProduct() method of the Northwind_Biz.Lookup component.

COM+ CONFIGURED COMPONENTS

Most of the components in the Northwind Traders Online application are COM+ configured components. Depending on the different COM+ services required, these configured components reside in several COM+ applications. Figure 13.8 shows all the COM+ applications and components used in the Northwind Traders Online application as they appear in the Component Services snap-in.

Figure 13.8: *Northwind Traders Online COM+ applications and their components in the Component Services snap-in.*

You can create, install, and configure these COM+ applications and their components by using the Component Services snap-in, as you did in Chapters 6, "Writing Transactional Components," 7, "Compensating Resource Manager (CRM)," 9, "Queued Components," and 10, "COM+ Events." You also can create, install, and configure these COM+ applications and components programmatically through the COM+ Administration object model, as you saw in Chapter 11, "Administering COM+ Applications Programmatically."

The following sections describe the Northwind Traders COM+ applications and the components installed.

NORTHWIND

Northwind is a regular COM+ application that hosts the following components that need transaction services:

- **Data.Access**—This generic data access component encapsulates all the data access APIs and interacts between business tier components and the data stores. The Data.Access component is configured as Support Transaction so that it can be enlisted in the caller's transaction context when requested. See Chapter 6 for detailed information about this component.

- **Northwind_Order.Order**—This legacy component supports existing versions of the Visual Basic Northwind Ordering clients. It is configured as Requires Transaction and will be the root of the transaction. See Chapter 6 for detailed information about this component.

- **Northwind_Order.Order2**—This component is an enhanced version of the Northwind_Order.Order component. You created this separate interface earlier to see how to use multiple interfaces to support component evolution. The new functionalities added to this component include a call that involves interaction with an Access database that is protected by the Compensating Resource Manager. This component is also configured as Requires Transaction and will be the root of the transaction. See Chapter 7 for detailed information about this component.

- **Northwind_Product.Product**—This component is used by the Order or Order2 component to deduct the number of units in stock in the Products table based on the quantity ordered. See Chapter 6 for detailed information about this component.

NORTHWIND CRM

Northwind CRM is a COM+ application that has the Compensating Resource Manager service enabled. It contains the following components:

- **CRMInvoice.CRMInvoiceWorker and CRMInvoice.CRMInvoiceCompensator**—These components were developed to use the extended transaction services provided by the COM+ Compensating Resource Manager infrastructure. The CRMInvoiceWorker component is configured as Support Transaction, whereas the CRMInvoiceCompensator component is configured as Disabled. See Chapter 7 for detailed information about these components.

- **Northwind_Invoice.Invoice**—This component inserts an invoice into the Invoice database in Microsoft Access. It performs the insertion through the CRMInvoice.CRMInvoiceWorker component so that the transaction can be protected by the COM+ CRM service. This component is configured as Support Transaction. See Chapter 7 for detailed information about this component.

- **Northwind_Credit.Credit**—This component checks the credit history of a particular customer and decides whether the transaction should be committed or aborted based on the results. This component is also configured as Support Transaction, although it involves only a Select type (query) database interaction. See Chapter 7 for detailed information about this component.

NORTHWIND SHIPPING

The Northwind Shipping COM+ application contains two Queued Components:

- **Northwind_Ship.Ship**—This QC is called by the Northwind_Order.Order2 component asynchronously through the COM+ QC service. It inserts shipping records in the Shipping database and invokes another QC, Northwind_Notify.Notify, to send a shipping notification message. See Chapter 9 for detailed information about this component.

- **Northwind_Notify.Notify**—This QC is called by the Northwind_Ship.Ship component through the COM+ QC Service to send a shipping notification message. See Chapter 9 for detailed information about this component.

NORTHWIND INVENTORY EVENTCLASS AND NORTHWIND INVENTORY SUBSCRIBER

The Northwind Inventory EventClass and Northwind Inventory Subscriber COM+ applications work together to provide COM+ LCE services to the Northwind application. They have the following components:

- **Northwind_Inventory.Inventory**—This EventClass defines the event interface. This component is installed as an EventClass in the Northwind Inventory EventClass COM+ application. It is invoked by the publisher and works with the COM+ event system to deliver the event to appropriate event subscribers. See Chapter 10 for detailed information about this EventElass.

- **Northwind_InvSubscriber.InvSubscriber**—This event subscriber is installed in the Northwind Inventory Subscriber COM+ application, a separate COM+ application from the EventClass. This component subscribes the event defined in the Inventory EventClass. See Chapter 10 for detailed information about this component.

NOTE

These applications also have another component: the event publisher named
Northwind_InvPublisher.Publisher. This publisher component is not shown in
Figure 13.8 because it is a nonconfigured component. See Chapter 10 for detailed
information.

The Data Tier: Data Services

The data services tier contains two SQL Server databases: Northwind and Shipping. It also has an Access database: Invoice.

Many stored procedures have also been implemented to simplify the database access and manipulation of the middle-tier components. The stored procedures are also called by database triggers to publish a COM+ LCE event. See Chapters 6, 7, 9, and 10 for descriptions of most stored procedures used in Northwind. Later in this chapter, you will see a couple of new stored procedures used by the Web pages.

Building the Northwind Traders Online Web Site

The following sections demonstrate how to build the Northwind Traders Online Web application that will leverage the Windows DNA architecture of the existing Northwind Ordering System you built in previous chapters.

This Web application is built as four ASP pages developed in Microsoft Visual InterDev 6.0, as you saw earlier in Figure 13.7. I'm not going to cover how to use Visual InterDev here because it is beyond the scope of this book. Instead, I'll walk you through the ASP page source code to explain how the Web site works.

EXAMPLE

The Login Page

The login page in Figure 13.1 is implemented in an ASP page, Login.asp. Listing 13.1 shows the code for this page. All the metatags inserted by Visual InterDev have been stripped out.

Listing 13.1 Login.asp

```
<html><head>
<title>Northwind Traders Online</title>
<script language = javascript>
<!--

function ValidateFields(theForm) {
    if (theForm.CustomerID.value == "")
    {
        alert("Customer ID is missing!");
        theForm.CustomerID.focus();
        return (false);
    }

    if (theForm.Password.value == "")
    {
        alert("Password is missing!");
        theForm.Password.focus();
        return (false);
    }
return (true);
}

//-->
</script>
</head>
<body>
    <center>
    <IMG height=242 src="images/northwindlogo.gif"
        style ="HEIGHT: 126px; WIDTH: 138px" width=258 >
    </center>
    <center> </center>
    <center><font color="darkred" face="Tahoma" size="5">
        Welcome to Northwind Traders Online !</font></center>
    <center> </center>
    <center>Please Enter Your Customer ID and Password</center>
    <center>Then Click the Login Button to login:</center>
    <center> </center>

<center>
<form action=login.asp method=post id=frmLogin name=frmLogin
        onsubmit ="return ValidateFields(this)">
  <table border="0" cellPadding="1" cellSpacing="1" width="75%"
    style="HEIGHT: 61px; WIDTH: 293px">
  <tr>
    <td>
        <p align="right"><em>
```

Listing 13.1   continued

```
            <font face="Arial">Customer ID</font></em></p></td>
      <td><input id="CustomerID" name="CustomerID"
          style ="HEIGHT: 22px; WIDTH: 158px"></td></tr>
    <tr>
      <td>
        <p align="right"><em>
          <font face="Arial">Password</font></em></p></td>
      <td><input id="Password" name="Password"
          style  ="HEIGHT: 22px; WIDTH: 158px" type="password"
 ></td>
   </tr>
   </table>
   <p><input id="submit1" name="submit1" type="submit" value="Login"
        style="HEIGHT: 24px; WIDTH: 61px">  
   <input id=reset1 name=reset1
        style="HEIGHT: 24px; WIDTH: 55px" type=reset value=Clear>
   </p>
</form>
</center>
</body></html>
<%
    if Request.Item("CustomerID") <> "" and Request.Item("Password")<> "" then
        dim oLogin
        dim rsCustomers
        dim sCustomerID, sPassword,sError
        sCustomerID = Request.Item("CustomerID")
        sPassword = Request.Item("Password")
        set oLogin = server.CreateObject("Northwind_login.Login")
        set rsCustomers = oLogin.VerifyLogin("Northwind",sCustomerID,
                                                    sPassword,sError)

        if sError="" then
            session("CustomerID")=sCustomerID
            session("CompanyName")=rsCustomers("CompanyName")
            session("Address")=rsCustomers("Address")
            session("City")=rsCustomers("City")
            session("Region")=rsCustomers("Region")
            session("PostalCode")=rsCustomers("PostalCode")
            session("Country")=rsCustomers("Country")
            Response.Redirect "Products.asp"
        else
            Response.Write "<center><b>" & sError & "</b></center>"

        end if
    end if
%>
```

The first part of the Login.asp code defines the JavaScript function ValidateFields(). The function is enclosed inside the <script></script> tags. It will be called inside the Web browser, not executed at the server side. This is called *client-side scripting*. Client-side scripting is used for simple data validation and calculations that do not require a round trip to the server to get feedback. I chose JavaScript instead of VBScript for client-side scripting here because, unlike VBScript, which is somehow Internet Explorer–specific, JavaScript is supported by most Web browsers. Therefore, using JavaScript for client-side scripting extends browser independence. The ValidateFields function checks whether the customer ID and password are entered by the customer. If the customer has not completed this information and tries to click the Login button, a message box pops up reminding the customer that some information is missing (see Figure 13.9).

Figure 13.9: The ValidateFields *function fires off a message.*

Following the ValidateFields function is the majority of the HTML code between the <body></body> tags; this code defines the interface of the login page as shown in Figure 13.1.

The rest of code in Login.asp, inside a pair of <%,%> tags, is the server-side scripting code executed on the IIS Web server. The server-side scripting is really what ASP is all about. This code in Login.asp creates an instance of the Northwind_Login.Login object and calls its VerifyLogin() method by passing in the customer ID and password. The script uses three internal objects. The Server object creates an instance of an object by calling its

CreateObject() method. The Session object stores global data so that it can be used by other pages. The script also uses the Response object. If the login succeeds, the script displays the product list (Products.asp) by calling the Redirect method of the Response object, as shown in Figure 13.2 earlier. Otherwise, it calls the Write method of the Response object to display the error on the login page (see Figure 13.10).

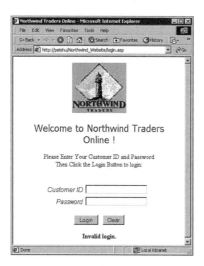

Figure 13.10: *An invalid customer ID and/or password.*

Notice that you use an HTML form object (frmLogin) to help collect information and submit it to the Login.asp page using the Post method.

The ASP code relies on the Northwind_Login.Login object to perform the login verification. Northwind_Login.Login is created in an ActiveX DLL project that has one class module named Login.cls (see Figure 13.11).

Figure 13.11: *The Northwind_Login.Login project.*

The Northwind_Login.Login component supports one method, VerifyLogin(), as shown in Listing 13.2.

Listing 13.2   The VerifyLogin() Method of the Northwind_Login.Login Component

```
Public Function VerifyLogin(ByVal sConnection As String, _
                            ByVal sCustomerID As String, _
```

Listing 13.2   continued

```
                                  ByVal sPassword As String, _
                                  ByRef sError As Variant) As Variant


    Dim oRs        As Object 'ADODB.Recordset
    Dim oData      As Object 'Data.Access object
    Dim sSQL       As String
    Dim lRows      As Long


    On Error GoTo VerifyLogin_Err


    Set oData = CreateObject("Data.Access")


    sSQL = "Exec Customers_VerifyLogin @CustomerID = '" & sCustomerID & "'" _
        & ", @Password = '" & sPassword & "'"


    Set oRs = oData.GetResult(sConnection, sSQL, lRows)


    If lRows = 0 Then
        sError = "Invalid login."
        Set VerifyLogin = Nothing
    Else
        Set VerifyLogin = oRs
    End If


    Exit Function
VerifyLogin_Err:
    VerifyLogin = 0
    sError = "Error " & CStr(Err.Number) & ": " & Err.Description & "."


End Function
```

As shown in Listing 13.2, the `VerifyLogin()` method creates an instance of the `Data.Access` object and calls its `GetResult()` method to execute a stored procedure, `Customer_VerifyLogin`. Listing 13.3 shows this stored procedure.

Listing 13.3   The `Customer_VerifyLogin` Stored Procedure

```
if exists(select 1 from sysobjects where id =
object_id("Customers_VerifyLogin"))
  drop proc Customers_VerifyLogin
go

create proc Customers_VerifyLogin
 @CustomerID nchar(5),
 @Password varchar(15)
```

Listing 13.3   continued

```
as

select      CompanyName,
     Address,
     City,
     Region,
     PostalCode,
     Country
from      Customers
where       CustomerID = @CustomerID
and         Password = @Password

if @@rowcount = 0
  raiserror ('Invalid login!.',16,1)
go
```

The `Customer_VerifyLogin` stored procedure returns a row from the Customers table according to the customer ID and password being passed in. If no row is found, the stored procedure raises an error to the `Northwind_Login.Login` component, which creates the error message displayed in the Web browser, as you saw in Figure 13.10.

You may notice that the stored procedure refers to a Password column in the Customers table that originally does not exist. To add this Password column in the Customers table and populate it with the default value (password), you need to run the Transact SQL script shown in Listing 13.4. The `alter table` keyword is used here.

Listing 13.4   Transact SQL Script That Adds a Password Column to the Customers Table and Populates This Column with a Default Value

```
use northwind
go

alter table Customers
add Password varchar(15) null
default 'password' with values

go
```

TIP

Prior to SQL Server 7.0, if you compiled a stored procedure that had a reference to a nonexisting object, such as a column name or table name, you got a compile error. In SQL Server 7.0, however, the names are not resolved at compile time. Rather, the names are resolved the first time the stored procedure is executed. This new feature of SQL Server 7.0 is called *deferred name resolution*. Refer to SQL Server Books Online for more information.

The Product Selection Page

After the user successfully logs in the application, he or she sees the Product Selection page shown earlier in Figure 13.2. Listing 13.5 shows the code for this page in Products.asp.

Listing 13.5 Products.asp

```
<%@ Language=VBScript %>
<html>
<head>
<title>Select A Product</title>
</head>
<body>
<p align="left"><font face="verdana" size="6">
    <strong>Product Selection </strong></font></p>
<p align="left"><em><font face="verdana">
    <strong>Select a product from the list:</strong></font></em></p>
<div align="left">
<%
dim oLookup
dim rsProducts

set oLookup = server.CreateObject("Northwind_Biz.Lookup")
set rsProducts = oLookup.GetProduct("Northwind")
%>
<table border=1>
    <tr>
        <td align="center" bgcolor="#C0C0C0">
            <strong>Product ID</strong></td>
        <td align="left" bgcolor="#C0C0C0">
            <strong>Product Name</strong></td>
    </tr>

<%do until rsProducts.EOF%>
    <tr>
        <td align="center">
            <a href="Order.asp?ProductID=<%=rsProducts("ProductID")%>">
            <%=rsProducts("ProductID")%></td>
        <td align="left"><%=rsProducts("ProductName")%></td>
    </tr>
<%     rsProducts.MoveNext
loop
rsProducts.MoveFirst
%>
</table>
</div>
</body>
</html>
```

The style used in Products.asp is a little different from Login.asp. In Login.asp, all the server-side scripts are located at the end of the file and enclosed inside a pair of <% and %> tags. In Products.asp, however, the scripts are mixed with the standard HTML code all over the page. The inline scripting syntax <%=...%> is equivalent to <% Response.Write ... %>. No matter which style you choose, however, the output is the same: a pure HTML page. The server-side scripts are not seen from the browser; they run at the server side as the name implies.

The first part of the page defines the table header in standard HTML syntax (between the <body> tag and the oLookup object declaration).

The next part of the page uses mixed HTML code and scripts to complete the table. Here, you declare two object variables. The first object variable, oLookup, holds an instance of the Northwind_Lookup.Lookup object. The second object, rsProducts, holds the ADO recordset returned by the GetProduct() method call. After the recordset is returned from the database, you loop through the recordset and populate the HTML table.

Notice that the first column, the product ID in the HTML table, is implemented as a hyperlink by using the <a> tag, which points to another ASP page, Order.asp. When a customer clicks a product ID on this page, the browser displays the Order.asp page with the information about the selected product. You establish this hyperlink by using the QueryString collection of the Request object. The Request object is another ASP internal object that collects information from the browser and passes it to the server. The query string uses the following syntax:

```
<target page> ? <parm1>=<value> & <parm2>=<Value> & ...
```

You can submit multiple parameter/value pairs, separated by an ampersand. Here, you pass the product ID to Orders.asp as follows:

```
<a href="Order.asp?ProductID=<%=rsProducts("ProductID")%>">
```

NOTE

Unlike Visual Basic, in ASP, every variable is a variant data type. For this reason, you declare variables using only the Dim keyword without using As Datatype.

EXAMPLE

The Ordering Page

After the customer decides which product he or she wants to order and clicks the product ID on the Product page, the Order page opens, as you saw in Figure 13.3. Listing 13.6 shows the code of the Order.asp page.

Listing 13.6   Order.asp

```
<%@ Language = VBScript %>
<html>
<head>
<title>Place an Order</title>
</head>
<body>
<script language = javaScript>
<!--
function ValidateForm(theForm)
{
  var checkOK = "0123456789-,";
  var checkStr = theForm.Quantity.value;
  var allValid = true;
  var decPoints = 0;
  var allNum = "";
  for (i = 0;  i < checkStr.length;  i++)
  {
    ch = checkStr.charAt(i);
    for (j = 0;  j < checkOK.length;  j++)
      if (ch == checkOK.charAt(j))
        break;
    if (j == checkOK.length)
    {
      allValid = false;
      break;
    }
    if (ch != ",")
      allNum += ch;
  }
  if (!allValid)
  {
    alert("Please enter only digit characters in the \"Quantity\" field.");
    theForm.Quantity.focus();
    return (false);
  }
  if (theForm.Quantity.value < 1)
  {
    alert("The \"Quantity\" field must be greater than 1.");
    theForm.Quantity.focus();
    return (false);
  }
  return (true);
}
//-->
</script>
<form action="Comfirmation.asp" method=post id=frmOrder name=frmOrder
```

Listing 13.6 continued

```
    onsubmit="return ValidateForm(this)">
<%

    dim rsProduct
    dim oData
    dim sSQL

    sSQL = "exec Products_GetByID @ProductID = " & Request("ProductID")

    set oData = server.CreateObject("Data.Access")
    set rsProduct = oData.GetResult("Northwind",sSQL,0)

    session("ProductID") = rsProduct("ProductID")
    session("ProductName") = rsProduct("ProductName")
    session("UnitPrice") = rsProduct("UnitPrice")

%>
    <center>
    <table border = 0 cellspacing="5">
        <tr>
            <td align="right"><strong><em>Product ID:
</em></strong></td>
            <td align="left"><strong><%=rsProduct("ProductID")%></strong></td>
        </tr>
        <tr>
            <td align="right"><strong><em>Product Name:    </em></strong></td>
            <td align="left"><strong><%=rsProduct("ProductName")%></strong></td>
        </tr>
        <tr>
            <td align="right"><strong><em>Unit Price :
    </em></strong></td>
            <td align="left"><strong>$<%=rsProduct("UnitPrice")%></strong></td>
        </tr>
        <tr>
            <td align="right"><strong><em>Quantity:    </em></strong></td>
            <td align="left"><input id="Quantity" name="Quantity" value=1
style="HEIGHT: 22px; WIDTH: 50px"></td>
        </tr>
    </table>
    </center>
    <center> </center>
    <center>
        <input id=submit1 name=submit1 type=submit value="Check Out">
    </center>
</form>
</body>
</html>
```

As in the Login.asp page, the first part of this page is a client-side validation function named `ValidateForm()` written in JavaScript. This function makes sure that a valid quantity value is entered before submitting the request to the server for processing.

Again, you use an HTML form (`frmOrder`) with a `Post` method to collect the information from the customer. The Confirmation.asp page is specified as the destination page of the Post action.

In Order.asp, you create an instance of the `Data.Access` object and execute a stored procedure by calling its `GetResult()` method. This returns a one-row ADO recordset, with the information for the product specified by the ProductID. Listing 13.7 shows the `Products_GetByID` stored procedure.

Listing 13.7   The `Products_GetByID` Stored Procedure

```
if exists(select * from sysobjects where id = object_id('Products_GetByID'))
 drop proc Products_GetByID
go

create proc Products_GetByID
 @ProductID int
as
select      ProductID,
            ProductName,
            UnitPrice
from        Products
where       UnitsInStock > 0
and         ProductID = @ProductID
go
```

The product information, such as product ID, product name, and unit price, is listed in a borderless table, along with one field for the customer to specify the quantity of the product he or she wants to order.

EXAMPLE

The Confirmation Page

When the customer specifies the quantity for the product and clicks the Check Out button, the code in Confirmation.asp is executed on the Web server. Listing 13.8 shows the code in Confirmation.asp.

Listing 13.8   Confirmation.asp

```
<%@ Language=VBScript %>
<html
<head>
<title>Order Confirmation</title>
</head>
```

Listing 13.8   continued

```
<body>
<%

    Response.Buffer = true

    dim oOrder
    dim iProductID
    dim sProductName
    dim cUnitPrice
    dim iQuantity
    dim sCustomerID
    dim dOrderDate
    dim dRequiredDate
    dim dShippedDate
    dim sCompanyName
    dim sAddress
    dim sCity
    dim sRegion
    dim sPostalCode
    dim sCountry
    dim cSubTotal
    dim cTotal

    iProductID = session("ProductID")
    sProductName = session("ProductName") & ""
    cUnitPrice = session("UnitPrice")
    iQuantity = Request("Quantity")
    sCustomerID = session("CustomerID") & ""
    dOrderDate = date()
    dRequiredDate = DateAdd("d", 21, dOrderDate)
    dShippedDate = DateAdd("d", 14, dOrderDate)
    sCompanyName = session("CompanyName") & ""
    sAddress = session("Address") & ""
    sCity = session("City") & ""
    sRegion = session("Region") & ""
    sPostalCode = session("PostalCode") & ""
    sCountry = session("Country") & ""
    cSubTotal =  cUnitPrice * cint(iQuantity)
    cTotal = cSubTotal + 15

    Response.Write "<h3>Your order has been processed as follows.<br>" _
                    & "Thank you for your business!</h3>"

    Response.Write "<strong><em>Customer Information</em></strong><br>"
    Response.Write "Customer ID: " & sCustomerID & "<br>"
```

Listing 13.8 continued

```
Response.Write "Customer Name: " & sCompanyName & "<br><br>"

Response.Write "<strong><em>Order Information</em></strong><br>"

Response.Write "Date Ordered: " & dOrderDate & "<br>"
Response.Write "Date Required: " & dRequiredDate & "<br>"
Response.Write "Product ID: " & iProductID & "<br>"
Response.Write "Product Name: " & sProductName & "<br>"
Response.Write "Unit Price: $" & cUnitPrice & "<br>"
Response.Write "Quantity: " & iQuantity & "<br><br>"

Response.Write "<strong><em>Shipping/Billing Information</em></strong><br>"
Response.Write "Ship to/Bill to: " & sCompanyName & "<br>"
Response.write "Address: " & sAddress & "<br>"
Response.Write "City: " &  sCity & "<br>"
Response.Write "Region: " & sRegion & "<br>"
Response.Write "PostalCode: " & sPostalCode & "<br>"
Response.Write "Country: " & sCountry & "<br>"
Response.Write "Subtotal: $" & cSubTotal & "<br>"
Response.Write "Freight: $" & "15<br>"
Response.Write "Total: $" & cTotal & "<br>"
Response.Write "Scheduled Shipping Date: " & dShippedDate & "<br>"

on error resume next
set oOrder = server.CreateObject("Northwind_Order.Order2")


oOrder.PlaceOrder iProductID, _
                  cUnitPrice, _
                  iQuantity, _
                  sCustomerID, _
                  10, _
                  dOrderDate, _
                  dRequiredDate, _
                  dShippedDate, _
                  1, _
                  15, _
                  sCompanyName, _
                  sAddress, _
                  sCity, _
                  sRegion, _
                  sPostalCode, _
                  sCountry, _
                  sCompanyName, _
                  "Web Order", _
                  "Speedy Express", _
```

Listing 13.8   continued

```
                        sProductName, _
                        cSubTotal, _
                        cTotal

    if err.number<> 0 then
        Response.Clear
        Response.Write "<h3>The following error has occurred.<br>" _
                        & "Your order has been cancelled!</h3>"

        Response.Write err.description
    end if

    Set oOrder = Nothing
%>
</body>
</html>
```

The code in Listing 13.7 creates an instance of the Northwind_Order.Order2 object, passing all the parameters from the variables stored in the session object. If the call succeeds, the browser displays a confirmation message along with the information about the order, as you saw in Figure 13.4 earlier. Should an error occur, the browser will display the error message. For example, if a customer tries to order more products than are in stock, he or she will get a message indicating that an error has occurred and the order has been canceled, along with the error information, as shown in Figure 13.12.

Figure 13.12: *The browser displays an error and tells the customer the order has been canceled because of the error.*

Testing the COM+ Enabled Web Application

At this point, you have walked through all the code in the four ASP pages. Conceptually, they are the same as the code in the Visual Basic order form you built in Chapters 6 and 7.

Now let's check the COM+ feature. These COM+ functionalities are built into the middle-tier components and have nothing to do with which type of client you are using, either a Win32 VB application or an HTML 3.2 Web application. Let's test the Web site to see if this is true.

First, test the transaction behavior, including the automatic transaction service and the CRM. To do so, log in as customer **Blondel père et fils** with customer ID **BLONP** and pick a product from the list. In this case, choose Aniseed Syrup by clicking Product ID 3 on the Product Selection page. The Order page then displays the product ID, name, and unit price information; it also displays 1 as the default quantity, similar to the page shown earlier in Figure 13.3. When you click the Check Out button, you see a page like the one in Figure 13.13.

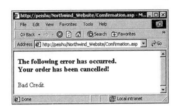

Figure 13.13: The browser displays an error, indicating the customer has a bad credit history.

Recall that, in Chapter 7, you intentionally gave all the customers whose names start with the letter *B* a bad credit history. So, this order is not processed, nor is the invoice. Therefore, you know that both Transaction Services and the CRM are working. You can confirm this fact by following the procedures outlined in Chapter 7.

Now that you know the transaction is working for both traditional DTC-based and new COM+ CRM-based transactions, what about the Queued Components feature? To test the QC, log in as customer **Cactus Comidas para llevar** with a customer ID of **CACTU**. Now try to order one item with Product ID 3, Aniseed Syrup. Figure 13.14 show the results: a confirmation page with a message from the Northwind_Notify.Notify Queued Component.

You can query the Shipping database to confirm the order, as shown in Figure 13.15.

So far, so good! The next thing you should check is the LCE event's functionality. If you check the Products table, you'll find that the current inventory level for Product ID 3 is 33. Now go back to the Order page by clicking the Back button on the browser's toolbar. This time, try to order 30 items of the Aniseed Syrup. So, type **30** in the Quantity box and click the Check Out button. This time, you get a message from the Inventory event subscriber, as shown in Figure 13.16, indicating the inventory for Product ID 3 is low, and you need to place a back order.

Figure 13.14: *The message from the Queued Component indicates that the shipping for the order has been scheduled.*

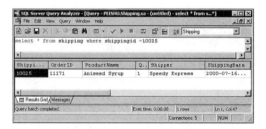

Figure 13.15: *Querying the Shipping database to confirm the shipping for the order.*

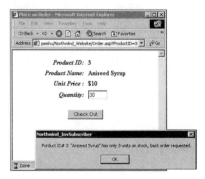

Figure 13.16: *A message from the COM+ events services (LCE) indicates that the inventory level for the ordered product is low.*

You can see that the LCE works just as it is supposed to. Everything is in order!

Conclusions

This chapter discussed in detail the architectural design of the Northwind application you built in the preceding chapters. It also demonstrated how to build a COM+ enabled, Windows DNA 2000 application by using Active Server Pages and the COM+ components you built previously. The purpose of this chapter was to demonstrate how to build a complete Windows DNA 2000 application that leverages all the important COM+ services.

The Web site you built in this chapter uses some very basic ASP and Web development techniques. It provides only the minimal functionality to support this sample application. The focus was on how to use the COM+ services from ASP pages.

I did not intend to teach you ASP programming. You can find plenty of books and resources out there that cover these topics, so I don't need to repeat them here. For this reason, I did not cover the parts of a regular Business-to-Consumers (B2C) commerce Web site, such as a shopping cart, cookies, and page navigation. These topics are beyond the scope of this book.

This chapter does, however, demonstrate the principles of good Windows DNA application design—that is, separating business logic from the presentation layer and putting it into the COM or COM+ components in the middle tier. In the ASP pages of this example, you can see that every request for data accessing and manipulation is done through the middle-tier components. The database back end is totally hidden from the ASP front end, which makes the distributed application more scalable, more flexible, and more maintainable. I have seen many poorly designed ASP applications in which several stored procedure calls and event-embedded SQL statements are put in the ASP pages themselves. This is actually a two-tiered approach, and it suffers from many scalability and maintainability issues.

The sample Windows DNA application you built in this and the preceding chapters will provide you with some general guidelines for developing distributed enterprise and Internet applications using COM+ services and the Windows DNA framework. It will give you a good starting point for building real-world Windows DNA 2000 applications using COM+ technology.

What's Next

In this chapter, you had a chance to examine a complete Windows DNA application using all the important COM+ services you learned in this book. In Chapter 14, "A Case Study: COM+ and Enterprise Application Integration (EAI)," you will learn how you can use COM+ services to solve many problems presented in a real-world Enterprise Application Integration (EAI) scenario.

A Case Study: COM+ and Enterprise Application Integration (EAI)

In the preceding chapter, you built a complete Windows DNA 2000 application using all the important COM+ services. In this chapter, you will learn how you can use COM+ along with the eXtensible Markup Language (XML) technology in the Enterprise Application Integration (EAI) arena to solve many problems. You'll use a real-world scenario for the case study.

This chapter teaches you the following:

- The fundamentals of EAI
- The issues involved in an EAI implementation
- How to use COM+ and XML to provide an EAI solution
- How to walk through the source code

Introduction to Enterprise Application Integration

In some large organizations, different computer systems have been built over the course of several decades, using various tools and technologies and running on different platforms. Even medium-sized companies have all kinds of computer applications, built at different times with different tools that are all running to support the business. Moreover, mergers and consolidations among organizations occur almost daily, bringing together different systems running at different physical locations. All these scenarios present a big challenge—how to make these diverse systems talk to each other without significantly rewriting any of them. This is where *Enterprise Application Integration (EAI)* fits in.

Enterprise Application Integration is a process that brings diverse computer applications together by using enabling technologies, such as message queuing middleware, and data exchange standards, such as Electronic Data Interchange (EDI) or the emerging standard—eXtensible Markup Language (XML). Message queuing middleware allows applications to interact with one another in a loosely coupled, asynchronous fashion. Open standards (XML, for example) allow different applications to exchange data with one another in a mutual understandable manner. Together, these enabling technologies help applications that are implemented in different languages on different platforms to seamlessly integrate with each other without having to modify any of these applications themselves.

Applications involved in EAI processes can be just about anything, from desktop applications to legacy systems to Web applications. The goal of EAI is to make all the disparate and dissimilar computer systems work together in an organization or between business partners as though they were one single system.

The Case Study

This section discusses a real-world EAI story so that you can see the issues involved in creating the original architecture. Then you will see how you can use COM+ to resolve the problems presented by this situation. For this case study, I have replaced the real names for the parties involved with fictitious names.

The Background

The E-LAWS company is a national leader in electronic filing (E-File) of legal documents through the Internet. The E-File services provided at the company's Web site replace the traditional method of filing, serving, storing, and retrieving court documents with a significantly more efficient electronic process. It reduces the manual process of duplicating, packaging, and delivering copies of documents to the court and serving parties.

The huge popularity of electronic filing services has brought E-LAWS many business opportunities. In the past few months, the company has built a business relationship with several government entities, including several state courts. Here, you'll review the company's EAI efforts with one of the state courts. The company is going to integrate a Web-based application with a Microsoft SQL Server 7.0 database, running under Windows NT 4.0 machines, with a legacy application that has a DB2 database running under the AS/400 systems.

The requirements of this EAI are as follows:

- The state court wants to utilize the existing E-LAWS Web site instead of building its own Web site that would simply duplicate the E-LAWS Web site's functionality.

- The modifications to the legacy system must be minimal. One main limitation is to allow the addition of only a few modules on top of the existing system to facilitate the integration process.

- A state court clerk will initialize or activate a case at the E-LAWS Web site. When this happens, this information needs to be stored in both the E-LAWS SQL Server database and state court's DB2 database.

- Updates to the status do not have to be in real-time but should occur as soon as all the data is stored on both sides of the integration.

- The integrated application shall be operational as soon as possible, preferably within six months.

Original Design

Figure 14.1 illustrates the original design developed by one of the major EAI venders in the country.

Let's walk through a case activation scenario for this integrated system. A state court clerk activates a case using a Web browser at the E-LAWS Web site. This activity causes the ASP page running at the E-LAWS IIS Web server to update the EFiling database and also sends a message to an MSMQ message queue.

A queue listener application developed in Visual C++ as an NT Service listens to the queue and picks up the message when it arrives. The application then instantiates one of the integration objects on-the-fly by using the Label property of the MSMQ message as the ProgID and the message itself as a single pipe-delimited (|) parameters string.

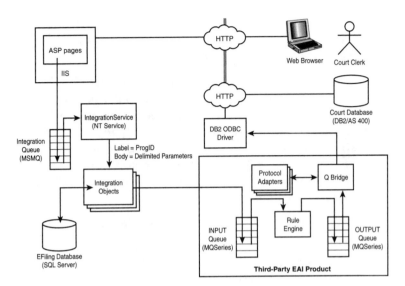

Figure 14.1: *The original integration design.*

The integration object parses the message into parameters and calls a stored procedure in the EFiling database to retrieve required data. Then it packs them together as a double pipe-delimited (| |) message and sends it to the INPUT queue of an IBM MQSeries queue manager.

The EAI Rule Engine then picks up the message from the INPUT queue and performs some lookup and validation tasks. It then sends a converted message as a single pipe-delimited string to another IBM MQSeries queue designated as the OUTPUT queue.

The EAI Queue Bridge listens to the OUTPUT queue, picks up the message when it arrives, and then converts the message into a SQL statement defined in one or more protocol adapters. The converted SQL statement is then executed against the DB2 database through the Internet using a third-party ODBC driver.

Several problems are associated with this design:

- The third-party EAI product supports only the IBM MQSeries as its message queuing middleware. This support may be desirable in a non-NT environment but does not make any sense in this scenario. Here, everything runs under the NT platform, the vendor specific requirement will only increase E-LAWS's cost for extra expensive MQSeries licenses, whereas MSMQ definitely meets all the message queuing functionalities the company requires. Besides, MSMQ has already been used in other areas of E-LAWS's applications.

- The Rule Engine and Queue Bridge used in this EAI product are both implemented as NT Services. It is very difficult to separate data flows (in-bound versus out-bound) and isolate failures.

- This EAI product doesn't offer sophisticated exception handling. Should the Queue Bridge fail to update the Court legacy database, the message will be lost. No retry or notification mechanism (using email, for example) is available.

- The protocol adapters store SQL statements, execution sequences, and other information and provide this information to the Queue Bridge at runtime. However, the database connection string (server name, database name, user ID, and password,) are embedded or hard-coded in these adapter files, making redeployment extremely difficult. There are more than 80 adapter files, and each adapter file contains one or more ODBC connection strings. If you want to move these files to another environment (for example, move them from the development servers to the quality control servers, or to the production servers), you need to reconfigure all these 80+ files by using a GUI tool provided by this EAI product. This would be extremely difficult to maintain!

- The MSMQ integration queue listener was developed in Visual C++ as an NT service. Should something go wrong, it will stop listening to the messaging events. Additionally, significant programming skills are required to develop and debug NT services.

- Although message queuing is used in this EAI product, it is used only on one side of the integration boundary—at the E-LAWS's system. The most critical path is the database update to the DB2 database through the Internet. This is a direct, synchronous action. This architecture is not robust. If the DB2 system is offline, all the attempts to update will fail.

EXAMPLE

The Solution: COM+ and XML

Now let's see how to resolve the problems in the original design by using COM+ and XML. Figure 14.2 illustrates the COM+/XML alternative to the original design.

This new design uses two important COM+ features: LCE events and Queued Components. It also uses XML to exchange data between systems. Let's see how it works.

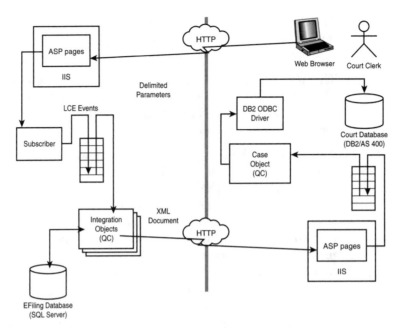

Figure 14.2: *The modified integration design using COM+ and XML.*

When a state court clerk activates a case through a Web browser at the E-LAWS Web site, the HTTP request is sent to an ASP page running under the E-LAWS IIS Web server. After updating the EFiling database, instead of sending a message to the MSMQ integration queue, the ASP page fires an LCE event.

In response to the LCE event, the event subscriber makes a call to one of the integration objects that is a Queued Component. Using Queued Components in conjunction with LCE improves scalability. The processing of the event messages do not block the events' firing because they are queued.

The integration object parses the input message into parameters and calls a stored procedure to retrieve related information from the EFiling database. It then generates an XML document based on the data returned from the stored procedure.

The XML document itself is sent through the Internet via the HTTP protocol to another ASP page running at the state court. The ASP page parses the XML document received, converts it to a SQL statement, and submits it to the database by calling another Queued Component.

This new design has many advantages:

- Using LCE events in conjunction with Queued Components provides a more durable solution, as opposed to developing an NT service to monitor an integration queue. The event subscribers and Queued Components are easy to write and can both be developed in Visual Basic. The rest of the job is to configure the appropriate COM+ applications.

- Configuring the integration objects as Queued Components improves the robustness of the integration. QC has a built-in retry mechanism. You can also specify a custom exception handling class, as you learned in Chapter 9, "Queued Components," to implement sophisticated exception handling and notification.

- Using the Queued Components on the other side of the fence—if the state court decouples the legacy system from the front end—again improves the robustness of the solution. It also uses fewer DB2 ODBC driver licenses because the database update requests are queued.

- Most importantly, the entire expensive third-party EAI product and the expensive IBM MQSeries are totally out of the picture. This is a big cost savings.

An XML Primer

Because eXtensible Markup Language technologies are used in this solution, I'll briefly introduce some basic XML here. I cannot, however, provide comprehensive coverage of XML. A more intensive study of XML is obviously beyond the scope of this book.

What Is XML?

Like Hypertext Markup Language (HTML), XML is also a tag-based language. Unlike HTML, which is used for *presenting* the data, however, XML is used for *describing* the data. In other words, HTML is about the representation of the data, whereas XML is about the data itself. XML is extremely useful in describing complicated hierarchically structured data. XML has become an emerging standard for data exchange. The XML standards are governed by the World Wide Web Consortium (W3C).

Due to the scope of this book, the rest of this section will only give you a quick introduction to XML so that you can better understand how XML is used in our sample application. To fully master the XML language, I highly recommend to you the book, *XML by Example*, also from Que.

An XML document that describes this book, for example, might look like this:

```
<Book type="Programming">
  <Title>Visual Basic and COM+ Programming By Example</Title>
  <ISBN>0789724588</ISBN>
  <Author>Peishu Li</Author>
  <Price>$29.99</Price>
  <Publisher>Que Publishing</Publisher>
</Book>
```

As you can see, everything in this XML document is wrapped in a pair of tags, `<Title></Title>`, `<ISBN></ISBN>`, and so on, pretty much like HTML.

The preceding XML document about the book is an example of a *well-formed XML document*. An XML document contains *elements*, such as `Book`, `Title`, `ISBN` and so on, in the preceding example. It can also have *attributes*, such as `Programming` in this example. The content between tags is called *text*. For example, `$29.99` and `Que Publishing` are text.

A well-formed XML document follows some basic rules. For example, start tags must match end tags, elements are not allowed to overlap, and tags are case sensitive (`<Book>` is not the same as `<book>` nor `<BOOK>`). You can also use a shortcut to represent an empty element; for example, `<book/>` is considered the same as `<book></book>`.

In addition to well-formed XML documents, there are also so-called *valid XML documents*. A valid XML document contains *document type* information that indicates the XML document must be validated against either a Data Type Definition (DTD) or an XML-Schema. Both DTD or XML-Schema are used for validating the document content by defining which elements can appear within the document and the attributes that can be associated with an element. They also define the structure of the document, which elements are child elements of others, the sequence in which the child elements can appear, and the number of child elements.

The DTD is a proven standard, whereas the XML-Schema is a proposed standard. XML-Schema, however, offers more flexibility because it uses the XML syntax itself to define an XML document. XML-Schema can be used for document validation.

Dealing with XML Documents

The W3C specification defines two interfaces for dealing with XML documents. You can manipulate an XML document using either the Document Object Model (DOM) or the Simple API for XML (SAX). DOM is an object-oriented programming model, whereas SAM is an event-based programming interface. This example uses only DOM, so I'll skip the discussion of

SAX. If you're interested, refer to Appendix A of this book for more information on SAX.

For this example, you will use used Microsoft's DOM parser that is shipped with Internet Explorer 5 (which comes with Windows 2000). So, the discussion focuses on the MSXML DOM model.

TIP

You can download the most recent version of Microsoft XML parser, The July 2000 Microsoft XML Parser Beta Release from the MSDN Web site at `http://msdn.microsoft.com/xml/general/msxmlprev.asp`.

DOM uses a tree structure to represent an XML document. The elements in a DOM tree are called *nodes*. Every XML document must have only one root node. The Book node in the earlier XML document is the root node. The root node can have child nodes, which, in turn, can have grandchild nodes and so on.

An XML document is represented by the DOMDocument object. The root node is represented by the DocumentElement object. You use the DOMDocument object to add nodes by calling its createNode() method. Another important DOM object is the XMLHTTPRequest object, which allows you to use the HTTP Post method to send an XML document object to a target URL, as you will see in the example later.

The Source Code

Now it's time to take a look under the hood. In this section, you will walk through the complete source code of this sample application to see how our solution described in previous section is actually implemented.

The EventClass

The EventClass and its definition (the code) are shown in Figure 14.3. It has an IEvent class model.

EXAMPLE

Figure 14.3: The CaseEvent EventClass.

Now you can compile the project file into CaseEvent.dll and install it in an empty COM+ server application as an EventClass.

The Event Subscriber

The event subscriber is an ActiveX DLL project that implements the IEvent class of the EventClass (see Figure 14.4).

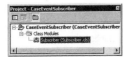

Figure 14.4: *The event subscriber.*

At this point, set a reference to the EventClass and type the code in Listing 14.1 in the Subscriber.cls class module.

Listing 14.1   The Implementation of the CaseActivated Event in the Subscriber

```
Option Explicit

Implements IEvent

Private Sub IEvent_CaseActivated(ByVal sMessage As String)
    Dim oInt As Object
    Set oInt = GetObject("queue:/new:Integration.Case")
    oInt.Process sMessage
End Sub
```

As you can see in Listing 14.1, the code simply creates a Queued Component and calls its Process method by passing the message as its input parameter.

Your next step is to compile the project to CaseEventSubscriber.dll and install it in a regular COM+ server application. Then subscribe the event defined by the CaseEvent EventClass.

The Integration Objects

Here, I'll discuss only one of the integration objects: the Integration.Case component. Figure 14.5 shows the project for this component.

Figure 14.5: *The Visual Basic project of the* Integration.Case *component.*

Now set references to ADO 2.5 and MSXML 2.0 in the project, as shown in Figure 14.6.

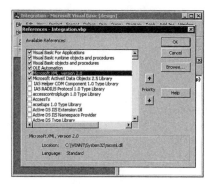

Figure 14.6: *Setting the reference to ADO and MSXML in the project.*

Listing 14.2 shows the code for this `Integration.Case` component.

Listing 14.2 The `Integration.Case` Component

```
Option Explicit

'Input parameter offsets.
Private Const COURT_TYPE = 0
Private Const COURT_LOCATION = 1
Private Const CASE_YEAR = 2
Private Const CASE_CLASS = 3
Private Const CASE_SEQUENCE = 4

'XML Schema location.
Private Const XML_SCHEMA = "x-schema:http://PEISHU/CaseSchema.xml"

'Target URL for posting the XML document.
Private Const POST_URL = "http://PEISHU/Court_Site/ProcessXMLDoc.asp"

'Module level XML document object.
Private m_oXMLDoc As New MSXML.DOMDocument

Private Function AddNode(ByVal sName As String, _
                        Optional ByVal oParent As MSXML.IXMLDOMNode, _
                        Optional sText As String) As MSXML.IXMLDOMNode

    Dim oNode As MSXML.IXMLDOMNode

    Set oNode = m_oXMLDoc.createNode("element", sName, _
```

Listing 14.2 continued

```
                    XML_SCHEMA)


    If Len(sText) Then
        oNode.Text = sText
    End If

    If oParent Is Nothing Then
        m_oXMLDoc.appendChild oNode
    Else
        oParent.appendChild oNode
    End If
    Set AddNode = oNode
End Function


Public Sub Process(ByVal sMessage As String)
    Dim oXMLDoc          As New MSXML.DOMDocument
    Dim oCase            As MSXML.IXMLDOMNode
    Dim oRecType         As MSXML.IXMLDOMNode
    Dim oCaseData        As MSXML.IXMLDOMNode
    Dim oHTTP            As New MSXML.XMLHTTPRequest
    Dim vMessage         As Variant
    Dim sDelimiter       As String
    Dim sCourtType       As String
    Dim sCourtLocation   As String
    Dim sCaseYear        As String
    Dim sCaseClass       As String
    Dim sCaseSequence    As String
    Dim sEFileFlag       As String
    Dim sConnection      As String
    Dim oConnection      As New ADODB.Connection
    Dim sSQL             As String
    Dim oRecordset       As ADODB.Recordset

    On Error GoTo Process_Err

    'Parse the input message.
    sDelimiter = "|"
    vMessage = Split(sMessage, sDelimiter)
    sCourtType = vMessage(COURT_TYPE)
    sCourtLocation = vMessage(COURT_LOCATION)
    sCaseYear = vMessage(CASE_YEAR)
```

Listing 14.2 continued

```
        sCaseClass = vMessage(CASE_CLASS)
        sCaseSequence = vMessage(CASE_SEQUENCE)

        'Build stored procedure call.
        sSQL = "Exec Case_Activation @CourtType = '" & sCourtType & "'," _
            & "@CourtLocation = " & sCourtLocation & "," _
            & "@CaseYear = '" & sCaseYear & "'," _
            & "@CaseClass = '" & sCaseClass & "'," _
            & "@CaseSequence = " & sCaseSequence

        'Connect to the database and run the stored procedure.
        sConnection = "DSN=EFiling;UID=sa;PWD=;"
        oConnection.open sConnection
        Set oRecordset = oConnection.Execute(sSQL)

        'Retrieve the EFileFlag.
        sEFileFlag = oRecordset("EFileFlag")
        Set oRecordset = Nothing
        oConnection.Close
        Set oConnection = Nothing

        'Build the XML document.
        Set oCase = AddNode("Case")
        Set oRecType = AddNode("RecType", oCase, "ECases")
        Set oCaseData = AddNode("CaseData", oCase)
        AddNode "CourtType", oCaseData, sCourtType
        AddNode "CourtLocation", oCaseData, sCourtLocation
        AddNode "CaseYear", oCaseData, sCaseYear
        AddNode "CaseClass", oCaseData, sCaseClass
        AddNode "CaseSequence", oCaseData, sCaseSequence
        AddNode "EFileFlag", oCaseData, sEFileFlag

        'Post the XML document to the remote site
        oHTTP.open "POST", POST_URL, False
        oHTTP.send m_oXMLDoc

    Exit Sub
Process_Err:
    Err.Raise Err.Number
End Sub
```

The Integration.Case object implements only one method: Process. It parses the message being passed into individual parameters to call the Case_Activation stored procedure and return EFileFlag. Then it calls the AddNode function repeatedly to generate the XML document. AddNode uses the createNode() and AppendNode() methods to create nodes and build the XML document.

After building the XML document, the Process method calls the Open method of the XMLHTTPRequest object, specifies that the HTTP Post method be used, and then sends the XML document object to the target URL—in this case, the ProcessXMLDoc.asp page.

Now you can compile Integration.dll and install it in a COM+ server application with queuing and listener enabled. Also, enable the queuing of the _Case interface.

EXAMPLE

The Receiving ASP Page

Listing 14.3 shows the code for the receiving page, ProcessXMLDoc.asp.

Listing 14.3   ProcessXMLDoc.asp

```
<%@ Language=VBScript %>
<%
    dim oXMLDoc
    dim oCaseXML
    dim sError
    dim rc

    set oXMLDoc = server.CreateObject("MSXML.DOMDocument")
    oXMLDoc.async = false

    'Load the XML from the Request object.
    oXMLDoc.Load request

    if oXMLDoc.parseError.errorCode = 0 then
        'Create the queued components.
        Set oCaseXML = GetObject("queue:/new:CaseXML.XMLDoc")
    Else
        sError = "Error: " & oXMLDoc.parseError.errorCode & vbcrlf _
                & "Line: " & oXMLDoc.parseError.Line & vbcrlf _
                & "Reason: " & oXMLDoc.parseError.reason & vbcrlf
    End If

    on error resume next

    if sError = "" then
        oCaseXML.Process oXMLDoc.XML
```

Listing 14.3 continued

```
        set oCaseXML = nothing
    end if

    if err<> 0 then
        sError = sError & err.description
    end if

    if sError <> "" then
        Response.Write sError
    else
        Response.Write "Case (XML) document processed!"
    end if
%>
```

You may notice that Listing 14.3 doesn't have any HTML tags at all. It is a pure ASP scripting page. This page is designed to be called by the Integration.Case component over the Internet and run completely behind the scenes.

The script in ProcessXMLDoc.asp is straightforward. After creating an instance of the DOMDocument object, this script sets the async property to False, which forces the XML document to be loaded synchronously. If this property is not specified, the default asynchronous loading behavior is used. In this case, you are responsible for checking the loading status by querying the onreadystatechange property until it is completed (it returns the value 4). The ASP code then loads the XML DOMDocument object from the request object. If the XML is successfully loaded, the ASP page will create an instance of the Queued Component, CaseXML.XMLDoc, and pass the contents of the XML document to its Process method.

> **NOTE**
>
> If you try to directly open ProcessXMLDoc.asp, it returns an error, as shown in Figure 14.7. When you directly open this page, no XML document has been passed to it.

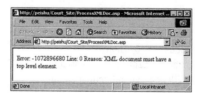

Figure 14.7: *Trying to directly open the ProcessXMLDoc.asp page results in an error.*

EXAMPLE

The `CaseXML.XMLDoc` Component

`CaseXML.XMLDoc` is another Queued Component that is called by the ProcessXMLDoc.asp page. Figure 14.8 shows the `CaseXML.XMLDoc` component in a Visual Basic project.

Figure 14.8: *The* `CaseXML.XMLDoc` *component.*

Next, you must set references of the project to both ADO 2.5 and MSXML 2.0.

The `CaseXML.XMLDoc` component implements a single method, `Process`, as shown in Listing 14.4.

Listing 14.4   The `Process` Method of the `CaseXML.XMLDoc` Component

```
Public Sub Process(ByVal sXML As String)
    Dim oXMLDoc        As New MSXML.DOMDocument
    Dim sRecType       As String
    Dim sCourtType     As String
    Dim iCourtLocation As Integer
    Dim sCaseYear      As String
    Dim sCaseClass     As String
    Dim lCaseSequence  As Long
    Dim sEFileFlag     As String
    Dim sSQL           As String
    Dim oConnection    As New ADODB.Connection
    Dim sConnection    As String
    Dim sXMLError      As String

    On Error GoTo Process_Err

    'Load the XML into the DOMDocument object variabale.
    oXMLDoc.async = False
    oXMLDoc.loadXML sXML

    If oXMLDoc.parseError.errorCode <> 0 Then
        sXMLError = "Error occurred at line : " & oXMLDoc.parseError.Line & "." _
                    & vbCrLf & oXMLDoc.parseError.reason & "."
        GoTo Process_Err
    End If
```

Listing 14.4 continued

```
'Make sure we get the right RecType
sRecType = oXMLDoc.documentElement.childNodes(0).Text

'In reality, we need to check all the RecTypes
'using a Select Case syntax, for example.
'Here we only check "ECases" rectype for simplicity.

If sRecType = "ECases" Then
    'Retrieve data from the XML document.
    With oXMLDoc.documentElement.childNodes(1)
        sCourtType = .childNodes(0).Text
        iCourtLocation = CInt(.childNodes(1).Text)
        sCaseYear = .childNodes(2).Text
        sCaseClass = .childNodes(3).Text
        lCaseSequence = CLng(.childNodes(4).Text)
        sEFileFlag = .childNodes(5).Text
    End With
End If

'Build the SQL string.
sSQL = "update  ECases" & vbCrLf _
    & "set EFileFlag = '" & sEFileFlag & "'" & vbCrLf _
    & "where CourtType = '" & sCourtType & "'" & vbCrLf _
    & "and CourtLocation =" & iCourtLocation & vbCrLf _
    & "and CaseYear = '" & sCaseYear & "'" & vbCrLf _
    & "and CaseClass = '" & sCaseClass & "'" & vbCrLf _
    & "and CaseSequence =" & lCaseSequence

'Connect to the database and execute the SQL statement.
sConnection = "DSN=Court;UID=sa;PWD=;"
With oConnection
    .Open sConnection
    .Execute sSQL
End With

Exit Sub
Process_Err:
    If Err = 0 Then
        Err.Raise vbObjectError + 500, "CaseXML.Process", sXMLError
    Else
        Err.Raise Err.Number
    End If
End Sub
```

Here, the Process method loads the XML string to the DOMDocument object by calling the LoadXML method. Then it parses the DOM tree to retrieve the context of nodes by using the childnodes collection. Finally, it builds a SQL statement using the data retrieved from the XML document and sends the SQL request to the Court database for processing.

Now you can compile CaseXML.dll and install it in another COM+ application with QC enabled. Don't forget to enable the queuing on the _XMLDoc interface as well.

The Databases

EXAMPLE

For this demonstration, you can set both databases on the SQL Server. This strategy was used for the real-world development, too. Notice that you specify the DSN in the connection string in Listing 14.4 so that during deployment all you need to do is reconfigure the DSN and point it to the DB2 database (using the DB2 ODBC driver, of course).

Listing 14.5 shows the Transact SQL (TSQL) scripts for creating and populating the CourtEFiles table on the EFiling database.

Listing 14.5 The CourtEFiles Table in the EFiling Database

```
use EFiling
go

if exists(select * from sysobjects where id = object_id('CourtEFiles'))
 drop table CourtEFiles
go

create table CourtEFiles(
 CourtType char(1) not null,
 CourtLocation tinyint not null,
 CaseYear char(4) not null,
 CaseClass char(2) not null,
 CaseSequence int not null,
 EFileFlag char(1) null,
    constraint pk_ECases primary key
      (CourtType,CourtLocation,CaseYear,CaseClass,CaseSequence)
)
go

insert CourtEFiles (CourtType,
          CourtLocation,
          CaseYear,
          CaseClass,
          CaseSequence,
              EFileFlag)
        Values ('D',
           21,
            '1999',
```

Listing 14.5 continued

```
          'DR',
          133689,
          'Y')
go
```

Listing 14.6 contains the `Case_Activation` stored procedure.

Listing 14.6 The `Case_Activation` Stored Procedure

```
if exists(select 1 from sysobjects where id = object_id('Case_Activation'))
  drop proc Case_Activation
go

create proc Case_Activation
 @CourtType char(1),
 @CourtLocation tinyint,
 @CaseYear char(4),
 @CaseClass char(2),
 @CaseSequence int
as

set nocount on

select      EFileFlag
from        CourtEFiles
where       CourtType = @CourtType
and         CourtLocation = @CourtLocation
and         CaseYear = @CaseYear
and         CaseClass = @CaseClass
and         CaseSequence = @CaseSequence
go
```

Listing 14.7 contains the TSQL scripts for creating and populating the ECases table in the Court database.

Listing 14.7 The ECases Table in the Court Database

```
use Court
go

if exists(select * from sysobjects where id = object_id('ECases'))
  drop table ECases
go

create table ECases(
 CourtType char(1) not null,
 CourtLocation tinyint not null,
 CaseYear char(4) not null,
```

Listing 14.7 continued

```
CaseClass char(2) not null,
CaseSequence int not null,
EFileFlag char(1) null,
  constraint pk_ECases primary key
    (CourtType,CourtLocation,CaseYear,CaseClass,CaseSequence)
)
go

  insert ECases (CourtType,
          CourtLocation,
          CaseYear,
          CaseClass,
          CaseSequence
)
      Values ('D',
          21,
          '1999',
          'DR',
          133689)
go
```

Putting It All Together

The ASP code that activates a case might look like the following:

```
<%
    dim oEvent
    set oEvent = server.createObject("CaseEvent.IEvent")
    oEvent.CaseActivated "D|21|1999|DR|133689"
    set oEvent = nothing
    response.write "Case Activated!"
%>
```

When the event fires, the subscriber calls the Queued Component, Integration.Case, which parses the pipe-delimited string into individual input parameters to call the Case_Activation stored procedure. It then uses the returned EFileFlag (Y in this case) along with other parameters to generate an XML document. Figure 14.9 shows how the XML document it generated looks in Internet Explorer, which has a built-in XML parser.

Notice that the first line in the XML document points to an XML-Schema document, CaseSchema.xml. The XML-Schema document defines all valid elements allowed in the case XML document, as shown in Figure 14.10.

Figure 14.9: The XML document generated by the `Integration.Case` component.

Figure 14.10: The XML-Schema document, CaseSchema.xml.

After the XML document is generated, the `Process` method calls the ProcessXMLDoc.asp over the Internet, passing the XML document object. The ASP page then passes the XML content to a Queued Component, `CaseXML.XMLDoc`, which builds a SQL statement based on the data and submits it to the Court database. It updates the `EFileFlag` of a corresponding row in the ECases table of the Court database to `Y`.

As you can see from this example, by using the COM+ services, you can greatly simply your development task whereas providing more robust solutions. E-LAWS gained numerous benefits by using the COM+ alternative in their EAI efforts: significant cost saving by avoiding some expensive third party products and tools, more robust and flexible exception handling by utilize the built-in exception handling capabilities of COM+ Queued Components, better fault tolerance by taking the advantage of the loosely coupled architecture provided by Microsoft message queuing services.

What's Next

In this book, you have read about all the aspects of COM+ programming from a Visual Basic developer's perspective. I have taught you how to program COM+ in Visual Basic by showing you abundant examples throughout the book. In the last part of the book, I provided a complete COM+ application and a real-world case study showing how to use COM+ to solve business problems. In addition to COM and COM+, this book also taught you other advanced technologies, including Windows DNA, ADO, MSMQ, design principles, UML, and XML. Most of the code in this book reflects code used in numerous real-world enterprise and e-commerce applications I have built for my clients. After you finish reading this book, you should have a solid starting point to build your own real-world COM+ applications by using Visual Basic. Empowered with the knowledge you gained from this book you will be able to build better solutions for your organization and/or your clients, and a brighter career in the future.

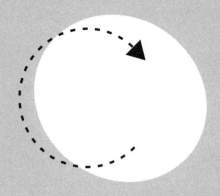

Appendix

Appendix A: COM+ and Related Web Resources

Appendix A

COM+ and Related Web Resources

This appendix lists some useful COM+ and other related Web resources.

COM, DCOM, MTS, COM+, and Other Microsoft Technologies

Microsoft COM site: `http://www.microsoft.com/com`

Microsoft DCOM site: `http://www.microsoft.com/com/tech/dcom.asp`

Microsoft MTS site: `http://www.microsoft.com/com/tech/mts.asp`

Microsoft COM+ site: `http://www.microsoft.com/com/tech/complus.asp`

This Web site contains comprehensive COM+ resources, including links to the "COM+ Resource CD Online," technical articles, white papers, presentations, books, and other related web sites.

Microsoft COM+ Platform SDK:
`http://msdn.microsoft.com/library/psdk/cossdk/betaintr_6qan.htm`

This is the official Microsoft COM+ online documentation.

Microsoft Windows DNA site: `http://www.microsoft.com/dna`

Microsoft MDAC site: `http://www.microsoft.com/data`

Microsoft MSMQ site: `http://www.microsoft.com/msmq/default.htm`

MSDN Active Server Pages Guide:
`http://msdn.microsoft.com/library/pskd/iisref/aspguide.htm`

ASP Today: `http://www.asptoday.com`

This is a developer-oriented forum hosted by Wrox publishing. It posts many very practical ASP and related articles on a daily basis. Contributors of these articles include Wrox authors.

Visual Studio Web site: `http://msdn.microsoft.com/vstudio`

MSDN Web site: `http://msdn.microsoft.com/default.asp`

Microsoft TechNet Web site: `http://www.microsoft.com/technet/`

Other Resources

A comprehensive XML Web site: `http://www.xml.com`

MSDN Online XML Developer Center:
`http://msdn.microsoft.com/xml/default.asp`

W3C Web site: `http://www.w3c.org`

This is the official web site of the World Wide Web Consortium (W3C). It contains specifications for XML, HTML and other protocols and standards.

Rational UML Resource Center: `http://www.rational.com/uml/index.jtmpl`

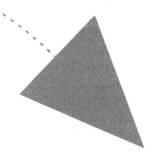

Index